Under Review

ANTHONY POWELL

Under Review

FURTHER WRITINGS
ON WRITERS 1946–1989

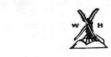

HEINEMANN:LONDON

William Heinemann Ltd
Michelin House, 81 Fulham Road, London SW3 6RB

LONDON   MELBOURNE   AUCKLAND

First published in Great Britain 1991
Copyright © Anthony Powell 1991

A CIP catalogue record for this book
is available from the British Library
ISBN 0 434 59929 8

Typeset in 11/12pt Linotron Baskerville by
Hewer Text Composition Services, Edinburgh
Printed and bound in Great Britain by
Mackays of Chatham PLC, Chatham, Kent

For
Kingsley Amis

ACKNOWLEDGMENTS

The pieces which follow were mostly published in the *Daily Telegraph*, others were in *Apollo*, *Punch*, the *Spectator*, and the *Times Literary Supplement*. Raffles appeared in *Raffles: The Amateur Cracksman* (Eyre & Spottiswoode): Verdant Green in *The Adventures of Mr Verdant Green* (Oxford University Press). I am grateful to editors and publishers of these for permission to reprint them here, also again to Tessa Davies, Roland Glasser, and Violet Powell, for making photocopies, when that was necessary.

CONTENTS

Contents

Some Novels and Novelists

Contents

The Europeans

Contents

INTRODUCTION

An earlier collection of occasional writings called *Miscellaneous Verdicts* contained, as well as reviews, odds and ends such as introductions and the like. The present assemblage, with a couple of exceptions, is all reviews, most of them about a thousand words long, written for the *Daily Telegraph*. The large audience addressed, small space available to express views, imposed certain limitations, but on the whole books reviewed represent my own choice (indulged by Literary Editors), a lot of them biographies. The trifling claim I would put forward for these relics of the past forty years or more is that, to borrow a term from painting, they achieve a kind of pointillist effect by massing together comments on single individuals over several decades, thereby displaying a literary landscape slightly different in lights and shades from that found in an historical or critical book on similar themes.

Miscellaneous Verdicts fell without undue strain into four sub-divisions. After a certain amount of arranging and rearranging, four sections too seemed appropriate for the present volume. These are called 'The Nineties: Forerunners and By-products'; 'Bloomsbury and Non-Bloomsbury'; 'Some Novels and Novelists'; 'The Europeans'. I have allowed myself a good deal of licence as to names included under the various headings; a diversity which – to borrow the painting metaphor again – seems to add contrast, even at times exoticism, to the colour values of the canvas.

The figures of Wilde and Beardsley dominate 'The Nineties', although all sorts of forerunners such as Walter Pater, John Addington Symonds, Havelock Ellis, and others, contributed to the final *fin-de-siècle* firework display, even George Du Maurier, with his long parodying of the Aesthetic Movement in *Punch*. On the other hand, a painter like Sargent, or actor like Beerbohm Tree (after all, Max Beerbohm's half-brother) provide reminders that there were different sides to the period than the *décadence*. An interesting thing is that several writers and painters, grouped here under 'The Nineties', could have been just as well accommodated in the next section, 'Bloomsbury and Non-Bloomsbury', in spite of the abyss that existed between them, anyway in the eyes of Bloomsbury.

This second section could equally well have been called 'The

1

Twenties' (when looked back on, remarkable for its concern with the Arts), but individuals considered are often Bloomsburies, while others, Wyndham Lewis, for example, are savagely anti-Bloomsbury. In fact Bloomsbury makes a useful landmark for comparison: Augustus John (praised by Virginia Woolf in her first novel), indifferent to Blooms-bury and all its works, to some extent running an opposition performance; T. S. Eliot on good terms with Bloomsbury without being in any way part of it; Arnold Bennett, himself attacked by Bloomsbury, humbly accepting Bloomsbury's pretensions.

Walter Richard Sickert (he would sometimes call himself Walter, sometimes Richard) not only ragged Bloomsbury up hill and down dale (though respectfully treated), but provides a perfect link with 'The Nineties'. For example, Wilde, on his lecture tour in the United States, explaining Aestheticism to the Americans in order to prepare them for *Patience*, Gilbert and Sullivan's satire on that, writes to Sickert's sister that the American landscape would provide good subjects for 'Walter's impressionist sketches'. Slightly more than twenty years later, Edith Sitwell (the Sitwells to be regarded as in competition with Bloomsbury) tells Sickert how much she admires his work, accordingly the artist gives her a drawing for being so 'mad'.

Edmund Gosse, included here under 'The Nineties', was well disposed to the Sitwells, but, anyway for a time, used to speak of 'an American poetaster called Eliot'. An example of the licence taken in this section is inclusion of James Joyce and D. H. Lawrence. Lawrence's association with Lady Ottoline Morrell gives him a tenuous Bloomsbury connection, though Joyce has none, except Virginia Woolf's dislike for his work. Incidentally, I withdraw my comment here that *Ulysses* must be read in its early Paris edition, having recently reread with enjoyment the Corrected Text. William Orpen, apotheosis of the academic painting Bloomsbury loathed, was at the Slade with John, a lifelong friend, which seems to give Orpen a ticket of admission among all these.

The Twenties brings up the matter of the First World War; its Dead, its Damaged, its Survivors. In the first category, Rupert Brooke (and his facetiously named Neo-Pagans) grew up side by side with proto-Bloomsbury, displaying amusing similarities and disparities. The Damaged are in one case represented by the stage designer Lovat Fraser (in the Memoirs of his widow), who left a mark on the period by his decor for *The Beggar's Opera*, to which, rather anachronistically, I have appended a piece about the infamous Jonathan Wild, on whom Gay based the Opera. Grace Lovat Fraser's Memoirs recall a wonderful Age of Innocence, when D. H. Lawrence could share a bed with Ezra Pound.

Bloomsbury, of course, disapproved of Lovat Fraser's art, as also the great Russian designer of Diaghilev's Ballets, Léon Bakst. Bakst was elbowed out by the Modernists (some of them brilliant stage designers too), but now recognised as the original artist he was. In quite another sphere from Lovat Fraser, another of the Damaged (wounded in Mesopotamia) was Geoffrey Madan. Madan's Commonplace Book shows him as perfect specimen of the war generation 'brought up on an English literary culture of intensive study of the Classics'. It was a culture even then on its way out, and, although Madan is an obscure figure, I think he is of interest.

Of the Survivors essentially associated with the War (as opposed to, say, Osbert Sitwell), Siegfried Sassoon and Robert Graves are here, though neither examined specifically as poets. The former represents an essentially Non-Modern approach; the latter Modern in his own particular manner. Does anyone in this country still remember Rabindrinath Tagore? He was once a well-known figure in the world of Edwardian mystical verse. D. H. Lawrence wrote an irritated letter about him to Lady Ottoline Morrell.

The third section, 'Some Novels and Novelists', a deliberately mixed bag, not necessarily chosen for quality, takes a look at all sorts: Aphra Behn to Sheridan Le Fanu; James Hogg to Compton Mackenzie; *The Prisoner of Zenda* to *Three Men in a Boat*; *Three Weeks* to *The Green Hat*. Sherlock Holmes to Raffles, those creations of brothers-in-law. Certain of these novelists might have been consigned to another heading, Arthur Machen, for instance, to 'The Nineties', as he was actually published in the Keynote Series, many of which had title pages designed by Beardsley. Machen is not a great novelist, but his short story 'The Bowmen' gave rise to the legend of the 'Angels of Mons', which allots him a small place in folk history, especially for anyone who remembers that strange fantasy sweeping the country.

Verdant Green, paradigm of all Oxford novels, is discussed at some length, because I wrote an Introduction to a recent reissue of that minuscule classic. I have followed *Verdant Green* up with a rather rare item, *Balliol Rhymes*, belonging to a later Victorian period, and dealing more with dons than undergraduates. Apart from their differences both give off the same unmistakable Oxford essence.

The fourth and last section, 'The Europeans', opens with a glance at translations from *The Greek Anthology*, followed by a study of *The Satyricon* of Petronius: the pair of them representing some of the foundations of European literature. I felt encouraged to reprint the notice of the former by having, at the time of its appearance, received an approving postcard from the then Regius Professor of Greek.

'The Europeans' includes, I think justifiably, a good many French names. Among those I should like to draw attention to a curious item, the caricatures, in the form of small statuettes, executed by Jean-Pierre

Dantan of such figures as Balzac, Hugo, Berlioz, Paganini (Dantan was specially keen on musicians), and many others. The Russians added a pungent flavour to European literature when they found out about writing, among whom Lermontov is not to be missed. The Continent is bound together at an earlier period by Casanova (usually totally unappreciated at his true value in this country). The Brothers Grimm combine an old-fashioned Teutonic simplicity (the way the Germans were regarded before the Franco-Prussian War) with salutary warnings to children that all sorts of sinister personages are to be encountered on life's road. Ludwig II of Bavaria suggests Teutonic romanticism; Strindberg, Scandinavian Modernism.

In my review (1961) of Dumas *père*'s Memoirs, I expressed a doubt as to whether some of the people who speak glibly of the Three Musketeers had ever read any of Dumas's novels. A correspondent wrote to me at the time, saying if you borrowed them from public libraries you had to wait weeks and weeks. I accepted that. Some thirty years later it was brought home to me just how wrong I had been, a country neighbour remarking, quite by chance, that he always read a Dumas novel in bed. When he came to the end of the canon, he started again.

As in *Miscellaneous Verdicts*, order of appearance here is, in principle, based on the year in which the subject was born, followed by the year in which the review appeared. Occasionally, in both cases, this proved inconvenient (for instance, although much younger than Verlaine, Rimbaud suitably follows him), chronology then being disregarded.

Anthony Powell

The Nineties:
Forerunners and By-products

WALTER PATER

Pater continues to be remembered for writing that Mona Lisa is older than the rocks among which she sits, and that success in life is to burn with a hard, gemlike flame.

Otherwise his books are forgotten, few people having much idea what Pater was like, or why he has any importance. I possess *Marius the Epicurean* (a school prize, in spite of its author's dubious reputation among his academic contemporaries), and can confirm its writing as the reverse of readable.

Nevertheless, Walter Horatio Pater (1839–94) was neither a dull nor an insignificant figure. He was well worth examination, especially as a scholarly biography of him has never before appeared. Michael Levey rightly avoids any hint of guying his subject, which could at times have been a temptation.

Perhaps the most remarkable aspect of Pater is that his attitude of mind, essentially an original one, should have been engendered by his own particular circumstances. The surname seems to have been less rare than its bearer supposed (a link, as he romantically hoped, with Watteau's pupil, J-B. Pater, is unlikely), the Paters seeming to have come from East Anglia. His more immediate forebears were surgeons in the East End of London.

Pater was educated at King's School, Canterbury (among its other literary alumni, Marlowe, Hugh Walpole, Maugham, Leigh-Fermor), then Queen's College, Oxford. Intended for the Church, he was a genuine believer, but a roving mind and sharp wit – qualities Pater obviously possessed, though almost impossible to preserve on paper – led him to make occasionally satirical comments on religious matters.

The consequence of this habit, unwise in a postulant cleric of the period, was that one of Pater's two closest friends wrote to the Bishop of London stating that Pater was not a suitable candidate for ordination. His friends' betrayal of him was really the sole dramatic incident of Pater's life. He managed, however, to win (among eleven candidates) a non-Clerical Fellowship at Brasenose College, Oxford (notorious for its athleticism and heartiness), henceforward becoming consciously agnostic.

Pater represents in an earlier generation the witty paradox, the belief that art belongs in the sphere of enjoyment rather than morals, a nostalgia for Greek homosexuality, all later popularised by Oscar Wilde in his individual manner. In these attitudes Pater was not alone among his contemporaries, but thet were to be found in what was on the whole a very different area of life from his own.

Swinburne and Rossetti, for example, creatively gifted, possessed backgrounds not at all unlikely to throw up social and intellectual rebels such as themselves. Pater, quiet and withdrawn by temperament, seems to have generated within himself, with a minimum of help from outside, a similar moral and aesthetic upheaval. The fact of Pater being a non-starter as a practising homosexual was no more important than Swinburne being a non-starter as a practising heterosexual, when it came to making a theoretical onslaught against mid-Victorian values.

It was not Pater's personal behaviour that caused him to gain a bad reputation early in life – though he seems to have mildly cultivated the better-looking undergraduates – but the book in which his much quoted passage about Mona Lisa appears, *Studies in the History of the Renaissance*.

This work was by implication an attack on the universally revered Ruskin, who had scarcely mentioned Leonardo's famous picture in his notes on the Louvre, beyond a few technical comments on the painting of the rocks, to which Pater held Mona Lisa anterior. *The Renaissance* appeared when Pater was in his middle thirties, creating a sensation among the stuffy from which his reputation never wholly recovered.

Pater achieved additional publicity by being included as the aesthete, Mr Rose, in W. H. Mallock's *The New Republic* (1877), which remains an amusing squib by a perhaps now underrated novelist. So far from being outwardly an aesthete, Pater was described as looking like a retired major in the Rifle Brigade, while others thought his features had some resemblance to Velasquez's many portraits of Philip IV of Spain. He lived with his two unmarried sisters (regarded as a somewhat formidable couple even by Henry James) and was very fond of cats, his own cat deliberately destroying an essay on Baudelaire presented to her master by Paul Bourget.

Pater was an extremely modest man, who never truly appreciated that in his later years he had become quite famous. The young Bernard Berenson wrote to ask if he might attend Pater's lectures, but, to Berenson's eternal irritation, Pater replied that he could not allow that because they were mere informal talks for Brasenose undergraduates.

Max Beerbohm executed one or two caricatures of Pater, and we may regret that Beerbohm did not include among them a picture of those lectures on art being delivered to a characteristic gathering of Brasenose undergraduates of the period.

The Case of Walter Pater, Michael   1978
Levey, Thames & Hudson.   *Daily Telegraph*

JOHN ADDINGTON SYMONDS

John Addington Symonds? About the best most of us could do in a General Knowledge questionnaire in which his name occurred would be to say he was a Victorian writer whose speciality was the Renaissance. Possibly some could add that he produced a study or pamphlet called *A Problem in Greek Ethics*.

However, in his day Symonds was a well-known figure as poet, critic and to some extent what would now be called art historian. He may have been knocked about by contemporary reviewers at times, but there were also those who regarded him as a man to step into the shoes of Ruskin and give a lead in that sphere where religion, philosophy, art and science met in a well-conducted and essentially Victorian dance.

But what does one mean by essentially Victorian? The more the true facts of that extraordinary epoch come to light, the less easy is it to define the Victorian way of life in any simple manner. Looking back, the Victorians seem to have possessed much that we lack today. Yet in many ways how unlike were their times to what is now popularly imagined. The one aspect that seems immovable as a rock is Victorian humbug.

John Addington Symonds was born in 1840, the son of a notably successful British doctor. He was educated at Harrow and Balliol, won the Newdigate Prize, toyed with becoming a don, then read for the Bar, married, had four daughters, suffered from bad health, lived much abroad, wrote poems, essays on the Elizabethan dramatists, translated the life of Benvenuto Cellini, edited Michelangelo's Letters, produced seven volumes on the Renaissance in Italy, wrote about the Greek poets and quite a bit more. He died in 1893.

Phyllis Grosskurth takes this rather unpromising material and relates it all, soberly, thoroughly, skilfully, to what was the motivating factor of Symonds's life. We are back with *A Problem in Greek Ethics*. The problem was, of course, homosexuality.

Here one must rather spoil the narrative by revealing the source of Phyllis Grosskurth's at times very extraordinary information. Symonds wrote memoirs towards the end of his life which he hoped might rival Rousseau's in telling the unvarnished truth about himself and his sex life.

9

His literary executor (not Symonds himself) made a stipulation that the memoirs should not be published until 1976. Phyllis Grosskurth has been allowed access to these memoirs and to make extracts from them, though only by paraphrase.

The knowledge that he wrote confessions should really be kept as a surprise after the reader has already absorbed the course of Symonds's life. This happens in the biography, coming as a dramatic climax to Symonds's long tale of uncertainties and incoherence where he himself was concerned. However, that fact must be made clear to explain how Phyllis Grosskurth knows some of the things she does know.

Symonds's early sexual experiences with his own cousins between the ages of eight and eleven seem so unusual that one is surprised that the rough-and-ready morals of Harrow came as a shock to him, at least so far as the boys were concerned. It was, on the other hand, not unreasonable that a series of very indiscreet letters from the Head-master himself to one of his pupils should upset Symonds when they were shown to him.

He told his father, who presented the Headmaster with the alternative of exposure or resignation. The Headmaster naturally resigned; but Dr Symonds added a rider that he must never again take a job involving heavy responsibilities. Some years later Palmerston offered him a bishopric, which was accepted. Dr Symonds weighed in again. Palmerston was suddenly told that the bishop-designate had changed his mind and wanted to remain a simple country clergyman.

This gives some indication of the remarkable picture of Phyllis Grosskurth's biography. Although she plays the psychoanalytical side only gently, Symonds's life provides an almost textbook case for some of Freud's theories.

Symonds's mother died when he was four years old, though not before he had had a terrifying experience with her in a carriage when the horses bolted. He was devoted to his father, a dominating man, who also fussed over him. It was only after his father's death, when he himself was in his middle thirties, that Symonds began to indulge his tastes: an interesting example of Freud's theory that the death of a father is the most important psychological milestone in a man's life. Freud's thesis is, of course, that homosexuality is a form of arrested development due to an infantile fixation on a female, and that inverts are not, as Symonds came to imagine, a select class of mankind.

In the earlier part of his life the pressures to keep his secret were in the main social. After the 'Labouchère Amendment' to the Criminal Law Amendment Act of 1885 Symonds was put in the position of a criminal and had to be even more circumspect outwardly.

At the same time one cannot help feeling that a certain hypocrisy is discernible in some of Symonds's writings on the subject, a fact that makes the ultimate production of his outspoken memoirs unexpected. Perhaps this is being unfair to him, so crushing was the weight of Victorian humbug, when for example, we find Swinburne – usually the first to advocate plain speaking – upset when the sixteenth-century charges of homosexuality against the poet Marlowe were printed.

The interesting point about Symonds is that in his early days, thinking his case quite exceptional, he methodically set about to cure himself by marriage. He was always attached to his four daughters, but it is not surprising that Mrs Symonds suffered nervous upsets. On the whole, though she is said to have refused to read her husband's books, she seems to have behaved extremely well in trying circumstances.

In later life Symonds followed up *A Problem in Greek Ethics* with *A Problem in Modern Ethics*. Both were privately printed only, and circulated among a few friends. Henry James, as usual (in a letter to Edmund Gosse, who seems to have been distinctly involved in the problem himself), puts his finger on Symonds's chief failing:

> It's on the whole, I think, your place to plant the standard of duty, but he [Symonds] does it with extraordinary gallantry. If he has, or gathers, a band of the emulous, we may look for some capital sport. But I don't wonder that some of his friends and relations are haunted with a vague malaise. I think one ought to wish him more *humour*, it is really *the* saving salt. But the great reformers never have it – & he is the Gladstone of the affair.

John Addington Symonds: A Biography, Phyllis Grosskurth, Longmans.

1964
Daily Telegraph

HAVELOCK ELLIS

The latter half of the nineteenth century precipitated a crisis in the sphere of sex. A hundred years before, George Selwyn's mild taste for necrophily merely amused society, though a de Sade might go too far and be sent to the Bastille; Beckford, too, overstepped the permitted mark, while people are still arguing as to why precisely Byron had to go into exile.

These things might happen in a small aristocratic world without demanding scientific investigation, but the rising tide of democracy, bearing with it a flood of ruthless publicity, brought the public face to face with, for example, the Wilde case, and the fact that all kinds of people, sometimes the most humdrum, often possessed abnormal tastes.

Doctors and sociologists began to turn their attention to the subject simultaneously all over Europe. In this country Havelock Ellis (1859–1939) more than any other man was responsible for what might be called the new attitude towards sex. There is, indeed, something particularly English about Ellis's combination of moral earnestness and amateur approach.

Arthur Calder-Marshall has written *Havelock Ellis: A Biography* very well indeed. He is right to have denied himself any concession to humour in a story which requires to be told in the terms in which it was lived. The smallest suggestion of irony, or digression from deep seriousness, would have put the picture out of focus. As presented, the narrative conveys with extraordinary aptitude the world and be-haviour of Ellis and those who surrounded him.

All the same, in spite of the book's sympathy and skill, Ellis, the man, somehow escapes us. His wife, and the various women with whom he was associated, are projected with at times painful realism; but, apart from a sense of overpowering egotism, of an entirely passive sort, protecting its possessor for his own especial work, we cannot guess what it would have been like to consult this shy, high-voiced sage.

Ellis was the son of an easy-going sea captain in the mercantile marine and a woman of unusually strong religious principles. Mrs Ellis was devoted to her son, but never allowed herself to practise the ordinary endearments of a mother towards him. On the other hand, she sometimes carried informality regarding natural functions of the body in her own behaviour to lengths which modern psychiatrists might condemn.

When Ellis was sixteen he sailed to Australia in one of his father's ships. On arrival he took a job as a schoolmaster. There he remained in lonely circumstances for some years, always feeling he had a mission in life. Finally, it came to him in a flash that he should train to be a doctor, and that his speciality should be sex.

He returned to England, passed the necessary examination at a modest level, and wrote a number of books. In 1898 he produced the work for which he is most famous, *Studies in the Psychology of Sex*. There was a prosecution. The books were withdrawn, though published at the time in Germany and the United States, eventually achieving their desired status as a serious pioneer contribution to the study of the subject.

Calder-Marshall writes with good sense:

> My own view of what is wrong with all the first *five* volumes of the *Studies in the Psychology of Sex* is that they are moral and educational books disguised as science. The climate of public opinion was such that Ellis could not say what he wanted to say to ordinary men and women in their own words.
>
> It all had to be wrapped up in the form of quotations from learned authorities, many of whom were engaged in the same sort of sex education, building up their mutual authority by cross-quotation of one another. The 'unwholesomeness' one feels when reading the *Studies* . . . arises from the uneasy sense that the author's real meaning is different from his apparent meaning.

This is excellently put. The fact was that Ellis was a prolific, well-read, but far from talented writer. He was usually preaching, lush in style, not always wholly objective, and – it has been suggested – sometimes had his leg pulled by correspondents. As against these weaknesses, he was a man of the strictest personal integrity. He lived in relative poverty for the whole of his eighty years, when the smallest talent for doing a deal would have brought in a fortune.

Unfortunately a lack of worldly wisdom, attractive in itself, does not always lead to happy results. For example, de Villiers, the publisher chosen by Ellis to launch the work he had so much at heart, was shady to a quite exceptional degree even in one of his profession.

Ellis's personal life was never easy. He appears to have been over sixty before he was himself able to achieve a normal physical union, although he was married and had strong emotional relationships with various women throughout his life. The first of these to play an important part was Olive Schreiner, author of *The Story of an African Farm*.

Nor was Edith Lees, who became Mrs Havelock Ellis, an ideal wife. She was primarily attracted to her own sex, but, in spite of this, there can be no doubt that a strong tie always existed between her husband and herself. Both she and Ellis were Socialists and believed that husband and wife should contribute equally to the family budget. This was fortunately made possible by her possession of a small private income.

One of the most enjoyable aspects of Calder-Marshall's book is the picture it gives of the curious politico-intellectual circles in which Ellis and his friends moved. At one end of the scale were figures like Shaw, soon to be rich and successful beyond the dreams of avarice; at the other, strange, forgotten folk who shade off into a ramshackle, near-criminal world. This was the community which largely formed so many views accepted in our own day.

It is impossible not to be struck by the fact that, peculiar in some ways as was the Ellis marriage, it also shared many of the characteristics of matrimony of a more banal kind. No couple in a comic strip could better represent a jealous wife than Edith, or, for that matter, though in his own particular manner, Havelock that of much tried husband.

Havelock Ellis: A Biography, Arthur   1959
Calder-Marshall, Hart-Davis.   *Daily Telegraph*

GEORGE DU MAURIER

The great illustrators of the nineteenth century, to whom *Punch* owes the fact that it is not as forgotten as the *Tomahawk* or *Lika Joka*, were of varied skills. Keene was the most accomplished draughtsman; Tenniel had the gift of presenting politicians as fabulous monsters, like those inhabiting his *Alice in Wonderland*; but Leech and Du Maurier possessed that rare, time-defying instinct for catching and recording with genius the social scene.

The interesting point is that neither Keene, nor Doyle, nor Linley Sambourne – to mention only three from several talented artists – ever bring off that particular difficult achievement: though at another level Phil May is again briefly successful. Today, one would look to cartoonists of quite different technique, Osbert Lancaster or Mark Boxer, as the dazzling castigators of the Nuclear Age.

George Du Maurier (1834–96) has another claim to fame as well as, say, 'The Curate's Egg' – an incident produced for him by a clergyman friend – and the immortal series guying the Aesthetic Movement. He was author of the novel *Trilby*, written at the age of sixty, an almost-perfect example of what George Orwell called a 'good bad book', or, to use Hugh Kingsmill's phrase (not, I think, claimed as original), 'inspired imbecility', in its combined absurdity and vitality in describing the bohemian life of Paris art students.

Du Maurier himself was a man of unusual gifts and complications. Leonée Ormond has done an excellent job in presenting his personal side, though she perhaps allows herself rather too many comments on the Victorian epoch, and gets a bit involved in the Laocoön-like task of trying to disentangle the Pre-Raphaelites from the Aesthetic Movement, and both from the *Décadence*.

We all know the Victorians had differnt standards from our own, but when Leonée Ormond remarks: 'It never occurred to him [Du Maurier] that Mrs Ponsonby De Tomkyns might have used her energy and intelligence more profitably than in social intrigues,' she invokes the New Puritanism of 'social conscience' that risks being even more silly, priggish and humourless than the Victorian brand. Besides, as Mrs Ponsonby De Tomkyn's life was devoted to snobbishness and social climbing, there is absolutely no question, given the period, that

15

she did not also spend much of her time on good works and charitable undertakings with those ends in view, a well-recognised method of making smart acquaintances.

However, that is by the way. One must not be ungrateful for Leonée Ormond's balanced and sympathetic picture of Du Maurier's own career, remarkably successful as it seems now, though apparently frustrating to himself at the time. One of the most interesting matters she sorts out is her subject's ancestry. Du Maurier himself thought that he came of minor French *noblesse*, a fact that played a considerable part in the imaginative fantasies of his novel-writing. These origins were, alas, a total invention.

Du Maurier's grandfather, a master glass-blower, had emigrated to England at the time of the French Revolution to avoid the repetition of a prison sentence he had already suffered for fraud. Leonée Ormond does not mention a relevant fact, that is to say that glass-blowing (owing to its economic importance) was the one trade open to the *noblesse*, so that no doubt many glass-blowers, when away from their own neighbourhood, claimed noble status. At a time of revolution, that must have been a special temptation. All the same, Du Maurier's grandfather did the thing in style and forged a relatively convincing pedigree.

In fact, Du Maurier had a much more amusing family tree than that supplied by French minor nobility, because the glass-blower's son married a daughter of Mrs Mary Anne Clarke, mistress of the Duke of York, notorious, among other things, for allegedly taking bribes for handing out army officers' commissions and promotions in the days of purchase.

Mrs Clarke also 'did time' (for libel), but whatever her frailties, she was a woman of great energy and wit. It is not suggested that Du Maurier's mother was of royal origin, but it seems probable she was not the daughter of Mary Anne's drunken husband.

This heredity, not surprisingly, caused all sorts of complexities in the third generation. One is constantly struck by Du Maurier's extraordinary mixture of gifts and stupidities, wit and insensitiveness, ambition and lethargy. He was also plagued (like Tenniel) with having the use of only one eye, and subject to recurrent melancholia. Although he seems to have had affairs as a young man, and suffered a nervous breakdown at the time of his long engagement to his wife, it was his mother, child of an earlier approach to sex, who suggested taking a temporary mistress, a solution Du Maurier himself indignantly refused.

Du Maurier had an enormous acquaintance among persons of interest. He shared a studio with Whistler (who ridiculously and spitefully brought a libel action against *Trilby*), and was a close friend of Henry James, to whom he first offered *Trilby* as a plot. A good literary exercise would be to rewrite that novel in the James manner. It was not Andrew K. Hichens, but Robert Smythe Hichens who was author of *The Green Carnation*, and about ten when described here as having 'quite lost his heart' to a beautiful girl.

George Du Maurier, Leonée   1969
Ormond, Routledge.   *Daily Telegraph*

THOMAS WISE

I

The Victorian age never ceases to produce fascinating characters and situations. Thomas Wise comes high in the gallery of its curiosities. The son of a tobacconist, he became a clerk in an essential-oil firm, in which he eventually rose to partnership.

From his early youth he was devoted to literature and bibliography; at the age of twenty-five somehow managing to pay the then record price of £45 for Shelley's *Adonais*. Pushing and vain, he ingratiated himself with most of the prominent men of letters of his period; and, to be just to him, his qualities as a collector, bibliographer and editor were high. There is a particular kind of unctuousness and pretension to modesty in some of his letters quoted in this book which must have put shrewd people on their guard. Even so, it would have hardly prepared them for the truth.

Briefly, Wise's forgeries of rare editions of eminent authors run into measurable distance of 500; to which he added a great many crude thefts from the British Museum, tearing out pages from seventeenth-century plays to build into his own copies and increase their value on the market when sold.

We learn from these essays that book collectors, as early as 1898, had begun to feel disturbed about certain Victorian items appearing in the salerooms. In 1934, John Carter and Graham Pollard published their tremendous piece of detective work: *An Enquiry into the Nature of Certain Nineteenth-Century Pamphlets*. Wise was still alive. He had no answer. He shut himself up in his house. He would see no one. In any case, he was by then a sick man, dying in 1937.

At first there was an effort in some circles to pass the whole thing off as a joke. Bernard Shaw, for example, always maintained that Wise did it for a lark – an example of Shaw's unreliability of judgment. It is perfectly clear from the book under review that Wise made a handsome income out of his forgeries. So far as his thefts and book-faking were concerned, these were effected in the face of perpetual denials on his own part that he ever even participated in book dealing at all.

Wise's friend, the author and critic, Edmund Gosse, has been under fire from time to time, since Wise's exposure, as a possible party to some of Wise's misdoings. It appears from evidence here adduced that Gosse was wholly ignorant that something underhand was taking place, and that any such innuendo is without foundation.

Wise's career in the essential-oil trade makes it clear that he was an able businessman. The glimpse of him in the company of Browning, supplied here by himself, is enjoyable. No doubt his misdeeds brought him not only money, but also a sense of power over the people who regarded him as an able, if not specially attractive, hanger-on of the literary world.

The Wise mystery would make an excellent Sherlock Holmes story:

' "Holmes," I said, "there are two men coming up Baker Street. I am sure from their serious air that they are on their way to visit you."

' "Bibliographers, both of them," said Holmes. "They are only calling to require me to confirm their findings on the Wise case. The elegantly dressed one is from Cambridge University; his companion, distinctly bohemian in aspect, an Oxford man." '

Thomas J. Wise: Centenary Studies,   1959
ed. William B. Todd, Nelson.   *Daily Telegraph*

II

John Carter, a contemporary, I knew only slightly at Eton. Later when for a time he abandoned Scribner's second-hand books for general publishing, Scribner's was my American publisher. Carter liked a touch of dandyism, always affecting a red carnation with evening dress, even (perhaps over lavishly) when wearing his CBE.

Graham Pollard, a few years older than me, was already earning a living as a second-hand bookseller while an undergraduate at Oxford, and was, I think, all but married. He was a (serious) Communist in those days, inclined to be dismissive of fellow-undergraduates, but I found him always friendly and entertaining. I never knew him later. Except when dressed as a small boy in shorts at the Hypocrites Club fancy-dress party his shock of hair and revolutionary demeanour made him look like Danton.

Throughout the latter half of the nineteenth century, rumblings had more than once been heard on the subject of forged books. In 1934 Carter and Pollard published *An Enquiry into the Nature of Certain Nineteenth-Century Pamphlets*, which chiefly involved about forty books by Matthew Arnold, Mrs Browning, Robert Browning, Dickens, George Eliot, Kipling and others.

The authors of the *An Enquiry* – now published in an annotated reprint – showed, chiefly by the technical means of type-founts and paper, that the works concerned could not have belonged to their supposed dates, and by a mass of other evidence demonstrated that almost all emanated from the celebrated bibliophile Thomas James Wise (1858–1937). The only thing lacking at that date was proof that Wise had actually instigated the forgeries.

The *Enquiry* was a bombshell, and a courageous one for two young men to explode. Wise, who had been given an Honorary MA by Oxford, and Honorary Fellowship of a College, did not lack friends. Indeed one of the most striking features in the story is how dozens of stuffy pundits leapt to this scoundrel's defence.

Wise, starting from scratch as an office-boy, had become director of a firm marketing essential oils (as opposed to fuel oils) and was an extremely able businessman. Books were his hobby, and he made himself an expert on them too. Probably about 1886 he fell in with another, somewhat older book-lover, H. Buxton Forman (1842–1917), a civil servant in the Post Office. Both men were inconceivably awful amateur poets.

A Sequel to an Enquiry, undertaken by Nicolas Barker and John Collins with an energy and scholarship worthy of their predecessors, adds all kind of interesting material to the original investigation, its main revelation being proof that Buxton Forman was every bit as criminal as Wise.

Wise was bullying, exuberant, comparatively gregarious. Buxton Forman, on the other hand, seems to have been an unsociable, tedious fellow (Swinburne called him 'Mr Fuxton Boreman'), but Forman too was successful at his job. In the Post Office he became second-string, and was awarded a CB. He liked association copies, and would create fictitious ones with scraps of autograph manuscript. He also treasured an apparently genuine lock of Keats's hair given to Fanny Brawne.

One of the funniest items here is that a General, Sir Anthony Coningham Sterling, KCB, printed a number of his poems, under his initials only, in *Fraser's Magazine* in 1849. Wise identified these as A. C. Swinburne's (who would have been eleven at the time), and Edmund Gosse accordingly incorporated the fact in his memoir of the poet in the DNB, hazarding the guess that Swinburne's mother had sent in the verses.

At one moment investigators suspected that Gosse might have been in the swindle, but that seems undoubtedly not to have been true, though he admittedly connived at Wise's piracy of Swinburne's *The Ballad of Bulgarie*. I still wonder why Gosse allowed an astonishingly feeble poem, attributed to Swinburne, first to appear in the *Eton Candle* (1922) a year or two before its inclusion without provenance in the Bonchurch Edition of Swinburne's Collected Poems which Wise managed to edit.

Finally – and possibly most extraordinarily of all – an irritable reply was found written from Wise to Forman in between the lines of a note from Forman to Wise actually referring to their malign activities. It is reproduced in facsimile in the Epilogue to *An Enquiry* and came from the collection of an American collector named Pforzheimer who would not allow it to be made public while Wise was alive. Nor was it, until Pforzheimer himself died in 1945 – a remarkable example of how people sometimes love shielding a criminal.

It is now known that Wise also stole some 200 items from the British Museum – and one notes that, by modern standards, he was not even a good bibliographer.

Further information about this lovely pair will almost certainly appear in due course, possibly with additional collaborators. Perhaps the best punishment for the pompous, self-opinionated, aggressive Wise (who held himself incommunicado during the last two years of his life) was to know that he had been exposed and made a fool of by two young men.

An Enquiry into the Nature of Certain Nineteenth-Century Pamphlets, John Carter and Graham Pollard; *A Sequel to an Enquiry*, Nicolas Barker and John Collins, two-volume set, Scolar.

1983
Daily Telegraph

OSCAR BROWNING

'What can those modern linoleum schools know of these ancient aristocratic vices?' demanded Mrs Warre Cornish, wife of the Vice-Provost of Eton, when someone spoke disparagingly of Eton's morals. If the modern schools were initially unversed in that field, they learnt with astonishing speed.

It was the enormous proliferation of boarding-schools in the nineteenth century, with boys living in monastic conditions, that brought about the Victorian obsessive horror of homosexuality. In earlier days at Eton, like being married or wearing a beard, it had merely been regarded as against the rules.

One might have thought that Oscar Browning (1837–1923) – the O.B. – would not stand up to more than one biography. An excellent book on him appeared in 1927 by his nephew H. E. Wortham, but Ian Anstruther finds much that is new to say about a strange figure, both interesting in himself and throwing light on all sorts of sides, reputable and disreputable, of the period.

Browning, a good scholar without being in anything like the top class, began life as an Eton master, where he soon acquired a house, which in the 1870s brought in £3,000 a year – a handsome sum from which the recipient was expected to put enough by to pension himself. Browning, with his mother, ran the house in a civilised manner, encouraging the arts and music, giving the boys eatable food, trying to stem the then growing worship of athletics, in general behaving in a manner that made his house, with as good a record at work as any other, celebrated and sought after by parents.

That was on the credit side. On the debit side were Browning's appalling egotism, his conviction that he was always right, his tactlessness, and above all his utter inability to avoid interfering in other people's business. Being himself a dyed-in-the-wool homosexual he not surprisingly had favourites, but does not seem to have gone beyond rather effusive handling of them. Where he drove many of his colleagues (and Dr Hornby the Headmaster) mad was in constituting himself guardian of the school's morals – regarding which he considered he knew much more than anyone else – including those of boys in houses not his own.

The final row came over a boy called Curzon – subsequently Marquess Curzon of Kedleston. Browning was sacked by Hornby over a technicality of having a slightly larger number of boys in his house than was laid down, something that had been allowed the previous year and for which he had forgotten to obtain renewed permission. There was a colossal rumpus, including a Question asked in Parliament; boys, parents, many colleagues, protested, but Hornby was within his rights.

There was no appeal. Hornby's action was understandable, but does not do him much credit. He himself was a philistine of the first water and quite unmemorable as a headmaster except for this incident.

Browning was able to take up a Fellowship at King's, Cambridge, at £300 a year. He had no pension – having made no provision for that even had he remained at Eton – and settled down to keep himself and his mother by his pen. At Cambridge Browning gradually became a famous figure, entertaining in his rooms, writing to the papers, standing for Parliament, using now what seems the very limited means at his disposal for drawing attention to himself. He was what was then called a radical, but something of an imperialist, and generally regarded as a snob without any serious contemporary rival in that sphere.

Painted, sculpted, caricatured by Max Beerbohm, associated with many admirable institutions and reforms, a centre of social life, an excellent teacher, he never managed to write a book of any real scholarship. Although personally popular with a great many dons and undergraduates, over and above being the sort of well-known buffoon who always gets a certain amount of applause, Browning continued to drive people mad. After thirty years Cambridge was almost as glad to get rid of him as Eton had been.

Ian Anstruther tells all this story with sympathy and humour. He also relates much that Wortham left out. Browning never threw away a letter; some 10,000 remain and it is these which give a peculiar vividness to this book. Parents fussing about their sons' behaviour at Browning's house are some examples (putting hands in pockets, not sitting up, etc.), among his pupils being the two apparently not altogether easy sons of Henry James's friend the American lawyer-sculptor, William Wetmore Story. On the whole, parents were uncompromisingly on Browning's side, including Curzon's, and years later Curzon himself had Browning to stay in India when he was Viceroy – five weeks of never equalled paradise for the guest.

Among the many letters are also literally thousands from boys Browning befriended or simply picked up. In this respect he showed no snobbery whatever, not even (in the social sense) inverted – all classes were grist to his mill. There is no doubt whatever that some of the relationships went beyond the bounds of pure friendship (at one

moment Browning seems to have become the victim of an infection) but
again the picture is not a simple one. There is also no doubt that he
behaved with great kindness and helped many out-of-work young men
to steady jobs. Again the letters, of a sort that usually do not get printed,
are interesting for their evidently genuine affection for Browning,
indeed love (even when he was an old man) does not seem too warm a
term.

When the Oscar Wilde débâcle took place there was a tendency for
homosexuals to make a trip abroad or at least behave more circum-
spectly than formerly. Browning – who knew Wilde and shared what
was then the embarrassment of the same first name – did not trim his
sails in the least. He continued to pick up young sailors, give exclusively
male parties, fondle any youth he found attractive. He died in Rome in
his eighty-seventh year, having been appropriately awarded (through
Curzon) an OBE.

<table>
<tr><td>Oscar Browning: A Biography, Ian
Anstruther, Murray.</td><td style="text-align:right;">1983
Daily Telegraph</td></tr>
</table>

OSCAR WILDE

I

Oscar Wilde (1854–1900) has been endlessly written about, always with prejudice. Here are more than a thousand letters from him, covering the whole of his life, from which it is possible to form an opinion of the man himself without anyone at your elbow indicating what you ought to think. It is a collection of absorbing interest.

In editing these letters, Rupert Hart-Davis has done a magnificent job. Hardly a name, hardly an obscure expression, is left unexplained, yet the reader is scarcely aware of the notes. This literary elegance is an example to the whole world of scholarship.

Wilde, as a man and a writer, is peculiarly difficult to envisage with clarity, largely because he thought so unclearly about himself. The letters help in assessing him as no biography could do. Wilde loved to insist on the fact that he was a Celt. The statement is always coming into his letters. Of course he had a lot of Irish blood, but, in fact, only a century and a half before his birth, his ancestors had been English builders from Durham.

He is perpetually emphasising his status as an 'artist'. He was certainly a man of remarkable talent, but here again the preponderance of his literary work was in the field of well-paid, publicly recognised achievement. Wilde was not in a position like the French Symbolist poets, for example, or James Joyce, who went on plugging away in poverty and discomfort at a particular line they wanted to perfect, and were, so to speak, artists or nothing.

The turning point in Wilde's career of success, as the Letters show, was when in 1882 he went to lecture in America. He was sent there in the not specially dignified role of showing the Americans what the Aesthetic Movement (so relentlessly caricatured by Du Maurier) and he himself were like, in order that the Gilbert and Sullivan opera *Patience*, which satirised both, should have a successful run on the other side of the Atlantic. It was rather as if, in our own day, it had been thought advisable to display an Angry Young Man to the American women's clubs before staging *Look Back in Anger* in New York.

The hearty, slangy letters of Wilde as an undergraduate, the apparently quite genuine interest in girls, are no preparation for what came out at his trial. They are incredible in the light of the utter abandonment to male prostitution that took place after release from prison; of which no complete picture has been given until now.

Wilde was a good scholar. At Oxford (having done three years at Trinity College, Dublin), he was that much older than his contemporaries, an important point in university life. He took a First in Greats, and would have been offered a Fellowship had he been less flippant with the dons.

Montgomery Hyde's book brings out Wilde's almost obsessive inability to handle money, which certainly increased as he got older. It would be true to say that he was never out of money troubles, even when doing quite well, though as a young man, one way and another, he was not too badly off. Charm, push, very real abilities, kept him afloat.

But because Wilde was well able to look after himself in the hurly-burly of publicity and journalism, a most efficient editor of *The Woman's World*, this does not mean that he lacked deeper gifts. It only means that his gifts were different from his own decidedly inflated view of them. *Dorian Gray*, of which its author thought so much, has sunk to being a book every intelligent schoolboy gets over at fifteen, but the two letters to a newspaper advocating prison reforms are quite magnificent of their kind: vivid, moving, sticking to the point, unexaggerated, everything that a protest of that sort should be.

The letter written in prison to Alfred Douglas, already published as *De Profundis*, but corrected here, and expanded by about a thousand words, is also in places a superb piece of writing. In it Wilde makes the essential point that the world believed his relationship with Douglas to be a gay riot of wit and champagne. On the contrary, it was a sinister, harassing, bickering partnership in which Wilde shelled out the money, while Douglas threw tantrums, wrote poisonous letters, refused to visit his friend when he had flu. All the same, the Wilde-Douglas association must, by its persistence, go down to history. Bosie was horrible, unspeakable, but Oscar could not escape. They were linked by indissoluble bonds.

Few friendships would have survived what Wilde said to Douglas in the *De Profundis* letter. Even if Douglas never received the letter (as he alleged), it expressed the writer's feelings. Yet within four months of Wilde's release from prison in May 1897, they were in Naples together. This reunion wrecked any possibility, not merely of social rehabilitation in even the most modest form, but also prejudiced the smooth running of arrangements for keeping Wilde going, through the efforts of his faithful friends, Robert Ross, More Adey and Reggie Turner.

Yet, in spite of all the horrors of his life, Wilde could still laugh. One of Hart-Davis's notes quotes a letter (17 April 1898) from Ross to Wilde's erratic publisher, Smithers:

Oscar is very amusing as usual but is very abstracted at times. He says that *The Ballad of Reading Gaol* doesn't describe his prison life, but his life at Naples with Bosie [Alfred Douglas] and that all the best stanzas were the immediate result of his existence there . . . Did you hear what he said to someone who objected that the guardsman could not have worn a *scarlet* coat as he was in the Blues? He amended the lines:

> He did not wear his azure coat
> For blood and wine are blue.

However impossible it was for Wilde to exist without such periodic bursts of humour, the Letters during the two and a half years of life left to him after his release make painful reading. If ever sending a man to prison for homosexuality with the object of reforming him failed abjectedly, it was Wilde's two years' hard labour.

Yet what was to be expected? How could such a man possibly live quietly in continental backwaters? On all sides he was exhorted to work. These exhortations, although understandable, show a complete lack of grasp of the art of writing. The writing is the man. Wilde, with extraordinary speed, sat down and produced *The Ballad of Reading Gaol*. When he had done that, he had said all he wanted to say about prison. He said it effectively.

From the point of view of a writer, he found all his former approach to life knocked out of him. He was at an end so far as writing went. He had no friend to live with, was socially ostracised even by some of those who had shared his pleasures. There were perpetual embarrassments about money; the latter, it must be admitted, largely through his own fault. Worst of all, there was nothing to do. Is it surprising that his financial dealings lacked integrity, that he took to drink, spent his days with the homosexual underworld?

The only thing that seems absolutely certain is that, if Lord Queensberry had not forced a libel suit, Wilde would have been confronted in some other way by the alternative of arrest or leaving the country. It was impossible that the recklessness of his behaviour should not lead to disaster.

I remember [wrote Wilde] as I was sitting in the dock on the occasion of my last trial listening to Lockwood's [prosecuting counsel] appalling denunciation of me – like a thing out of Tacitus, like a passage in Dante, like one of Savanarola's indictments of the Popes at Rome – and being sickened with horror at what I heard. Suddenly it occurred to me: 'How splendid it would be if I was saying all this about myself!'

It is interesting that when Wilde wrote to Ross about Lord

Queensberry's insulting card he used the phrase 'The tower of ivory is assailed by a foul thing'; early employment of the metaphor.

'There is good and bad in every one of us,' observed a male prostitute after attempting to blackmail Oscar Wilde, who replied, 'You are a born philosopher.'

The Letters of Oscar Wilde, edited by Rupert Hart-Davis, Hart-Davis.   *1962*
                                        Daily Telegraph

Oscar Wilde: A Biography, H. Montgomery Hyde, Eyre Methuen.   1976
                                        Daily Telegraph

II

The Wildes had come to Ireland from Durham in the middle of the eighteenth century – descent from a Cromwellian or Orange colonel of Netherlands origin seems quite apocryphal. Sir William Wilde was the grandson of this eighteenth-century English immigrant, by profession carpenter, builder and land agent.

Lady Wilde's family, the Elgees, originally from Scotland (perhaps, a long way back, from Italy), were of similar background, building also playing a part, with legal and ecclesiastical connections taking the place of medicine and surgery. She wrote nationalist verse under the name of 'Speranza'. Terence de Vere White failed to find any information about Speranza's father, a Dublin attorney, who died inexplicably at Bangalore. One would agree that her own lifelong silence on the subject suggests that all might not have been well.

Sir William Wilde (b. 1815), an eye and ear specialist, was knighted for his work on the Irish census, in which he certainly seems to have shown superhuman energy, in addition to his other work and interests. He was an antiquary of unusual perception for his period, immediately grasping the resemblance between the tombs at Mycenae and those at New Grange in Ireland. He was also keenly concerned with Celtic origins, at that date cumbered with all sorts of ludicrous suppositions which he helped to clear away.

His intelligence and enterprise were not allied to discretion, and he managed to father three illegitimate children before his marriage to Speranza in 1851. By this time his bride was well known for her writings and nationalist activities. She was obviously a remarkable young woman – not so young, de Vere White thinks, as she gave out – but with the best will in the world one cannot feel great enthusiasm for her verse.

Speranza's politico-poetical life and Sir William's progress in his career include a lot of disparate elements. A striking aspect of his account of the Wilde's Dublin ménage is that it oddly recalls what might be termed the nostalgic strain in Joyce's *Ulysses*.

If formal letters, dinner parties, thrilling glimpses of vice-regal society, constituted one side of this Joycean phantasmagoria, there was another Joycean aspect, too, but in a different manner. Sir William had already shown some irresponsibility about women who attracted him, and, although the impression is that the Wilde household was a relatively happy one, marriage did not alter him in this respect.

The extraordinary thing about his entanglement with a certain Miss Travers is the manner in which, *mutatis mutandis*, this paralleled in at least one form his son Oscar's disaster.

Sir William had treated Miss Travers for ear trouble when she was nineteen, and continued to be her doctor and friend, for ten years, including occasional help with small sums of money when she was hard up. It is perfectly clear that he was attached to her. One would say it was equally clear that she was not his mistress; though it seems possible at one moment that things went a shade further than she herself cared to confess.

Finally, when she was twenty-nine, she accused Sir William of raping her in his surgery, producing in protest a shower of writings and pamphlets, the latter giving a fictional version of the attack. She also put garlic into the soap-trays of the surgery, to annoy the other patients. The fact was that Miss Travers, if not mad, was at least in such a neurotic state that the word could be reasonably used of her.

Among many grotesque features of the whole affair was the fact that Sir William and Miss Travers continued on comparatively friendly terms after the alleged incident had taken place. She wrote asking him, for instance, to cut a corn on her foot, which he had operated on without entire success a short time before, addressing him as 'spiteful old lunatic'.

In short, the legal storm burst not from action on the Wilde side – Miss Travers had a virulent hatred for Speranza – but when Speranza herself, greatly tried, wrote a letter of remonstrance, regarding the wording of which she should certainly have consulted a lawyer.

The Travers parents now brought a libel case against the Wildes. All this row had been going on, incidentally, just at the moment when Sir William was knighted. The case was dismissed, but a good deal of mud had been stirred up, not only in Dublin, because, naturally enough, the scandal made London headlines.

The affair was, indeed, a classic example of how mud sticks. The story has often been repeated that Sir William was accused of raping a patient under an anaesthetic, whereas that was merely Miss Travers's fictional account of a deed done by an imaginary doctor called Quilp. In fact, the actual assault was alleged to have taken place in about ten minutes while other patients were waiting to enter Sir William's surgery. Another extraordinary item was that a letter written by Miss

Travers saying 'take up your I O U' was very generally misprinted in the newspapers as 'take up your *son*' – a most unfortunate error.

When Sir William died, his widow came to live in London. Speranza was in straitened circumstances. Oscar was now beginning to make a name for himself, but her elder son, Willy, never managed to put his own financial position on a satisfactory basis; his continued dependence on his mother finally causing a rift between himself and his brother Oscar.

Under all her absurd posing, one wonders if Speranza really knew a good deal. Obviously she was immensely tough. His parents explain Oscar himself in all sorts of ways.

The Parents of Oscar Wilde: Sir
William and Lady Wilde, Terence de
Vere White, Hodder.

1967
Daily Telegraph

III

Wilde said with truth that he put his talent into his work; his genius into his life. The former is finite: an amusing comedy, *The Importance Of Being Earnest*, together with other plays that can still be performed; ingenious stories like *Dorian Gray* and *Lord Arthur Savile's Crime*; *De Profundis*, which Richard Ellmann defines as a tragic love-letter; some rather awful poems, redeemed by *The Ballad of Reading Gaol* (a shade too long); occasional writings of varying merit.

Wilde's life, on the other hand, in its rise and fall, has the quality of myth. That is as he would have wished. Although the cast of characters is much smaller, Wilde's drama possesses some of the timeless fascination of the Dreyfus case in its display of human vileness and human nobility.

With regard to *L'Affaire*, it is characteristic of Wilde that his Letters show that he dined in the company of Esterhazy, the true villain of the Dreyfus case, and his mistress, the registered prostitute, *la fille Pays*, 'a most charming woman – very clever and handsome', with an unerring instinct for getting into a mess, thereby causing a faint stir among the French security authorities.

That Wilde was a brilliant classical scholar is sometimes forgotten, when he was making his way by what is hard to regard otherwise than as a lot of aesthetic buffoonery, especially during his tour of the United States. There, it should be noted, Walt Whitman kissed him, and (agony, surely, for Wilde) they split a bottle of home-made elderberry wine brewed by Whitman's sister-in-law.

Ellmann is particularly convincing in the manner in which he traces Wilde's gradual transfer into active homosexuality. It should be emphasised that Wilde always accepted the contemporary view that this was a 'purple sin'. Nothing would have been less sympathetic to him than a clinical approach to sexual divergence, or for that matter, the exuberances of 'Gay Liberation' – a phrase he would not have approved.

When first in London, Wilde set up house with a painter friend, who possessed a fashionable clientele. Wilde's flirtation with Lily Langtry (it is just conceivable they had an affair) was perfectly genuine. When he married Constance Lloyd a slight feeling that there was something fishy about his goings-on (mostly owing to his exotic clothes) was largely set at rest, especially as his wife gave birth to two sons in quick succession. A characteristic engagement was for the newly married couple to dine with the young American painter John Singer Sargent.

For a time Wilde contented himself in a quiet friendship with a Cambridge undergraduate, gradually separating his writing from domestic life at home in Tite Street, Chelsea, by doing it elsewhere. Success now came thick and fast; then the first encounter with Wilde's evil genius, a young man of startling good looks and unparalleled nastiness, Lord Alfred Douglas. He was one of the younger sons of the Marquess of Queensberry, inventor of the rules for Boxing, who at nastiness could give his son a game any day, though nastiness of a somewhat different order.

I have always been struck by the extraordinary suddenness of Wilde's plunge into an utterly disreputable world of blackmailing rent-boys, even if he had been increasingly moving in more or less homosexual circles of an intellectual sort, which nevertheless included sturdy heterosexual elements like Frank Harris. A question that has always posed itself is: what were Wilde's physical relations with his wife during this period? He was outwardly on the best of terms with her, even if frequently away from home, supposedly working.

Ellmann provides a persuasive answer to this. When Wilde was at Oxford (he went up to the University rather older than most) he is believed to have contracted syphilis from a prostitute. Ellmann agrees there is no absolute proof of this, but several matters point to its truth, especially Wilde's autopsy. Ellmann thinks that Wilde told his wife that, after supposing himself completely cured, symptoms had reappeared, which made avoidance of sexual relations wiser.

Something else about the marriage in the dire year of 1894: Constance Wilde may have had a brief affair. Ellmann shows that certainly she was in love. By this time Lord Queensberry had begun the campaign against his son's association with Wilde. Two factors additionally exacerbated this onslaught: Queensberry's second wife divorced him for impotence, an undignified predicament for a champion of masculinity. Almost at the same moment his eldest son, Lord

Drumlanrig, died in circumstances that suggested suicide, possibly from fear of blackmail in connection with Lord Rosebery, whose sexual tastes were suspect.

The rest is well known: the libel action; the two years' hard labour; the dreadful Continental exile before Wilde's death, diseased, penniless, almost impossible to help because of his own loss of all control. It was a terrible end for a man who had been a wit in the top class (his jokes stand up today far better than Whistler's) and a man of unrivalled generosity of heart.

One thing is certain. Disaster would have come sooner or later. Perhaps a mad Marquess was more picturesque than a police raid on a homosexual brothel. English hypocrisy has been much decried where Wilde was concerned. In fact the French and Americans were not much better, even the Italians not showing up particularly well. I think Ellmann takes too seriously Wilde's boast that he 'made' Aubrey Beardsley, a far truer artist than himself; and to call Max Beerbohm ungrateful for caricaturing Wilde is surely to misunderstand the art of the caricaturist. Still, those are small points in a resounding book.

Oscar Wilde, Richard Ellmann,   1987
Hamish Hamilton.   *Daily Telegraph*

IV

In 1887, two or three years after their marriage, Oscar and Constance Wilde took a young Canadian, Robert Ross, as paying guest in their house, 16 Tite Street, Chelsea. Why they knew him is not clear. There were several plausible possibilities as to how that happened. Robbie Ross was cramming at the time to take the examination for King's College, Cambridge.

Ross's father had been Attorney-General of Canada, his mother also coming from a prominent political family in the Dominion. He was one of several children, the family comfortably off, so that if not rich Ross always had something to fall back on. It seems to have been recognised from the start that he was homosexual, regarded as a matter for regret, but not a condition unheard of before.

Ross behaved with such resolute unselfishness towards Wilde, visiting him in prison, raising money for him when he was released, putting up with a great deal of ingratitude, that one is apt to think of him as a tractable figure. On the contrary, Ross was extremely aggressive, not to say litigious.

The importance of Maureen Borland's book is in making this clear. Her style is a shade rough and ready, from time to time she allows her own prejudices a canter, but there is much interesting information told in a manner sympathetic to its subject.

A tradition has flourished that Ross, as an undergraduate, introduced Wilde to active homosexuality. No evidence whatever exists for
this belief; indeed when Ross was PG-ing at Tite Street relations seem
to have been completely formal. Like so much to be observed in Wilde's
career, intimacy seems to have sprung up between them almost from
one day to the next.

Another aspect of Ross's life unfamiliar to me was his friendship with
Lord Alfred Douglas (possibly something even warmer), which
continued at least in theory well into the period after Wilde's death,
when Douglas (who has claims to being one of the nastiest men of his
generation) had already begun his persecutions of Ross. I had
supposed Ross and Douglas always hated each other.

Here, I think, one may underestimate the brotherhood of homosexuality, especially when it was the love that dared not speak its name.
This atmosphere of a secret society is often to be noticed in Maureen
Borland's book; for instance, when Reggie Turner takes Douglas's side,
after what might be thought his inexcusable conduct. Ross's relations
with Douglas were always exceedingly complex, as also with many
other homosexuals who people the narrative.

The undoubted streak of madness in Douglas does not vindicate his
innate and repulsive unpleasantness. He found an appropriate hench-
man in a now forgotten hack called T. W. H. Crossland, heterosexual,
but similarly paranoiac. Together they ran a paper, spattering Ross
with filth that in Douglas's case was also hypocritical filth, as Douglas
himself was tarred with the homosexual accusations he levelled at his
victim.

The final crescendo of all their libels and lawsuits, although
ostensibly something different, was the Pemberton-Billing case in 1918,
with its '47,000 perverts'; perhaps the most grotesque display ever
featured in our newspapers, making, say, the Profumo proceedings
seem like a leader in the parish magazine.

Apart from the side of his life dominated by friendship with Wilde,
and all that derived from it, Ross was an extremely able connoisseur of
pictures, although he stopped short before Post-Impressionism. He
was for some time partner in the Carfax picture gallery in St James's,
coming near being made at different moments Director of the Tate, and
the Wallace Collection. He would have liked the latter appointment.
Ross was also for a period valuer of pictures for the Inland Revenue.

Maureen Borland remarks, certainly with truth, that Ross needed
Wilde in a broken-down state to help. It was part of his nature – if you
like, part of a desire for power – which drew him to the unfortunate. So
shrewd an onlooker as Ada Leverson, the Sphinx, commented: 'I think
he rather resented any friend who was not in need of him.'

Maureen Borland speaks of Ross's habit of introducing a quiet joke into what he wrote. An example of that is his (possibly somewhat apocryphal) encounter, as a child in Chelsea, with Carlyle: 'He was the first, and perhaps most interesting, of all my street acquaintances.'

Ross was responsible for the Epstein sculpture over Wilde's grave in Père-Lachaise, about which there was the inevitable outbreak of rows. Incidentally, those broadminded French (who always laugh so heartily at Anglo-Saxon pruderies) objected to the figure's private parts being slightly prominent.

Epstein refused to modify them, so a bronze fig-leaf was installed. This was, of course, immediately stolen. Accordingly, the Paris authorities put a tarpaulin round the tomb, which remained until early in 1914. The French Customs also claimed £106 for importing a work of art.

I think Maureen Borland might have included a line or two about Christopher Millard as subsequently a distinguished bookseller. Millard only appears as a homosexual always getting into hot water (which he was), bibliographer of Wilde, secretary to Ross. He was rather more than that, a man of notable intelligence and charm.

Wilde's Devoted Friend: A Life of   1990
Robert Ross 1869–1918, Maureen   *Daily Telegraph*
Borland, Lennard.

V

Ada Leverson, if she were notable for no other reason, has earned a certain immortality, like Sir Philip Sidney, by one kind act. During the interval between his trials, when no hotel would take him in, she offered Oscar Wilde a refuge in the nurseries of her house, where, known only to the servants, he lived in secret. It was Wilde who named her The Sphinx.

Violet Wyndham, her daughter, conveys a vivid picture of The Sphinx's world. This is a world increasingly forgotten in the over-simplification of social history. More than once one is reminded of the less exalted but at the same time rich and cultivated circles described by Proust, to which there is now no real parallel.

A wit and novelist of considerable gifts, The Sphinx was not cut out for domesticity, while Ernest Leverson, twelve years older than his wife, was no Ideal Husband. One of the most striking sides of the picture here presented is the mixture of what would now be regarded as comfortable circumstances, a house in Mayfair and so on, combined with ever threatening financial disaster. In the end, the blow fell. Ernest Leverson parted company with The Sphinx and set off to Canada to repair a fortune lost on the racecourse.

Wilde complained bitterly of the way Leverson recouped himself from a fund made over to Wilde of which Leverson was trustee. More than ever one sees that Leverson's behaviour was not unreasonable, and that, so far from being 'bourgeois', he was, already in a financial sense, living almost as dangerously as Wilde himself.

I used to meet The Sphinx sometimes years ago. The vision of her remains as a little old lady, always in black, swathed in stoles and veils, picking her way, as she smiled gently to herself, through an infinitely rackety party of persons most of whom were at least forty years younger. She had all the air of a celebrity.

It is characteristic, when Wyndham Lewis's *Apes of God* appeared, causing annoyance among those who were so bitterly, and often unfairly, lampooned there, that The Sphinx was absolutely delighted by her own appearance in those pages.

Among the persons who appear momentarily in the circle of The Sphinx are John Gray and André Raffalovich, subject of the series of essays in *Two Friends*. Here we have a very different development from the 1890s and very different treatment of their commemoration.

John Gray, author of *Silverpoints*, a book of poems, famous even in those days of exotic book production for the breadth of its margins, was a young civil servant of modest origins, who brought a libel action against a newspaper for saying he was the model for Dorian Gray. It seems undeniable that he signed at least one of his letters to Wilde 'Dorian'.

With the best will in the world, it is hard to reread Gray's work without thinking him an astonishingly bad poet. All the same, he was obviously extremely good-looking and lively as a young man, on familiar terms with all the nineties notabilities.

Gray's lifelong friend André Raffalovich was of Russian origin. In his early days he wrote a pioneer study of homosexuality and several novels. Violet Wyndham says that Raffalovich was so ugly as a baby that his mother sent him to England, determined never to see him again.

At the age of thirty-two Gray took orders as a Roman Catholic priest, a Church to which Raffalovich also belonged. They went to live in Edinburgh, where Gray became a canon, well known for his saintly life and black linen sheets on his narrow bed. Raffalovich was equally noted for his benefactions to religion and charity. Their combined luncheon parties in Edinburgh were rather famous.

I found the story of Gray's and Raffalovich's moral regeneration less stimulating than The Sphinx's complete inability to be a good example to anyone. Perhaps Gray sometimes felt that too. 'Sunday is a miserable day,' he once murmured (so Father Edwin Essex records), then adding apparently in the depths of gloom, 'It's a miserable life altogether.'

The Sphinx and Her Circle: A   1963
Biographical Study of Ada Leverson,   *Daily Telegraph*
1862–1933, Violet Wyndham,
Deutsch.
Two Friends: John Gray and André
Raffalovich: Essays Biographical and
Critical, edited by Father Brocard
Sewell, St Albert's Press.

VI

In the history of the world there may have been two greater narcissists than George Bernard Shaw (1856–1950) and Lord Alfred Douglas (1870–1945), but where vanity, certainty of being in the right, self-advertisement, were in question there cannot have been many competitors.

This view is by no means weakened by each drawing attention to such characteristics in the other, while claiming total humility where he himself was concerned. With such marked traits in common, they were bound to come together. It is only surprising that this did not happen until Shaw was seventy-four and Douglas sixty.

In the aftermath of Oscar Wilde's débâcle, violent quarrels had broken out among Wilde's friends and hangers-on as to who had, and who had not, behaved well throughout the drama. In the course of these polemics Shaw, generally speaking, remained on good terms with all the chief combatants, though evidence in Mary Hyde's well-edited collection of letters suggests that he was not above stirring up a bit of surreptitious trouble in that area from time to time.

Douglas, although possibly behaving slightly better after Wilde's downfall than some of those who disliked him alleged, at the same time cannot be said to have cut a very attractive figure. But, as Shaw put it:

It is inevitable that you should appear in these [Wilde's] biographies as a sort of *âme damnée* beside him, not in the least because you were a beautiful youth who seduced him into homosexuality (how enormously better it would have been for him if you had: you might have saved him from his wretched debaucheries with guttersnipes!) but because you were a lord and he was a snob.

The case in point was a book by Frank Harris to which Shaw had contributed a preface, where Douglas thought he had been badly treated. Everyone knew that Harris was a scoundrel, though in certain respects an amusing one. Shaw's malicious side caused him to have an undoubted weakness for Harris (who died in 1931) especially in his capacity as a buccaneer disrupting society. In justice to Shaw, he also wanted to do what he could for Harris's widow, left in a state of near destitution.

A correspondence now began between Shaw and Douglas which was to last for more than a dozen years. It was really a kind of flirtation between two elderly men, one not without its embarrassments, when Douglas addresses Shaw as 'St Christopher', and Shaw – as Douglas had asked to be called Childe Alfred – begins his letters 'Dear Childe'.

Douglas was at this period in a far from prosperous state, living in a flat in Hove for which he was always on the point of being unable to pay the rent. He received a small allowance from his wife with whom he was on good terms, though they did not live together.

He had done six months' imprisonment for libelling Winston Churchill, and – Shaw pointed out – possessed a taste for litigation that made many papers unwilling to mention him at all for fear of Douglas bringing a case. Writing in April 1939, Douglas says: 'After all I am the best living English poet.' In that field it must be admitted that at least 'the love that dare not speak its name' has established a place for itself.

Shaw asserts here more than once that he did not dislike Wilde, but there can be little doubt that, as a fellow Anglo-Irish literary adventurer making a career in England, he felt a certain jealousy, as he showed in his denigration of *The Importance of Being Earnest* as a play.

The line between being a professional wit and a professional bore is one only too easily crossed. Wilde, one feels, however trying his behaviour at some moments might have been, remained on the right side, while the same cannot be said for Shaw. Douglas, where his own obsessions are concerned, scarcely pretends to be anything other than a bore. I met him only once but his potentialities in that direction were clearly colossal.

Where Douglas wanted Shaw to alter certain things in his preface (when another edition of Harris's book appeared) Shaw is shown here at least twice in saying he had made the requested alterations when he had in fact done nothing of the kind. Nevertheless the two correspondents remained on good terms.

There is an amusing discussion of Shakespeare's Sonnets (about which Douglas was writing a book) during the course of which Shaw shrewdly comments:

I think your view of Shakespeare's complaints of senile decay and decrepitude as proofs that he was a very young man indeed when he wrote them is brilliantly sound; but you had better keep at the back of your mind the fact that such complaints have two characteristic ages.

One of them is twenty and the other forty. Forty, which decisively ends all pretensions to youth, makes a fearful impression.

If I were you I should take the complaint as proving Shakespeare was either twenty or forty, and then show that forty was out of the question.

Shaw's praise of Mussolini, Hitler, and Stalin is well known. Even allowing for such political orientations, his sheer inability to form correct judgments as to what was going to happen make one wonder how he could ever have been taken seriously. For instance in April 1939, Shaw writes:

Of course the war scare is all nonsense. Now that the last page of the Versailles treaty has been torn up and flung in our faces (it being quite certain we would not fight for it), and that we are frightened into a combination with Russia at last, there is no sane risk f war on the cards.

<table>
<tr><td>Bernard Shaw and Alfred Douglas:</td><td>1982</td></tr>
<tr><td>A Correspondence, ed. Mary Hyde,</td><td>Daily Telegraph</td></tr>
<tr><td>Murray.</td><td></td></tr>
</table>

FRANK HARRIS

Quite a lot of books have been written about Frank Harris (1856–1931). The fascination he exerted – and must to some extent still exert – remains to some degree inexplicable. Philippa Pullar starts off in rather a jaunty style, summarising events with plenty of the four-letter words that Harris himself so much loved, but by the last quarter of the story one feels that she, like everyone else who had dealings with Harris, has been a little worn down. This is largely because the awful muddle of his later years is almost impossible to chronicle in anything like intelligible narrative. It is also hard not to be facetious about him. Perhaps there is no reason for even trying to avoid that.

The story of Harris's beginnings are better set out here than in any other work I have read. They were origins sufficiently diverse to offer unusual opportunities for a fantasist, and Harris was a fantasist in the top class – one of the greatst who has ever lived. Both his parents were Pembrokeshire Welsh, not altogether like the rest of the principality in character. His father was a coastguard, stationed in Ireland, where his son was born. Harris himself went to America when he was about fifteen or sixteen, after going to school at Ruabon in Denbighshire.

Ruabon was likely to figure as Rugby in his later days, though paradoxically he usually wore Old Etonian ties (as in most of the photographs in this book), of which he was always asking his admirer, Hesketh Pearson, to send him a fresh supply.

The difficulty faced by the Harris biographer is: what can be believed? In short, what is the real point of Harris? It is not an easy question to answer. A few undeniable facts as to his abilities are worth recording. He arrived in the United States with about £15, and certainly had a hard struggle at first. Nevertheless, by the time he was nineteen he had passed the exams required for the American Bar.

While still quite a young man he could talk excellent French and German. The stories he told about his methods of learning these languages may be absurd. The fact remains that it is on record that he spoke them well. What can only be guessed at are his powers of persuasion – half charm, half bullying – the effectiveness of which was really his own downfall.

Philippa Pullar, no doubt rightly, emphasises that much of Harris's time was spent in a state of deep melancholy. He suffered from fearful depressions and fear of illness. This was the other side of his womanising and high living, aspects to which he himself gave much prominence. The ludicrous nature of most of the stories he told about himself still obscures some of the extraordinary things that really did happen to him.

There seems absolutely no doubt that when, as a young man, Harris returned to England, he made a great impression. He was a worshipper of Carlyle. The story of the Sage confiding the fact that he was impotent to Harris has been much ridiculed. Philippa Pullar shows that, from evidence available, it is by no means impossible that Carlyle should have said something of the sort. Carlyle's letter recommending Harris to Froude – thought by some debunkers not to exist – is referred to in a letter written by Froude produced here.

All this early part of Harris's life, his journalism and friendships with the writers of the 1890s, particularly Wilde, makes comparative sense. He is to be seen as a lively, if not particularly reputable, adjunct to the literary world of the period. He seems to have gone off the rails in his late thirties, interesting himself in financial ventures of a risky sort, notably the promoting of an hotel in the south of France.

One of the good points about Harris was that he made no bones whatever about standing up for Wilde when he was sent to prison. This was a courageous thing to do at the time. He also helped Wilde financially, but there were the inevitable rows about that, which happened to all Wilde's benefactors. Harris himself sooner or later had rows with everyone he dealt with.

Of his adventures with women told in *My Life and Loves*, written in a desperate need of money, there is nothing particularly unbelievable except the absurdity of the circumstances described – Harris was entirely devoid of humour. He may well have enjoyed experiences of more or less that sort, even if the details were less picturesque. His relations with Nelly, life-long mistress, and finally third wife, are not without fascination, Harris casting her for a certain role in his emotional life, and through thick and thin, insisting that she was playing that role, no matter how differently she was in fact behaving.

Harris seems to have had a perfectly genuine desire to fight against some of the hypocrisies and injustices of his age, but he entirely lacked the balance required to get such things improved. One of the most convincing accounts of him comes from Thomas Bell, an accountant (later Harris's secretary), who was interviewd by him for a job, without knowing who his prospective employer might be. In the course of later conversations it was mentioned by Bell that he knew Dutch. Harris asked about Dutch literature. When Bell spoke of a Dutch author who wrote under a pen-name Harris at once referred to him by his real name. That may have been a bit of luck, but it was the sort of luck Harris often showed.

Latterly he was inclined sometimes to identify himself with Christ, at others with Shakespeare. There was no doubt a touch of paranoia.

Frank Harris, Philippa Pullar,   1975
Hamish Hamilton.   *Daily Telegraph*

JOHN LANE AND THE
BODLEY HEAD

The Bodley Head was established in London in 1887 by Charles Elkin Mathews and John Lane. Elkin Mathews, whose family background was shipbuilding at Gravesend, had a little bookshop in Exeter, home town of Sir Thomas Bodley, founder of the Bodleian Library at Oxford. That settled the name. Lane, only son of a Devon farmer, was a clerk in the Railway Clearing House at Euston Station, a job found him by the Revd. Stephen Hawker, parson-poet of Morwenna ('and shall Trelawney die', etc.), who was a friend of Lane's mother.

Lane, as well as being keen on business, was already a confirmed bibliomaniac by his early thirties, when the firm came to birth, and probably possessed as good a collection of books as his means allowed. To that extent he may be regarded as a promising publisher for the 'list' that the Bodley Head was to produce. At the same time, he was moved to tears by William Watson's sonnet, 'Life is still life, not yet the hearth is cold' – hardly characteristic of the spirit of the *Décadence*.

Elkin Mathews did not possess even these basic qualifications to publish *The Yellow Book*. He found it difficult to make up his mind on any subject, but at least knew that he did not care for the Decadents. Like Lane, he enjoyed commercial success, and is described as a 'neat, dapper little man, rather fussy and old-maidish in his ways'. To add to the burden of Decadent writers and artists published by the Bodley Head, Richard La Gallienne arrived from Liverpool, where he was learning to be a chartered accountant, to become a London poet and the firm's chief reader.

Le Gallienne – whose very name, someone said, suggested incorrect grammar – was actively opposed to the whole Movement, but it is characteristic of how much the period is misunderstood that, if he is remembered at all, he is usually lumped in with its members. Nothing was further from his own view. He wrote:

> To notice only the picturesque effect of a beggar's rags, like Gautier; the colour scheme of a tippler's nose, like M. Huysmans; to consider one's mother merely prismatically like Mr Whistler – these are examples of the decadent attitude. At bottom, decadence is limited thinking, often insane thinking.

This publishing background, in many ways so incongruous, adds point to the laughing irony of such Beardsley drawings as the frontispiece to John Davidson's *Plays*, which caricatures, among others, Le Gallienne. Davidson was himself an anti-Decadent, though a more interesting man and much better poet.

Wilde, extremely competent when it came to transacting literary business, did not get on with Lane, whose name he gave to the manservant in *The Importance of Being Earnest*. The Bodley Head's stock boy, William Shelley, played a squalid part in the Wilde trials, which really put an end to the period. Lane does not come particularly well out of the panic that followed.

James G. Nelson's book is by no means limited to the personalities of the Nineties, dealing thoroughly with the bibliographical and typographical side of the Bodley Head. It is probably true to say that well-printed and designed books at a reasonable price have never been bettered than by, say, the Keynote Series.

Of course all Bodley Head writers were not Decadent figures. Among the others who deserve a mention is John Leicester Warren, third and last Lord de Tabley, by no means a bad poet, and a melancholy man. He had written a pioneering work, *A Guide to the Study of Book-plates*, which had fallen flat on publication, but when reissued by the Bodley Head sold out. De Tabley was far from delighted:

> I have failed in literature, I have failed in politics. I have failed in such a miserable thing as being a landlord, which any fool can manage. Nothing remains except these contemptible book-plates! It is like poor Lear, whose pictures are all wrong, whose serious writing is all wrong, but who made his one hit with a book of nonsense.

I think that insistence on the Nineties being a reaction from 'Victorian materialism' has become rather a cliché. Human beings, when examined, do not greatly vary in their 'materialism' from one age to another, even though its pursuit may take different forms.

The Decadent side of the Nineties can be traced back a long way, while many of its other ingredients show new attitudes towards art and society taking shape. It is interesting, for instance, that as early as 1891, the playgoer is described as having to sit through naturalistic dramas which prove that burglars are:

> The Psychical Epitome
> Of Labour struggling to be free.

The Early Nineties: A View from the Bodley Head, James G. Nelson, Oxford University Press for Harvard.

1971
Daily Telegraph

AUBREY BEARDSLEY

I

The 1890s have been written of *ad nauseam*; and are usually accepted – at their own estimation – as the over-ripe fruit of the Victorian terminal. Whether such a view of them is no more than the final piece of romanticism to crown their own prevailingly romantic mood, or whether they were, indeed, a little renaissance, set neatly at the end of the reign and standing apart in the history of art and letters, is a question that might well be asked. They are, after all, as much the beginning of one period as the end of another, and their most characteristic ideas and sentiments, traceable to far earlier epochs, lasted, many of them, to the 1920s. The luxuriance, the despair, the diabolism, the self-conscious indifference to the laws of destiny, all in some degree legacy of Byron, Swinburne, Pater and a host of others (supported by Gautier, Baudelaire and many more nineteenth-century writers in France), possess a long pedigree in the record of what has been well called the Romantic Agony; while, in the graphic arts, Pre-Raphaelites or painters like Fuseli and Dadd had toyed earlier in the century with themes that came to be thought of as typically *fin de siècle*. Even on the Continent the tendency was to move in other directions only by easy stages. The theatrical designs of Léon Bakst or sad clowns of Picasso's 'blue period', might equally well have been accommodated before the turn of the century.

It might be suggested, for example, that two main, and apparently hostile, concepts govern the period: first, that self-indulgence is best; second, that life should be approached in a spirit of abnegation. To some extent, of course, examples of obvious blendings of these notions are to be found (in novels and short stories, notably through the mouthpiece of such characters as renegade priests and disillusioned noblemen); and the images assume from time to time new and complicated patterns, according to the vagaries of mutually opposed political, aesthetic or social creeds. They are, however, adequately illustrated, in a general way, by the extreme antitheses of Wilde and Kipling, the former affirming from the house tops (at any rate until the moment of débâcle) that the pursuit, in decidedly artificial forms, of beauty and pleasure was the true object of existence; the latter, with scarcely more delicacy and restraint, advocating a path of duty that lay through a jungle of sombre and disagreeable realities.

Both these apprehensions – at any rate the manner in which they were ventilated – were in some degree products of an age of wealth, order, security. They are complementary to each other and reflect different aspects of the same picture, making in a strange manner the nineties of a piece. We see all at once that there could have been no Dorian Gray without the Absent-minded Beggar: Trilby's singing was the answer to Salome's dancing: Bernard Shaw's pragmatical heroines become the inevitable antidote to a repletion of Cynaras; *The Yellow Book* lies at peace beside the *Pink 'Un*, while the cigar-smoke from Romano's mingles with the incense of the Black Mass.

Wilde's name is commonly invoked as the high priest of the period; and certainly the side of literature which he represents is not otherwise strong in eminent figures. There is, however, another name which has become increasingly employed to indicate the essence of the period, and for this reason is often spoken of as if representing a similar approach to Wilde's. It is that of Aubrey Beardsley. Beardsley is *par excellence* the figure which embodies the austerity and the licence, oddly fused together, that represent the conflicting sentiments of those years.

Between delighted commendation for beauty of 'line' and outraged censure of 'morbidity' of subject, there remains, even after fifty years, some doubt regarding Beardsley's status in the gallery of the English School. *The Best of Beardsley* reproduces 130 or more of his drawings, with an introduction by R. A. Walker, acknowledged expert on the subject. The collection provides an excellent survey of the artist's outstanding work. Ideally speaking, there might have been a shade less shine in the paper on which these examples are reproduced; but such refinements are not always possible nowadays. Here at least is a volume at a reasonable price, which would give someone who knew nothing of Beardsley an excellent idea of the scope of his work. The new edition of Arthur Symons's essay on Beardsley (first published in 1898) also contains sixteen plates, and supplies, perhaps, the answer to the question of shiny paper; because the drawings on this rougher surface are distinctly coarsened in reproduction.

Aubrey Beardsley was born on 21 August 1872. Walker mentions an ancestral prompting of some interest: his paternal grandfather was a jeweller, or working goldsmith. An hereditary and businesslike interest in elaborate design is therefore established at the outset. By the age of eleven he was a musical prodigy, performing in public, a few years later, acting in amateur productions in the appropriate setting of the domes and cupolas of the Pavilion at Brighton. When, at seventeen, he entered the Guardian Life and Fire Insurance Office as a clerk his reading was already extensive and varied. He died in his twenty-sixth year on 23 March 1898, leaving behind him a number of remarkable drawings which, for the term of his working life, is enormous. To speculate on how he might have developed, had he lived, is to ignore the cause of his illness; for tuberculosis undoubtedly played its part in the feverish and unnatural energy packed into so few years. It may be of assistance, critically speaking, to consider him under three headings, that is to say, as a draughtsman, as an illustrator, and as the epitome of the Nineties as an epoch.

Beardsley's fortune, or misfortune, was that almost every available scrap to which he ever set his hand should be put before the public. There is nothing that he would have cared for less; but although a book like *The Uncollected Work of Aubrey Beardsley* (1925) added in no way to his reputation, it gave the opportunity (withheld in the case of most artists) of peeping behind the scenes. Certainly nothing could be more extraordinary than the bound he made from these crude – if not uninteresting – sketches (which might have appeared in any school magazine) into technical virtuosity and an atmosphere of inspissated *décadence* of a year or two later.

The influences that follow so quickly upon the steps of these immature designs are clearly innumerable. On what might be called the Anglo-Saxon side there are Burne-Jones, Walter Crane, Whistler, Phil May (as Walker points out), and, of course, Hogarth: Continental models were supplied by Crivelli, Mantegna, Callot, Longhi, Watteau, Goya, Prud'hon, Toulouse-Lautrec, and Gustave Moreau: Greek vases and Japanese prints also finding a place. From this diversified, but not incoherent, assemblage something entirely original emerged; indeed, so individual was the result that imitation of Beardsley was uniformly unhappy. This was not because there were few imitators. On the contrary, their name was legion. France was distinctly impressed; while in Germany and Austria the Beardsley impact was so strong as to be observable in book illustration or theatrical décor within a few years of the Second World War. The later Beardsley drawings – *Mademoiselle de Maupin* and *Volpone* – have for some reason a peculiarly Teutonic flavour, which no doubt explains this.

To deny the skill of Beardsley's draughtsmanship would today be scarcely tenable as a critical position; though Roger Fry found 'meanness' in certain of his pictures: for example, in the subsidiary decoration of the scenes from *The Rape of the Lock*. Few would attempt to deny that a perfectly straightforward drawing like 'Garçons de Café', from which extraneous elements or comment have been excluded, shows mastery of his medium; and keen grasp of the possibilities of modern reproductory processes, which was his almost revolutionary contribution to the decorative arts. There can be no doubt, however, that he is also a great illustrator. A generation of critics, reacting from

Victorian representational painting, have preached – sometimes with irascible pedantry – that since pictures are merely a matter of colour and design, they might just as well be hung upside-down, a position in which such qualities might be equally well appreciated; while any question of 'telling a story' would in this fashion be removed. If, in fact, pictures *were* hung upside-down to absolve them from all imputation of anecdotage, few would come out of that ordeal better than Beardsley's, whose delicate and intricate lines make as indestructible a pattern as his reasoned masses of black and white.

The English have always shown an aptitude for illustration; and the proclivity does supply a place for Beardsley in a long and distinguished dynasty of English illustrators: Gilray and Rowlandson, Cruickshank and Phiz, Leech and Keene.

Taking a stand, therefore, on the view that he was at once an illustrator and draughtsman of first-class ability, we are still left with the characteristic to which his antagonists are least reconcilable: that is to say, his manner of looking at life. Some correction of a misunder-standing is necessary. This, as suggested earlier, is in the disregard often shown for the different – and, in fact, violently opposed – standpoints of Beardsley and Wilde, who have scarcely anything in common, except that both died in the rites of the Roman Catholic Church. Wilde was, of course, at the height of his success when Beardsley first appeared on the scene; and, although it was natural enough that Beardsley's drawings should sooner or later find their way into Wilde's books, it might be safely said that, unlike Beardsley, there is about Wilde little or no distaste for life. Witty, romantic, and *au fond* sentimental, he has no real criticism to make of the world around him. One may like Beardsley or leave him alone, but his drawings indicate an entirely contrary attitude. We may even feel at times that he used the idiom of the moment simply because it *was* the idiom of the moment: therefore expressed best his bitter and sardonic cast of mind in satirising his surroundings. He was without sentimentality. We can readily understand that, when shown his drawings, William Morris could see nothing in them.

The rope in the picture called 'The Footnote' (a bond removed on the cover of *A Second Book of Fifty Drawings* (1899), but restored in *The Best of Beardsley*) yokes Beardsley's self-portrait to the statue of Priapus. That must be admitted (with its implications) as his own *apologia*; but, even in *Lysistrata*, Beardsley is never salacious in the manner of, say, Félicien Rops – a much inferior contemporary to whom he is sometimes compared, and Arthur Symons, rather surprisingly, commends in his essay. After all, Aristophanes himself does not mince his words; though it should be added that on his deathbed the artist asked that all equivocal drawings be destroyed. It is Beardsley's inflexible severity that shocks rather than any promise he holds out of forbidden pleasure. If this truth cannot be derived from a study of the drawings themselves, it may be borne out by the records that remain of Beardsley's personal relationships. He disliked Wilde, caricaturing him in the *Salome* series. There was an undoubted tendency among the milder aesthetes of the period – while they bowed to Beardsley's genius – to regard him as a cocky young man from the City, perhaps even a rather bumptious young man, whose demeanour was out of place in a world where conventions had become established in snugly epigrammatic, if somewhat old-maidish, terms. In Robert Ross's excellent 'Eulogy of Aubrey Beardsley' which introduces *Volpone* (1899) some of these things are hinted at; and there are lines in a letter written by Beardsley in May 1897 (*Last Letters of Aubrey Beardsley*, 1904), describing a meeting with a French priest, which reveal almost startlingly how far removed were some of his impulses from the popular idea of him:

> He asked me if I had completed my military service yet in England, and I felt quite ashamed to confess that we were not expected ever to do anything at all for our country.

Sickert showed Beardsley how to paint in oil, setting on the palette for him the colours for 'A Caprice', and in Sickert's vigorous and trenchant canvases there is perhaps to be found something more in common with Beardsley's orientation than superficial resemblances in the tailpieces of Ricketts or the fans of Conder; for Beardsley had a vitality and power of self-criticism that put his work far ahead of the majority of his contemporaries in any of the arts. In an era of Ivory Towers, in so much as it was possible, suffering as he did, he lived within one; but with a keen eye for what was going on outside. There can be no doubt that he struck the best moment for the display of his genius; though, equally, such a genius could not have remained hidden long in any age. It was, perhaps, as well that he did not survive to our own time, when there are few Ivory Towers available; for as someone was saying only the other day – now that so much of the Empire has gone, one simply cannot get the ivory.

The Best of Beardsley, edited and compiled by R. A. Walker, Bodley Head.
Aubrey Beardsley, Arthur Symons, Unicorn Press.

1949
Times Literary Supplement

II

This volume of Beardsley's Letters is of great interest, revealing more of the artist himself and the people who surrounded him, at the same time providing a dramatic, amusing, in the end appallingly harrowing story. As a boy of ten Beardsley was performing at concerts, and would probably have become a professional musician had his health allowed. At that age he was also earning money for his hard-up family by designing menus. His unsatisfactory father worked in a brewer's; his mother, a dominating figure in his life, daughter of a Surgeon-Major in the Army.

At Brighton Grammar School Beardsley was contemporary and friend of C. B. Cochran, the impresario, who produced at Brighton Pavilion a play Beardsley wrote as a schoolboy. Just before he was sixteen, a job was found for him in the Clerkenwell and Islington surveyor's office; then he became an insurance clerk.

One of the most dramatic letters describes how Beardsley and his sister went to Burne-Jones's studio, where they had been told the pictures could be seen on application. This turned out not to be the case. They were walking away, when Burne-Jones himself ran after them, saying they must come in, having made the journey on such a hot day. Beardsley, then eighteen, had by chance some of his own drawings with him. He showed them to Burne-Jones, who at once recognised their qualities. The Oscar Wildes were at tea, and the young Beardsley travelled back with them. From that moment Beardsley moved into the extraordinary vortex he was to inhabit for the rest of his life.

Roger Fry called Beardsley the 'Fra Angelico of Satanism'. This strikes me as an exceedingly silly remark to come from an eminent, if humourless, critic. Apart from his technical mastery of black and white masses, the essential character of Beardsley is that he was a supreme comic artist. The phallic Lysistrata drawings, once thought so wicked, are these days published in the ordinary way and to be bought across the counter.

Such a view of Beardsley himself is certainly brought out by the Letters. Although he may have, so to speak, dealt in affectation, he was himself the most unaffected of men. His letters to Leonard Smithers, an effective publisher but undeniably disreputable figure, show Beardsley's directness and wit. They are an instance – regrettably rare – of freedom to print four-letter words providing something really funny.

Although for a time Beardsley was the rage, and money came in with relative ease, Wilde's trial and conviction put a stop to that. The frightened John Lane sacked Beardsley from *The Yellow Book*, and it was not long before increasing ill health, owing to his tubercular lung, threatened financial disaster.

When an article described him as 'unclean and sexless', Beardsley wrote a letter saying that, as to the first, he took a bath every day; and, if the critic thought the second, he could come and see him in it. A matter cleared up in the Letters is the accusation that Beardsley cut Wilde in

Dieppe after his release from prison. The reverse appears from Wilde's own Letters, and it is now clear that Beardsley hoped to give the former impression to André Raffalovich. Raffalovich was a Roman Catholic convert, who played a great part in Beardsley's own conversion, which took place five months before his death at the age of twenty-five. Raffalovich was on bad terms with Wilde, but was supporting Beardsley in his illness with £400 a year. This also explains Beardsley's letter telling Smithers he would work for a projected magazine only if Wilde were not a contributor.

The conflicting sides of Beardsley's character are well displayed by concurrent letters to Raffalovich and Smithers. They make an extra-ordinary contrast, sometimes written on the same date. One is perpetually struck by Beardsley's way of expressing himself in a manner – as opposed to, say, Wilde or Beerbohm – that might perfectly well be used today.

Scrope Davies ('reference untraced') was a friend of Byron's. In Stanley Weintraub's 'Beardsley' (1965) 'whom the gods love, etc.' (to Smithers, M. S. Huntington) reads (Weintraub, p. 208) 'whom the sods love, etc.'

The Letters of Aubrey Beardsley, edited   1971
by Henry Maas, J. L. Duncan and   *Daily Telegraph*
W. G. Good, Cassell.

III

This new (fourth) edition of *Le Morte Darthur*, a facsimile of the third, includes three additional drawings, and the cover Beardsley misspelt. Many of the designs are magnificent, though the figure-work, astonish-ing as it is for an artist of twenty, still echoes Burne-Jones.

Beardsley's death at twenty-five, showing no sign of failing powers, left behind scanty biographical material. What does exist has been excellently sifted and arranged by Malcolm Easton in *Aubrey and the Dying Lady*. This is certainly the best study of its subject up to date. Easton brings to the story not only scholarship and understanding, but also that worldly wisdom and humour which are almost equally required. He can praise Beardsley, show his exceptional gifts, without disparaging those among whom he moved, like Wilde, who knew himself no match for Beardsley where the arts were concerned.

There are, of course, those who can see in Beardsley no more than sneering, masked faces, pierrots, dwarfs, hermaphrodites, but (setting aside his marvellous drawing) the myriads of imitators never managed to achieve anything approaching his 'moral' vision, his deep and biting irony. Not one could ever be mistaken for a genuine Beardsley by those familiar with the real thing.

Naturally the question arises in Easton's book of Beardsley's own sexual orientation. It has been suggested – I think insensitively – that he was homosexual. There can be no doubt that he attracted homosexuals, sometimes he wrote them what seem rather flirtatious letters, and he was, when dying, saved from absolute penury by the generosity of André Raffalovich, admittedly one of them.

As against that, Beardsley himself, more or less in so many words, stated he was not homosexual. Certainly he went on jaunts to Brussels and elsewhere with his publisher Smithers, where the goal would have been women, though no doubt prostitutes. There seems no evidence that Beardsley ever claimed anyone remotely to be described as a 'regular girl-friend' – still less 'boy-friend' – though efforts to seduce him by Ada Leverson, 'the Sphinx', are alleged. We do not know with what result.

Something else is indicated in a letter to another of his publishers, John Lane. 'I'm going to Jimmie's [the St James's Restaurant, off Piccadilly] on Thursday night dressed up as a tart, and mean to have a regular spree.' Was he pulling Lane's leg? Apart from the fact that transvestites are by no means necessarily homosexual – and this was (if carried out) undoubtedly a rag – another question arises, which is the crux of Easton's study. Was Beardsley accompanied 'in drag' by his sister Mabel?

Mabel Beardsley, a year older than her brother, a beauty, an actress of some note, was also an extraordinary person. She died in 1916. She is the 'Dying Lady' of Yeats's poem, and the title of Easton's book. How incestuous was the relationship? There can be no doubt whatever that mutual devotion felt by Beardsley and his sister went far beyond feelings between most brothers and sisters. It should be noted that Beardsley (considering the textbook psychology of his situation), was by no means obsessed with his mother.

There seems reliable evidence that Mabel Beardsley had a miscarriage in her early twenties. Suggestions that her brother was responsible (never very credible) are specifically denied by Easton on available evidence. One would guess that nothing of the sort ever took place, but Easton draws attention to Beardsley's undoubted preoccupation with pictures of embryos.

Beardsley's father, usually spoken of as a ne'er-do-well, emerges with glowing testimonials from Crowley's Alton Ale Stores. Was Aleister Crowley's father (a well-to-do brewer) one of the directors? The Beardsley children were brought up as the Highest of High Anglicans. This played a great part in Beardsley's life, his deathbed conversion to Roman Catholicism being no last minute hustle into religion, brought about by Raffalovich. Malcolm Easton is admirable in the way he deals with many painful yet fascinating questions, his delicacy and intellectual appreciation always tempered with good sense and good jokes.

Aubrey and the Dying Lady: A   1972
Beardsley Riddle, Malcolm Easton,   *Daily Telegraph*
Secker & Warburg.
Le Morte Darthur, Sir Thomas
Malory, illustrated by Aubrey
Beardsley, Dent.

IV

Simon Wilson's new selection, *Beardsley*, has the merit of including a hitherto unpublished Beardsley drawing, *The Impatient Adulterer* (1897) in which I take special interest, as I was offered it at a very reasonable price in the late 1940s. *The Impatient Adulterer* is one of Beardsley's phallic designs, and there seemed the difficult problem of where to hang it, which would arise even in these days. One wonders if – as so often with Beardsley – the adulterer himself is a portrait. Most of the fifty drawings here have been rephotographed, and I have the impression that the large Café Royal mirror behind *The Fat Woman* (Mrs Whistler) comes out better than usual. I am not sure that I agree, in *L'Education Sentimentale*, that the elder woman is 'corrupting' the girl, who looks well past that, but then I don't really think Beardsley 'corrupting'. I find him merely our greatest satirical artist. Wilson's notes are sometimes a little obvious, as when he remarks of one of the Lysistrata drawings that occur here: 'The marvellous black stockings are less ancient Greek than modern Parisian'. Surely they are more *Belle Epoque* than modern? It would be more useful to find an explanation for why the lady whipping Earl Lavender is left-handed.

Beardsley, Simon Wilson, Phaidon.   1977
                                                       Apollo

MAX BEERBOHM

I

The wit and sense of Max Beerbohm's theatrical criticism written for the *Saturday Review*, between 1898 and 1910, where Beerbohm succeeded G. B. Shaw, is emphasised by the cloud of wearisome and cantankerous bombast that finally emerges from so much of Shaw's writings. Here, for example, we learn the feelings of a critic at the first night of *Quo Vadis?*, *Peter Pan*, and *The Passing of the Third Floor Back*.

In 1898 George Robey, 'who was educated at Cambridge and is, in my opinion, one of the few distinguished men produced by Cambridge within recent years', was already going strong. In point of fact Beerbohm did not find the manner of such comedians – 'the Cambridge manner, I suppose' – immensely sympathetic, except for Dan Leno, whose obituary notice is perhaps the most delightful of the essays collected here. Leno, 'whose theme was ever the sordidness of the lower middle class, seen from within', was a man of true genius:

> the moment he capered on, with that air of wild determination, squirming in every limb with some deep grievance, that must be outpoured, all hearts were his . . . that face so tragic, with all the tragedy that is writ on the face of a baby-monkey.
>
> I have always thought [writes Beerbohm] that the speech over Yorick's skull would have been much more poignant if Hamlet had given Horatio some specific example of the way in which the jester had been wont to set the table in a roar. We ought to have seen Hamlet convulsed with laughter over what he told, and Horatio trying to conjure up the ghost of a smile.

What a pity that Beerbohm does not himself offer some appropriate example of what Hamlet might recall.

In dealing with *Macbeth* he does, however, provide a little historical booby-trap. It would be interesting to know if it has remained unquestioned for fifty-five years.

> According to Aubrey the play was first acted in 1606, at Hampton Court, in the presence of King James. It is stated that Hal Berridge, the youth who was to have acted the part of Lady Macbeth, 'fell sudden sicke of a pleurisie, wherefor Master Shakespeare himself did

53

enacte in his stead'. One wishes that Aubrey had given some account of the poet's impersonation.

'Stated' this may have been, but not by Aubrey. One Mackyse Byerbohemme, Gent. (later dubbed Knight) may have contrived it – and, after all, Shakespeare would have been forty-two.

While on the subject of Shakespeare, the Beerbohm comment on the Bensons is worth quoting:

I wish Mr Benson would, in his very genuine devotion to Shakespeare's memory, ask himself, whenever he is meditating a new production, 'If the poet were alive today, and I were asked to dictate the cast, would he make me and my wife play the two leading parts? If not, which are the two parts he would assign to us?'

In rather the same manner, Sarah Bernhardt is taken to task for playing l'Aiglon:

Some years ago I found in a musical hall an 'artiste' made up as Faust on one side and Marguerite on the other singing 'Notte d'Amor' in alternate voice and profile. If Sarah had seen him, I am sure she would have taken the hint.

We are given a glimpse of George Alexander 'wearing a wig that was evidently a mat of oakum woven by a convict'. Gerald du Maurier, playing in Björnson in 1901

as the Pastor's son, had the kind of part in which a self-conscious young Englishman would be bound to feel that he was making a fool of himself . . . But Mr du Maurier did nothing of the kind. Advancing years have made an artist of him.

Of W. B. Yeats:

There is a prologue to 'The King's Threshold,' and in the printed copy of the play, Mr Yeats notifies that this prologue was 'not used in Dublin, as, owing to the smallness of the company, nobody could be spared to speak it'. Of course, the pride of poverty is not in itself less ridiculous than the pride of wealth. But it has, for the London playgoer, at least, the charm of newness.

The essay, 'Literary Men on the Stage' (1904), is one of the best.

The histrionic and the literary temperaments are of all temperaments further asunder. Actors, having so little in common with writers, see as little as possible of them. When an actor cast for the part of a literary man conscientiously penetrates into literary circles to observe, he is very much disappointed. He wants good make-up –

something typical and sharply distinctive; and he looks for it in vain. Their art, unlike the actor's, stamps no special seal upon their features and their gait. As for costume, and hair-dressing, the modern writer carefully shuns anything in the way of specialism. His dearest ambition is to be taken for a soldier. His ambition is unfulfilled; but he often succeeds in looking rather like a doctor. To make himself up rather like a doctor would be perhaps the most artistic course for an actor in the part of a literary man.

Around Theatres, Max Beerbohm,   1953
Hart-Davis.   *Punch*

II

Rupert Hart-Davis is hesitant in speaking absolutely categorically on the subject of Reggie Turner's parentage. It seems almost certain, however, that Reginald Turner was the illegitimate son of Lionel Lawson (originally Levi), uncle of the first Lord Burnham. Turner, a few years older than Max Beerbohm, was with him as an undergraduate at Merton College, Oxford. He had been left fairly comfortably off, if not rich, by his father, later inheriting a considerable fortune from a half-brother. Everyone who knew him agrees that Turner was a conversational wit of the highest order.

His tastes made it advisable, as well as congenial, to live out of England. Writing to Turner in 1906, Max speaks of a move from his own hotel at Florence: 'rooms hallowed by your tenancy – rooms with a ceiling crude painted over with flowers, and with small human faces which have, I feel, looked down on scenes which I should not have approved of.' This is an interesting remark in the light of wholly unjustified suggestions that Beerbohm was homosexual.

However, the main interest of the Letters is in the portrait they provide of Beerbohm himself, a document untouched by another hand, from which all can judge. The letter is, perhaps, the most revealing of media. However semi-consciously composed, it can never wholly hide the character of the writer. In the first place, we are struck by the very fact of a friendship that lasted nearly fifty years in unbroken affection. If, as there is some suggestion, it began on Turner's side with a rather too excessive warmth, the durability that held up through two world wars, in that turmoil of an exigent and critical intellectual world, is not to be despised.

This is not to say that the young Max – even the older Max – appears always as an attractive character. There is a hard egotism that is only justified by the high standard of his work. When, in later life, it must be admitted Max failed always to keep up, and became in some respects rather a middlebrow, a certain narrowness of interest and concentration on himself are apt to display a less endearing side.

Yet the gifts are definite. The obituary (reproduced in a note here) of Oscar Wilde for the *Saturday Review* is a masterpiece of conciseness and grasp of Wilde's qualities and defects as a writer. In another manner, there is Max's dislike of hypocrisy:

At Madame Tussaud's, I saw (this reminds me) the waxen effigy of G.B.S. when I was in London.

I thought it might form a good basis for a caricature. Some days later I was lunching at his place, and mentioned the effigy to him; at which he flushed slightly, and waved his hands, and said he had had to give Tussaud a sitting, as 'it would have seemed so *snobbish* to refuse'!

Considering that it had been the proudest day of his life, I was rather touched by this account of the matter. I am afraid he is afraid of me. I met him also dining at Philip Sassoon's, and he seemed decidedly uncomfortable at being caught by me there.

Nor was Max without modesty.

I haven't nearly so amusing a mind as you have [he wrote to Turner], but I've always taken so much more pains over my writing than you have – or so *many* more pains, I should prefer to say, thus corroborating what I have just said about my painful carefulness.

One has the impression that Max Beerbohm and Augustus John did not greatly care for one another. Max refers to John dressing like a tramp but buying a pair of patent-leather boots after his marriage. John, on the other hand, speaks of Max 'misrepresenting' the company at the William Rothensteins, and, apparently, of liking to do himself too well at table.

Max Beerbohm: Letters to Reggie   1964
Turner, edited by Rupert Hart-   *Daily Telegraph*
Davis, Hart-Davis.

III

From his personal appearance, there can be little doubt that Turner was a member of the Lawson family. Besides, he inherited a small income from these sources, and later a capital sum that made him, if not rich, independent. He was brought up by a clergyman and his wife, to whom – unlike the pattern of most such stories – Turner was deeply attached. He went to school at Hurstpierpoint, a minor public school in Sussex, not far from Bristol, then to Merton College, Oxford.

At Merton, Turner met Max Beerbohm. The stage was now set for his subsequent career of conversationalist and dilettante; if anyone who produced a dozen novels truly can be called the latter. The novels must be admitted to lack talent, and, although it is universally agreed that Turner was an amusing talker, his *mots* do not hold up very well either. However, the entertaining remark depends on raising an immediate laugh, not on being written down and read half a century later.

Turner was a member of the Wilde circle, one of those who behaved extremely well at the time of Wilde's disaster. He not only coped with Wilde's extremely difficult, often ungrateful behaviour on emergence from prison – thereby risking his own source of income for consorting with such a disreputable person – but he was there at the deathbed and helped with the appalling subsequent problems. No one, it might be thought, except a man with admirable qualities, could have written Turner's letter to Wilde here reproduced, protesting at the way Wilde was treating the friends (not Turner himself) who were devoting their lives to trying to make his position easier.

In an odd way one sees, through the personality of Reggie Turner, how 1890 characteristics devolved and did not entirely die. D. H. Lawrence especially has 1890ish traits, particularly noticeable in the Turner context, though of course not the most obvious one in the popular mind. All the emphasis on 'genius', the emotionalism, the actual life lived in Florence and elsewhere (although of a kind Lawrence himself was always deploring), seem to show a real affiliation with the earlier (rather than later) intellectual period.

One cannot agree with Stanley Weintraub that the portrait of Turner as Algy in *Aaron's Rod* (here quoted) is well done. It seems, on the contrary, to demonstrate once again Lawrence's almost total inability to write convincing dialogue in his novels. It is possible that Lawrence also used Turner's physical appearance to describe the name-part in *Kangaroo*, otherwise supposedly modelled on the Australian general, Sir John Monash.

A more convincing picture of Turner was probably given in Maugham's short story – one of his best – 'The Outstation', where the exiled Warburton reads the *Times*, which reaches him six weeks after publication, each day six weeks back, never, so to speak, delving into the future, always at hand with letters of congratulation and condolence to former friends in London. In this connection, one feels it right to note that 'Una, Lady Troubridge' appearing in these pages as 'Lady Una Troubridge' would have been painful to Reggie.

Turner's last years were haunted by illness and unhappiness. The best that can be said is that he died before the outbreak of the 1939 war, which would have posed insuperable problems.

Reggie: A Portrait of Reginald Turner,   1966
Stanley Weintraub, W. H. Allen.   *Daily Telegraph*

IV

Max Beerbohm was about six months younger than William Rothenstein. They had met – Beerbohm not yet twenty-one – when Rothenstein had come up to Oxford to make portraits of notable dons. Beerbohm was already considered sufficiently prominent as an undergraduate to be included. They became friends from that moment, and the friendship – with one serious fracture that was immediately repaired – lasted a lifetime.

They were both, perhaps, in a sense disappointed men. This may sound an odd thing to say about Beerbohm, who enjoyed a superlative success even if what he did never brought in much money. My reason for supposing disappointment lurking somewhere in the background is that a writer who could do things as good as 'Enoch Soames', 'Maltby and Braxton', or the visit to Swinburne in Putney, must have wanted to continue with stuff of equal merit. In fact Beerbohm was not able to produce their equivalent later in life; and the good cartoons too are always the relatively early ones.

Rothenstein, although he achieved the same official recognition as his friend in knighthood, was far more explicitly conscious that something was wrong; beginning to voice dissatisfaction with his own work quite early on in the Letters. Rothenstein, like Beerbohm, was something of a phenomenon in his early twenties, not as a painter, but as a tirelessly energetic, outwardly self-confident little figure pushing himself in all circles where the arts were concerned, knowing everybody from Meredith to Verlaine, Goncourt to Gissing. He later wrote interesting Memoirs. The superiority of Beerbohm's wit can be appreciated by comparison with Rothenstein's since they both used the idiom of the period.

We get a sudden vivid picture of Wilde in a stray phrase when Beerbohm writes (September, 1893) that he has just met Willie Wilde at Broadstairs:

> Quel monstre! Dark, oily, suspect, yet awfully like Oscar: he has Oscar's coy, carnal smile & fatuous giggle & not a little of Oscar's esprit. But he is awful – a veritable tragedy of family likeness.

I looked back to Rupert Hart-Davis's edition of Beerbohm's letters to Reggie Turner and found a somewhat milder version:

My only consolation has been Willie Wilde, brother of Oscar, of whom I have seen a good deal. He is very vulgar and unwashed and inferior, but if I shut my eyes I can imagine his voice to be the voice of Oscar . . . if Oscar had not been the success in life he has he would be the image of Willy.

The row between Beerbohm and Rothenstein took place in 1909, when they were in their middle thirties. Rothenstein throughout his life – perhaps like not a few people who make friends easily – was famous for having no tact. Beerbohm had control of his pen, but possessed an obvious vein of cruelty, never hesitating to tease Rothenstein for his vulgarity. Rothenstein seems to have taken this in good part on the whole, but, when he tried to riposte in the same tone, had none of Beerbohm's skill.

In May 1908, Rothenstein, who had visited a show of Beerbohm's cartoons, wrote:

One word of warning: in one or two drawings I notice an inclination to draw like a 'professional' artist; this brought tears to my eyes & misgivings to my heart: you might in time I admit draw as well as Pegram [a *Punch* artist], but why not go on drawing better than anyone else?

Rothenstein's general comments in the way of art criticism do not strike one as particularly apt, but in this case it is easy to believe that he was speaking good sense. On the other hand, this is not the way to give advice to a friend, however close. The bomb seems to have burst nearly a year later. In March 1909, Rothenstein sent a letter beginning: 'Dear Max – I am so staggered by your letter that I cannot easily answer it . . .' He goes on to say that he cannot imagine that his 'crude chaff' could have put Beerbohm out, and that Beerbohm's letter 'shows, in spite of its ending, a real dislike of me.' This letter is followed up by another saying 'I am not so self-righteous as you think,' and apologising abjectly for being 'stupid' and 'heavyhanded'.

Unfortunately two letters from Beerbohm are missing. Rothenstein must have felt them too painful to preserve. This is to be regretted because a really angry letter from Beerbohm would be worth reading for its phraseology. The row does seem to have been entirely patched up, and all went well after that until Rothenstein's death.

An interesting angle on Beerbohm's point of view – anyway as a man in his fifties – is given in a letter dated November 1929. Rothenstein had recently become friendly with Ramsay MacDonald, when Prime Minister. Beerbohn presses Rothenstein on this occasion and in a later letter, to suggest to MacDonald that C. P. Scott, editor of the *Manchester Guardian*, would be a suitable recipient of the Order of Merit.

Max and Will: Max Beerbohm and   1975
William Rothenstein, their Friendship   *Daily Telegraph*
and Letters, 1893–1945, edited by
Mary M. Lago and Karl Beckson,
Murray.

V

The rather over-sugary tone with which it has long been customary to speak of Max Beerbohm and his work has done something to obscure his position as caricaturist and writer. The strength of Beerbohm's personality widely imposed his own legend, perhaps in the long run not wholly to his advantage. There is no reason why he should not be considered in the rational way a critic might consider the work of, say, 'Spy', 'Ape' or Osbert Lancaster. Accordingly, Rupert Hart-Davis's *Catalogue* of all Beerbohm's known caricatures – more than 2,000 – is an enormous help in assessing the overall picture; who was caricatured; how were they treated; what percentage is remembered.

Hart-Davis's skill at this sort of job being what it is, I am hardly going too far in saying that *Catalogue* can be read almost as a piece of narrative writing dealing with the best-known figures of the period covered. In addition, he includes 100 caricatures, none of which has appeared in any of Beerbohm's own books before, all chosen to illustrate different aspects of the artist's best work.

It is right that Beerbohm's two-sided gift should be simultaneously memorialised by the publication of a series of prose pieces that also cover his whole life. *A Peep into the Past* gives an excellent idea of his abilities in that field too, if at times it also reveals certain limitations. For example, the purely discursive essays tend to dictate, while something like the account of Andrew Lang, met only a couple of times, tells you with extraordinary vividness just what Lang must have been like.

There is a certain flatness in having to insist that an 'amusing' performer is also 'serious'. Beerbohm himself was well aware of this, speaking in one essay of the manner in which Wilde and Whistler were regarded in their day as *farceurs*. 'Both, apart from their prominence, were doing serious work; but neither was taken at all seriously. Neither was thanked.' Whistler got a farthing damages, Oscar Wilde two years' hard labour. Wilde, he adds elsewhere, was 'academic', never 'decadent'. Beerbohm himself, on the other hand, was to some extent killed with kindness, put in a showcase for ornaments.

The first thing to be stated unequivocally about Beerbohm's

drawings is that he is a true caricaturist. He knows by instinct what is slightly grotesque about an individual's appearance and behaviour and draws a picture emphasising these aspects. He does not – as do many caricaturists today – copy a photograph more or less accurately, then simply place the head on a disproportionate body. Beerbohm knows his victim, knows the apt situation in which to place him. He also had a true originality of attack. On the whole his likes and dislikes affect the impact of the caricature remarkably little. Obviously he approved of Henry James, was outraged by Kipling. Caricatures of both are equally funny, equally savage – indeed James 'meeting his other self' is an acute comment on the novelist's character.

An exception to a generally retained posture of calmly ironic comment is Beerbohm's treatment of the Royal Family. Here something snapped. A raw psychological wound is somehow revealed. Why did they upset him so appallingly? True, Edward VII apprised of his accession, or thinking a convent is a brothel, are both reasonably funny here, but the *Catalogue* lists pages more of not very subtle anti-royal bludgeoning, and there can be no doubt the subject was a little obsessive. One has only to look at a French comic paper of the early 1900s like *L'Assiette au Beurre* for anti-British-Royal-Family caricature to see how indifferent many of Beerbohm's were.

He is not, of course, without his failings as a draughtsman, and these on the whole increased rather than diminished. One of the useful points of the drawings reproduced here is to know how good the later caricatures would sometimes be; for example, the proposed frontispiece for 'that dreadful work *Joseph Conrad and His Circle*' (written by Jessie Conrad), done in 1935.

More than once Beerbohm quotes Disraeli's saying, 'the disappointed are always young'. One cannot help wondering how deeply he felt that comment to apply to himself. Appearing fully armed with all his gifts as an undergraduate, he was immediately launched on to a world of picturesque personalities, asking for just the handling he was so well qualified to give. Self-satisfaction, the legitimate weapon of the brilliant young man, carried him on through the next decade, but things never got quite adjusted – considering what a lot of talent was there – after the First World War.

This enjoyably narcissistic approach naturally resulted in several pages that list self-caricatures. One of the best (reproduced) is 'Homage to Praxiteles paid by Max', in which Beerbohm, in morning clothes, poses to resemble Hermes holding the infant Dionysus – Beerbohm, a Dutch doll. On the whole one would say he is more at ease with writers, painters, musicians, social figures (some of the last now totally forgotten) than politicians, yet one feels that Beerbohm would have been not at all unwilling to operate politically had his own grasp been stronger. The several unidentified drawings are tantalising, all obviously intensely characteristic of their subjects, and most reminiscent. Is the side-whiskered figure in bowler, stock and leggings, George Belcher, the comic artist?

A Catalogue of the Caricatures of Max Beerbohm, Rupert Hart-Davis, Macmillan.
A Peep into the Past and other Prose Pieces, Max Beerbohm, collected and introduced by Rupert Hart-Davis, Heinemann.

1972
Daily Telegraph

WILLIAM ROTHENSTEIN

No picture or caricature of the Café Royal, or of any other bohemian gathering in the 1890s, is complete without the mountainous figure of Oscar Wilde and the tiny, black, bespectacled form of William Rothenstein. There can be no doubt whatever that this was Rothenstein's supreme moment. Once the Nineties are over, the rest of the story must be a falling off. This does not mean that Robert Speaight's biography lacks interest. On the contrary, it provides a great deal of material to ponder on. It is well done, but was Speaight quite the man to do it? His urbanity is only equalled by his fairness. Only once, at the thought of Omar Khayyám, is he stirred to faint asperity.

Perhaps someone who thoroughly disliked Rothenstein should have undertaken the task. What has happened, one wonders, to the student who, at the opening of an exhibition at the Victoria and Albert in the 1920s, shouted: 'I wish to take this opportunity of protesting against the petty pomposity of Sir William Rothenstein, which is turning the Royal College of Art into . . . ?'

No one ever heard what Rothenstein was turning the RCA into, because the interrupter was hustled from the room like a pro-Bomb enthusiast at a CND meeting, but a critic of that calibre might have been the best person to write the life. Then the reader's reaction would have been to insist on Rothenstein's many good qualities. As it is, we rebel against Speaight's reasonableness, his tireless persuasiveness, directed to making us take Rothenstein seriously; since it is clear from the attitude of Max Beerbohm and the other friends of his golden period that the whole point about Rothenstein was *not* to take him seriously, in fact to treat him as a colossal joke. 'Will, don't look so sensible,' Wilde used to beg; and Beerbohm's cartoon of Rothenstein's Old Self saying to his Young Self: 'Take off your hat, Sir! – and leave the room!' perfectly sums up the change that took place.

It was a strange progress. Born in Bradford in 1872, of a business family of German-Jewish origin, he was sent to study art at the Slade and to Paris. During the Paris period, Rothenstein knew – with innumerable other people – Verlaine, by that time considered too much of a handful by even the most hardened café-frequenters: and, at the other end of the scale, Degas, who wished to meet only very few persons hand-picked by himself. Degas even had Rothenstein's drawings hanging on his walls.

Well-known names plaster these pages, but at a certain moment the reader is aware that some inner change has taken place. The quality of the people suddenly wanes. From Degas and Verlaine, we find ourselves jostling Cunninghame Graham, Maeterlinck, Tagore, Drinkwater . . . all at once one is gasping for breath, feeling that, whatever its contemporary failings, Modern Art did a magnificent job in the way of letting in much-needed fresh air. Among other things, incidentally, we learn that 'a common admiration for Brueghel' drew Ramsay MacDonald and Rothenstein together.

This is not the place to discuss Rothenstein in detail as a painter, but his work does not hold up well. There is a certain period charm about, for example, the portrait of the artist's wife and Augustus John, titled 'The Doll's House' (1899), but it could hardly be called an important contribution to the English School; while the collection of Portrait Drawings, published in 1926, are, with a few exceptions, depressing, even, in certain cases, devastating, to take from the shelf and look through.

What happened to Rothenstein? To some extent the book explains. He mistook solemnity for seriousness: 'William Rothenstein paints very much like the rest of us, only from higher motives,' was the comment of Wilson Steer. Even if Rothenstein's talent was never a large one, too much high thinking played hell with it, such as it was. Honest, ambitious, immensely hard-working, intoxicated with people, he never managed to disentangle himself from theory, yet at the same time never took on any theory of painting that brought good results. It is extraordinary that he should have found time to write the immensely long explanatory letters about himself and his work, some of which are quoted by Speaight, some recorded only by mention in the letters of others. It was, of course, the fashion in his time to write long letters, even so, Rothenstein seems to have been more sensitive to criticism than most, more willing to enter into long rigmaroles and generalisations to combat hostile opinion.

Speaight speaks of the 'embryonic vorticist' in Rothenstein and certainly the stories here recall more than once the 'bourgeois-bohemians', depicted so well by Wyndham Lewis (inventor of Vorticism) in his novel *Tarr*. In the end one reluctantly feels that Rothenstein represented an 'establishment' more stifling than any Royal Academy. His claim to remembrance belongs to a rather different area: as one of the characters in *Seven Men*, and, with other generous acts, as a friend who was kind to Wilde when he came out of prison.

William Rothenstein: The Portrait of   1962
An Artist in his Time, Robert   *Daily Telegraph*
Speaight, Eyre & Spottiswoode.

HERBERT BEERBOHM TREE

The title of this book – perhaps not an altogether happy one, as Tree's importance does not lie mainly in his love affairs – can be justified by *The Great Lover* being the name of one of his later productions at His Majesty's. At the same time it is not to be denied that Tree did have a family of six children by a mistress in Wandsworth, as well as three by his wife, and one by an English actress in America in his sixty-fourth year; not to mention various more casual affairs.

Herbert Beerbohm Tree (1852–1917) was the son of a well-to-do corn merchant, and half-brother of the much younger Max Beerbohm – remarkable progeny for their father. The Beerbohm family were German Balts from Lithuania, granted an estate by Frederick the Great in the mid-eighteenth century. The pear-trees on their coat of arms were probably the reason why Tree took that name to act under.

Madeleine Bingham has already written a biography of Irving, Tree's older contemporary – and in many respects a strong contrast, both as man and actor – so it is right that she should also consider a figure who not only left an enormous mark on acting and theatrical management, but built His Majesty's Theatre – still standing in its fine but, alas, architecturally mutilated block in the Haymarket – and founded RADA, nursery of a good deal of talent in his profession.

Tree began as an amateur, and never wholly adapted himself to professionalism, getting bored by long runs, and liking to do everything in an expansive way rather than an economically prudent one. Nevertheless he left a fortune of about £100,000, a largish sum at that date, which was divided between his two households, the Wandsworth family including the distinguished film producer, the late Sir Carol Reed.

One of the many interesting aspects of Tree is that he spans a period in theatrical history between the old-fashioned ranting of the first half of the nineteenth century, and Hollywood in its early days, where, towards the end of his life, he worked and quite enjoyed himself, in spite of barbarisms already in evidence there. All this is taken at a brisk pace by Madeleine Bingham, who is a trifle too addicted to such phrases as 'snowy shirt-fronts', 'the fair sex', 'waxed wroth', though these might be held to give a period flavour. I do not think she says enough about

65

the background of Lady Tree (née Maud Holt), nor quite does justice
to her as a personality. When I was a young man Sir Herbert Tree
seemed a legend of the past, but one was always being told of witty
remarks made by Lady Tree, though admittedly she outlived her
husband.

I feel too that the author somewhat exaggerates, as so often happens
nowadays, the primness of Tree's era. No doubt there were a lot of prim
people about, but not in the world in which Tree himself moved, even if
things were not talked about explicitly, as they are today. An instance
of this seems given by the following anecdote that is told here about
Tree's production *Nero*.

> Esmé Percy played Brittanicus. A story has come down in theatrical
> circles, presumably through the late Mr Percy, that Tree was
> attracted to him. He is supposed to have been having supper with
> Maud [Lady Tree] and Herbert [Beerbohm Tree], when she got up
> from the table, wished the two men good night and then turned and
> said: 'Remember Herbert, it is *adultery* all the same.'
> In viewing the progress of Tree's life, it is impossible to believe this
> story to be true. It is incontestable that Esmé Percy was very
> beautiful in a very feminine way at about this time, and in his Roman
> costume had great charm. But, in middle age, people, both men and
> women, are apt to exaggerate both their charms and their conquests.

But surely the story is perfectly true, and a joke. Esmé Percy was the
embodiment of what is now called 'camp', and Maud Tree, who was a
person full of fun, made the crack as she left the room, and Esmé Percy
repeated it as a good joke – as indeed it was. This seems an illustration
of the point of a story, as so often happens, being completely lost in later
repetition.

Tree was, in fact, one of those in the theatrical world who wrote to
Wilde and sent him money when disaster fell, which could not be said of
everyone with whom Wilde had been associated in the theatre. Indeed,
one has the impression that, matrimonial vagaries apart, Tree behaved
well, and even in those matters took steps to look after his illegitimate
children, notwithstanding, his will turned out a shock to his legitimate
family.

Tree was not incapable of telling stories against himself. He was at
his best in roles like Svengali or Paragot (does anyone now remember
W. J. Locke's *The Beloved Vagabond*?) and when he played Hamlet was
felt to over-romanticise the part. Tree installed his friend John Hare in
the Royal Box to watch it, and afterwards they had supper together.
Hare said not a word about Tree's performance. Tree saw Hare into his
carriage, then put his head through the window and said: 'At any rate it
is a fine play, Johnnie, isn't it?' calling to the coachman to drive off.

He was also fond of recounting how the commissionaire at his own theatre observed to him: 'You may think I'm out to flatter you, but a gentleman coming out of the pit said there was not more than a dozen actors in your line of business that could play the part better!'

'The Great Lover': The Life and Art of Herbert Beerbohm Tree, Madeleine Bingham, Hamish Hamilton.

1979
Daily Telegraph

ARTHUR SYMONS

I never heard it stated that Enoch Soames, in Max Beerbohm's *Seven Men*, was specifically modelled on Arthur Symons (1865–1945), but, when one rereads Symons's verse and learns more of his life, it is hard not to suspect that Beerbohm had him in mind.

For example, take Symons's lines to the musician Dolmetsch:

> A melancholy desire of ancient things
> Floats like a faded perfume out of the wires:
> Pallid lovers, what unforgotten desires.
> Whispered once, are re-told in these whisperings?

They are probably today less known, in truth, than the imaginary Soames's famous poem from *Fungoids*:

> Pale tunes irresolute
> And traceries of old sounds
> Blown from a rotted flute
> Mingle with noise of cymbals rouged with rust . . .

To suggest this is, of course, to be grossly unfair to Symons, who was a genuine poet, if a minor one, an interesting, though somewhat woolly-minded critic, and a man of varied and remarkable intelligence.

He was born in 1865, son of a Wesleyan minister, of a Cornish family of some antiquity, who, a generation or two before, had owned an Elizabethan manor house of great beauty. Enoch Soames, too, it will be remembered, was of nonconformist background – in any case a rich field in the literary ancestries of this country.

Early photographs make Symons look surprisingly like a young Dylan Thomas. Both were born in South Wales, though Symons was of old Cornish stock on both sides of his family. His father's cure of souls changed every three years, so the only son was brought up all over the place.

Symons from his earliest years reacted against the atmosphere of his home, though he was not on bad terms with his parents, who seem to have stood up surprisingly well to the considerable shock of producing a poet of the *Décadence*. Like most of the other well-known 1890s writers, he was a remarkable scholar in his way, though inability to deal with certain subjects, like mathematics, prevented him from turning this to account from the point of view of matriculation.

Symons was obviously an extremely bright boy. He went to various Devonshire schools, and, as often in such cases, found a master interested in his development. As a result he was writing remarkably sophisticated prose when a boy of fifteen. At nineteen he was employed on prefaces to editions of Shakespeare, the sort of work which put him in a position to earn a living as a literary journalist.

Symons's ambition was always to be a poet. His real ability as critic has been, to some extent, obscured by the Nineties legend of decadence and death from absinthe with which he is associated, and to which Symons himself extensively contributed.

The really surprising thing is the way in which Symons was determined to earn a living as a writer, and did so. He had no literary connections. To have a long article on the Provençal poet, Mistral, accepted by the *National Review*, even though he had already had a great number of other pieces turned down by editors, was a striking achievement at the age of twenty.

This capacity to exist on his books, essays and introductions to the classics continued until Symons was thirty-five. He had a flat in the Temple, travelled as much as he wished, indulged his taste for music-halls, ballet girls and 'the chance romances of the streets'. Some felt he had gone too far when he wrote of the last of these:

> I too have sought on many a breast
> The ecstasy of love's unrest,
> I too have had my dreams, and met
> (Ah me) how many a Juliet . . .

That it should be possible for a writer to live comfortably, while restricting himself to works aimed at so comparatively limited a public, is an interesting aspect of nineteenth-century life. However, money difficulties set in acutely when he married in 1901.

Symons married the daughter of a Newcastle shipbuilder in 1901, a union which was a very fair success, though naturally overcast by total breakdown in his middle-forties. This sudden seizure was attributed by 'all the best men in London' to GPI – or insanity. He was given eighteen months, at most two years, to live. Not for the first time the doctors made a mistake.

All things considered, the marriage was not an unsuccessful one so far as the mutual relationship was concerned, but Symons's wife was far from a competent manager of their domestic affairs, and the financial situation went from bad to worse.

Finally, when Symons at forty-three went off his head, they were travelling in Italy. The result was a series of nightmare experiences, which fully justified all the gloomy imaginings of his poetry at its most gruesome. Dreadful incarcerations followed in asylums. However, after about two and a half years of treatment, Symons recovered, and lived on till 1945, when he was eighty.

W. B. Yeats remarked: 'Symons has always had a longing to commit great sin, but he has never been able to get beyond ballet girls.' This was undoubtedly true, and one feels that fantasy played a fair part even in the 'adventures' to which he referred throughout his life. In fact, when a girl to whom he was attracted talked of becoming an actress, he wrote her a long letter warning of the moral dangers of that profession.

On the other hand, Symons had an unusual gift for getting to know foreign writers, also for languages. His book *The Symbolist Movement in Literature* (1899) introduced Mallarmé, Verlaine, Villiers de l'Isle Adam, Tristan Corbière, Laforgue and others to the English-speaking world.

T. S. Eliot wrote that it was entirely due to this book that he learnt of those French poets, who had immense influence on his own work. Symons went so far as to have Verlaine stay with him at his flat in the Temple, a risky undertaking which passed off pretty well.

The Letters, well edited by Karl Beckson and John M. Munro, involve all sorts of people and opinions, from the Pre-Raphaelites to d'Annunzio. Symons had not a vestige of humour, but he got about a great deal.

His money affairs are rather mysterious. He himself never made more than what came in from books of verse, literary criticism, an occasional job writing theatre or art notices. He had no money of his own. His wife, on the other hand (although said to be very extravagant), left over £40,000 in 1936. They seem to have conducted their financial affairs most incompetently, because Symons continually writes as if about to starve to death.

An incident that shows Symons as a man to be taken seriously was his visit (1898) to the Castle of Dux in Bohemia, where Casanova had ended his days as librarian. Symons, who was interested in Casanova, routed about in the castle, where he found two chapters of Casanova's *Memoirs*, which had been lost for half a century, also some relevant love-letters.

Symons's own Letters contain, from time to time, comments on contemporary matters that throw light, for instance (1891): 'Henry James's play [*The American*, based on James's novel of that title] was lamentable. It has the combined qualities of a mild farce, high-faluting French drama of an extinct school, and an Adelphi melodrama of the present.'

In 1894, in a letter in French to Verlaine, Symons gives the address of Morton Fullerton, for whom James showed a *tendresse*, and with whom Edith Wharton had an affair.

Symons knew the young James Joyce and liked his rather watery poems. However, he was never able to make the transition from the literary approach of his own early days to that of the very different literary world which grew up round him.

He visited the Swinburne/Watts-Dunton ménage at The Pines, Putney, leaving an account of it that does not greatly differ from Max Beerbohm's or A. C. Benson's. Swinburne told him that all the plays he wrote at Eton were modelled on Webster and Tourneur, 'duchesses, poison, murders'.

When Symons stayed with Thomas Hardy at Max Gate another guest was A. E. Housman 'who wrote some verses'. When (1906) Hardy sent Symons the second part of *The Dynasts*, Symons called it an 'unparalleled spectacle', but could not approve, disliking narrative poems, for instance 'condemning wholly Wordsworth's "The Excursion".'

Symons himself always recognised the indelible mark a Methodist upbringing had left on him. His life is well and sympathetically described by Roger Lhombreaud, *Professeur de lettres* at the NATO International School. It is appropriate that a Frenchman should write the definite biography of a poet and critic who did so much to propagate greater knowledge in this country of French poetry and French criticism.

Lhombreaud writes in English with fluency. As a biographer, he is perhaps too good-natured, resisting temptation at any stage to smile at Symons's total lack of humour. He also takes the trouble seriously to rebut Frank Harris's highly coloured stories about Symons, no doubt the purest imagination. Symons's mental breakdown, diagnosed as GPI, appears in fact to have been the consequence of hereditary insanity.

I met Symons in the 1920s at luncheon. By that time he was not immensely coherent, having never wholly recovered from going off his head in 1908. In his sixties, he looked infinitely aged. He talked much of a party at Lady Diana Cooper's.

Betjeman's lines 'On Seeing an Old Poet in the Café Royal' refer to him.

> Devilled chicken, devilled whitebait,
> Devil if I understand.

Arthur Symons: A Critical Biography, Roger Lhombreaud, Unicorn Press.

Arthur Symons: Selected Letters, 1880–1935, edited by Karl Beckson and John M. Munro, Macmillan.

1963
Daily Telegraph
1989
Daily Telegraph

JOHN DAVIDSON

I

John Davidson (1857–1909) had a hard life, the circumstances of which recall the horrors suffered by Gissing's literary men, although Davidson was not given to self-pity, even when his poems treat of misery and want. On the contrary, he had in him a strong streak of dandyism. His philosophy has been described as materialistic and aristocratic. Fascinated by power, and the menacing development of modern science, he was also devoted to the past, and to the life of the individual as opposed to the mass.

Davidson was the son of an Evangelical minister, and brought up in Greenock. His not very successful, at the same time far from obscure life, he made an end of by drowning himself. Like George Orwell, whom he somewhat resembles (in the manner that persons who take precisely the opposite view of things sometimes resemble each other), he wished no biography of himself to be written.

Caricatured by Max Beerbohm, a contributor to *The Yellow Book*, Davidson is thought of as a Nineties' poet. There was a side to him that certainly belonged to that epoch. In the poem (not included in this collection) which forms a prologue to his novel, *A Full and True Account of the Wonderful Mission of Earl Lavender* with its frontispiece by Aubrey Beardsley, he gaily identified himself with that age:

> Though our eyes turn ever wave-ward,
> Where our sun is well-nigh set;
> Though our century totters grave-ward,
> We may laugh a little yet.

> Oh! our age-end style perplexes
> All our elders time has tamed;
> On our sleeves we wear our sexes,
> Our diseases, unashamed.

All the same, Davidson was not altogether of the Nineties. It might be argued that he was born too soon. With plenty of original talent of his own, and different as he is from both, if there is something in him of Orwell, there is also something of Betjeman.

The ballads are too numerous and too long, yet in spite of a tendency to be turgid, most of them contain good lines. The 'Fleet Street Eclogues' are odd, original productions, in which, as in 'Earl Lavender', a surrealist strain is to be detected.

Probably Davidson's best remembered poems are:

> As I went down to Dymchurch Wall,
> I heard the South sing o'er the land;

or:

> When the pods went pop in the broom, green broom,
> And the apples began to be golden skinned . . .

Others, equally notable, are to be found in R. D. Macleod's selection – for example 'A Loafer', verse of peculiar and haunting poignancy.

Shaw's statement, here quoted, that Davidson committed suicide because of £250 he had lent him to write a poetical drama which turned out a failure, should perhaps be accepted with reserve. Davidson may have felt despair; his strong personality suggests that, in itself, this debt would have provided an insufficient reason to cause him to make away with himself.

Poems and Ballads, John Davidson,   1959
selected, with an introduction, by   *Daily Telegraph*
R. D. Macleod, Unicorn Press.

I I

There really might be said to be a John Davidson revival in progress. Two years ago his Poems and Ballads were collected together and reprinted, with an introduction by R. D. Macleod. Now we have a further selection of Davidson's verse, only a few items repeated from that earlier volume. A preface by T. S. Eliot acknowledges certain influences exerted by Davidson's work on himself.

Maurice Lindsay gives an excellent account of Davidson. He emphasises that too high claims must not be made for him as a poet, and he sweeps aside Davidson's novels as worthless; although I confess to have a sneaking regard for *The Wonderful Mission of Earl Lavender*. However, moderation in praise is undoubtedly the right approach. Davidson is not a poet to thrust down people's throats. Some of what he wrote was undoubtedly mediocre. At the same time, there are also many memorable lines: while his own personality grows in retrospect.

Fascinated by the idea of power, by the extraordinary advances of science, he was also straining after a new poetic language. If he had been born half a century later he might have lined up with, say, Roy Campbell, making, intellectually speaking, a formidable opposition to W. H. Auden and his school.

Both Maurice Lindsay and Hugh McDiarmid (in an essay included in this book) are, perhaps rather naturally, all out to emphasise the 'Scotchness' of Davidson. In doing this they seem to miss at times some of his amusing points. It is a little as if a keen pacifist fastened on Davidson's poem inveighing against armies and wars, and drew the conclusion from this that Davidson did not believe in force; which in fact preoccupied and attracted him enormously.

For example, Lindsay (one of the chief authorities on Burns) writes:

It is odd to find Greenock-born Davidson referring to Burns as being possessed of 'a great English imagination', but it is clear from the context that what he really means is 'British' and equally clear from his exposition of Burns's views on marriage that he has not read his Burns very carefully.

It seems to me that if Davidson had wanted to write 'British', he would have written 'British'. I suspect that part of the fun of writing 'English' was taking a rise out of compatriots like Lindsay – who, I repeat, has done his job here exceedingly well. Davidson obviously enjoyed pulling legs that emerged from kilts. This seems to me to be borne out by the ballad of St George's Day (not included here) in the 'Fleet Street Eclogues', which ends with Menzies and Sandy joining in with Basil and the rest, with the final verse:

> By bogland, highland, down and fen.
> All Englishmen, all Englishmen!
> Who with their latest breath shall sing
> Of England and the English Spring!

I do not believe Davidson meant the British spring for a moment. In case this may be thought to be labouring a small point, let me add that McDiarmid in his interesting essay states: 'In short, like Byron, he [Davidson] was a Scottish, not an English poet, although he used an alien language, and had apparently no knowledge of the independent Scottish tradition.'

If McDiarmid is going to claim Byron, I really do not see why Davidson should not give England Burns in return.

Some of Davidson's insight into the future in such a poem as 'The Triumph of Mammon' is remarkable:

> No world-god, but a god Teutonic, foe
> Of Latin races, Slavs and yellow men
> Of negroes, Hebrews, every other folk . . .

This vein of prophecy was at work in one of his best known poems, 'The Runnable Stag', in which the form of his own death was envisaged:

Three hundred gentlemen, able to ride
Three hundred horses as gallant and free,
Beheld him escape on the evening tide,
Far out till he sank in the Severn Sea,
Till he sank in the depths of the sea –
The stag, the buoyant stag, the stag
That slept at last in a jewelled bed
Under the sheltering ocean spread,
The stag, the runnable stag.

John Davidson: A Selection of His   1961
Poems, edited, with an introduction,   *Daily Telegraph*
by Maurice Lindsay and essay by
Hugh McDiarmid, Hutchinson.

ERNEST DOWSON

The Letters of Ernest Dowson (1867–1900), admirably edited by Desmond Flower and Henry Maas, are full of interesting points. The introductory pages to the various groups of correspondence make the volume into almost a biography, entirely disposing of previous very general misconceptions. *The Poetical Works of Ernest Dowson* are also newly available, a complete edition appropriately edited by Desmond Flower. If gigantic claims cannot be made, there can be no doubt that Dowson wrote a number of good poems. In 'Cynara', whatever its period mannerisms, even absurdities, Dowson pinpoints a mood that probably few persons have entirely escaped at some time in their life.

Largely owing to a highly coloured article about him by Arthur Symons in the *Savoy*, a legend has descended of Dowson as drunken, drug-addicted, sponging, down-at-heel, disreputable, sunk in hopeless passions for Soho waitresses. This is far from just.

Dowson's family owned a small dock in the East End of London, where they had been in the shipping business for at least four generations. His father and grandfather, both with literary leanings, had known Browning and other writers. There is no record of Dowson going to school, and his better than average education seems to have been owed to his father. When he went up to Queen's College, Oxford, in 1887, a modern note is struck – racial and narcotic – by an Indian undergraduate introducing Dowson and some others to *bhang*. After two almost totally unsuccessful *bhang* parties after hall, the dose was intensified, with the result that an emetic had to be procured from a nearby chemist. Henceforward *bhang* was out.

Dowson's temperament was certainly melancholy, no doubt affected by a history of mental instability on his mother's side. However, the ultimate failure of the dock appears to have been chiefly due to changing demands from shipping, rather than any gross inefficiency on the Dowsons' side. Dowson, who helped his father manage the docks for several years, undeniably had a taste for very young girls, though he merely fell romantically in love with them. His passion for the daughter of a Polish restaurateur (she was the prototype of Cynara and inspiration of most of his poems) went on for years. He proposed to her two days before she was fifteen. The editors speculate on how different things might have been had she accepted him, and Dowson succeeded in getting a job as a librarian. One cannot help feeling the mess would merely have been one of a different sort. As it was, Dowson lived in France, starved, went downhill, his writing not on the whole improving.

When he called on Toulouse-Lautrec, the painter insisted on Dowson staying to dinner:

> It was a most charming and original dinner; his younger brother shares his apartment, and cooks and apparently does all the house work . . . after dinner which was most creditable to the Lautrec culinary talent we drank rum and worked hankey-pankey with planchette . . . We then took haschish, and eventually all, with the exception of the elderly Professor, slept on sofas and mattresses at Lautrec's.

That was an exceptioal party. Drug-taking seems, on the whole, to have been a rare and fairly amateurish affair, as the occasion when Beardsley took hashish, which had a delayed action. He was overcome with laughter in a crowded Paris restaurant.

One is struck by Dowson's extraordinarily 'modern' taste in books as a young man – Stendhal, Laclos, James, for example. Beardsley illustrated Dowson's *The Pierrot of the Minute*, which play, for some unaccountable reason, was performed at Aldershot, when the stringed band of the Royal Horse Artillery played 'the Moonlight Sonata' softly at intervals throughout.

The Letters of Ernest Dowson, edited   1967
by Desmond Flower and Henry   *Daily Telegraph*
Maas, Cassell.
The Poetical Works of Ernest Dowson,
edited by Desmond Flower, Cassell.

VINCENT O'SULLIVAN

Of the few people familiar with the name of Vincent O'Sullivan (1868–1940) today, some probably know his book on Wilde; others remember Aubrey Beardsley's remarkable cover design for O'Sullivan's novel *The Houses of Sin*. Like Enoch Soames, the nineties' poet in Max Beerbohm's story, who made a pact with the Devil, O'Sullivan has been long forgotten; but now there are signs of a renewed awareness of his work. Certainly no one interested in this period should miss *Opinions* – essays written in the 1930s, which deal with George Moore, Ouida, Gissing, Gertrude Atherton, Frank Harris, 'John Oliver Hobbes', 'Corvo' and Wilde.

O'Sullivan was an American of Irish origin, whose father had made a fortune in the Civil War. He was sent to England to be educated. By one of those tricks of fate that brought Galsworthy to voyage in a passenger ship, on which Conrad was First Mate, it happened that Frederick Rolfe ('Baron Corvo') was an assistant master at O'Sullivan's school.

In 1892 O'Sullivan went up to Exeter College, Oxford, but did not outlast his first term. A couple of years later he was to be found in the midst of the nineties' group, a friend of Dowson and Beardsley; tolerating – which few seemed able to do – Smithers the publisher; knowing but not closely associated with Wilde, until after his release from prison.

Alan Anderson gives a good account of all this in his introduction. O'Sullivan wrote poems, essays, novels and plays, one of which was produced at the Court Theatre. He also published a book of short stories with the perfect Nineties' title of *A Dissertation Upon Second Fiddles*. His book, *Aspects of Wilde*, which appeared in 1936, is an excellent study.

Little is known of O'Sullivan's later middle years. He lived in France, apparently – probably on account of the Slump in America – getting poorer and poorer, although his father had left a million dollars. Finally, in 1932, he was injured in a street accident in Bayonne, and the expenses of French hospital treatment ate up his few remaining resources. From that time he was increasingly destitute. The war did the rest. He died penniless under the German occupation. It is a very tragic story.

O'Sullivan does not emerge from these essays as a great writer, but his style is lively and personal. He has all kind of small things to record which illuminate the people he knew. He finds a good word to say for Ouida; he hotly defends Corvo, even to the extent of suggesting that *The Quest for Corvo* was unjust to that rather unalluring personality, who, apart from a small group of enthusiasts, was largely put on the map by A. J. A. Symons's book.

Mrs Craigie, who used the pseudonym 'John Oliver Hobbes', and Gertrude Atherton, novelist and memoir-writer, were once well-known names in the literary field. O'Sullivan, who found both ladies intensely irritating, pitches into them here with a will. He also has a good deal to say about George Moore, another now unfashionable author who shows a decided posthumous vitality as a character.

There is an amusing account of Frank Harris, wearing a pullover and a red scarf round his neck as appropriate vestments, going to a sanatorium near Berlin to visit Maxim Gorky. He was to be introduced by a Russo-American journalist. Harris asked O'Sullivan to lunch with him the following day to hear about the 'star' writer of the Bolshevik Revolution.

> The visit to Gorky had proved a disaster. Gorky had received them in the hall of the establishment. He did not ask them to sit down, and while Harris was talking to him in German, he turned and walked away and did not come back. The journalist sent one of the servants to find him, but Gorky refused to come down again.
>
> Harris was in a great rage. And he might well have been. It is hard to explain Gorky's conduct; it is impossible to excuse it. I cannot think what could have induced Gorky to act as he did. It is all very well to be a barbarian, but the most primitive barbarian would hardly thus treat a man who had driven thirty miles on a winter day to see him.

What a splendid Max Beerbohm picture the scene would have made. One cannot help feeling a sneaking sympathy for Gorky, however uncultured his behaviour, in feeling unable to face Frank Harris that afternoon. Which of us, ill in a German sanatorium, can swear he would not have acted in a similar manner?

Wilde remains the personality in whom O'Sullivan is chiefly interested, although he considered Beardsley the only 'genius' he had ever encountered in the course of his life. He emphasises sides of Wilde often overlooked, for example, his passionate attachment to Lily Langtry.

Opinions, Vincent O'Sullivan, with   1959
an introduction by Alan Anderson,   *Daily Telegraph*
Unicorn Press.

JOHN SINGER SARGENT

'Yes, I have always thought Sargent a great painter,' said Henry James. 'He would be greater still if he had one or two little things he hasn't – but he will do.'

James was an early friend of John Singer Sargent (1856–1925), whose portrait of him is one of the best Sargent painted. James was about fifteen years older. They came from somewhat similar American expatriate backgrounds, although Sargent, in spite of being for most of his life associated with this country, never felt inclined to take British nationality. His family, though not particularly distinguished, dated back to the seventeenth century in Massachusetts. His father was a doctor, who pottered about Europe with a hypochondriac wife. It was on her money, not a great deal, that they lived.

Sargent was born in Florence. There was some idea that he should go into the US Navy, but his talent for drawing appeared early, and he was exhibiting at the Salon at twenty-one. His master was Carolus-Duran, a not particularly inspired painter, though he left a mark on Sargent's work. Carolus-Duran's studio was one in which the often brutal ragging of new students (touched on in *Trilby*) was not allowed. That would not have been at all to the taste of the always frock-coated, well-turned-out Sargent.

Sargent is a puzzling figure. When he became successful he was one of London's most inveterate diners-out, yet always remained reserved, rather shy, to the end of his days incapable of making the shortest and simplest speech. Women thought him attractive. Once or twice he was suspected of love affairs with his patronesses. On the whole evidence seems against that. The (inevitable) suggestion of a homosexual slant on his relations with a male model called Nicola, who became his factotum, is even less probable. In short, Sargent seems to have had no serious love affairs of any kind.

I have not read Evan Charteris's life of Sargent (1927), said by the Sargent family to be full of mistakes. Charles Merrill Mount's biography (1957) gave the facts, but was on the stodgy side. Olsen is livelier. He is happier with vignettes than chronological narrative, the style jerky at times, but Sargent himself emerges rather more, although remaining an enigmatic figure. How could this enormous energy and –

to say the least – considerable talent, confine itself within such conventional walls?

The fact probably is that Sargent's life was no more than what is here told. Max Beerbohm (who loved to caricature Sargent in such situations as looking apprehensively out of his window in Tite Street at the unending queue of smart ladies in huge Edwardian hats waiting to be painted) speaks of him as 'the most sensitive and correct of men'. In the end he settled down with his crippled sister, who, so to speak, acted the part of wife to him.

Although Sargent was well into his forties when the King came to the throne, and had painted many of his important pictures in the nineties, it is with the Edwardian Age that one associates him. In fact, if someone asked what was most characteristic of the period, Sargent's name would immediately spring to mind. Sargent himself became immensely sick of painting portraits, begging hostesses to ask him to paint their fences or their stables, rather than themselves, but it was themselves that he was best at.

It might be urged that Sargent did not possess a particularly interesting mind, lacked intellectual stamina. That would be hard to sustain. He was more or less bilingual in French, spoke German and Italian well, was extremely conversant especially with French literature, which he preferred to English. This wide reading is notable considering the scrappy education he was given, while his parents rambled from one European town to another.

When the Post-Impressionist Exhibition of 1910 took place, Sargent came down rather too heavily on the 'wrong side'. He had, after all, been friends with several of the Impressionists (who were admittedly lukewarm about his own painting), and it might be added that Sickert displayed the same disapprobation. This attitude made Roger Fry and Bloomsbury passionately anti-Sargent. But when the chips are down, was Duncan Grant really a greater painter? A more sensitive one certainly, but blood and guts count in the arts too.

Sargent's not very subtle side comes out in the supposedly satirical touch he lends to some of his portraits. Examples could be multiplied almost indefinitely. Lord Ribblesdale and Asher Wertheimer will do. That Lord Ribblesdale is a 'good likeness' can scarcely be doubted, because the features so closely resemble those of his grandson, the late Hugh Fraser, MP, but the head would 'go' at least ten times into the body, and the painter's comment is rather heavy-handed.

Distortion is forgivable in, say, a Matisse, but Sargent would not have approved of Matisse or those painters who habitually distort. Yet he himself uses this method to exaggerate the elongated aristocratic figure in hunting kit. In contrast we have Mr Wertheimer (who took it in extremely good part) with his cigar. Again one doesn't doubt that the picture is 'like' this Jewish collector, but it can't be said to tackle a potentially more interesting side of him. All in all, Sargent remains somewhat inexplicable, perhaps because there was nothing to explain.

John Singer Sargent: His Portrait,   1986
Stanley Olson, Macmillan.   *Daily Telegraph*

EDMUND GOSSE

When I was at school Edmund Gosse came down in about 1921–22 to judge the reading aloud in a Declamation Prize. He was in his early seventies, looking exactly like Max Beerbohm's many caricatures of him, and made some eminently sage remarks on the subject of reading aloud.

I don't think even the most self-satisfied of contemporary writers (perhaps the next selection of the Book Marketing Council?) could quite achieve Gosse's overwhelming assurance. It gave a marvellous glimpse of an earlier epoch.

Gosse's assurance by no means came from lack of being knocked about by life, as Ann Thwaite's enjoyable biography shows. She very reasonably subtitles her book a landscape. It is almost a panorama; in one sense a success story, in another a chronicle of much dreariness endured and critical savaging for woolliness and inaccuracies. Even when he rose to the top Gosse was often depressed and disturbed by hostility in a literary world he would have liked to dominate.

Ann Thwaite rightly takes the line that there was much to be said for Gosse whatever his failings. At worst he wrote a minor classic in *Father and Son*, the autobiographical work produced in his late fifties. This book – first published anonymously with broad hints as to authorship – describes Gosse's upbringing in the fanatical atmosphere of the Plymouth Brethren, a home life in which scarcely any pleasures or normal social contacts were allowed. Gosse's father, a distinguished zoologist (the tradition of French Huguenot origins was quite imaginary), firmly believed until just before the end that, rather than die, he would be personally translated to the Next World.

Gosse's mother had died when he was a child. In spite of the trials of life at home he got on well, in a sense, both with his father and step-mother. He had an extraordinary toughness and energy which enabled him to stand up to a depressing and badly paid job in the British Museum, where he copied catalogues in a malodorous underground den. He lived in lodgings in Tottenham with two amiable but straitlaced spinster friends of the Gosse family.

All the time Gosse was struggling away to place articles. He looked upon himself as a poet to the end of his days. One is amazed how soon he came to know Swinburne and William Bell Scott, both in their different ways fairly violent tonics for a young man brought up as Gosse had been. When he managed to escape from the British Museum it was only to a relatively better paid but scarcely less boring job at the Board of Trade.

One of the keys to Gosse's career was that during a fairly haphazard schooling he had a facility for picking up languages. He had learnt German well and – distinctly rare – the Scandinavian languages. Accordingly, he was the first person to mark down Ibsen, which he did not from Ibsen's plays but from an early book of poems. Later he did not wholly approve of the plays. Here is to be noted what seems an essential Gosse characteristic: he could quite often recognise genius, but also, often, the genius he recognised was too hot for Gosse to hold.

An interesting example of this is Dostoevsky, whose *Crime and Punishment* Gosse read in French in 1887, and thought 'the most powerful, the most daringly successful novel I have ever read'. When, however, he was an old man corresponding with André Gide, Gosse wrote:

> We have all in our time been subjected to the magic of this epileptic monster. But his genius has only led us astray and I should say to any young writer of merit who appealed to me – Read what you like, only don't waste your time reading Dostoievsky. He is the cocaine and morphine of modern literature.

There in a nutshell is what was wrong with Gosse, and it is something by no means simple to explain. He was a man of extremely complicated psychology. Many thought him the most amusing talker they had ever met. Ann Thwaite wisely does not attempt to explain too much. She spreads out a generous amount of information to choose from. However, she does express a judgment on two aspects which have cropped up of late years.

It has been suggested that Gosse was secretly homosexual. There seems no indication of that as a young man. He thought of marrying several girls before he found his wife, and when married was unquestionably happy in that state. On the other hand, Gosse himself made no secret of being what can only be called in love with the sculptor Hamo Thornycroft. This relationship was perhaps comparable to Tennyson's with Hallam, except that Thornycroft did not die; he too married and sculpted, among other works, Cromwell outside the House of Commons.

Gosse also sometimes expresses what might now be regarded as rather suspect pleasure in the society of good-looking undergraduates. He was a friend of J. A. Symonds, of whose writings on homosexuality he disapproved, as he did those of Gide. In short, Gosse might have had bisexual leanings but certainly never allowed these to get out of control.

Ann Thwaite also dismisses the smear that Gosse was a party to the book forgeries of T. J. Wise. She produces excellent reasons for clearing Gosse absolutely. Again, if for no other reason, one would think him much too cautious, apart from any such criminal act being utterly alien to Gosse's character. How anyone could ever have trusted Wise with a face like that is nevertheless a mystery.

Gosse knew Tennyson, Browning, Arnold, was a close friend of Stevenson, James, Kipling, Hardy and lots more. Particularly after he became Librarian of the House of Lords, he added most of the British aristocracy (for which he had a weakness) to his acquaintance and politicians like Balfour, Asquith, Haldane. Gosse, in short, was what comparatively few writers of this country are, a character straight out of Proust. In every respect he would have fitted perfectly into Mme Verdurin's dinner-parties, not least in possessing faintly enigmatic sexual tastes. Perhaps he was there.

Edmund Gosse: A Literary Landscape,   1984
1849–1928, Ann Thwaite, Secker.   *Daily Telegraph*

Bloomsbury and Non-Bloomsbury

LYTTON STRACHEY

I

I never met Lytton Strachey, but of the group popularly classified as Bloomsbury, his was the personality which came over most strongly to the outsider. By the late 1920s the Bloomsburies were already thought of by the young as a curious embalmed residue of another age, not unimpressive, but out of touch and quite unjustifiably pleased with themselves. When Strachey died in his early fifties in 1932, there was a real feeling, both within and without the circle, that Bloomsbury too, in its essence, had passed away with him, whatever relics might remain of the original sect.

That is, of course, merely the superficial impression of the moment. Nevertheless, it seems worth mentioning as tribute to Strachey's individual status. Michael Holroyd's excellent biography shows what a complex affair Bloomsbury really was. His first volume deals mainly with the period before Strachey achieved eminence. Holroyd negotiates with adroitness and understanding the years when Strachey was unknown. Once or twice we are allowed to look into the future, when certain things have to be explained, in general it is the wretchedly unhappy, near-invalid young man who is pictured here.

The Strachey family has been of unusual distinction since the days of Elizabeth I. To mention only two among many: one of them wrote a book almost certainly made use of by Shakespeare in composing *The Tempest*; another was Clive's right-hand man in India. The family still inhabit the house in Somerset they have owned for 300 years. With all this enterprise, intelligence, public service, together with plenty of eccentricity, something seems missing in the later stages. A more light-hearted element was needed to leaven the lump.

By the time Strachey's parents – a general and his second, much younger wife – were living in Lancaster Gate with their large family, they seem to have accumulated much of the worst of all possible worlds – physical discomfort, seediness, intellectual snobbishness, intense family pride, quite unrelieved by the frivolity of a slightly higher social echelon. It was like the Forsytes, all the worse for being old-established and intelligent.

Partly on account of his bad health, partly because there had been some trivial schoolboy scandal there about his brother, Strachey was not sent to Eton. He went, instead, to an establishment of 'The New School Movement', which 'aimed at producing wholesome, healthy citizens' by the 'natural method'.

There was the usual headmaster with a strong, hypnotic personality, who felt that books produced peril to 'body, mind and character'. Emphasis was on cold baths, military drill and manual labour. Water-closets considered decadent, the whole school assembled each morning in a field.

After a couple of terms of this régime, Strachey's health broke down completely. He was removed to what he later described as a 'semi-demi-public school'. This was followed by two years at Liverpool University, failure to get into Balliol, and entry to Trinity College, Cambridge. Strachey's educational *via dolorosa* needs detailing, because it obviously had an effect on his later development. Its handling had been cranky in the extreme on the part of his parents, and it is worth noting that it was crankiness rather than conventionality that he was, in fact, later reacting against.

When he went up to Cambridge, a new world blossomed. He was older than the average undergraduate, an odd mixture of naïvety and sophistication. The really extraordinary thing is that Strachey found there, in his first term, the entire nucleus of the Bloomsbury group, and, roughly speaking, they all lived in close contact for the rest of their lives. Bloomsbury could never have come into being without these Cambridge foundations. At Oxford – for which great dislike was felt by Strachey and his friends – things would undoubtedly have been somewhat different.

Strachey was throughout his life homosexual. Holroyd treats this fact without the slightest evasion and much good sense, not hesitating to allow a joke on the subject, if need be. In this connection, the rather thin story recorded here about Constant Lambert has little or no point, unless it is known that Strachey had made an unsuccessful pass at the entirely heterosexual Lambert on an earlier occasion.

Strachey's homosexuality was torture to him. Hopelessly susceptible, he was painfully conscious of his odd, unattractive appearance, while troubles with his digestion kept him in an almost permanent state of taking cures and diets. Much of his time after he came down from the university was spent in acute misery.

In addition to this, money was permanently short. He had failed to get a fellowship and lived uncomfortably in a chilly room in Lancaster Gate on what he could get from writing reviews. Later these reviews were for the *Spectator*, then a kind of Strachey reserve, though, as it turned out, one of the few papers to attack 'Eminent Victorians'.

The subsequent stage of the formation of Bloomsbury was the social alliance of the Cambridge young men with Vanessa (Bell) and Virginia

(Woolf), daughters of Sir Leslie Stephen. Of these ladies, too, Holroyd provides convincing sketches. In one of his most depressed moments, Strachey, in spite of a bad cold in the head, visited Virginia Stephen and proposed. To his horror, he was accepted. One cannot help feeling that this was one of her supreme moments for exerting malice to which she sometimes felt herself impelled. However, matters were satisfactorily arranged. Strachey wrote to friends and relations describing the incident, begging them to tell no one.

This habit of living in public is one of the most striking features of Strachey himself and the whole group, even though that public might be a small one. They seemed to have enjoyed little or no privacy from each other. This helps the book. Holroyd writes with sympathy of his subject, though not ignoring Strachey's envy, unkindness and appalling poems. He was a remarkable figure, even at an early age. The whole story is an enthralling one.

Lytton Strachey: A Critical Biography.   1967
Vol. I: The Unknown Years,   *Daily Telegraph*
1880–1910, Michael Holroyd,
Heinemann.

I I

Strachey as a writer does not wear well. He could be intelligent, witty, the master of a phrase, and was usually genuinely absorbed by his subject matter. These qualities are vitiated by a giggling egotism that at its best often offers no more than the Victorian approach turned the other way up, and, at its worst, a deliberate falsification of history.

The impact *Eminent Victorians* made was extraordinary, but this impact was on Strachey's contemporaries, rather than the younger generation. Strachey himself was astonished at the favourable manner in which these daring studies were received. He had expected resounding attacks from all sides. On the contrary, he succeeded in precisely expressing the mood of the moment – a rare coup which from time to time electrifies different kinds of books or plays.

Strachey was born in 1880. For those a quarter of a century younger the idols he was destroying had been largely laid low. This is not to say that *Eminent Victorians* was not in many ways a notable book, but it was essentially a 'Victorian' book, obsessed with Victorian values. *Queen Victoria* is less interesting; *Elizabeth and Essex*, a middlebrow historical reconstruction, positively to be regretted. However, this was not felt by the public at the time, especially in America, where the sales of *Elizabeth and Essex* especially were unprecedented for what passed as serious history. This hitherto unsuccessful, physically weak, inhibited, eccentric highbrow essayist suddenly became a well-known public figure and something not much short of a bestseller. What was the reason for this?

The personal – and far the most striking – side of Holroyd's book gives an answer to that. For all his apparent weaknesses, Strachey had an immensely strong will and incredibly violent emotions. Also, he was ambitious, with a truly Victorian desire to impose his own moral judgments on the rest of the world. He is on record as admitting that.

What follows, as his life story is unfolded, is a kind of Greek Tragedy. Certainly those who complain about the world today being 'permissive' will be made to sit up at what was happening, even before the First World War. Strachey was homosexual, but even his homosexuality was oddly adjusted, and from time to time he would be attracted to women in a shy undergraduate sort of way. From this fact arose the really extraordinary love affair – for it can be called no less – of Strachey and 'Carrington'.

Carrington (although her Christian name was Dora she was always called by her surname) almost steals this second half of the biography. She was a colonel's daughter, a talented art student in rebellion against her home, about fifteen years younger than Strachey. They were brought together by friends, and, going for a country walk, Strachey suddenly kissed her. Carrington, who despite her later adventures with both sexes, was at this time a prude, was furious at this assault. She planned to take her revenge on Strachey by stealing into his room in the early morning and cutting off his beard. He woke up before she could do this, their eyes met, and she fell in love with him for life.

Any attempt to summarise what followed would be to maul about Holroyd's masterly account of the whole unbelievable story, which, in its simplest terms, resolved itself into Carrington, Strachey and Carrington's husband, Ralph Partridge (who had won an MC in the war and commanded a battalion at the age of twenty-three) all living in the same house. Carrington was in love with Strachey; Strachey in love with Partridge; Partridge in love with Carrington: the first two couples being platonic, it was generally supposed. The developments that followed on from this basis were no less unusual. No doubt a fair amount of the distributions, and redistributions, that took place between the couples and trios here concerned did not rise above a self-indulgence that would have been better controlled, or at least better not openly paraded in the Bloomsbury manner. More than once one feels that a little less malice and a little more hypocrisy would have made everyone's life easier, without seriously altering the general moral tone. What lifts the story from the banalities of sexual promiscuity is the fact that some sort of a compromise was eventually hammered out; and Carrington's final suicide. One feels that there is much to ponder; much that is moving.

If Strachey wanted fame, he certainly found it, but the side for which he was famous does not seem to be his most remarkable side. Perhaps he, too, somehow felt that he never truly achieved the self-expression that he deserved. Again and again one is struck by what might be called Strachey's 'anti-Bloomsbury' literary judgments, a kind of desire in him to escape from Bloomsbury, just as he wanted to escape from Victorianism. It is astonishing, at a 'highbrow' level, that he could only read Proust with an effort and refused even to embark on Joyce. Incidentally, it is worth pointing out, apropos of his famous reply to the Tribunal (asking him what he would do if a German soldier attempted to rape his sister), 'I should try and interpose my own body,' that, when something of the sort had, in fact, happened, as is recorded in the first volume of this biography, Strachey had frightened the assailant off by pretending to be insane.

Lytton Strachey: A Critical Biography.   1968
Vol. II: The Years of Achievement,   *Daily Telegraph*
1910–1932, Michael Holroyd,
Heinemann.

III

Among a great many Bloomsbury reputations at one time considerably over-inflated, Dora Carrington has hardly had her due as a talented painter. She was chiefly known, even in her own day, for the odd ménage in which she lived. After mentioning that, people would add that her pictures were quite good too. This volume of Letters, well and magnanimously edited by David Garnett, is possibly the most interesting item that has yet come out of Bloomsbury. Its interest is, of course, largely due to the fact that the Letters were preserved by the persons concerned. They therefore supply what can be read as an enthralling psychological novel. Characters and situations are introduced, develop, decay. Finally, there is the climax, which the reader feels inevitable as the latter pages are reached, when the writer takes her own life after Strachey's death.

Carrington, born in 1893, was the fourth child of a family of five, her father then over sixty. She showed great promise as an artist, was sent to the Slade at its peak period as an art school. There Mark Gertler, the painter, immediately fell in love with her. His published letters tell his side of the story. A strong character, if not always a wholly attractive one, Carrington not only inspired and experienced love, but was able to express her feelings on paper in an odd, sometimes deliberately naïve, but essentially effective manner. Her passion for Lytton Strachey makes an extraordinary story. There can be no doubt now that her love for him was in a large measure returned, and, although Strachey was predominantly homosexual, it took for a time a physical form.

David Garnett, in his account of the general background, points out that Carrington, in spite of her close association with the Bloomsbury world, was never entirely at ease in it. That very different ethos of Augustus John was more to her taste. One has the impression in the Letters that the Bloomsburies (in their own particular genre, snobs of the first water) were not happy about Carrington's lack of what they regarded as polish. Garnett also draws attention to Carrington's taste for reopening an amatory relationship immediately after closing it down. In this she was certainly not unique among women, but it is rare to have letters set out, as they are here, showing how a lady may string along several men at the same moment.

'I believe I am a perfect combination of a nymphomaniac and a wood-nymph!' she wrote to Gerald Brenan. 'I hanker after intimacies, which another side of my nature is perpetually at war against.' This seems to summarise her point of view very fairly. She was also involved in love affairs with her own sex.

The letters are illustrated with some of her drawings. Carrington's descriptions show a remarkable power of conveying the look and feel of the English countryside. For example:

As I approached our village, a hundred memories crowded and jostled, like human beings getting on a bus: the wooden Flying Fox, the weather vane on the malting house, our kitchen garden with its high wall and pear tree, the sunk leads on the roof of the house, where I used to climb through a skylight and watch the river below me on hot summer afternoons, my attic bedroom window, the garden with the variegated holly tree, and the Ilex in the corner, all the farmhouses and particular trees along the road. I had lunch with the Scotch MacKilligans.

One is reminded of Kilvert's Diary. There is the same absolute certainty about what the writer sees and feels. Carrington's scraps of poetry are also not to be ignored.

The book should do something to persuade people that eccentric sexual situations were not all invented during the last ten years, and that many soldiers (Ralph Partridge, Gerald Brenan, and so on) came out of the First World War (the Bloomsburies, as such, did not go into it, of course) with just the same sentiments as those so much propagated now – that anything is better than a commercial struggle for existence.

Carrington: Letters and Extracts from   1970
her Diaries, edited by David   *Daily Telegraph*
Garnett, with a biographical note
by Noel Carrington, Cape.

LEONARD WOOLF

Leonard Woolf, just short of eighty years of age, has had a distinguished career as a writer and editor, husband of Virginia Woolf, pillar of that group of Cambridge intellectuals whose activities gave new meaning to the name of Bloomsbury. *Sowing* takes its author only to the age of twenty-four and his entry into the Ceylon Civil Service, but, as the various personages who played some part in his life are introduced, Woolf says something of each and of their subsequent influence upon himself. One is struck by the fact of how early friends and ideas were formed into what was to remain an almost unaltered pattern throughout his career.

The narrative of the years which culminated in Cambridge is extraordinarily well done. Appropriately enough, Leonard Woolf lived as a child in Bloomsbury – in one of those large, almost country houses, of which few now remain – on one side of Tavistock Square, under the caryatids of St Pancras Church. His family was Jewish on both sides, with Belgian connections; his father a successful barrister. He was educated at St Paul's. A dramatic slant is given to the story by the father's death, when wife and nine children were reduced from comparative wealth to comparative poverty.

Woolf writes in an incisive, rigorous prose, suited to his own uncompromising view of life. He gives the reader a clear idea of his upbringing and what he was like as a boy. His account of this sudden decline in the family fortunes, and the manner in which it was weathered, is adept in handling. At the same time one has the feeling that the author's at times almost brutal directness conceals a good deal of sensitiveness that has suffered in the past some hard blows. The trembling of his hands – sometimes so great that he could not write down on paper the sentence of prisoners who came before him in Ceylon – indicates this.

Accordingly, like others of the group, he found, in what was perhaps a certain basic lack of self-confidence, support in becoming a member of Bloomsbury; that community which had about it something of a small religious sect in the attitude of its adherents towards each other and to the outside world.

His recurrent theme is rebellion against Victorianism, and he takes the Dreyfus case as the rallying point.

> Over the body and fate of one obscure Jewish captain in the French army a kind of cosmic conflict went on year after year between the establishment of Church, Army, and State on the one side and the small band of intellectuals who fought for truth, reason, and justice, on the other.

This sentence seems to me a typical piece of Bloomsbury over-simplification, characteristic of a view of life which divided the world into 'good' intellectuals (provided they were of the approved sort) and 'bad' outsiders.

Of course the acquittal of Dreyfus was a triumph of justice over injustice, but in point of fact Major Picquart, a soldier (and more than a bit of an anti-Semite), first sought justice for Dreyfus at extreme risk to himself; while Dreyfus – to his great credit – refused, in spite of the pressure applied, ever to lend himself to the powerful political forces which hoped to make him their pawn. The military authorities and the Roman Catholic Church may not have shone during the Dreyfus episode, but it is surely a completely inadequate picture to suggest that the conflict was untinged on the Dreyfusard side by all the normal impurities and violence of power politics, or that the panorama was not an infinitely complicated one.

This may appear a pedantic point – taken at random from many other subjects here – but it seems an important one in the examination of the Bloomsbury attitude, an examination which Leonard Woolf by implication demands.

Sowing: An Autobiography of the Years 1880–1904, Leonard Woolf, Hogarth Press.

1966
Daily Telegraph

ARTHUR WALEY

Even in his lifetime Arthur Waley (1889–1966) was something of a legend. In his particular way a prodigious scholar, he translated and promoted in this country the literature of China and Japan in a manner that might be said almost to have introduced their historic writings to the West. In addition to that, he was a personality very much in his own style. Although not a member of the inner praesidium of Bloomsbury he certainly graded as a Bloomsbury in the eyes of the outer world. The extraordinary social discomfort that his manner could produce is referred to more than once in these pages.

The first half of this book consists of brief memoirs of Waley himself: the second, extracts from his own articles, prefaces and translations of Chinese and Japanese poets and prose writers. In the Japanese field his most famous translations are, of course, *Tale of Genji*, the long, almost Proustian novel written by Lady Murasakai ('Lady Violet'), and *The Pillow-Book of Sei Shonagon*, works belonging to the tenth and eleventh centuries.

Ivan Morris, who edits this volume, Waley's star pupil, is himself a translator and chronicler of Japan in the top class. It is therefore not surprising that, among the interesting collection in *Madly Singing in the Mountains*, the Editor's piece is the most authoritative and informative on the professional side. Morris brings to his appreciation just the right amount of personal prejudice, excluding, for example, from this anthology Waley's translation from the Chinese, 'Monkey' (praised by several contributors), because he personally does not like it. That is an approach Waley himself would have respected. Morris also includes one or two of Waley's own poems, though commenting that no great claims can be put forward for them. On the other hand, he really does show what an astonishing job Waley did.

Among many revealing contributions it is hard to quote from some without seeming unjust to others. One might pick out Carmen Blacker's anecdote of the Ministry of Information during the war as a typical example of Waley's treatment. Carmen Blacker, who had just left school, was deciphering from the Japanese. Introduced to Waley and overcome with shyness at meeting the great man, she said: 'I often find Japanese dreadfully ambiguous.' Waley, in his high, quiet, but

97

essentially smacking-down tone, replied: 'Oh, really, I have never come across a single case of ambiguity in my whole life.' The reply is worth noting, because it is perfectly clear from what follows in this very book that Japanese *can* be ambiguous. The fact is mentioned more than once by Westerners, by a Japanese, and implied, if not stated, by Waley himself. Yet it is also true that Waley could be the kindest of men. I am not prepared to believe that he was wholly unaware of his manner, as some here suggest. There was, it seems to me, a fair amount of aggression, or at least an agonised wall of self-defence.

Although I never knew him at all well, I can vouch for Waley's kindness. He once rang up and invited me to come with him to Patrick Hamilton's play *Rope* (about two undergraduates who commit a murder) for which he insisted on paying for the tickets. When we left the theatre, I expressed a minimum of conventional thanks. Waley listened for a second to make sure what I was talking about, then with apparent contempt, walked away into the night without a word.

I am glad that Sacheverell Sitwell chronicles here the famous remark of Ada Leverson (Oscar Wilde's 'The Sphinx'): 'I expect you often go to *The Mikado*, Mr Waley': Peter Quennell records the occasion when Cyril Connolly invited Waley to luncheon at a new and relatively luxurious Mediterranean hotel. Waley, on the safe side, arrived with a salad he had bought in the market-place carried in a string bag.

Roy Fuller interviewed Waley for the BBC in 1963. Their talk is reproduced here. It contains some good stuff on the subject of translation and poetry generally. Waley – whose *A Hundred and Seventy Chinese Poems* had been published in 1918 – was one of the group that included T. S. Eliot, Wyndham Lewis, Ezra Pound, Ford Madox Ford and others, who used to dine weekly at a restaurant in Frith Street.

Waley could be an extremely amusing talker and loved gossip. He was not unaware of his reputation for being difficult, and told me that when he met F. F. Urquhart ('Sligger'), the Dean of Balliol, 'not wanting to be Cambridge', he made some trivial remark to which Urquhart, in general noted for his mild manner, replied: 'Need we talk about the weather?'

Asked what Chairman Mao's poems were like, Waley replied that they were 'better than Hitler's pictures and perhaps not quite so good as Winston Churchill's'. He was sometimes irked by the contemporary theatre, and was overheard to say: 'I don't think one need wait any longer,' as he strode out of the first act of *Waiting for Godot*. I last saw Waley when he must have been at least seventy at the Private View of some paintings executed by two chimpanzees. He was absolutely

unchanged. We agreed that the female artist was the more sophisticated, the male with the deeper feeling.

Madly Singing in the Mountains: An
Appreciation and Anthology of Arthur
Waley, edited by Ivan Morris,
Allen & Unwin.

1970
Daily Telegraph

VANESSA BELL

A month or two ago I read, straight off, the six volumes of Virginia Woolf's Collected Letters. In that amusing, painful, malicious, finally tragic chronicle of the writer's life, her relations with her sister Vanessa Bell (1879–1960) are certainly well up among the most interesting exhibits. There was perhaps no alternative for Frances Spalding but to cover a great deal of familiar ground. Understandably, she has not the skilful touch of Quentin Bell as an historian of Bloomsbury, above all lacking his humour, so necessary in describing the individuals concerned; though sometimes the Bloomsburies' dealings with each other, and the rest of the world, are sufficiently droll in mere narrative. None the less Frances Spalding has done a painstaking and thorough job. If she is a bit solemn about it all at times, the material is there.

We get off to rather a slow start with the two Stephen sisters deciding they did not like conventional social life, one marrying Clive Bell (1907), the other Leonard Woolf (1912). It is here, at this early stage that some analysis of their lifelong relationship might have been a help: Virginia Woolf's almost incestuous love for Vanessa Bell was combined with jealousy and dependence on her elder sister for calm advice.

Clive Bell, a genial, somewhat ludicrous, figure, of *nouveau riche* background, had exchanged hunting and shooting for what was then the latest art criticism from France. He was evidently much in love with his wife when he married her, and she with him. Virginia Woolf was three-parts lesbian, but liked leading men or women on; and there seems no doubt that her flirtations, in the early years of his marriage, with Clive Bell (a push-over emotionally speaking throughout his life), though certainly not physical, did undermine things chiefly on account of this complex sisterly relationship, which is never quite sufficiently emphasised.

The next stage was for Vanessa Bell to embark on a passionate affair with Clive Bell's fellow art-critic (from whom he learnt a good deal) Roger Fry, who brought a Quaker religiosity to aesthetics. Clive Bell took his wife's affair in his stride, and for the rest of their marriage he and she lived separate lives though remaining on good terms – he with a succession of mistresses of all ages, preferably thirty years younger; she with a strange association, which constitutes the body of this book.

100

Frances Spalding does not make undue claims for Vanessa Bell's painting. Clearly she had a talent, though not an original one. It is as a decorator that she is often seen at her best. This does not mean that she was not an absolutely dedicated artist within her limits and a remarkable woman. Her own fear that Duncan Grant always sat above her as a superior painter was perhaps not always justified. It may be, however, that this professional sense of a supposed superiority on Grant's side had something to do with her determination to capture him, a congenital homosexual, who never ceased throughout the union to be involved with men, sometimes to the extent of making her fear that their ménage would be broken up even in her seventies.

After bearing two sons to Clive Bell, his wife had a daughter by Duncan Grant, though the pretence that she was Bell's daughter was kept up for a time even by those likely to guess the truth. Clive Bell himself showed the greatest good nature about this event, even being rather put out when years later the paternity of Duncan Grant had to be openly acknowledged.

David 'Bunny' Garnett, the writer, although later enormously addicted to women, had some years of homosexual association with Duncan Grant and tried to seduce Vanessa Bell. When this daughter, Angelica, was born, he is alleged to have said: 'I think of marrying it; when she is twenty I shall be forty-six – will it be scandalous?' This, indeed, Garnett did, after first beginning with an affair with Angelica. That, for some reason, was too much even for the Bloomsburies, who had preached for years, sexually speaking, you ought to do exactly what you liked best, irrespective of what other people thought. The parents Vanessa Bell and Duncan Grant, wrote literally (as Clive Bell would have put it, '*textuellement*') asking Garnett whether his 'intentions' were 'honourable'.

It need hardly be said that matters like Duncan Grant's boy-friends need a good deal of sorting out, and Frances Spalding does that sort of thing with admirable industry. She looks at everything from a Bloomsbury window, and is a bit naïve about Edwardian conventional morals. The Bloomsburies didn't invent easy-going sexual behaviour. Their terrible sufferings during the 1914–18 war are touched on ('Bunny saw a Zeppelin on Friday night and heard some explosions').

The Surrealist Exhibition of 1936 was not by any means, as Frances Spalding supposes, the Post-Impressionist Exhibition of 1910. It was not far from being a damp-squib, as everyone interested in these sort of things had known about Surrealism for at least a decade. Edward Sackville West was cousin, not nephew, of Vita Sackville-West (who never ceased talking and writing about being an only child). Lady Gerald Wellesley, 'Dotti', the poet, appears as Lady Dorothy Wellesley and Lady Wellesley indiscriminately. It was Lady Tree, not Vanessa

Bell, who asked Asquith, then Prime Minister: 'Are you interested in the war?'

Vanessa Bell, Frances Spalding,
Weidenfeld.

1983
Daily Telegraph

THE BLOOMSBURIES

Leon Edel's method is to tell Bloomsbury's story as if it were a novel. In doing this he is immensely smooth, carrying the reader along with easy skill. He does not conceal Bloomsbury's blemishes, but somehow we feel ourselves a long way from the gritty reality. The Nine Worthies chosen by Edel to represent the Bloomsbury team (batting order alphabetical) are: Clive Bell; Vanessa Bell; Roger Fry; Duncan Grant; Maynard Keynes; Desmond MacCarthy; Lytton Strachey; Leonard Woolf; Virginia Woolf.

Let us look at the score, taking painters and painting first. Duncan Grant and Vanessa Bell were goodish painters, concerned chiefly with their own work, which could well have developed individually. Neither of them would come to mind as the outstanding painter of the period. Roger Fry (twenty years older than the rest) was a bad painter, but a strikingly original art critic. To art criticism he brought a Quaker puritanism that sometimes led to bigoted exclusions within the field of painting. Clive Bell was his understrapper, a *farceur* with some appreciation of pictures, a distinctly ludicrous womaniser, who nevertheless managed uncomfortably to stir his sister-in-law, Virginia Woolf. His most distinguished memorial is as father of Quentin Bell, who has written knowledgeably and sensitively on the subject of the Bloomsbury of his parents.

In the field of writing, other than 'creative', Maynard Keynes was an economist of great influence, even if his views have been by no means universally accepted. Leonard Woolf, an efficient civil servant in Ceylon, retired to become a literary or political journalist (who was at least once, when editing, made a fool of by a Communist), lived to ninety and wrote accomplished memoirs. Desmond MacCarthy (who in fact inhabited Chelsea, but for certain technical reasons rates as a Bloomsbury) was a not very adventurous literary critic, a nice man, asked to shooting parties, which was felt to give Bloomsbury tone, and the only Bloomsbury to have a gallant war record.

The two most successful and ambitious Bloomsbury writers were Lytton Strachey and Virginia Woolf. Strachey's success came comparatively late with *Eminent Victorians* and *Queen Victoria*, but when it came it was overwhelming, bringing him fame and the social lionising for which he longed. His books now seem giggling, cliché-ridden,

103

inaccurate, but there can be no doubt of the impact they made at the time. To say that, of all Bloomsbury, the most inflated reputation is Virginia Woolf's does not mean that Virginia Woolf did not possess a considerable talent, but she was not the only writer of her time to see that there were other ways of writing a novel than those of, for instance, Arnold Bennett, whom she attacked. *The Old Wives' Tale* certainly has its naïveties, and tails off in the latter half, but I am not sure that any novel Virginia Woolf wrote outpaces it.

Virginia Woolf's dominant personality has stood in the way of judging her books coolly. Her failing is a lack of creative imagination within her own terms of reference. It is perfectly true that she could grasp the importance in life of apparently trivial things, but in the last resort she is not sufficiently interested in other people. She has none of the understanding and wit of, say, Ivy Compton-Burnett. Her first two quite conventional novels are possibly her best. The later more experimental ones play with moods, but never deeply examine them like Proust.

Pretentious and self-regarding as Bloomsbury may have been, no one would deny that here was a remarkable collection of personalities, nor the fact that they hung together. The last was certainly not because they were so devoted to each other. Lytton Strachey found Roger Fry 'a most shifty and wormy character'; used to refer to Clive Bell's 'fat little mind', though he appealed to Bell, 'Can't you or Vanessa persuade Duncan [Grant] to make beautiful pictures instead of these coagulations of distressing oddments?'

The First World War weighed Bloomsbury in the balance, and on the whole found them wanting. In their much admired France the men would have been conscripted if fit. Duncan Grant began by thinking of joining up, but seems to have been moved to pacifism by his affair (in spite of being homosexual) with Vanessa Bell. Lytton Strachey's famous answer to the Tribunal asking 'What would you do if a German tried to rape your sister?' 'I should attempt to interpose my body between them,' turns out to have been planned comedy.

Clive Bell was perhaps the most ignominious, a hearty, healthy, self-indulgent man pottering about as a 'land-worker' at Garsington, where he got on even Lady Ottoline Morrell's nerves. Edel's chief piece of research lies in putting Desmond MacCarthy's war record on the map. By the late 1920s Bloomsbury was looked upon in the world of the arts as scarcely less stick-in-the-mud than the philistines they had formerly attacked. Where does Bloomsbury stand now? 'We were in the van of the builders of a new society,' wrote Leonard Woolf, 'which should be free, rational, civilised.' He should take a look around now.

Bloomsbury: A House of Lions, Leon   1979
Edel, the Hogarth Press.   *Daily Telegraph*

JULIA STRACHEY

I think it would be reasonable to say that Julia Strachey (1901–1979) was a beauty in her younger days; her two novels, *Cheerful Weather for the Wedding* (1932) and *The Man on the Pier* (1951) are both decidedly talented; her stories and shorter pieces are often funny. Indeed her briefest note is always written in a personal yet quite unaffected way. At the same time neither her good looks nor her writing was precisely the 'point' of her. Her father Oliver Strachey, a rather unsuccessful member of his tribe, though with all its idiosyncrasies, was a Superintendent of Railways in India where Julia lived blissfully until the age of four. Oliver Strachey's first wife was Swiss, and neither party took their marriage bond with undue seriousness; indeed Julia's mother had an illegitimate baby in Italy on the way to deposit Julia in England – as the custom was for parents employed in India – and finally parted from her husband.

Julia was now brought up by her 'Aunt Loo', former wife of Bertrand Russell, a member of the American Quaker family of Pearsall Smith, to which Oliver Strachey's second wife, Ray, belonged on her mother's side. It is the characteristics of this group of Julia's relations that are so well described by her half-sister. Here it will be sufficient to say that Aunt Loo made Julia at the age of twelve draw and colour an enlargement from a medical book of a drunkard's intestines poisoned by alcohol – a dreadful warning to be used at a lecture at a Women's Temperance Meeting. Soon after, in a crowded railway station Aunt Loo explained, at the top of her voice, the mechanics of cohabitation, demonstrating with one clasped hand and a finger of the other. She also told Julia she could never love her.

Julia was sent to the co-educational establishment Bedales, which she whole-heartedly disliked, and her account of its high-thinking 'healthiness' and 'progressive' attitudes certainly makes Jane Eyre's Lowood sound infinitely preferable as a girls' school. She was ticked off by a female prefect for playing a Boston one-step in the morning, and told that if she wanted a record lighter than classical music why not something healthy like a sea-shanty?

This narrative of Julia Strachey's life is made up partly from her own autobiographical writings, partly from her diaries, partly from letters to Frances Partridge who, with her husband Ralph, provided an ever-available refuge at their house Ham Spray. Frances Partridge also supplies explanatory paragraphs to show the course of events and sometimes modify Julia's by no means always just judgments of other people.

Julia's first husband was Stephen Tomlin (always called Tommy), the sculptor, who could not be regarded as an easy man to live with. Of him Julia wrote:

> If only, oh if only Tommy could have been content with the actual sins he committed. If only he would have done without this aftermath of tortured guilt! Then, ah then, there would have been a little time over for companionship with me. And yet I was aware in my secret heart that I only truly felt at home with such spectres and revenants as my husband.
>
> I had always made a bee-line for refugees and exiles hailing from the same far-off and despoiled kingdom from which I, too, had long ago been driven. They were my own people. I understood them, how their hearts and minds worked, having all my life known what it was to have been forced to scratch up, with bleeding fingers, some sort of a living upon alien territory.

That was all no doubt very true, but it makes a sad story. One of the troubles was Julia's appalling lethargy. Even with starvation at her heels she would scarcely be induced to get up in the morning or perform the commonplaces of domestic housekeeping without dreadful effort. She could be charming and amusing but was also hopelessly selfish and thought it a Strachey's duty to be critical of everything and everyone.

Even the devoted Frances Partridge (herself with Strachey connections and plenty of troubles of her own) was sometimes reduced to rage by being treated by her friend like a half-witted kitchen maid.

In 1939 Julia began her association with the painter (Sir) Lawrence Gowing, whom she was subsequently to marry, though nearly thirty years later they were to part. It is clear that much of her time with Gowing, who was much younger than her, was happy, yet the impossibility of Julia seeing her life with any sense of proportion is shown by the fearful complaints about living in Newcastle when her husband was teaching there, and by invocation of Newcastle as a lost paradise when they had returned to the South.

Julia: A Portrait of Julia Strachey
by Herself and Francis Partridge,
Gollancz.

1983
Daily Telegraph

FRANCES PARTRIDGE

Frances Partridge is the oldest living Bloomsbury (she has just celebrated her ninetieth birthday) and – I don't think it would be disputed, after reading her diaries – the nicest. Whether that would have been regarded as commendation in the old Bloomsburian world is another matter. Perhaps not. All the same, she is free from the overwhelming intellectual self-satisfaction that Bloomsbury used to project, and has her kindly moments.

Hanging On: Diaries December 1960–August 1963 begins painfully with the death of Ralph Partridge, the husband she adored through many ups and downs of complicated relationships. It would, indeed, be true to describe this diary as an almost wholly sad document, so far as the diarist's personal life is concerned, did it not end with the birth of a grandchild, which occasioned delight all round.

If Frances Partridge is the least disfigured of the Bloomsburies by undue assumptions, this does not mean that she is not herself a Bloomsbury to the core. However, if she feels that Bloomsburies are the only real people, she also has all the astringency they were accustomed to show about each other. This makes the diary very enjoyable, and sometimes so funny that one laughs aloud.

There are also some admirable vignettes of non-Bloomsburies: Cyril Connolly, for instance:

> The arrival of the Master [Connolly]: at first a crossish baby expecting to find himself alone and have a literary talk, but finding Johnny [Gathorne-Hardy] and Julian [Jebb] in occupation. I led him to my bookcase and shamelessly offered him baits to ingratiate him. He was soon on the floor, happy with his fat legs splayed out and hair flying wildly: then his own jokes and embroidered fantasies brought twinkling geniality and he was busy signing my copies of *The Unquiet Grave*.

A perfect picture, though a problem for the biographer. One of his wives, Barbara Skelton, described Connolly in her diary as having 'coolie legs'. Surely coolies don't have fat legs? Whose physical description should be believed?

To return to the Bloomsbury atmosphere, Frances Partridge's old friend Julia Strachey had to be dealt with carefully as she possessed all sorts of burning enthusiasms. Frances Partridge, for example, once spoke disparagingly of vitamins; this sneering at science caused dreadful trouble that took twenty-four hours to get over. There is also a richly comic account of their being snowed up in a house, alone together.

Duncan Grant, with Vanessa Bell, Bloomsbury's star painter, is neatly hit off:

> In his stained, ill-fitting suit he looks rather like a Jewish pawn-broker, standing a little apologetically and as if about to shuffle off or rub his hands together; rather hunched, looking up and blinking anxiously at us from his still forget-me-not blue eyes in a crumpled rose-petal face. Yet his air of apology seems to say, 'I don't really know how to behave. I'm not concerned with the world and its value.' This child-like innocence wouldn't take in anyone, nor does it take in Duncan himself. He has an excellent opinion of himself, and quite right too.

The last years of Clive Bell are sketched in sympathetically, but without extenuating his self-indulgence, selfishness and self-pity. Bell was lucky enough to have a nanny-like female friend to look after him, though one feels Partridge was right when she drew the line: 'And yesterday *pour comble*, Barbara wanted me to stay in the room while Clive *fit pipi* as they will both call it. That settled it.'

Finally, there is a splendid glimpse of Arthur Waley, the authority on Chinese and Japanese literature:

> Seventy-four, but I must say one wouldn't guess it from the smooth, graven, oriental mask he presents to the world, and the head well-covered with only partly grey hair. He goes to the British Museum on a bicycle every day and seems wiry and athletic – though rather like Charlie Chaplain seen from the back, with his legs in their baggy trousers under a short tight jacket. It is not this, though, that gives one a hilarious desire to laugh in his august presence – but rather the elaborate air of superiority, the desperately flawless face he presents to the world.

However, Waley did produce one fascinating reminiscence:

> He admitted having 'adored' Rupert Brooke at Cambridge, but he was eager to tell me how they had both taken their translation of Propertius to their tutor, who said Arthur's was much the best, and how this made Rupert turn scarlet with rage.

Hanging On: Diaries December 1960–   1990
August 1963, Collins.   *Sunday Times*

EDWARD GARNETT

Edward Garnett (1868–1937) was first employed at the age of nineteen in the packing department of the publisher T. Fisher Unwin. Proving to be wholly incompetent at doing up parcels, he was transferred to the less demanding job of reading manuscripts. For the next fifty years this was Garnett's mission in life, and he has some claims to be the most remarkable publisher's reader the craft has ever seen. Garnett's father was the celebrated and eccentric Richard Garnett, Keeper of Printed Books at the British Museum. The family was one of Yorkshire paper-manufacturers and clergymen. At the age of twenty-one Garnett married Constance Black, half a dozen years older, whose subsequent translations from the Russian – even if now to some extent superseded – almost singlehanded introduced the great Russian writers to the English-speaking world.

By the 1890s the three-decker novel was on the way out. From an early age Garnett was associated with shaping the works of a high proportion of the new race of novelists, now thought of as Edwardians. He left Fisher Unwin for Heinemann; then for Duckworth, The Bodley Head (John Lane), and finally Jonathan Cape.

It would be in general true to say that few writers cannot benefit from sound advice; while equally few – who are any good – are prepared to be messed about professionally by a publisher's reader. The interesting thing about Garnett is that he held very strong views himself as to what writing should be, and did not at all mince his words in making criticisms; but on the whole the authors who underwent his surgery were devoted to him, even if there was also a tendency to jettison Garnett's opinions as the writers concerned became well known. Garnett's brightest stars were Conrad at one end of the scale and D. H. Lawrence at the other. He also worked over Galsworthy to some purpose. Arnold Bennett, Somerset Maugham, Ethel M. Dell, Ford Madox Ford, James Joyce, with lots of others, appear within Garnett's orbit, only to disappear again with varied commendations or the reverse.

For anyone concerned with the history of novel writing in this country there is much to reflect on here. That Garnett had an extremely sharp eye for ability – whether Joycean or Dellian – seems undeniable but one is inclined to think that he adroitly managed always to deal with authors, able or less able, whom he himself found sympathetic. The others somehow were winnowed out. He got on well with, for instance, Norman Douglas, but that is about the farthest limit of coverage to include a fairly frivolous, while still accomplished, area of the literary field.

How would it have been had Garnett had to operate on, say, Saki, Aldous Huxley, the Sitwells, Evelyn Waugh? When the Hogarth Press was set up, it was to Virginia Woolf's enormous satisfaction that Garnett would no longer monitor her books.

George Jefferson deals with a kaleidoscopic scene competently if a trifle soberly. Many of the exchanges in which Garnett was involved are hilarious, and Jefferson inclines to play them down rather than get the best out of comic situations. However, he does enjoyably reproduce in full the caustic letter Garnett wrote to Jessie Conrad (saying he disapproved of the book she had written about her late husband), and the equally brisk letter she wrote back, which showed she was by no means unable to express herself.

Again, when Garnett read the manuscript of Galsworthy's *The Patrician* he complained that it showed up Galsworthy's ignorance of aristocratic life – a point Jefferson somewhat obscures by merely speaking of 'fidelity of characterisation'. Galsworthy, nettled by Garnett's criticism, wrote back that Garnett wasn't familiar with aristocratic life either, at the same time enclosing a list (has it been preserved?) of 130 aristocrats he, Galsworthy, knew. This incident seems relevant as well as funny, because it shows Garnett's instinct, whether he knew the milieu or not, for material in a novel that did not ring true.

In speaking of Garnett's relations with the publishers who employed him, Jefferson indicates that T. Fisher Unwin was not a very likeable character and Jonathan Cape was not above horse-dealing, but he does not attempt to characterise S. S. Pawling or William Heinemann, both quite interesting personalities. Gerald Duckworth's idiosyncrasies also deserve a line since such traits must have played a great part in Garnett's presentation of his literary reports.

One of Garnett's later associations was with the books of Henry Green (Henry Yorke), whose background might also have been described a little more fully, for the relationship was an interesting one which Yorke greatly valued. The two of them had an enthusiasm in common for the writings of C. M. Doughty (*Arabia Deserta*), whose style is by no means everyone's taste.

Garnett wrote several plays which, although never a great success, were put on briefly, and, in 1907, he was involved in a projected demonstration against the Lord Chamberlain's censorship which was in practice undertaken by a forgotten and inept figure called G. A. Redford. The deputation was to meet the then Prime Minister Campbell-Bannerman, but, alas, the demonstration never took place.

The Dramatic authors of England are to assemble in Trafalgar Square. Barrie will address them from the base of Nelson's column, and the Savoy orchestra will play 'Britons will never be slaves'. The procession will then form, and will be headed by Pinero and Shaw walking arm in arm. Immediately behind them will come Garnett and Galsworthy, each bearing the pole of a red banner with the inscription 'Down with the Censor'. An effigy of Redford, which is being prepared by the Savoy property-man, will be carried by Frederick Harrison and W. B. Yeats, and over its head will wave a banner, carried by Gilbert Murray, with the inscription 'Ecrasez l'Infame!' Arriving in Downing Street, Swinburne will declaim an 'Ode to C. B.'.

Edward Garnett is the biography of a gifted, cranky, generous, utterly incorruptible man, who left a distinct mark on writing during his period.

Edward Garnett: A Life in Literature,   1982
George Jefferson, Cape.   *Daily Telegraph*

ARNOLD BENNETT

From November 1926, to February 1931, the month before he died, Arnold Bennett (b. 1867) wrote a book column, 'Books and Persons', for the *Evening Standard*. All the articles are collected together here, unobtrusively but efficiently edited by Andrew Mylett. They make a most interesting volume which stands on its own both as a picture of the literary scene of the period and expression of Bennett's own views about writing.

Bennett's chosen image, the successful author, bowler-hatted, puffing a cigar, quaffing champagne, laying down the law about literature, was obviously vulnerable. It is a commonplace to add that this image covered a considerable amount of uncertainty, sensitive feeling, nervousness about sex, and, above all, a really passionate dedication to writing. All these things come out here with astonishing clearness, journalism always having its own *in vino veritas* side. Bennett was attacked, notably by Wyndham Lewis and Virginia Woolf; the former objecting to an alleged 'dictatorship of the book racket', and the latter on account of Bennett's cocksure materialism. To be fair to Lewis (b. 1884) and Virginia Woolf (b. 1882), they themselves represented a younger generation that aimed above all at the perfectionism of the artist; a very necessary reaction against much that had gone before, and Bennett was an obvious target.

One of Bennett's chief weapons, however, was that he was a man – above all a writer – wholly without envy. He also notes here (referring to Tolstoy) the opinion that 'spiritual pride' is 'possibly the worst human vice, except self-pity'. In short, Bennett was morally equipped to withstand these particular two opponents. What he says about Lewis's novel *Tarr*, and the Virginia Woolf novels in general, remains valid. *Tarr* had good chapters, but lacked 'ability to marshal'; *Mrs Dalloway* was lightweight, *Orlando* tedious. When it comes to highbrows attacking Bennett for his philistinism, it can easily be shown that, in writing his column (which certainly applauded many items now sunk without a trace), he also selected for praise deserving young writers who needed just the help that Lewis complained was no more than an attempt to pick a winner. Neither Virginia Woolf, nor the rest of Bloomsbury (let alone Lewis), were ever to the fore in seeking younger talent, while well-known figures like, say, Galsworthy (Bennett's exact contemporary), were non-starters when it came to awareness of what was happening in the world of writing.

It is true that Bennett could sell a book by a mere mention (to my own knowledge a novel about China called *Sun and Moon*, by Vincent Gowan, sold 200 copies or more on the strength of this), but in fact it was not so much current books, as Balzac, Stendhal, and the Russian classical novelists that he was constantly dinning into the public's ears as necessary reading. Bennett was an admirer of Joyce (about whom Virginia Woolf had considerable reservations) and a recommender of a host of writers who had not by any means then come into their own. He was taken by Proust, though always discomposed by techniques bearing no relation to his own. On the other hand, he possessed the necessary gift in a literary critic of grasping that a book can be good in parts.

One is struck, not for the first time, by the fact that critics are to be known by what they praise, much more than by what they attack. All people have their prejudices as to books they don't like, and it is easy to be rude about the authors of these. It is far more difficult to give the right reason why a book is good. Bennett may sometimes overdo his recommending, but he had taken on the writing of the column, one object of which was to give a broad survey.

A novel that is any good rarely lends itself to a straight read through, with written criticism of it in the same week. Nevertheless, Bennett wrote (October, 1928) that Evelyn Waugh's *Decline and Fall* showed 'a genuinely new humorist has presented himself . . . in my opinion comes near to being quite first-rate', and (May, 1929) of I. Compton-Burnett's *Brothers and Sisters*, 'by no means easy to read, it seems to me to be an original work, strong and incontestably true to life'. At first rather anti-Hemingway, he became a supporter after *A Farewell to Arms*, and he was keen on Faulkner when that writer was not much known, even in America. He also had a good word to say for Firbank.

Bennett was unexpectedly anti-Dickens – *A Tale of Two Cities* was the only one he had even been able to finish. He thought George Moore the greatest novelist of the day, but his own admiration for Moore did not prevent him liking Moore's *bête noire* Hardy, whose faults and virtues Bennett well appreciated. He recommends the nineteenth-century Swiss diarist, Amiel, still hardly known in this country, draws attention to Svevo's *Confessions of Zeno*, and Lermontov's *A Hero of Our Time*. Bennett seems to me over-impressed by T. E. Lawrence, Sinclair Lewis, E. M. Forster, and quite a lot of others.

Although he advocated more freedom in what was written (then ludicrously circumscribed by the Law), Bennett had a strain of primness. He thought *Ulysses* a masterpiece, but that it should not be allowed to be published in this country. That surely does not make sense.

Arnold Bennett: The Evening Standard   1974
Years, 'Books and Persons', 1926–   *Daily Telegraph*
1931, edited and introduced by
Andrew Mylett, Chatto.

LADY OTTOLINE MORRELL

When, in 1927, the Morrells sold their by then rather famous country house, Garsington Manor, the prospective owners asked where to buy meat and fish. Lady Ottoline Morrell is alleged to have replied: 'Don't talk to me of fish. You may talk to me about poetry and literature but not fish.' That was perhaps why, in the end, she felt her life a frustrated one. She never really understood that the arts are 'about' something. In her eyes the arts were the sum of the individuals who practised them; therefore the best thing to do in life was to collect as many of the latter as possible round yourself. She did not grasp that poetry and literature might just as easily be about meat and fish as anything else.

Ottoline Cavendish Bentinck (1873–1938) was daughter of a general (soldiers, by the way, have 'pay', not a 'salary'), a fairly distant cousin of the eccentric 5th Duke of Portland who honeycombed Welbeck with underground rooms. Her half-brother succeeding as 6th Duke, she was given precedence as a duke's daughter, becoming Lady Ottoline. Sandra Jobson Darroch is apt to indulge in clichés like 'the claustro-phobic Victorian age', but she tells the story in a good, straightforward, no-nonsense style, with a lot of emphasis on sex, which certainly bulked large on her subject's horizon. This is all right, provided readers allow for the fact that no one can ever be absolutely certain what was going on even when, as in this case, Lady Ottoline's daughter has – very sensibly – preferred to release letters and papers rather than leave matters to the imagination of unofficial biographers without access to these sources.

Unusually tall, not a beauty, though of compelling appearance, with a taste for exhibitionistic dress, Lady Ottoline reacted away early from conventional upper-class life. She was gifted with no exceptional mental equipment, but possessed an immensely powerful will, and a fanatically romantic feeling for the idea of the intellect. She was also highly sexed – being first seduced before marriage, apparently *en plein air*, by Axel Munthe; later possibly by Asquith, who undoubtedly made a pass at her.

Lady Ottoline was nearly twenty-nine when she married Philip Morrell, a solicitor, in due course a Liberal MP. Even if she gave him rather a rough time, they were pretty well suited, and it is possible that Sandra Darroch underrates Morrell's capacity for finding consolation.

The story of Lady Ottoline's long affair with Bertrand Russell has been told by Russell in his autobiography. Russell's feelings were certainly deeply involved, but, as reflected in his letters, he emerges as vain, pompous, selfish and rarely knowing his own mind. Lady Ottoline's strong attachment to him did not preclude occasional carryings-on with two other lovers simultaneously. The Bloomsbury Group came into her life early (she herself lived in Bedford Square, and at the end of her days in Gower Street). They made fun of her behind her back, but liked associating with her both for snobbish reasons, and for the curious fascination she exerted. Lytton Strachey was possibly the person best suited to deal with her temperament: humourless, but not without all skittishness, delighting in gossip and intrigue. Strachey would put on her high-heeled shoes and dance round the room.

In D. H. Lawrence was a figure cut to measure for her – a relationship (not physical) which satisfied his own favourite myth of the humbly born man and the great lady. His silliest side (dark gods, communities of the chosen few) found an enthusiastic echo in Lady Ottoline's boundless optimism about artists and writers, not to mention painters. Lawrence's love for interfering in other people's lives was, if possible, greater than her own, and trouble inevitably resulted.

D. H. Lawrence, Aldous Huxley, W. J. Turner, all put unflattering portraits of Lady Ottoline into their books, which greatly upset her. It is of interest that when – as with Henry James and Conrad – she dealt with writers of a severely professional attitude toward their work, such friction was not obvious.

During the First World War Garsington was a refuge for the Bloomsburies and other Conscientious Objectors, who giggled, acted charades, grumbled about their hostess's parsimony regarding jam, and allowed the hen-house to remain so long unclean that food-poisoning broke out. Sandra Darroch shows signs of thinking this approach preferable to efforts that might lead to the defeat of the Central Powers. She also oddly describes Jean de Menasce (who corresponded a lot with Lady Ottoline) as a 'comparative flop' – but Menasce has written a string of books of enormous erudition about Arab philosophy, Iranian religion, the Book of Daniel, and goodness knows what else. She also remarks:

At times the undergraduates [invited to Garsington] would not know how seriously to take Ottoline's questioning. C. M. Bowra recalls her saying to Anthony Powell: 'Mr Powell, do you prefer spring or autumn?' He thought for a moment and then replied that he preferred the autumn, to which she commented: 'At my age you'll prefer the spring.'

As Bowra has rather mauled the story I told him, may I put the record straight? – it illustrates how an emphasis can go wrong. Henry Yorke (Henry Green, the novelist) and I had lunched at Garsington *à quatre* with Lady Ottoline and her daughter Julian. After luncheon we went for a walk. On the way out I walked with Julian, Yorke with Lady Ottoline. After about a mile, Lady Ottoline, indicating we should return, crossed to me. It was an autumn afternoon. She said: 'Mr Powell do you prefer the autumn or the spring?' I replied (I did not have to 'think') that I liked the autumn. Several hundred yards further on, in her inimitable hiss, she said: 'I think when you are young, you prefer the autumn.' We continued for another quarter mile or so, when she added: 'And when you're old, the spring.' The interesting fact is that Lady Ottoline was absolutely right.

Ottoline: The Life of Lady Ottoline
Morrell, Sandra Jobson Darroch,
Chatto.

1976
Daily Telegraph

AUGUSTUS JOHN

I

The legend of Augustus John (1878–1961) began when he was quite young. Like most legends it diverged a good deal from what actually happened. Michael Holroyd has accomplished an extremely difficult task in assembling his account of years reasonably to be called innocent – in a rather special sense of that term – years which present considerable complications in accurate chronicling. They take the story to about 1910. As with all biography, it must never be forgotten that documentation is often a matter of luck. A passing mistress, for example, may keep letters, or a great love burn the lot, leaving no record. The impression here is that everything important has been well covered.

Reading of Augustus John's origins, one cannot help being reminded of Ivy Compton Burnett's, as outlined in Hilary Spurling's biography: a labourer great-grandfather, two generations of professional hard work, then a sudden flowering of talent in the arts. John's father and grandfather were Haverfordwest solicitors. Through them musical tastes were transmitted. Drawing ability came from his mother, daughter of a Sussex master-plumber. John himself had detested his upbringing, though he always loved Pembrokeshire. I don't think there is anything 'snobbish', as Holroyd suggests, in considering the 'men of Pembrokeshire' different from the rest of Wales – because, largely descended from twelfth-century Flemings and Normans, they *are* different. The John family may have been tedious to Augustus as relations, but they were by no means humdrum. It gives one a jolt to learn that John was briefly destined for the army.

Perhaps the most interesting single aspect of Augustus John's life that emerges from the first volume of Holroyd's biography is the part played by his sister, Gwen. Retiring in certain respects, somewhat ambivalent in sex relationships, Gwen John subsequently became the sculptor Rodin's mistress. Her brother considered her painting superior to his own. She had none of his exuberance as a painter, being even a trifle limited in range, but undoubtedly possessed great gifts. What is new, as revealed here, is Gwen John's influence in the complex relationship between her brother and his two wives, Ida Nettleship and Dorelia McNeill.

The risk to his work run by any painter, writer or musician who turns himself into a picturesque figure in the popular imagination, was by no means lost on John himself. He was well aware of it. How far he could ever have controlled it is another matter. Two elements dominated John's life in addition to painting: the particular form taken by his womanising, and – great man as he was and much as one liked him – a strain of undeniable crankiness.

The paradox of John's temperament was that, on the one hand, no man had a greater liking for being, if not alone (though he liked that too), at least on his own; on the other, so far from being an habitual lover-and-rider-away, his ambition was to be in patriarchal style surrounded by women and children. At one moment he quite seriously planned to increase the number of the former to four under one roof; and at another time he fathered three children within a week or two. Holroyd throws much light on the convoluted troubles of the simultaneous relationship with Ida and Dorelia. He is a little hard, I think, on the Nettleship family, when, after Ida died, they tried to get control of their grandchildren who were eventually kidnapped by John. Ivy Nettleship's charm and courage come out in her letters here.

A point that this biography makes clear is that much of John's behaviour was no carefree bohemianism, but a deliberate policy of shocking, which might almost find a parallel in some of the later acts of the Surrealists. On the other hand, his interest in gypsies was not only genuine, in that he lived with them and talked their language, but seriously anthropological as well. At this period John might be regarded as the John the Baptist of an 'alternative society', and the book gives a vivid, if daunting, picture of what such a life is like in practice.

But what effect did all this have on his painting? John had begun at the Slade at the age of sixteen, and by the time he was twenty, it is hardly going too far to say he had made his name. To some extent the womanising and eccentric goings-on stimulated bursts of painting, but even for a man of John's altogether remarkable physical strengths, they were dangerous stimulants, bringing on dreadful bouts of guilt and gloom.

Holroyd prefaces his biography by saying it is 'not an art book', but naturally he has to consider John's position as a painter: above all, the dividing of the ways when John chose to have no part in the Modern Movement – although the not very well instructed conventional art critics of his day considered him offensively 'modern'. I think Holroyd rather over-simplifies that dangerous word 'Victorianism' in treating of painters born in the 1870s. The choice was John's own conviction, rather than any chance of time. After all, in Paris he had got on with Picasso; Wyndham Lewis (enjoyably mentioned on a French beach wearing an Old Rugbeian blazer and cholera belt) was a friend at the Slade. The potential modernist contacts were there.

A figure referred to intermittently in Michael Holroyd's biography as a friend of John's, Michel Salaman, deserves rather more description than 'art-student turned foxhunter'. He was one of the nicest of men, generous, amusing, eccentric, and great devotee of John.

Augustus John: A Biography, Vol. I: 1974
The Years of Innocence, Michael   *Daily Telegraph*
Holroyd, Heinemann.
The Art of Augustus John, Malcolm
Easton and Michael Holroyd,
Heinemann.

II

This second volume of Michael Holroyd's biography of Augustus John completes the story; a sadder one than I was quite prepared for. I saw a certain amount of John in the year before he died, and, although very deaf, he liked to talk of the past – bursts between long silences – and never seemed in quite the state of despair the book convincingly shows him to have been. It is no good being pompous about John, and Holroyd does not attempt that. Indeed, the author is often presented in the role of great comic figure, his intense melancholy an essential part of that. To assert, as some do now, that John had less than a remarkable talent seems to me altogether absurd, if one examines some of the early drawings; but there is no doubt that it was a talent not all suitable (few are) to be dragged along at the tail of a lot of cheap publicity. Reaction was inevitable.

Nevertheless John was an impressive figure. Reynolds painted Garrick torn between Tragedy and Comedy, and that was almost literally John's case. His appallingly complicated and co-existent love affairs entangled him in ludicrous situations, on the one hand; suicides and death, on the other. Not to mention his drinking.

After his visit to Pittsburgh in 1923, a museum official accompanied John to Buffalo, and warned his host there of the painter's alcoholic habits. 'I replied, somewhat haughtily, that I thought Buffalo men could take care of themselves on the drinking line. Pittsburgh might have suffered but I had every confidence in my fellow citizens.' The host wrote afterwards, 'I was wrong.'

There is an inimitable quality about the comic incidents. In 1924 John went to Dublin as guest of the Irish Nation for some festival. The climax was a banquet at which the Commander-in-Chief of the Free State Army delivered a long speech in Gaelic. John had sunk into a pleasant stupor, but during the speech the municipal gas and electricity

workers staged a two-minute strike, and the lights went out. The Irish
general courageously went on with his speech in the blackness. John
suddenly came to. Where was he? He thought he had gone mad.
Compton Mackenzie, sitting opposite, was, with difficulty, able to
reassure him.

The incident of Lord Leverhulme, the soap millionaire, removing the
head from his portrait by John is probably no longer remembered, but
in 1920 it caused a tremendous furore. Newspapers in this country, the
Continent and America, even as far off as Japan, were full of the affair.
Students of the London art schools marched in Hyde Park, bearing a
huge replica of Lord Leverhulme's headless torso. In Italy a twenty-
four-hour strike was called of everyone involved in painting, including
models, colourmen and frame-makers. Another effigy of 'IL-LE-VER-
HUL-ME', made of soap and tallow, was burnt in Florence. What
happy days – compared with our own – when the world was interested
in art.

In 1939 John began a painting of the Queen (now Queen Elizabeth,
the Queen Mother) and elaborate arrangements were made at the
Palace. John was by no means unstirred by the prospect of working on
this royal portrait, but developing a temperature on the day appointed
had to send a message postponing the sitting.This was intended to
describe himself as suffering from an attack of influenza but, by a slip of
the pen, he wrote that he was suffering from 'the influence'.

During this period John painted a great many portraits of celebrities
of one kind and another, work about which he grumbled, though he
needed the money for his increasing retinue and progeny. In spite of
possessing a good many traits in common, he got on badly with Lloyd
George, the North and South Welsh being traditionally at odds. The
vanity of the various sitters, Yeats, Shaw, T. E. Lawrence, and so on, is
well worth reading about.

Meanwhile, what was happening to John as a serious artist? He
himself was absolutely aware that he had lost his grip. Holroyd makes
this quite clear. It was torture to the painter himself, but by this time he
could not make a recovery. The self-discipline was simply not there.
The 'life style' that he had himself largely invented had overwhelmed
him. This was not precisely because he did not work. In a certain sense
he worked at times very hard, and was preoccupied by work until the
end of his days.

Holroyd cannot be blamed for bringing in a lot of trivialities, because
it was these trivialities that caused the trouble. At the close of one of the
huge parties given at Mallord Street somebody standing by the door as
the guests left, heard John saying goodbye, add to woman after woman:
'You know how much you mean to me.' The disastrous thing was that
he felt it. If it had only been cynical there would have been less time

wasted. Michael Holroyd supplies a brief résumé of what happened to the extensive offspring, which helps to complete the story. Although plagued by an overpowering need to be a parent, John was not a very satisfactory one, generous about money, but jealous and possessive. He was perhaps a little afraid of his own father – who would not die – until the end. Edwin John must have had a touch of greatness too. In his ninety-first year, he shouted down from his bed to his housekeeper: 'Goodbye, Miss Davis. Goodbye.' When she got upstairs he was dead.

Augustus John: A Biography. Vol. II: 1975
The Years of Experience, Michael   *Daily Telegraph*
Holroyd, Heinemann.

WILLIAM ORPEN

When the Royal Academy held a joint memorial exhibition which included Orpen in 1933, Henry Tonks, spiky instructor at the Slade School of Art, wrote a characteristic letter to the painter's widow:

> I have already had the idea that in becoming a portrait painter he [Orpen] missed his real mark, there was in him much more of the comic and the satyrist [sic] . . . it is the same thing in his drawings . . . until he is again inspired by that strange impish spirit he had.

Few would deny that something seriously impaired the natural skills as a painter with which Orpen was born, but it is the supposed satire and the impishness that make so much of his work so awful. Nothing could be more unfunny, for instance, than the comic drawings scattered through his letters and profusely illustrated in Bruce Arnold's book – a biography with rather a slow start, but packed with good material once in its stride.

William Orpen (1878–1931) came of a Southern Irish Protestant family dating from William III. The Orpens were fairly well-to-do and had wide connections. His father was a solicitor. Owing to Orpen's remarkable early promise no difficulties seem to have been made about his becoming a painter. He was contemporary with Augustus John and William Rothenstein. Orpen never seems to have had any strong line of his own, though early on painting very capably in a manner influenced by Rembrandt, Watteau, Peter de Hooch, Vermeer and several more. Before he was twenty he brought off 'The Play Scene from Hamlet', proving this ability, and one would agree with Arnold in not thinking it Orpen's sole picture of any merit, as has often been suggested.

In the early 1900s Orpen had a teaching job in Dublin and came into contact with the group then making great efforts to bring cultural amenities to a community where riots could be caused by mentioning the word 'shift' (woman's body garment) in a play, or displaying a picture called 'A Lutheran girl being taken to Execution'. Orpen saw a great deal of (Sir) Hugh Lane, the art-dealer who worked untiringly to provide the Irish capital with some good pictures and was often ungratefully treated. Orpen used to tease and bully the homosexual Lane unmercifully, and call him 'Petticoat'.

In about 1906 Mrs Evelyn St George, an American lady married to an Irish landowner, became Orpen's mistress, a love affair that was to play an important part in his life. Orpen's picture of Mrs St George in 'Interior at Clonsilla' might be thought one of his best examples of Romantic Realism, though it is always hard to judge a painting from a reproduction.

When war came in 1914 Orpen would have had no difficulty in slipping away to Ireland, where he could certainly have earned a living. Instead he most honourably identified himself with the war Great Britain was fighting. After joining the army, he was transferred as one of the first War Artists. Portraits of the military and political leaders at the time of the Peace Treaty in Paris are probably Orpen's best-known pictures. The war had a strong effect on Orpen, obsessing him with its horrors, but one cannot say that when he tried to express the undoubted genuineness of his feelings in symbolic form such a style had a satisfactory influence on his painting. He was much more at ease in portraits of his luscious, tousled, blond, twenty-year-old French mistress, Yvonne Aubicq, whose subsequent history is one of the most extraordinary stories in Arnold's book.

After the war – although like everyone of his temperament Orpen was quite often in financial difficulties – money poured in. During the last few years of his life he was making £45,000 a year. By that time he had drifted apart from his wife (who seems to have been devoted to him), was producing inferior work even by his own standards, and drinking a great deal, this last apparently finishing him off in his fifty-third year.

Orpen was in certain respects a tragic figure. He worked prodigiously hard, was very ambitious, liked worldly success, but was always modest about his own achievements in relation to Sickert and John. His portraits, such as that of Foch, may be only a form of the higher journalism in painting, but give a perfectly adequate notion of what the sitter looked like, one not necessarily inferior to a photograph. Yet something was badly wrong. Many painters have a taste for painting themselves, but Orpen was peculiarly given to this form of narcissism. His facetiousness about himself seems to express some profound inner handicap. Like many unremittingly joky men he was deeply melancholy. Models liked him. He could be kind. If his knockout humour is often trying his description of painting Woodrow Wilson is very funny.

Shabby behaviour on the part of the Treasury should always be publicised and in Orpen's case the Treasury (though unsuccessfully) tried to subtract his army pay from the sums promised for pictures he painted. In the event he presented all this war work to the Imperial War Museum, representing a large sum given away. Even if one cannot share all Arnold's enthusiasm there is much here worth reading about.

Orpen: Mirror to an Age, Bruce   1981
Arnold, Cape.   *Daily Telegraph*

THE PEARSALL SMITH FAMILY

I

Logan Pearsall Smith observed: 'The husband of a niece of mine once told me that after his marriage he found out his wife was an Ogress, was the daughter and granddaughter of Ogresses, and had become the mother of a fourth of the species.' We may give the author of this book, Barbara Strachey, the benefit of the doubt as the last in the line designated above, because information about herself here is scanty. With regard to the others there can be no doubt that her great-uncle's words leant towards understatement.

The Smiths – later Pearsall Smiths – came from Philadelphia. They were Quakers. There was also a history of mental instability. Robert Pearsall Smith (1827–98) married Hannah Whitall, another of the Quaker community, and chief 'Ogress'. Indeed, compared with Hannah Pearsall Smith (or Hannah Whitall Smith as she always insisted) even the other female relations were Ogresses of a minor breed.

Robert Smith's father was a publisher who had done well out of pirating English books in America before the Copyright Convention. His son began in the same profession, but, deviating a little from orthodox Quakerism, found that he was an enormously successful revivalist preacher. Hannah, his wife, was equally adapted to that vocation, which became their way of life. Hannah was a feminist, a ferocious proto-Women's Libber, with all the advantages of being also an Ogress in the top class.

The Pearsall Smiths, Robert and Hannah, had five children, but only three play a main part in the story: Mary (1864–1945), Logan (1865–1946), and Alys (1867–1951). The Quaker tradition was intensely anti-worldly and anti the arts but from the beginning Logan Pearsall Smith especially displayed a taste for books, pictures and music. This involved having Walt Whitman to stay. The visit was regarded by the parents with some apprehension while the poet, on his side, was sometimes forced to 'slip out and round the corner for a drink'.

So advantageous had the Pearsall Smiths found their religious activities in their own country that they decided to try their luck in Great Britain. Here too they met with an instantaneous response. One of the few trite comments in Barbara Strachey's amusing, informative, above all well-organised book is to refer to the 'intensely stratified and snobbish society of Victorian England'. Clearly in certain senses it was not in the least 'stratified', the Pearsall Smiths (not at all grand in American social terms) sailing into high society, as Henry James had done a few years before.

Then came disaster. Robert had always indulged in religious emotionalism of an almost overtly sexual tone, which Hannah equally believed was the path of the spirit. Then he overstepped the ill-defined barrier between what was and was not allowed. There was a scandal about a lady in the congregation. Hannah stuck to it that there may have been indiscretions, but there had been no moral lapse. In the light of Robert's character and later conduct one would suspect that things went further. In any case the family returned to the United States under a cloud.

Later the Pearsall Smiths came back to live in England permanently. In due course Mary married an Irish barrister with political ambitions, Frank Costelloe, but, after having two daughters, started an affair with Bernard Berenson, then a young up-and-coming art historian. This uncomfortable situation was resolved after a few years by the death of Costelloe, when Mary married Berenson. By then her sister Alys had become the first of the four wives of Bertrand Russell, at that period a studious, puritanical young man, who had been brought up by his grandmother, known as 'the Deadly Nightshade'.

Oliver Strachey married as second wife one of the daughters of Mary (Costelloe) Pearsall Smith, and therefore in later generations Stracheys too are brought into the story, which naturally touches on many other stories that have been written during the last decade or so. This version remains very readable.

Logan Pearsall Smith, man of letters, deserves to be remembered for some of the epigrams in *Trivia* and for his passionate defence of the English language, though the word he coined 'milver' to denote someone truly congenial and possessed of the same interests, did not pass into common use. His first (salaried) milver was Cyril Connolly, who left to get married; then Robert Gathorne-Hardy, victim of his employer's manic-depression. For some reason Logan Pearsall Smith's final milver, John Russell, the art critic, gets no mention.

The Strachey connection brought in new and disparate elements to the later generations, entertaining to hear about, if not quite up to the great Pearsall Smith days. However awful Bernard Berenson and Bertrand Russell may have been – and there is much here to suggest that both of them could be pretty awful – we must always remember that they had Hannah for a mother-in-law. Hannah's reaction on visiting the Eternal City was:

I confess it does give me solid satisfaction to see *men* [priests] obliged to walk around in this muddy Rome with long flapping skirts twisting round their ankles at every step. It seems to introduce a little more fairness into things.

On the death of her husband, so Bertrand Russell reported, she sold his teeth to a second-hand dealer.

Remarkable Relations: The Story of the   1980
Pearsall Smith Family, Barbara   *Daily Telegraph*
Strachey, Gollancz.

I I

Barbara Strachey's entertaining book *Remarkable Relations* (1980) gave an account of the American Pearsall Smith family in which her grandmother Mary Pearsall Smith briefly figured. This is Mary Pearsall Smith's individual story, almost entirely presented by herself through the medium of letters and diaries. It is excellently edited and possesses the advantage that letters and diaries have in interposing no biographical opinion between the subject and the reader. The subject in this case (b. 1864) married first an Irish barrister called Costelloe, had two children by him, then ran away with Bernard Berenson, an American (of recently Jewish-Lithuanian origins) already becoming well-known as an expert on the Italian painters.

A good deal has already appeared about Berenson, and the legendary villa *I Tatti*, near Florence. This is Mary Berenson's side of the story which she tells with a great *brio*. Americans are not brought up either to conceal their feelings or to restrict talking about themselves; indeed a tendency to circumscribe either is looked on with a certain degree of suspicion. In addition to this national characteristic the Pearsall Smith family had been Quakers, so that Mary Berenson's conviction that she knew exactly how the world ought to be set right was an unusually strong one, which she reinforced by constant self-examination. Nor did she have any doubt that the dictates of Love had to be immediately followed.

In dealing with Berenson, however, she was up against an equally tough customer. Berenson undoubtedly knew a great deal about the Italian Masters. He was an exceptionally intelligent and gifted man in many other respects, but he could cause offence by claiming omniscience as to matters other than Giotto or Botticelli, while even about Giotto and Botticelli there were those who felt that they had a right to disagree.

Berenson was no less keen on having love affairs than his wife (as Mary Pearsall Smith became in due course, though not until Costelloe died), and it might be thought that some sort of an understanding could have been arrived at in this field. To some extent it was; but each was always passionately jealous of the other and right up to the end of Mary Berenson's life (she died in 1945, he continued into his nineties) colossal rows took place during which Berenson would sometimes kneel on the ground making horrible faces, and beat his head against the wall.

Everyone must live their marriage in their own way and although the Berensons' way from many points of view could not be called ideal, each had genuine feelings for the other. Although Mary Berenson seems, at first, beyond words, silly, hypocritical, self-regarding, dishonest, interfering, in the end it is hard not to begin to like her.

Since his death Berenson's reputation has become decidedly battered. No bones whatever are made by his wife in her letters and diaries as to such matters as bribing monks to sell pictures from their monasteries and smuggling such works of art out of Italy, if necessary in trunks constructed with false bottoms. The matter of making attributions with a view to disposing of a doubtful picture to a rich buyer, or accepting a sweetener from a dealer who wanted a Berenson guarantee, was clearly more complicated. There are specific occasions recorded here when Berenson refused such a temptation. His wife is often perfectly outspoken in saying she herself would have accepted the money. The striking thing is what both were admittedly prepared to do without surrendering a particle of their own high-mindedness.

Berenson was determined to have no children. When Mary Berenson was once pregnant (he was also not wholly convinced of the paternity), he caused her to have an abortion. He was much irked by his step-children, though in the end seems to have become resigned with a fairly good grace to step-grandchildren.

There are naturally a great many enjoyable vignettes here of the visitors to *I Tatti*, where a normal day would be a house-party and important visitors to luncheon; less important visitors and bearers of introductions to tea; and real nobs to dinner. Sometimes period views catch the reader's attention:

16 March 1903. Gilbert Murray threw a bomb into our midst last night by saying that the far-greatest poets of England were Chaucer, Shakespeare, Shelley and – Tennyson!! Keats and Milton were 'not in it' in his estimation. It was a thrilling moment, which was relieved by his exquisite reading of 'Maud'. This, however, failed to convert us to Tennyson's poetic gifts. . . . Murray is an angel, it is charming to discuss differences of taste with him. One night he defended Dickens.

One of the funniest incidents recorded here is the story of the frescos in the Big Library at *I Tatti*. There were certain alcoves to be decorated and the Berensons asked a French painter called Piot to undertake the job. I knew the story but had never seen a photograph of the frescos themselves. They are reproduced here. They look awful by any standard, far less those of a world-renowned art-expert. They were also mildly indecent. When the outraged Berensons wanted to paint them out the painter threatened to sue and they were covered with screens. There is also, incidentally, an inexpressibly funny photograph among the illustrations of one of the Berensons' Italian friends, kneeling on the ground reading his love letters, apparently, with a grey bowler beside him (1895).

Mary Berenson: A Self-Portrait from
her Letters and Diaries, edited by
Barbara Strachey and Jayne
Samuels, Gollancz.

1985
Daily Telegraph

RUPERT BROOKE

Rupert Brooke was born in 1887, the same year as Edith Sitwell; a year after Siegfried Sassoon; a year before T. S. Eliot. He was named after Rupert of the Rhine ('who never comes but to conquer or to fall'), a hero of his father's who was a housemaster at Rugby. The Edwardian era was the Golden Age of cranks, a flowering of Victorian dissidents free to burst out of the bottle now the stopper was removed. Paul Delany begins his book with a lively description of some of these, which at first I thought over long, but, by the end of the story, was absolutely necessary to show why the people he writes about (quite a large cast) behaved as they did.

Among the Victorian oddities were Edward Carpenter, Cecil Reddie and J. H. Badley, all of whom were involved in education, determined to make that 'progressive'. This included Socialism, the Simple Life, sexual reform, loose tweeds, sandals, nudity and so on. Carpenter and Reddie were homosexual, but Badley, who founded Bedales, a co-educational school, where sex was deprecated as 'silly', is said to have liked to give the girls a squeeze from time to time. Old Bedalians, notably the Olivier family, others too, played a considerable part in the Rupert Brooke story.

Brooke himself had been cloudlessly happy at Rugby, dazzlingly good looks and charm (which comes through a bit in Paul Delany's book) were reinforced by playing cricket and football well, with ability at work that promised a brilliant career, all quite apart from becoming a great poet. He won a scholarship at King's College, Cambridge, where his uncle was Dean. Delany's story is entertaining because detailed. For that reason it cannot be adequately summarised. At Cambridge, Brooke continued a path of rising reputation even if he behaved like an old-fashioned aesthete, and scored only a Second in Classics. He wrote poetry, attended holiday camps, studied Beatrice Webb's Minority Report of the Poor Law Commission, fell in love. He also became friends with various Bedalians, including a young Frenchman, Jacques Raverat (later to become a friend of Gide, though heterosexual), a fifth of Bedales pupils coming from the Continent.

The label 'Neo-pagans' was pinned on the group to which Brooke belonged by Virginia Woolf, one of the aspects of Delany's picture being the difference between the Neo-pagans and Bloomsbury: the latter homosexual and intellectual; the former predominantly hetero-sexual, keener on nakedness, sunbathing, living close to nature, a Walt Whitman programme. The core of Neo-paganism was provided by the daughters of Sir Sydney (later Lord) Olivier, with several of whom Brooke fell in love, beginning with Noel, aged fifteen. There was also up at Cambridge a girl called Ka (Katherine) Cox, daughter of a rich Fabian stockbroker, who had died, leaving her ideally independent to practise Socialism. She too (though no beauty) was to cause Brooke a lot of emotional trouble, and he her.

Up to a point all this is what might be expected from the Brooke legend. What comes as a complete surprise is the extreme difficulty Brooke found in gearing himself on to any form of physical relationship. Here was a young man with every virtue, every grace, who never managed to get to bed with anyone at all by the age of twenty-two. Brooke felt this deeply. As a desperate remedy he arranged, quite cold-bloodedly, to sleep with a Rugby contemporary slightly younger than himself. Two years later the situation was scarcely improved, merely by the addition of a modicum of heavy necking with Ka Cox. Many people live perfectly happily without sexual relations, but this did not fit in with being a free spirit.

The fact was that Rupert Brooke possessed a tenacious streak of puritanism, coupled with a tendency to hysteria. The heavy weather everybody made about each other showed no advance at all on Victorian behaviour; indeed it might be thought the Victorians often displayed more common sense with their problems than the people described here.

What emerges is an extremely amusing picture of the Neo-pagan (for want of a better term) relationship with Bloomsbury, a world into which figures like Lady Ottoline Morrell, Augustus John, Bertrand Russell, occasionally erupt. Russell (understandably when one remem-bers their respective features) loathed Rupert Brooke. Augustus John was generally regarded as taking the Simple Life too far. Just when Brooke seemed to be fixing himself with Ka Cox, the painter Henry Lamb, my late brother-in-law, then in the train of Augustus John, intervened, from Brooke's point of view disastrously. Lamb is accord-ingly treated rather severely here, but he had many good points, and won an MC a few years later.

Brooke finally suffered a nervous breakdown, went to Tahiti, had an affair with a girl whom 'it would be unfair to call a prostitute', returned to London to become protégé of Eddie Marsh, private secretary of Cabinet ministers. Marsh introduced Brooke to smart society, which he found great fun. Winston Churchill commissioned him into the Naval Division. The rest we know. One likes Brooke better without a lot of the nonsense that blurred his image. He may not have died in battle, but his end was more glorious than the wartime antics of Bloomsbury, and it's something to have written verses everyone remembers, even if nowadays they are not regarded as great poetry.

The Neo-Pagans: Friendship and   1987
Love in the Rupert Brooke Circle, Paul   *Daily Telegraph*
Delany, Macmillan.

ETHEL SANDS

Years ago, when I was to meet at dinner Ethel Sands (whose paintings I had known long before that), my hostess briefed me with the words: 'She's supposed to have been Maisie in Henry James's *What Maisie Knew*.' Reading Wendy Baron's enjoyable book, the resemblance of Ethel Sands to Maisie – a little girl neglected by both parents and left in the hands of lovers and mistresses – seemed to become at every line more remote. Then, towards the end of the book, it was revealed that Ethel Sands was perhaps to some extent the model for Nanda in James's *The Awkward Age* – an unglamorous young girl, ill-at-ease in the household of her glamorous mother, a very different situation. This is a warning against identifying real people with characters in novels.

Ethel Sands (1873–1962) was the eldest child of patrician Americans who lived a good deal in England. Her mother was a beauty, and although happily married, and apparently models of respectability, she and her husband were much in the world of Edward VII, when Prince of Wales. The Sands parents both died young. Their daughter, in her middle twenties, had to bring up two younger brothers. She was left well off (after an initial muddle about money). She had already shown her gifts as a painter, and formed a passionate friendship with another American art student in Paris, Nan Hudson. Their ménage lasted a lifetime, but, on available evidence, the relationship seems not to have been a physical one.

From pictures in Wendy Baron's book it is clear that Ethel Sands was not good looking, and her plainness, on first impact, seems to have struck letter-writers and diarists. This comes as a surprise to me. She was in her late seventies when we met, but so great was her elegance, charm, capacity to be amusing in a no-nonsense manner, that I could well have believed her to be good-looking in her youth. The photographs here show that not to have been the case. It was still the impression carried away.

Sickert was very much the master of both Ethel Sands and Nan Hudson, so far as painting was concerned. His relations with them and the other painters they met when they were working with him make one of the best parts of the book. Sickert himself seems to have favoured

Nan Hudson's pictures, anyway at first, perhaps not later. Ethel Sands appears to me to have been the preferable painter.

As well as working as a serious painter, Ethel Sands, who had an enormous amount of energy for such things, lived a very social life; increasingly so as she grew older. She got on with Bloomsbury and Lady Ottoline Morrell as well as a great many other people, not necessarily well disposed towards such circles. For those who feel that enough has been said of Bloomsbury at the moment, this side of Miss Baron's book is not overdone, though there are one or two dreadfully arch letters from Virginia Woolf.

A figure who appears a good deal is the American expatriate man of letters, Logan Pearsall Smith. Smith found Bernard Shaw genial, talkative, but an appalling bore. When Lytton Strachey and the rest of the Bloomsburies, not content with avoiding all war-effort themselves, tried to organise a non-conscription movement during the First World War, Logan Pearsall Smith wrote: 'It would be rather amusing if the whole lot of them get clapped into prison. But I don't think the authorities take them very seriously.' Bloomsbury pacifist antics were not at all in the line of Ethel Sands and Nan Hudson, who worked with the greatest devotion in military hospitals; not only then, but also in the Second World War when neither was at all young.

One of the merits of Wendy Baron's book is that it does not flag as time passes. Indeed, some of the best bits are the latter years of Ethel Sands's life, a period that has not yet been much worked over. We are, for example, given a vignette of the American art critic, Stuart Preston – 'The Sergeant' – and the furore he caused in London in the latter part of the war by his good looks, charm and the extent of his reading. Preston seemed to have stepped straight out of the pages of Henry James, or Edith Wharton who could certainly have made a story of The Sergeant's meteor-like passage through blitz-weary London. Another friend of Ethel Sands, a much closer one, of whom something is said here, is the novelist L. P. Hartley, several of whose letters are quoted. Hartley was a man of considerable eccentricity in his unobtrusive way. The letters confirm what I have thought before, that they should be collected. They might turn out to be a considerable contribution.

Wendy Baron writes in a deceptively quiet manner, always going for the non-scandalmongering method of describing the relationships of the many persons who came into her subject's life. At the same time she can occasionally land an unexpected rap over the knuckles to the celebrated, when they have been silly.

Miss Ethel Sands and Her Circle,   1977
Wendy Baron, Owen.   *Daily Telegraph*

WALTER RICHARD SICKERT

I

A few weeks after the opening of my first term at Oxford – I suppose about November 1923 – certain undergraduates were invited, in connection with the Slade Lectures, to hear Sickert say a few informal words after dinner at University College, of which the Master was then Sir Michael Sadler. I am ashamed to say I cannot remember much of what Sickert talked about, although it seemed very amusing at the time, but his tall figure, in what remains in my mind as a light greenish loudly checked suit, the cigar he flourished in the air, the pink face, grey hair, resonant voice, capacity to fill the room with his personality, remain vivid. I mention this occasion, the sole one when I set eyes on the great painter, not merely as a personal reminiscence, but also because Marjorie Lilly's admirable book states that not much is known of Sickert's life in 1923, a period when he had sunk into deep depression after the death of his second wife three years before. This gloom was not at all revealed to the young men he addressed. On the contrary, he seemed the essence of lively no-nonsense art criticism, though most of his audience, if they were like myself, did not know what good stuff they were listening to and how valuable in the light of much aridly doctrinaire aesthetics with which Bloomsbury was at that moment trying to cram the country. It does Sickert credit to have put on this good performance, when feeling in the depths of gloom himself. Marjorie Lilly's friendship with Sickert begins in 1917 when she rented a studio in the same Fitzroy Street house. A painter herself, she has a thoroughly professional approach to Sickert's life and work; so much so that it is hard to think of the Sickert story better told than in these comparatively informal recollections. This personal knowledge of the background immensely adds to the picture.

Sickert spent much of his time in France and Italy, but lived usually in London, really inventing the beauties of North London, especially Islington. No one had noticed before the material Sickert used in this area – he had, of course, other lines of painting too – but, just as, in a literary way, Dickens expressed all sorts of things that had never been previously expressed, Sickert, in painting, developed a form of urban landscape as original and essentially local as, say, that of Canaletto or Utrillo.

He was never much good at making money. One of Marjorie Lilly's many interesting points is showing the reader exactly why that was so: the odd sensitiveness, refusal to sell himself, of this in many ways extrovert man. Sickert was first married to Ellen Cobden (giving him the unusual distinction of having a father-in-law to whom a London statue had been raised); then to Christine Angus; finally to a fellow painter, Thérèse Lessore. Asked at a party, which included George Moore and Max Beerbohm, what was his favourite kind of woman, he replied 'My own particular brand of frump', but that does not seem fair to any of the ladies who became his wife.

While his own country was so comparatively unaware of his work, there were others who felt differently. In 1918 the Japanese Ambassador arrived at the Fitzroy Street studio with *carte blanche* from his Government to choose as many Sickerts as he thought fit and ship them to Japan. Sickert and the Ambassador had a *tête-à-tête* luncheon. They shared a Bath chap and a bottle of Madeira (Sickert was in general an abstemious drinker, though large eater), and a van appeared later to swell the Tokyo art gallery.

Sickert fans will be interested by Marjorie Lilly's identification of the male model in *Ennui, What shall we do for the rent?* and *Jack Ashore*. This figure was apparently a broken-down school fellow of Sickert's, who had become a vagrant and minor criminal. The help Sickert gave him was due to sheer good nature on the painter's part, not in the least to any of that attraction for criminal types which is sometimes found in intellectual circles. It is interesting to note, speaking of criminal activities, that as early as 1917 Sickert himself was able to point out to their owner eight forgeries of his paintings.

A notable aspect of this book is the series of pen portraits of minor personalities of the time, such as the celebrated dragon of the Slade, Henry Tonks. Tonks is not important enough to be owed a book to himself, but he crops up sufficiently often for those who know about him to want to hear a balanced judgment as to his merits and defects. Marjorie Lilly supplies exactly that. Her story of Tonks's one misjudgment in the war he waged against social butterflies at the Slade, when he was caught out by the beautiful Phyllis Boyd, is very funny. Tonks made a howler about Matthew Smith, but in many respects he did a good job, and his relations with Sickert are interesting. Interesting too are several letters to Nina Hamnett (whose work he admired), written by Sickert from Bath, and reproduced in the book. Bath was one of Sickert's favourite haunts, and he died there. The book is, indeed, full of lively stories about 'the servant of Abraham', as he called himself in one of his self-portraits. There are unexpected angles on its subject – for example that in 1914 Sickert made a determined effort to join the French Army and was furious when, at the age of fifty-four, he was judged unfit.

Sickert: The Painter and His Circle,   1971
Marjorie Lilly, Elek.   *Apollo*

I I

Several excellent accounts of Walter Richard Sickert (1860–1942) have apeared from time to time, including his own occasional writings about himself and his opinions, but there has been no complete biography. Denys Sutton supplies what must have been a difficult chronological record to assemble. The result is a much more coherent picture of Sickert than hitherto available; in fact a narrative packed with information about a really extraordinary figure.

On his father's side Sickert was a Schleswig-Holstein Dane, both father and grandfather professional painters. His mother was the illegitimate – but recognised and accepted – daughter of an Englishman, briefly a clergyman, then a distinguished astronomer. Although the Sickerts emigrated when Prussia moved into Schleswig-Holstein, they were naturally imbued with certain Teutonic influences, and Sutton points out that there is always a touch of the German tradition in Sickert's painting.

Since his father had never been very successful in his profession, Sickert was discouraged from becoming a painter, and he started life as an actor, a calling for which he possessed a strong leaning. Indeed, his own life, in different characters, was acted out by him as if it were a play, and with the greatest enthusiasm and energy. Finally it became clear that a painter Sickert must be. In 1881 he entered the Slade, then under the genial, if uninspiring Frenchman, Alphonse Legros.

The Sickerts (there were four other sons) were not well off, but they knew a great many people in the world of the arts. This early background, and the ease with which Sickert circulated later in a rich and smart society, is one of the interesting aspects of Sutton's book; Sickert's brilliantly depressing Camden Town interiors – and his own chronic financial difficulties – somehow obscured the grander side of life to which he was not at all indifferent, though in contrast he liked sordid environments.

A fascinating light is cast on both writer and painter by a letter (quoted by Sutton) from Oscar Wilde to Sickert's sister in 1882, written from America, saying that the Nebraska silver-miners at work 'would make beautiful motives for etchings, and Walter's impressionist sketches'. It is notable that Wilde's taste in painting, sometimes erratic, had marked down Sickert, still only twenty-one.

Sickert came heavily under the influence of Whistler, and, more rewardingly, of Degas, with whom he formed a friendship. Many of Degas's splendid *mots* are quoted here. In 1885, at Dieppe, Sickert ran across Gauguin, 'a sturdy man with a black moustache and a bowler', who had not yet decided to take the plunge and become a painter. With characteristic honesty Sickert wrote many years later that 'the sketch I saw him doing left no distinct impression on me, and I expressed the opinion that his desire to abandon business for art was rather imprudent than otherwise'.

It is hard to grasp now how revolutionary Sickert's painting was in the England of its day. But Sickert himself, so to speak the first English Impressionist, was also sent into the world to tease in due course the pedantry of Bloomsbury's preaching that Impressionism and Post-Impressionism were the only kinds of painting to be allowed. Sickert's own skill, and his delight in pulling the legs of pompous doctrinaires, did a great deal to maintain some aesthetic balance in the 1920s.

Sickert married three times, maintained a long liaison with an attractive fishwife of Dieppe, by whom he had a son. One of the most interesting aspects of Sutton's book is the manner in which it reveals the melancholy and lack of personal co-ordination that was the other side to Sickert's ebullience and high spirits. The actor in him led to all sort of odd situations connected with his own emotional life.

Sickert detested critics who tried to make a distinction between modern and earlier art. He wrote:

> To understand modern art at all you must have understood Poussin, since it is by way of Poussin, among other channels, that modern art has become what it is. What would you think of an English historian who, in writing of this century, should remark, incidentally, that he didn't care much about Queen Elizabeth, and had never heard of Bismarck?

He also wrote:

> I am sure so-called advanced work should not be grouped together. I would like to see John Collier ['A Fallen Idol', 'A glass of wine with Caesar Borgia', etc] & say Roberts [William Roberts, the Vorticist] hung side by side to fight it out on the walls with their brushes, not with words. In that way you would force the public to make its own comparisons.

Sickert made no secret of his reservations about the technique of Van Gogh, and Denys Sutton notes the 'acute' remark that Cézanne 'conducts, and compels us to accept the time and the rhythm he chooses to impose.' Much of Sickert's criticism was, of course, produced to score a rise, but at the same time he held views that were, however eccentric, essentially his own.

In one of his letters to a lifelong friend, the painter Jacques-Emile Blanche, Sickert wrote: 'unutterable happiness in no way abolishes profound chagrin'. The sentence contains much to explain this great and in many ways enigmatic man.

Walter Sickert: A Biography, Denys   1976
Sutton, Michael Joseph.   *Daily Telegraph*

THE SITWELLS

I

'If poetry was taken away from her,' remarked Dylan Thomas, at a party of Edith Sitwell's we were both attending, 'she might not die, but she'd be bloody sick.' This sums up the position pretty well. Any consideration of Edith Sitwell, or her writing, must always be made against the background of accepting her absolute dedication to the art of poetry as such.

It is necessary to begin with this pronouncement, because, if you start, as some do, from the fact that she sometimes said silly things when involved in controversy, you get nowhere. This book, for example, tails off into a lot of trivialities about people Edith Sitwell had rows with, which were certainly not worth chronicling. If the opinions of the persons in question were so worthless, why record them? The answer is, of course, that such polemics are, as literary history unfortunately shows, a characteristic psychological trait in many poets. Time, in the end, sorts out what should be preserved, while the rest is forgotten.

These failings in *Taken Care Of* cannot be ignored, because people who never knew Edith Sitwell might not guess what a kind, amusing, basically simple person she was, as well as being uniquely talented. What this autobiography does do, however, is to provide an extraordinarily vivid and compressed picture of her childhood and early life, the world already made familiar by Osbert Sitwell's autobiographical volumes, but one to which she brings her own penetrating eye and descriptive powers.

In her brother's tapestry of life at Renishaw, their father, Sir George Sitwell, looms as a comic, incredible, yet finally almost genial figure. Edith Sitwell, too, has her own anecdotes about that inimitable man, in that purely grotesque role. For example, Osbert (then a subaltern in the Grenadiers), with her connivance sent his mother a supposed anonymous letter accusing her husband of 'squandering money on the Scarlet Woman'. On finding out that the letter emanated from his son, Sir George wrote: 'To accuse *anyone*, let alone a parent, of adultery is a crime punishable by life imprisonment.'

Where Edith Sitwell adjusts the balance is to indicate how sinister, how truly horrible, much of the early life of herself and her two brothers was. Their father may have been grotesque and absurd; he was also menacing and charmless. Quite how she strikes this rather different note from Osbert's book, when much the same ground is covered, is not easy to say. Perhaps because she is more severe about that unhappy lady, their mother. The combination of the ludicrous and the dreadful, the aristocratic and the vulgar, fantastic ostentation and petty meanness of the most cheese-paring kind, that all went into the Sitwell upbringing, takes on a new hair-raising dimension in this account.

If ever a family had a right to feel that their own circumstances, apparently enviable in certain respects, were very decidedly not so in others, that family was the three Sitwells. A small example of the strange mixture that fate doled out to Edith Sitwell herself is that at the age of seventeen, when all the machinery was in motion to turn her into a routine debutante ('Little E', she was always known as) she met the painter, Sickert, who was at that time looked upon as a very 'advanced' artist. The friend who introduced them said: 'This woman admires your pictures.' 'Either she is mad or she is very intelligent,' Sickert replied, 'Which are you?' 'Mad,' said Edith Sitwell. The painter was delighted. He immediately presented her with a drawing. Such incidents were, of course, highlights in a life that seems to have had most of the disadvantages, and few of the advantages, of half a dozen different social worlds.

At a time when Edith Sitwell was very hard-up – much of her life was lived, financially speaking, in decidedly modest conditions – she happened to mention to her father that she had earned £15. ' "I hope," he said to me, "you are saving up for the Little Men" – his grandsons . . . I forget what I answered, but he remained silent, looking indescribably mean . . .'

Sir George had various plans for his daughter earning a living in her early life. Referring to one of these, years afterwards, he outraged his son's former soldier-servant, Robins.

When Osbert was dining alone with my father at Renishaw, waited on by Robins, my father said to Osbert: 'If Edith had done what I told her, she would be earning £1,000 a year now.'
This was too much for Robins.
'Yes. But would she be getting it?'
'Leave the room, Robins.'

Taken Care Of: An Autobiography,   1965
Edith Sitwell, Hutchinson.   *Daily Telegraph*

II

This is an exceedingly good book about the Sitwells – informative, thorough, sympathetic, without being in the least subservient. A great many delicate matters have to be handled. John Pearson never shows reluctance to deal with them, but he does so in a manner that remains extremely lively, while never descending to anything like malicious comment. He also keeps up an absorbing narrative for over 500 pages. Pearson begins with a brief but sensible account of Sitwell origins, about which there have been flights of fancy in the direction of the Plantagenets. The Sitwells were an old Derbyshire family of no exceptional distinction, whose final heiress married into another old local family called Hurt, owners of coal and lead mines, who took the name Sitwell in the eighteenth century. Dozens of aristocratic families had similar backgrounds and there was little justification for the megalomaniac family pride of the 4th baronet, Sir George Sitwell, father of Edith, Osbert and Sacheverell.

Sir George – 'Ginger' to his offspring – is the villain of the piece, a family tyrant more grotesque than any invented by Ivy Compton-Burnett in her novels, but very like those. A man of considerable intellectual attainments, cold-hearted, treacherous, Sir George was at once boundlessly extravagant and pinchingly mean, unusually shrewd and unbelievably obtuse. His fantastic dealings with his children are on record in Osbert Sitwell's memoirs. It was through Sir George's misplaced confidence in his own absolute wisdom that his wife, Lady Ida, was sent to prison after getting in a mess about her gambling debts.

John Pearson is not primarily concerned with a critical assessment of the three Sitwells as writers, though he seems to me sound on this, notably in seeing Sacheverell Sitwell as probably the most gifted. It is rather the panorama of Sitwell life as it unfolds – in what for two of them can hardly be regarded as less than tragedy – that is set out here with quite remarkable skill.

The place of Edith Sitwell (1887–1964) as a poet is still being argued, but that she will have a place can hardly be in doubt. The paradox of her life was that the public recognition of her later years left her unhappier than before, in spite of a passion for platform appearances and a delight even in Hollywood. The familiar enough concept of the 'emptiness' of that sort of success never seems to have crossed her mind, though in many respects she was full of kindness and understanding. It was sometimes thought – utterly mistakenly – that Edith Sitwell preferred her own sex. On the contrary, she had virginal but intense passions for men, chiefly the White Russian painter Pavel Tchelitchew who battened on her admiration and does not emerge as a particularly likeable personality. Pearson has much to say that is new regarding the 'seriousness' of this relationship.

Osbert Sitwell (1893–1969) will be remembered for his voluminous memoirs, but his place was as a wit, public figure, friend of great charm. It is well to recall two forgotten items which illustrate the acuteness of the early instincts of Osbert and Sacheverell Sitwell, as opposed to the lack of that quality in their far from aesthetically uninstructed father. In 1919, the two brothers arranged a show at Heal's Mansard Gallery in the Tottenham Court Road of the Paris School of Derain, Vlaminck, Matisse, Soutine, Utrillo, Picasso, Dufy, etc. At the close of show they tried to persuade Sir George to buy the lot for a few hundred pounds. He refused. Later it was suggested that Picasso (for £1,000) should do frescos in the Sitwell castle of Montegufone in Italy. Again Sir George refused. As a bloomer on the part of a man obsessed with money this is worth putting on record.

Pearson gives a tactful though finally painful account of Osbert Sitwell's lifelong homosexual affair with David Horner, an upper-class young man who was left a competence early in life by a French nobleman. There are also enthralling vignettes – which I take to be unpublished portions of Osbert Sitwell's memoirs – of T. S. Eliot's first marriage. John Pearson comments with truth that Osbert Sitwell was an excellent journalist, and also an accomplished courtier, somehow never quite finding a place as either.

Out of the mass of engrossing material collected here, if any general idea persists in coming to the surface, it is a sense of the sterility, the utter waste of time, of literary vendettas and offensive exchanges. From these Sacheverell Sitwell kept clear so far as possible. He was married, with a family, living in the country in England when not travelling to remote places of which he has written with such understanding. There were also his poems to write.

In days when Wyndham Lewis, then still on good terms with the Sitwells, was in Venice 'challenged to a match of draughtsmanship by an Italian painter', the subject seems to have been William Walton rather than, as captioned here, Sacheverell Sitwell. Pearson perhaps overestimates Osbert Sitwell's giving 'not the slightest sign' of his annoyance with D. H. Lawrence over the resemblances deliberately suggested (added to in subsequent versions of the Lawrence novel) between himself and Sir Clifford Chatterley. I have seen Osbert Sitwell kick a copy of Sons and Lovers across Duckworth's office to express his feelings on the subject – though he did add: 'But that *is* a good book.'

The Sitwells had a famous bowl full of press-cuttings in their anteroom at 2, Carlyle Square. John Pearson records how their friend, Lord Berners, to tease them, placed an even larger one in his hall containing only one cutting, 'a two-line announcement from the *Times*

that his lordship had returned to London from abroad.' It may have
been the one in which was noted: 'Lord Berners has left Lesbos and is
on his way to the Isle of Man.'

Façades: Edith, Osbert and   1978
Sacheverell Sitwell, John Pearson,   *Daily Telegraph*
Macmillan.

HAROLD NICOLSON AND
VITA SACKVILLE-WEST

I

When, some years ago, Harold Nicolson's Diaries appeared, people aware that both husband and wife preferred their own sex, felt that emphasis there laid on the Nicolsons' happy married life (already much publicised by the two of them in various public appearances), was at least a little inappropriate, if not actually irritating in the implication that a marriage of that sort avoided more normal matrimonial wear-and-tear. Nigel Nicolson's account of his parents' marriage which forms part of this book puts that right. He has provided a necessary footnote, and done it well. Objection may be raised to such plain speaking, but painful as some of the revelations are, the air has been cleared, a good deal of nonsense dispelled, and good qualities given their due.

The Sackvilles, builders of the vast house, Knole, by Sevenoaks, had died out in the male line in 1864, and become Sackville-West. The Sackville-Wests were given the peerage of Sackville in 1876. The 2nd Lord Sackville, unmarried, had several illegitimate children by a Spanish dancer, romantically designated a gypsy, but, in fact – as Nigel Nicolson firmly points out – simply widow of a barber at Malaga, good-looking, of strong personality, but no great star in her profession. One of these illegitimate children married her own first-cousin, the 3rd Lord Sackville, her father's nephew, who had succeeded to the title. This Lord Sackville and his half-Spanish wife produced an only child, a daughter, Vita Sackville-West (1892–1962), who married Harold Nicolson.

Harold Nicolson (1886–1968) was one of the younger sons of Sir Arthur Nicolson, 11th baronet, a distinguished diplomatist created Lord Carnock for his services. The Nicolsons were an able family, but not at all rich. Harold Nicolson joined the Foreign Service, like his father, and was expected to make a brilliant career. Vita Sackville-West inherited from her mother a pride of family which, even allowing for the undoubted splendour of Knole and Edwardian nobs giving themselves great airs, was excessive, especially in the light of the illegitimate Spanish strain. A wild tomboy, Vita from her earliest years showed talent as a middlebrow novelist. Although her parents disapproved of her writing, she had completed several historical novels by the age of seventeen, all showing the uncritical fluidity that marked her later work.

Nigel Nicolson draws partly on the account of herself his mother left behind her, partly uses his own narrative. In spite of having more than one extremely eligible young man showing signs of wanting to marry her – and some outdoor wrestling with the hall-boy, while growing up – her first strong passion was a lesbian one, which is described here by herself. Her great love was to be Violet Trefusis; a lesser one, Virginia Woolf.

The strangest thing about the whole story seems to be why Harold Nicolson and Vita Sackville-West were married in the first instance. She was only just twenty-one and already engaged on this affair with a woman. The Sackvilles liked Harold Nicolson, but were by no means wholly encouraging. All the same, the marriage formed the basis of Harold and Vita being 'in love' with one another, a situation which lasted throughout their lives on the odd terms set out in this book.

One would wish, if possible, to avoid moral judgments, to consider *Portrait of a Marriage* simply on grounds of interest and credibility. It is, however, hard to be objective, to believe in – or at least to understand – the alleged strength of their mutual love. Harold Nicolson seems to have been the first to withdraw from a physical relationship, and one can perfectly accept that they loved each other deeply without this need. What is harder to fathom is Vita Nicolson's apparently total disregard for her husband's feelings, not only in the exhibitionistic and incredibly inconvenient nature of her goings-on but also by continued lack of any goodwill to him in his chosen profession.

If a personal note may be excused, Harold Nicolson, on one or two occasions, was kind to me with help about jobs, but I never found him at all easy to get on with. I was quite unaware what he had been through in his marriage, which goes a long way to explain his unpredictable manner. His wife's lesbian activities, about which he behaved with great forbearance, at times had certainly given him intense pain. I think few people gave him the credit for this.

Nigel Nicolson makes no attempt to gloss over his father's homosexuality, though adding no doubt with truth that sex did not play a major part in his life. A fact entirely new to me is that Harold Nicolson did not leave the Foreign Office on account of pressures applied after his publication of *Some People*, a book that made fun of diplomacy. On the contrary, he resigned because his wife would not play a part in his official life, something that made his position increasingly difficult as he rose in the service. This is why he became – made his name as – a miscellaneous writer.

Portrait of a Marriage, Nigel
Nicolson, Weidenfeld & Nicolson.

1973
Daily Telegraph

I I

Harold Nicolson, not much of a success at Wellington, only moderately so at Balliol, was not expected to pass into the Foreign Service at all. In fact he was placed second in the list. He seems to have found his feet almost immediately as a diplomat in Madrid and Constantinople and, although he was to write later that he 'hated women, especially virgins', he married Vita Sackville-West at the age of twenty-six. When war broke out in 1914, Nicolson was at the Foreign Office, where he remained. This was a delicate matter for a man still in his twenties whose contemporaries were soon to be killed one after another on the Western Front. Nicolson might or might not have managed to obtain release at the outbreak of war, though that is doubtful, and he was certainly more useful to the country in Whitehall than he would have been in the army. Later release would certainly not have been allowed. In this otherwise enjoyable and understanding biography, I don't think James Lees-Milne emphasises quite sufficiently the guilt Nicolson felt about this, which – though I never knew him well – always seemed to me almost obsessive.

Nicolson's role was in being a brilliant subordinate. Although undoubtedly marked out for ambassadorial rank one feels doubts as to how his volatile and romantic temperament (which he would have been himself the first to acknowledge) might have reacted in a position of high responsibility. As things were his relations with his superiors, notably Balfour and Curzon, make very amusing reading, and these detailed presentations often throw light on the happenings of the period.

After League of Nations assignments Nicolson was sent *en poste* to Persia (it was the moment when Reza Pahlevi had just made himself Shah). All the elements that make dealing with Iranians difficult were present, and Nicolson's own descriptions are both witty and depressing so far as hope for more Iranian coherence is concerned.

Vita Nicolson, who had caused her husband much pain and embarrassment by her lesbian goings-on (his own affairs with, for instance, Raymond Mortimer, were quietly conducted), came out to Teheran for a short time, but she was too bored by diplomatic society to stay with her husband when abroad. By this time she was herself making some name as a writer. Her poetry is lifeless and pretentious, her novels worse, but they were by no means without admirers.

Harold Nicolson was already thinking of resigning before *Some People* – which naturally roused a certain amount of irritation among those in authority – was published. Resignation was a wise decision. He wrote with extreme facility, and was to become an able popular biographer and literary journalist. Lees-Milne scarcely quite conveys the trickiness of Nicolson's manner (you never knew if he would be friendly or cut you dead) but that does not detract from a book packed with all sorts of different material to hold the attention, which ends in 1929 with a change of profession.

Harold Nicolson: A Biography. Vol. I: 1980
1886–1929, James Lees-Milne,   *Daily Telegraph*
Chatto.

III

James Lees-Milne's second volume of biography is as entertaining as the first: indeed for comic incidents in a story that is quite often painful (certainly ends in one of the tragedies of old age), the final instalment is even more highly picked out in lights and shades. Harold Nicolson, who had many good qualities – kindness, generosity, zest for life, immense energy, a good deal of humour (at its best very funny, but sometimes drying up) – often appears in what can only be regarded by his own standards as an unedifying light. His view of himself seems to have been as lacking in understanding as his view of other people. He could never grasp that persons of another class to his own, or Americans, might exist within their own perfectly reasonable terms of reference. At the same time he regarded himself as a writer, a man of the world, on the whole a politician of the Left, and a bohemian.

In fact, many of his best qualities were those of the highly trained civil servant: he was upset in literature by the least sign of obscenity; his snobbishness was almost wholly undigested; and although himself homosexual, he objected to one of his sons merely sharing a flat with another young man, and to the other son, as an MP, voting for alleviation of the laws about homosexuality.

To the end of his life Nicolson lived entirely on his earnings; and although his wife had some money, most of that went on the famous garden they established at Sissinghurst Castle, which is their memorial. On ceasing to be a diplomatist he had to get a well-paid job. He worked at various forms of journalism, much of which he disliked but on the whole did well, and wrote a stream of books – no one was better at giving the essential facts about, say, Benjamin Constant or Sainte-Beuve.

Where entry into politics was concerned Nicolson at first tried to get adopted for a Conservative seat. Then he joined Oswald Mosley's New Party with its Fascist undertones. Eventually he reached the House of Commons as National Labour. At the election of 1945 he stood as a Nationalist and failed to get in. Then he attempted to be returned on the Labour ticket, the last ending as a peculiar disaster in North Croydon.

Nicolson now made desperate efforts to be made a peer. If he had not tried so hard it is by no means unlikely that he would have found himself in the House of Lords where his debating powers and mixture of qualities might well have been useful. As it was the tactlessness of his various approaches are scarcely credible. At times he had cold feet at the thought of being inducted wearing ermine and an Admiral's hat, at others he felt a barony was in the bag and the only thing to settle was his title:

> He decided that a name beginning with 'S' would be preferable because of the engraved cigarette-case of his father-in-law [Lord Sackville] which Vita had given him, and the letter 'S' embroidered on her towels. It was a pity for instance that the fields round Sissinghurst [ruled out for the 'Sissy' implication] were suitable for fields, not for persons. For instance, Frogsmead and Plague-spot would hardly do. Then Vita, having raked through an old map of the Sissinghurst property, came upon another field, which she suggested might not be inappropriate. It was called Lower Bottom.

Alas, it was not to be. Nicolson merely continued his unceasing round of lecturing, broadcasting, producing books, writing up his diary (a good if not over-exciting journal), then being entrusted with the biography of King George V. At the termination of that task he was more or less forced to accept a KCVO, though he had begged to be given the lesser grade of CVO which would not have saddled him with a knighthood.

Nicolson's career was an extraordinary one. Some years after leaving the Foreign Office he was invited to return there. His terms were too high. Some years after that he himself felt that he would like to go back. This time it was the Foreign Office that refused. There seems no doubt that Nicolson was a brilliant subordinate. In foreign affairs he believed that what mattered was not conversations between statesmen but carefully drafted treaties and conditions. Even by 1945 he had not taken in the implications of the Soviet Union's policies (which to do the USSR justice had never been in the least concealed), and thought 'the tide of Russian aggressiveness will sooner or later recede.' He also maintained a correspondence after defection with his old friend, in Lees-Milne's phrase, the 'drink-sodden crapulous traitor Guy Burgess'.

Harold Nicolson: A Biography. Vol. II: 1981
1930–1968, James Lees-Milne,   *Daily Telegraph*
Chatto.

WYNDHAM LEWIS

I

Wyndham Lewis, although most books of reference during his lifetime gave his birth as 1884, was born in 1881. One can imagine what contempt he himself would have heaped on any contemporary of his caught falsifying his age (Cocteau, for example, who did that very thing), and an innate moral inconsistency in Lewis of just that sort makes it hard to be fair to a man of diverse and extraordinary talent. He is still hard to place. Two new books are concerned only with Lewis's painting, drawing and art criticism, but it is not easy to ignore the rest of his writings entirely, because, by breaking off from time to time to write, he ceased to paint. It is also true to say that all his writing is heavily impregnated with the mark of a painter's vision. That he could have been merely one or the other is inconceivable in the light of his great gifts for both, but one may at least regret that he did not limit himself to painting and imaginative writing of one sort or another. *The Wild Body* and *Tarr* are extraordinary works: *One Way Song* contains some remarkable verse. It is the philosophic and political side of his work which sets such an obstacle in the way of his reputation and was so largely a waste of time and talent, when he might have been better employed.

Walter Michel's admirable volume of Lewis's paintings and drawings gives opportunity, never available before, to consider his graphic art as a whole. A promising figure at the Slade towards the turn of the century, Lewis's claim to have founded, in the Vorticists, the one pre-war 'modern movement' in painting can scarcely be denied. William Roberts, another painter of notable talent, survives but the rest of the small band have gone. Looking back, it is extraordinary to see how few of them there were, and what a mark they made.

It was one of Lewis's perennial grouses that Bloomsbury critics – Roger Fry and his understrapper Clive Bell – were so enraptured with France and the Impressionists that no other painting seemed to them of any interest. That was in one sense true enough, and a great deal that may have been instructive to the public in the way of leading them towards one sort of good painting was negatived by Bloomsbury provincialism and self-applause. Lewis, in his art criticism, collected in *Wyndham Lewis on Art*, knocks Fry and Bell about very thoroughly.

There is undoubtedly a case for saying that he himself was badly treated by the art critics of the Twenties, their hostility usually taking the form of more or less ignoring his work. Walter Michel says with truth that the books under review are not the rediscovery of a hitherto obscure figure, but the just tribute to a major artist of the period.

Having made this position clear, it must be admitted that there was a good deal about Lewis, as both artist and man, that was difficult to handle even by those who admired his work and wished him well. He died of a tumour on the brain. One cannot help wondering whether something had not already begun to go medically wrong in his forties, when persecution mania and an aggressive offensiveness to almost everyone and everything became so pronounced. This was the time when he named himself 'The Enemy'. It could be argued that the financial difficulties he suffered all his life, together with the determination to run against the stream, inevitably leading to a contemporary lack of appreciation, not to say hostility, in powerful quarters, were, in combination, enough to make any artist feel persecuted. At the same time a change not for the better appears a year or two after the First World War. In the earlier sections of *Wyndham Lewis on Art* I found myself marking passage after passage that seemed of notable interest. Suddenly this need to mark good points ceased; then, much further on, began again. I found that all the later paragraphs marked were, in fact, reprints from pre-war articles.

If we turn to the Lewis pictures themselves, the earliest drawings strike one as talented, if not particularly attractive. It is not until Lewis is in his late twenties that an individual style, with somewhat Cubist overtones, develops. By about 1912 this style has become decidedly interesting, not least on the 'abstract' side, an aspect of art that, as it happens, Lewis himself almost consistently attacks and – one of his many wrong prophecies – sees as having no future. Whether you like abstract painting or not, that was obviously a mistaken guess. Incidentally, some of Lewis's rather 'Egyptian' style drawings seem to have had influence on Graham Sutherland's work.

During the war Lewis served for about eighteen months in the ranks, and as an officer in the Gunners; then became an official war artist. The odd thing about the immediately pre-war drawings is that they seem directed towards a manner that was soon to be particularly suitable to Lewis's treatment of war subjects. Michel implies that Lewis himself does not seem to have set any specially high value on his work at this time, in spite of the great merits it possesses. One would agree that much of it might be thought Lewis at his best. The hard, 'mechanised' line of the drawings themselves, the treatment of the figure subjects, restrained yet somehow full of emotion, modern yet like people in a medieval manuscript or winter scene by Brueghel, are just what was required. The drawing 'The Rum Ration' (no. 308 of 1918) might be instanced, or 'A Battery Shelled' (pl. VIII, 1919). The admirable figure group on the left of the latter picture, the grave, almost naturalistic soldiers, makes a striking and dramatic contrast with the stylised demoniac figures of 'vorticist' shape rushing about under the immediate hail of fire. These war pictures might well be contrasted with the equally remarkable paintings of Renaissance war scenes such as 'The Surrender of Barcelona' (Pl. IV, 1936).

There are some excellent drawings of the early 1920s, among which the three very different studies of Edith Sitwell (nos 485, 487, 488 of 1921) deserve mention. The first of these Edith Sitwell portraits is now in the National Portrait Gallery. The 'Tyro' series, and their fellows of about the same date, I find less sympathetic. By the middle Twenties the style changes somewhat – influenced by later Cubism without being in itself Cubistic – and towards the end of the decade and beginning of the thirties some almost naturalistic portrait drawings occur. Osbert Sitwell – the Sitwells were on bad terms with Lewis by this time – said maliciously of these portrait drawings that he felt them 'too much influenced by Olive Snell' (a fashionable portraitist of the period). One would agree that, good as some are, some fall below the highest standard Lewis could produce. The portrait of Thomas Earp is, for example, a most accomplished drawing, exactly like him.

These comparatively naturalistic drawings continue on and off throughout the 1940s, reaching a peak of 'naturalism' when Lewis was in Canada, very hard up, marooned there through no fault of his own throughout the war. To make some money he painted almost ikon-like portraits of the Basilian Fathers, sometimes from photographs of oils. To the immediately post-war period belong some studies of T. S. Eliot. These are worth comparing with the full-length portrait of the poet refused by the Royal Academy in 1938, about which there was a great fuss, Augustus John temporarily resigning. Professor Hugh Kenner in his Introduction rightly draws special attention to the many pictures of Ezra Pound. It is greatly to be regretted that the Lewis portrait of Proust planned by Sydney and Violet Schiff never came off. It would have been a fascinating contact of personalities.

The sense that one has in looking through this collection of Lewis's pictures and drawings is of a definite reaction in oneself, but a reaction hard to put into words. The artist seems somehow to be *trying too hard*; putting too much intellectul energy into what requires feeling rather than thinking. One has much the same sense in reading Lewis's books. The brilliant descriptions that occur in *The Wild Body*, that marvellous opening paragraph of *Tarr*, are what Lewis felt; but so often later he forced the pace, and often one seems aware of that in the painting. There is a kind of uncertainty, a lack of conviction, masquerading as a swashbuckling self-assurance. I say this within the terms of accepting him as a figure of great distinction in both writing and painting.

One final word should be said. Lewis made himself disagreeable to a lot of people, and went out of his way to make enemies. He is not in general thought of as a generous critic. It turns out that a lot of the criticism to be found here is not only acute, but also generous. That is not solely when Lewis is dealing with painters younger than himself. The obituaries he wrote – reprinted here – of his own contemporaries Frederick Spencer Gore and Harold Gilman are models of their kind. That should be remembered.

Wyndham Lewis: Paintings and Drawings, Walter Michel, with an introductory essay by Hugh Kenner, Thames and Hudson. *Wyndham Lewis on Art: Collected Writings 1913–56*, edited and introduced by Walter Michel and C. J. Fox, Thames and Hudson.

1971
Apollo

II

Percy Wyndham Lewis (1881–1957) sometimes implied that his family was the one to which Wyndham Lewis, M P, first husband of Mrs Benjamin Disraeli, belonged – which well may have been the case some way back. In fact, Lewis was at least a fourth-generation American, with an admixture of Quaker and French-Canadian blood. Even his mother had close Canadian affiliations, and in this full and informative biography, Jeffrey Meyers states that Lewis held a Canadian passport. Only by chance was he not brought up in America.

The separation of his parents caused Lewis to be sent to Rugby, which was not a success. He left after two years to study art at the Slade. There, so I have been told, he had drawings in the Slade Magazine before his senior, Augustus John, who remained a friend. John was one of the few with whom Lewis always kept relatively on the right side. The Slade was followed by seven years abroad, mostly in Paris, but also in Spain, Holland, and Germany. When Lewis returned to England he became unquestionably the outstanding 'Modernist' figure in the country, possessing as he did a mastery of both painting and writing.

Lewis's revolutionary programme in the arts was energetic and coherent. It ran counter to the doctrines of the just emerging Bloomsbury group and the views of most other intellectuals of that very interesting pre-1914 period. Much influenced by Nietzsche and Sorel's *Réflections sur la violence*, Lewis was, for instance, anti-Romantic, anti-Proust, anti-Joyce, anti-Freud. His view of writing was that, like painting, it should deal only with what can be seen from the outside.

There is something to be said for this theory, which he demonstrated in his novel about bohemian life in Paris, *Tarr* (1918, revised 1928), and in the Breton short stories in *The Wild Body* (1927). Although published later, both these books belong to this period before the First World War, and constitute, in my opinion, Lewis's best work as a writer.

As a painter Lewis was anti-Impressionist (a school just beginning to be fully appreciated in Great Britain), and he founded the Vorticist Movement, an offshoot of Cubism and Futurism. Lewis was certainly the dominant figure, though (*pace* Meyers) William Roberts, by no means a bad painter, was justified in being annoyed when Lewis took the whole credit for Vorticism in the catalogue of the Tate Gallery exhibition of 1956.

After two years of active service in the Royal Artillery (he seems to have been a competent NCO and officer) Lewis was appointed a war artist. The circumstances of war were suited to his harsh and joyless style of painting. All this laid foundations for a brilliant post-war career, even for a painter and writer running against the main stream of highbrow fashion. That was not how things worked out. Lewis poured forth books, did a certain amount of painting, but remained in a fearful state of poverty, raging against the corruption of the world of art and letters, and his own unhappy condition. This period saw the publication of *The Apes of God* (1930).

Lewis had an extraordinary mastery of words and his aim to describe from the outside was wholly successful, but in *The Apes of God*, an immensely lengthy attack on the London world of intellectuals, it is impossible to grasp the characters described unless they have been met. Lewis was entirely without the power to 'digest' individuals he knew for representation in a novel. Indeed he was not (like, say, Pope) interested in those he attacked. Meyers says that Ratner in *The Apes* is meant to be James Joyce. It is just possible that some elements of Joyce have been included, but the main description is that of a far more obscure figure, John Rodker, as there indicated, a Jewish intellectual from the East End, who became a writer, translator and publisher, and frequented the world which Lewis excoriates.

Another misunderstanding is when Meyers, speaking of a portrait-drawing by Lewis, refers to the 'foppish preciosity' of Constant Lambert. Lambert was about as little 'foppishly precious' as would be possible for a man to be. He is wearing 'morning clothes' in the picture because that was the day uniform of a conductor, and the drawing is, in fact, not much like him.

These criticisms are certainly not meant to suggest that Meyers has not done a good job, handling a complicated narrative clearly, showing the other side of the picture in Lewis's many controversies, and at last doing some justice to Lewis's heroic wife Froanna. Lewis's real trouble seems to have been that he believed himself an omniscient political philosopher, which led him to write much that is now unreadable, including a very silly short book praising Hitler. It might be argued that many equally silly books have been written praising Stalin, but Lewis's came out at the wrong moment. Lewis's egoism, quarrelsomeness, utterly ungrateful behaviour to his friends (all passing the bounds of normality) were perhaps in some degree attributable to recurrent attacks of venereal disease.

The Enemy: A Biography of Wyndham Lewis, Jeffrey Meyers, Routledge.

1980
Daily Telegraph

T. E. HULME

The 1890s provide a neat ending to Victorian intellectual life. The next step in art and letters – 'the Modern Movement' – has the air (quite an erroneous one) of appearing fully armed, at the end of the First World War. The period between 1900 and 1914, in contrast, seems peculiarly shapeless; in some ways unproductive. This view of the Edwardian decade is, of course, not at all just. In truth, it was the field of fascinating struggles between opposed forces and ideas; but even now the smoke has scarcely cleared away sufficiently to see what was really happening.

When people talk of this pre-1914 period in England, they are apt to invoke, sooner or later, the name of T. E. Hulme. Wyndham Lewis, for example, is often said to have derived some of his theories from Hulme. One gets the impression of an *éminence grise* of considerable power. In this book Alun R. Jones gives an account of *The Life and Opinions of T. E. Hulme*. It is a lively account. In fact at the end of it you almost feel you have met Hulme himself.

Hulme was born in 1883 of a Staffordshire land-owning family who had gone into business in the Potteries. His early life was not very happy. He was never on good terms with his parents, both Victorianly authoritarian and uninterested in matters of the mind. In fairness to the Hulme parents, Hulme himself does not appear to have been an easy son. At an early age he was attracted by mathematics and philosophy, but was at the same time lazy and undisciplined. He was a great controversialist at school and is said to have reduced the headmaster to tears by arguing so heatedly. He was sent down from Cambridge, travelled to Canada by cargo boat, returned to London where, more or less disowned by his father, he lived on an allowance provided by a cousin of his mother's.

Jones pieces together with ingenuity Hulme's manner of life in London. The result is a document of great interest which goes a long way to show the difficulty, mentioned above, of conveying a coherent picture of the highbrow and Bohemian society of the time. The Eiffel Tower Restaurant in Percy Street, as one of Hulme's backgrounds, makes an appearance in 1909 – to continue its vivid career until the 1930s – and we find ourselves in the midst of contrasting names like

157

Sickert and Epstein, John Drinkwater and Ezra Pound, Wyndham Lewis and J. C. Squire, T. S. Eliot and Rupert Brooke.

Hulme came early under the influence of Bergson, who may (so we are told) be exploded as a philosopher, but obstinately refuses to be forgotten. Bergson thought that 'man's primary need is not knowledge, but action,' an idea that appealed to Hulme. Hulme's principal stock-in-trade was Original Sin (although he could scarcely be said to belong to any specific church) and a detestation of Romanticism, as opposed to Classicism; for each of which he provided his own definition. These convictions led him to a dislike of the Renaissance, and writers like Montaigne.

In art, he was greatly impressed by Byzantine mosaics and accepted the ideas of Wilhelm Worringer. Worringer was one of the earliest art critics to point out that non-representational painting, from Egyptian times onwards, was the result of deliberate choice on the artist's part, and not, as the nineteenth century often supposed, pictorial incompetence. It is worth noting that Modern Art came to Hulme from Germany, not France – a fact characteristic of Edwardian England.

His views on politics and poetry, as well as philosophy (writes Jones) all reveal this basic dichotomy. In poetry he insists on classicism according to romantic canons; in politics he demands a strong central authority and the maximum of individual liberty; in philosophy he embraced the work of Bergson and the logical positivists.

Hulme thought that all art was motivated by 'a passionate desire for accuracy'. You start off, he says, with some actual and vividly felt experience.

You find that when you have expressed this in straightforward language that you have not expressed it at all. You have only expressed it approximately. All the individuality of the emotion as you experienced it has been left out. You persist in an endeavour to so state things that the meaning does not escape, but is definitely forced on the attention of the reader. To do this you are forced to invent new metaphors and new epithets.

The artist, Hulme thought

is the man who is born detached from the necessities of action, and who, by reason of this detachment, is able to pick out of reality 'something which we, owing to a certain hardening of our perceptions, have been unable to see ourselves'.

Hulme was, therefore, an adherent of 'Modern Art' (he included the Diaghilev Ballet as 'Classical') and of a new approach to poetry.

Physically, he was a big man, and appeared to some people argumentative and aggressive, to others quietly ironical and full of charm in making his brilliant points. His own prose style, as may be seen from the quotation above, was unattractive; nor do I find the poems reproduced here impressive. There seems no doubt that Hulme had some taste for horseplay. He is said to have hung Wyndham Lewis upside down from the railings of Soho Square by the turn-ups of his trousers – a very practical manner of influencing him. Hulme's relations with women were extensive. Jones says – with perhaps a small touch of priggishness in an otherwise briskly told story – that Hulme liked girls 'of what Ashley Dukes quaintly calls "the shop-girl class"'. But you can't make the Classless Society retrospective. Surely Ashley Dukes spoke not 'quaintly', but factually.

Alun Jones comes to the conclusion – with which it would be hard to disagree – that as a philosopher Hulme was derivative and self-contradictory. At the same time Hulme did represent a very genuine reaction from what might be called Bloomsbury and Bertrand Russell; an opposition with plenty of wit and energy, that was at the same time not itself philistine. He was killed in action in 1917, a few days after his thirty-fourth birthday.

The Life and Opinions of T. E. Hulme,   1960
Alun R. Jones, Gollancz.   *Daily Telegraph*

LÉON BAKST

In 1921 *The Sleeping Princess* ballet (*La Belle au Bois Dormant*) put on at the Alhambra, with costumes and décor by Léon Bakst, was one of the great flops of all time. I saw it as a schoolboy, enjoyed every moment (having been brought up on *The Decorative Art of Léon Bakst*, from its appearance in 1913), and was pained, also rather ashamed, to find the production contemptuously dismissed by the intellectual pundits of the time as a 'glorified pantomime'.

Writing in 1930, Sacheverell Sitwell – quoted here in Charles Spencer's enjoyable book *Léon Bakst* – bears out that situation. Sitwell says of Diaghilev: 'the most exciting thing I remember was his revival of *La Belle au Bois Dormant* . . . It was a wonderful evening altogether, and the now despised Bakst had excelled himself.' The wheel has come round again. The aesthetic puritanism of Bloomsbury (chiefly to be blamed for its lack of imagination) is no more. Bakst is recognised as the greatest theatrical designer of the century.

Léon Bakst (1865–1924) was a Russian Jew, whose family were well-to-do though he himself suffered periods of penury in his younger days. His story is of interest for a variety of reasons. Charles Spencer has dug out a lot, but much remains unknown, perhaps will never be known. In Bakst's period, as now, there was an upsurge of Jewish persecution in Russia. He was expelled from the Academy art school for representing the set subject, 'The Madonna Weeping over Christ', in the crude terms of a Lithuanian ghetto.

Bakst established himself first as a painter. His ability to deal with 'Society' portraits brought him within measurable distance of settling down to what would have been a lesser career. He was also associated with the group connected with *The World of Art*, a magazine founded by Diaghilev, which in the early 1900s brought together a great deal of contemporary Russian talent. As a personality, Bakst was at that time regarded as something of a buffoon, veering between obsequiousness and conceit. Nevertheless his powers as a draughtsman were immense. The keenness of his intelligence may be gauged by the fact that in 1905, on a visit to Greece he went to Crete – an island even in the middle 1930s regarded by travel agents as scarcely worth bothering about –

and was much impressed by the Minoan artefacts Arthur Evans was uncovering. This Minoan influence is later visible in Bakst's own designs.

Bakst, who once spoke of himself as the 'Russian Veronese', always liked to think of his painting, rather than designing, coming first. He would have preferred to be remembered for his picture 'Terror Antiquus' – roughly speaking a Symbolist canvas, representing the destruction by earthquake of the Ancient World – rather than his theatrical masterpieces, *Schéhérazade*, *The Good-Humoured Ladies*, *The Firebird*, *Le Dieu Bleu*, *L'Après-Midi d'un Faune*, *Thamar*, and the rest. That did not mean that he was anything but exceedingly autocratic about his theatrical work, which had to cover aspects of music and choreography, as well as the demanding pictorial side.

Then came conflict, the break with Diaghilev. When Bloomsbury, in the early 1920s, disapproved of Bakst, it was only reflecting, in its provincial way, what was happening everywhere else on a much larger scale. Fashions were changing. Diaghilev was, of course, painfully anxious always to be *avant garde*, but, even had the great impresario been less obsessed in that direction, Bakst could hardly have failed to be on the way out. He does, in fact, supply one of the most interesting links between the nineties (he was much influenced by Beardsley) and the Modern Movement. Spencer rightly says that much nonsense has been talked about Bakst's 'Orientalism', but it is true that this side of him is in no way at odds with, say, Delacroix. At the other end, Bakst touches – but never wholly assimilates – the 'modernism' of Picasso with which he is not at ease in spite of enormous facility. Bakst belonged essentially to an earlier generation.

The relationship with Diaghilev, the parting of the ways, Bakst's connection with Ida Rubenstein, are all fascinating to read about. The décor of the ballets was handed over to (among others) Braque, Chirico, Picasso – great painters certainly, but not necessarily theatrical designers superior to Bakst. Still, past fashions have to give way, especially in the theatre. Bakst was briefly married to a daughter of Pavel Tretiakov, whose great art collection formed the basis of the Gallery bearing his name in Moscow. Characteristically, Bakst only had a son by his former wife after they had been divorced. He was much attracted by women, but never managed to establish a permanent relationship with one. Often spoken of as 'depraved', it is not clear where his tastes lay, but they seem to have caused him a good deal of trouble and depression, possibly bad health.

Chagall was a pupil of Bakst, and Lovat Fraser – himself a distinguished artist in the field of theatrical design – learnt a lot from him when the Russian Ballet came to London in 1909. There is much else in Charles Spencer's book, all chronicled in a straightforward, well-informed, sensible manner, characteristics not always to be found in a study of this sort.

Léon Bakst, Charles Spencer,   1973
Academy Editions.   *Daily Telegraph*

T. S. ELIOT

I

At the end of the war, on leaving the Army, I spent a few months in the country. T. S. Eliot was staying in the neighbourhood, and we saw quite a bit of each other. Later in London he dined with us once or twice, we with him, and met occasionally at parties. I mention this merely to emphasise what an unusually difficult person Eliot is to describe. That was not because he 'kept to himself', or refused to join in conversation. On the contrary, he was prepared to talk on almost any subject, and was anything but self-important. There was, at the same time, something withdrawn, unapproachable, in his personality that seems to defy definition.

William Turner Levy, aged twenty-two and serving with the United States Army in England, first made some sort of contact with Eliot, through introductions, in 1944. They did not actually come face to face until three years later, when the poet was fifty-nine. A friendship developed; there were letters and reunions over a period of eighteen years until his death. Victor Scherle, by interrogating Levy (subsequently ordained as Episcopalian minister), played a part in shaping this account of Eliot into narrative form.

If one may so put it, Americans – at least some Americans – have a simplicity of outlook that makes it possible to describe individuals in a manner so straightforward that it almost spills over into absurdity, yet still conveys acceptable and unslanted information. Lilian Ross's *New Yorker* Profile of Hemingway might be instanced. In this country, for some reason, no one can bring off that sort of thing in quite the same way. For better or worse the narrator always obtrudes, even when anonymous. Levy is a good example of this guileless approach:

> Eliot enjoyed the food enormously. At the table my father talked with him about the shipping business, particularly with respect to English contracts during both wars. My mother spoke of her stamp collection and chanced to comment on the commemorative stamp picturing Whistler's Mother. Eliot said that he had been highly amused in his childhood by a painting of Whistler's Mother which parodied the original, showing the venerable lady standing up! This continued to amuse him inordinately, and was my first experience with Eliot's extremely droll sense of humour.

The scene impresses itself in a way that more pretentious writing would have spoilt. It continues no less vividly, with Eliot telling a favourite joke. On a later occasion: 'To be polite, I asked the Eliots if they would like another martini. I was thunderstruck when Tom immediately accepted the offer. We all had a third, ice-cold, bone-dry, Beefeater martini.'

These artless vignettes give, in a sense, just what one wants to know about people, but not everyone can draw them without self-consciousness. Naturally some of the discussions were on religious subjects, and, among others, the theologians Reinhold and Richard Niebuhr are invoked. There is also the occasional interesting literary opinion: that Eliot was unimpressed by *Moby Dick*; thought 'The New English Bible' a matter for 'dismay' in its translation.

One of the most characteristic incidents in the book is that of the Roosevelt plate 'used at Hyde Park in F. D. R.'s time, bearing the initials of the President's father, James Roosevelt – a rare and historical item', and presented to Eliot by Levy. Eliot wrote back that he believed that natives of West Africa, when they gave a present to anyone they held in esteem, chose only a gift they themselves coveted. The plate was in that class, because he knew of Levy's admiration for Franklin Roosevelt. He himself, on the other hand, did not share that admiration. His conscience told him he must send the plate back.

> Nor do I overlook the great generosity of Lend Lease; or am I mindless of what the outcome of the war would have been for England, if America had taken no part in it. But what I also cannot forget is that Mr Roosevelt was no great friend of England; that he was suspicious of British policy and disapproving of the existence of the (now almost inexistent) British Empire. Oh my dear William, the harm that has been done in the world, the disorder that is only now [1956] too evident by the ju-ju of those words 'colonialism' and 'imperialism' working in American breasts! Was it this perhaps that led Mr Roosevelt to embark on the disastrous policy of agreeing with Stalin rather than with Churchill? . . . Anyway, I regard Mr Roosevelt's foreign policy as a colossal folly.

This conveys Eliot very well. Most of us, I think, however much we agreed with this condemnation of Roosevelt's foreign policy, would have kept the plate, not risked hurt feelings. Not so a man of Eliot's integrity. William Levy, though – anyway at the time – unconvinced of Eliot's rightness of judgment, took the incident well.

The attractive simplicity of this brief collection goes some way to convey essential elements. An omission seems to me to be no reference to Eliot's peculiar agelessness – but perhaps the disparity of age at the beginning of their friendship was too great for that to be apparent. It is surprising to find Eliot on a favourite subject of his – cats – stating that pedigree cats are 'no good, stupid, nervous and of feeble character'. That generalisation could only have been the result of inexperience.

Affectionately T. S. Eliot: The Story of   1969
a Friendship 1947–1965, William   *Daily Telegraph*
Turner, Levy and Victor Scherle,
Dent.

I I

These two volumes, a worthy tribute to the Eliot Centenary, are so engrossing that it was hard to know which to put first. The admirably edited Letters win on chronological grounds, though Lyndall Gordon's subtle and scholarly biography of the later years of T. S. Eliot (1888–1965) often throws light on his earlier career in the Letters. Lyndall Gordon makes the point that Eliot rejected American pursuit of Happiness, America's easy optimism, but not American belief in Perfectibility. He never lost his New England roots in Calvinism and deep moral seriousness. His ancestors had burnt witches; his cousin Charles William Eliot, President of Harvard (1870–1909), deploring Henry James's frivolity, wrote in 1919: 'It seemed to me all along that his English residence for so many years contributed neither to the happy development of his art nor to his personal happiness.' If Henry James were to be regarded as wasting time, this was a tough heredity. Eliot's immediate forebears, after three generations on the Mississippi, had become – like Empire-builders changing for dinner in the jungle – more Bostonian than Boston. Eliot's background must always be remembered when considering him and his work; perhaps not least in the sense of latent violence that lurks behind an apparent urbanity.

There are far too many fascinating aspects of the story illustrated by the Letters to mention here. Perhaps the most remarkable is the manner in which Vivienne Haigh-Wood, Eliot's first wife, comes to life in her own letters. Hitherto one had the vaguest picture of her: that she was a relatively 'liberated' pre-1914 girl, who, after a desperately unhappy marriage, gradually went mad, having to be eventually confined, and dying in 1947, leaving Eliot with a ghastly sense of guilt.

This is an unfair judgment, though Vivienne Eliot had disastrous failings. Throughout the years chronicled in these Letters the Eliots were devoted to each other, though Vivienne's incessantly bad health, lack of balance, tactlessness and desire to be 'in on the act' often made things difficult. Above all there was their grinding poverty. None the less Eliot often asked her advice; on at least one occasion actually sent for her to help him out when she was having a brief spell of rest in the country. It was Vivienne who suggested the name the *Criterion* for the severely highbrow quarterly Eliot was editing when this period of the Letters ends.

One of Eliot's relations said: 'Vivienne ruined Tom as a man, but made him a poet.' There seems much truth in this. The same might to some extent be said of the bank in which Eliot worked. He was not shovelling money about with a trowel (as was popularly supposed at the time), but reporting on the balances of foreign banks and so on, work which he distinctly enjoyed and was evidently proficient at. What would *The Waste Land* be without King William Street and the City references?

Writing (December 1914) to Conrad Aiken (an American poet he later did not regard highly) Eliot says: 'I should be better off, I sometimes think, if I had disposed of my virginity and shyness several years ago; and indeed I still think it would be well to do so before marriage.' Eliot was then twenty-six. To the same correspondent, a month or two before, he had written: '[Ezra] Pound is rather intelligent as a talker: his verse is well-meaning but touchingly incompetent.' He was to revise the latter opinion.

Another point that the Letters reveal is the desperate efforts Eliot made to join the United States navy or army, when America entered the First World War. He was far from medically fit, but he could have been usefully employed in either service in Intelligence, being prevented by a bureaucratic imbroglio that would have been impressive even in a Communist country.

One of the most interesting things about the Letters is how often one notices the rhythms of Eliot's poetry in their phrasing. In the light of his support of literary expression generally, especially James Joyce's *Ulysses* (though he admitted its enthusiasts annoyed him almost as much as Joyce's detractors), it is amusing to find him showing a faint note of anxiety (February 1920) to his brother Henry as to whether their mother might be shocked by *Sweeney Erect*.

Turning from the Letters to Lyndall Gordon's biographical study, there can be no doubt that its central character is Emily Hale, an American girl Eliot nearly married in 1913. There continued to be a strong bond between them, as Eliot seems to have remained in love. When Vivienne died the question of marriage again rose, but Eliot retreated, although he still seems to have loved Emily Hale in a sense, and (as Lyndall Gordon indicates) she occurs frequently in the poems. Eliot allowed it to be understood that although this was so, he preferred to remain unmarried. It was therefore something of a shock to Emily Hale when he married Valerie Fletcher in 1957 – an event that gives a fairy-tale ending to what is often a sombre story. Emily Hale adds a complete dimension to what was previously known of Eliot, and Lyndall Gordon's book must be read to appreciate the skill with which she deals with this delicate matter, and Eliot's additional feeling of guilt.

The Emily Hale relationship was on quite a different footing from Eliot's friendship with Mary Trevelyan (who proposed to him twice), even if this association too is of considerable interest. In fact the attendant lords and ladies, who start a scene or two in Eliot's life, and move through both Letters and biography, make a vivid procession.

Arnold Bennett, 'a successful wholesale grocer . . . with a most disagreeable Cockney accent' (March 1917), rudely interrupts Eliot's conversation with W. B. Yeats, but they later become friends. Eliot prefers Wyndham Lewis's drawings (which he considers 'classical') to his writings. There is something not far from flirtations with Brigit Patmore and Mary Hutchison (wife of St John Hutchison, barrister; mistress of Clive Bell, art critic).

Brigit Patmore was mistress of Richard Aldington, a friend of Eliot's later to become an enemy, who begins to play an equivocal role towards the end of the Letters. (Aldington, called American by Lyndall Gordon, was English, though he worked for some years in the USA.)There is an interchange in the *Athenaeum* magazine between Eliot and a man called William H. Pollack, in which Eliot, quoting *Hamlet*, remarks: 'So look'd he once when in an angry parle he smote . . .' There is obviously a joke to be made, but it was in fact Eliot who was smiting a 'sledded Pollack', not vice versa.

Lyndall Gordon is good on John Hayward, the crippled man of letters who for some time shared a flat on the Embankment with Eliot. Hayward's complex personality, his somewhat terrifying manner and appearance, are not easy to put over, and she does this outstandingly well. In Eliot's later poems Hayward was at least as important an influence as Pound had been on earlier ones.

Finally, when (August 1921) negotiations were in progress with solicitors in connection with the launching of the *Criterion*, Eliot wrote to Sydney Schiff (his Proustian friend): 'I have seen Mr Broad'; could this have been the redoubtable Reggie Broad, balletomane, who looked like Stroheim, and, as a matter of routine, arranged that at every entr'acte two drinks (doubles) should be waiting (for himself) at the bar at Sadler's Wells? Reggie Broad *was* a solicitor.

The Letters of T. S. Eliot: Vol. 1:   1988
1898–1922, edited by Valerie Eliot,   *Daily Telegraph*
Faber.
Eliot's New Life, Lyndall Gordon,
Oxford University Press.

ROBERT GRAVES

Martin Seymour-Smith's penetrating, quirky, informative, unpompous approach is remarkably well adapted to the Graves story. In addition, Seymour-Smith, since the age of fourteen, has known and corresponded with Robert Graves, for a time tutoring one of the Graves children. In short there has been a close and uninhibited relationship for forty years, which makes for an extremely entertaining book.

Robert Graves, born in Wimbledon in 1895, came on his father's side from an Anglo-Irish family of some intellectual eminence, the same being true of the family of his German (half Schleswig-Danish) mother. This mélange of national characteristics seem to have set up something of an inner conflict from early childhood, causing a tendency to be at odds with other people. From boyhood existed also the determination to be a poet.

Graves's mother was a woman of deep piety, and in a sense, in spite of ups and downs in matters of sex, he himself has always retained a strong element of puritanism. While at Charterhouse – continued for a short time after leaving – he had a wholly innocent 'pash' for a boy and was greatly upset by the boy turning out less than well-behaved. By that time Graves had been swept into the war at the age of nineteen, serving with the Royal Welch Fusiliers, being severely wounded. His account of trench-warfare in *Goodbye to All That* (1929), an early autobiography written to make some quick money, is the best on record in English.

Graves's puritanism comes out in the trials of his first marriage to the fanatically feminist Nancy Nicholson (daughter of the painter William Nicholson), which bust up (one uses the colloquial phrase advisedly) some ten years later when, out of the frying-pan into the fire, he moved in with the American poet Laura Riding. If matrimonial entanglements were not in their way painful to read about, Seymour-Smith's account of both ladies, Nicholson and Riding, having simultaneous affairs with an Irish literary buffoon called Phibbs (which resulted in Riding jumping from a fourth-storey window, Graves from a third), would be side-splitting. Graves finally achieved a happy marriage and settled down in Mallorca, a base from which he was intermittently displaced by wars, but where he remained and grew famous. His own distrust of Fame always persisted, together with what Seymour-Smith speaks of as an external optimism tempered by an intense gloom and terror; a condition from which poetry offered the only escape.

Seymour-Smith deals skilfully with Graves's poetry, giving plenty of quotation, and showing the manner in which it has been, in its day, both 'traditional' and 'modern' – in a sense seeing 'modern' poetry out by its own vigour and endurance – and he notes that Graves remained consistently anti-Yeats, anti-Pound, anti-Auden.

A necessity for Graves's poetry to have a 'Muse', a role long filled by Laura Riding (with an extraordinary submission on Graves's part) so that Graves's later years, one can only say, have been plagued by love affairs with girls decades younger than himself. The poetry must be produced; the poetry cannot be produced without suffering; the suffering is generated by the girls. That at least appears to be the process. Although, in one sense, not caring for conventional forms of social life, in another Graves has never lived at all privately. Accordingly, there is nothing particularly indiscreet in going into his emotional involvements. At the same time, these sunset love affairs are not easily expressed in simple terms owing to the complications of Graves's temperament, one side of which is not without a certain naïvety.

Graves's prose writings are also well handled. They are astonishing in number, falling roughly into scholarly and pot-boiling, the last mostly historical novels. These are sometimes a shade stodgy, but include so lively a work as *I Claudius*. For a time Graves was caught up in the movie world, and projects to make a picture of Claudius were in the air long before the eventual serial on television.

The scholarly books (the degree to which they deserve that epithet is sometimes argued) fall roughly into the anthropological, like *The White Goddess*, or biblical/historical, like *The Nazarene Gospel Restored*. There are also translations from the Classics, and the work on Greek Myths. Graves's treatment of the Greek Myths is at times impaired by insistence that one or other of his views is the right one (to be found in others of his world too), but he has an enormously wide knowledge and his speculations are always unexpected and worth hearing. Naturally, all sorts of celebrated persons crop up in the story made impossible to reduce to any pattern by the sheer improbability of some of the episodes. I found it all compulsive reading.

Robert Graves: His Life and Work,   1982
Martin Seymour-Smith,   *Daily Telegraph*
Hutchinson.

SIEGFRIED SASSOON

I

Siegfried Sassoon (1886–1967) would have been the first to agree that he had rather an uncomfortable temperament. Such is indeed the main subject of this first published volume (1920–1922) of Diaries which he began in 1905, and carried on until 1956. The earlier diary material was more or less absorbed into the largely autobiographical volumes about Sassoon's alter ego Sherston, who first appeared as the Fox-hunting Man and the Infantry Officer. Sassoon told Rupert Hart-Davis (who has done here his accustomed impeccable job) that he gave up writing these semi-fictional memoirs because he found himself merely copying out the Diary; by which he set probably greater store.

I think Hart-Davis's self-effacement as editor might have allowed a short paragraph in the Introduction to state how odd Sassoon's position was in 1920. After war service of notable gallantry in which he had won an MC and had been recommended for a DSO, he had written a letter to his Commanding Officer saying that he would no longer obey orders as he disapproved of the war. This attempt to be court-martialled failed chiefly through the efforts of Robert Graves; Sassoon was sent to an army psychiatric hospital, in due course returning to another battalion, from which he was invalided after a wound.

In *Siegfried's Journey* Sassoon subsequently wrote that he did not regret this course of action, but in the light of future events thought a negotiated peace in 1917 would not have been permanent; an ambiguity of mind that is often reflected in the Diary. None the less Sassoon is remembered for his anti-war poems; limited perhaps but in their way memorable. Thus after the war ended Sassoon was left in a sense high and dry. He was in theory an ardent Socialist, in practice lived a life divided between fox-hunting or steeple-chasing (where he found the people boring), or London literary cliques (where he found the people boring too). He seems to have had about £1,100 a year, comfortable for a bachelor at that time, with which he was unusually (if slightly self-applaudingly) generous to other people.

The opening pages of the Diary are, to tell the truth, a bit stodgy. When Sassoon gets into his stride there is plenty of interest, both about the diarist himself and social life at the beginning of what was to be a

170

gaudy decade. The underlying theme is always the disquiets Sassoon suffered with his own homosexuality. In spite of his Socialism, and nine months in 1919 as Literary Editor of the *Daily Herald*, Sassoon existed as a well-to-do dilettante. He had two rooms in the house of W. J. Turner and his wife in Westminster. Sassoon on the whole got on well with Turner, an Australian poet and music critic, who had a name in literary circles for being polemical.

Sassoon's homosexual involvements (which appear to have been not at all of a promiscuous order) had begun with two young men before this volume opens, both of whom figure here. The first of these, in England, was Gabriel Atkin, an artist-illustrator; and P. (who remains anonymous, possibly still alive), evidently a young upper-class German. Although Hart-Davis does not mention this, Gabriel Atkin has gone down in history as having been given a pound by the rich Ronald Firbank who wanted to be taken out to dinner.

A figure who occurs quite often in Sassoon's pages is Nellie Burton (always referred to simply as Burton), who kept rooms for 'single gentlemen' at 40, Half Moon Street, and deserves a niche in the chronicle of the period. Wilde's friend Robbie Ross spent the last years of his life in her rooms, and among those who were also accommodated there known to Sassoon were Lord Berners and (Sir) Roderick Meiklejohn (sometime fellow secretary with Eddie Marsh of Asquith). Osbert Sitwell once took me to see Burton, a kind of Rosa Lewis of the Cavendish (but really quite different), with whom people would drop in to have tea. Of the retired nanny or lady's maid pattern, Burton had an inimitable style. In one entry Sassoon records: 'Her room was full of flowers, "sent," she explained, "on account of it being the anniversary of Robin Hollway shooting himself".'

Sassoon was on good terms with Thomas Hardy with whom he would stay from time to time, and appears to be unique in liking Hardy's irascible terrier Wessex; even writing a poem to Wessy. Edmund Gosse, when Sassoon dined with him, referred to 'an American poetaster named Eliot', and 'for Marcel Proust and James Joyce expressed the utmost abhorrence'. This last comment was in June 1922. In one of the notes Sassoon appended to the Diary at a later date he says: 'January 8th 1923: I am astonished to see Gosse's name among the nineteen signatories to the *Nouvelle Revue Française* (a memorial number dedicated to Proust's memory)'; a perfect Gosse story.

Sassoon himself did not find T. S. Eliot at all easy, and was upset by Eliot saying that 'all great art is based on a condition of fundamental boredom – *passionate boredom*.' Some little time after that Sassoon admitted he saw something of what Eliot meant. Sassoon's weakness as a diarist is in not being able to convey in a couple of words individual character – for instance giving no picture of strange personalities like

Roderick Meiklejohn (whom he saw quite often), or Christopher Millard, the bookseller.

Siegfried Sassoon Diaries, 1920–1922,   1982
edited and introduced by Rupert   *Daily Telegraph*
Hart-Davis, Faber.

II

There was presumably some substantial reason for publishing these war diaries of Siegfried Sassoon subsequently to the diaries covering the years 1920–22. Not only would the strictly chronological order have been more natural, but the diarist's immediately post-war mood and sense of flatness is much more understandable if the personal record of Sassoon's heroic period – the term is applicable both literally in connection with himself and historically because great events were being decided by battle – is available to the reader. I am, as it happens, only a rather moderate admirer of Sassoon's celebrated fictionalised narrative of those years, *The Memoirs of an Infantry Officer*, which so often has the air of being over-written. The war verse – 'scarifying' as Rupert Hart-Davis truly calls it – seems to me more effective as anti-war propaganda than poetry; even if a line like 'To mock the riddled corpses round Bapaume' haunts the memory. Whatever his own objections to being thus categorised, it is certainly as a war poet that Sassoon makes a valid claim to fame as a writer of verse.

The Memoirs of an Infantry Officer presents a comparatively mild and reasonable Sassoon, while the poetry displays a man at the end of his tether with horror and disgust; but the diary volume under review illustrates Sassoon's extremely complex nature, which could be aggressive and bellicose in the extreme. For example (June 1916): 'I rather want to see the summer out, and get the experience of a big battle which must surely come next month'; or (April 1917, only a few months before the 'wilful defiance'). 'But the fact remains that if I had the choice between England tomorrow and the battle, I would choose the battle without hesitation.' When, after his spell in an army psychiatric hospital to which he was sent, Sassoon returned to duty, he records (January 1918): 'I want to go back to one of the regular battalions. The other place is only a side-show, and I'd be with an inferior battalion.'

The following month, after he had been sent to Egypt: 'No tragedy. Nothing heroic. I *must* have the heroic.' (May 1918):

Damn leave; I don't want it. And I don't want to be wounded and wangle a job at home. I want the next six weeks, and success; do I want death? I don't know yet; but the war is outside life; and I'm in it.

Two things strike one in the story; first, the extraordinarily sensible manner in which the military authorities (against whom Sassoon was always railing) handled the situation when he made his statement about refusing to obey orders. At least some of the 'scarlet Majors at the Base', through whose hands the Sassoon case inevitably passed, took a balanced view. Secondly, how strange it must have been to return to normal regimental duty overseas after being the centre of an affair that at the time surely rocked anyway the more informed end of the Army. Sassoon was doing a very risky thing. He could easily have been shot. What would have happened, even with a reputation for bravery, without his having the ribbon of the MC on his tunic? He had, too, as friends, a lot of prominent people, but some at least of these were likely to be as much an embarrassment as a help. One cannot help feeling that when Lady Ottoline Morrell appears to have urged him, after return to England, to continue with his demonstrations against war, there was at least some parallel with those patriotic girls Sassoon was always complaining about who, just because they enjoyed the glamour, persuaded men to become soldiers.

An interesting aspect of this volume of war-time diaries is the almost wholly muted attitude towards Sassoon's homosexuality, more or less explicit in the volume already published, though the fact of his intimacy with Robbie Ross and others of the Old Guard of the Wilde circle is in its own way revealing enough. When Sassoon circularised writers and others known to him personally with his document of protest, Arnold Bennett wrote a notably rational reply, ending with the words: 'What is the matter with you is spiritual pride.'

Hart-Davis has done his usual excellent job of editing, but when Sassoon, complaining of the lowbrow tastes of his brother officers, writes: 'Their chief standard seems to be the *London Mail* and the illustrated papers with pictures by "Kichener" and (for a treat) *La Vie Parisienne*', the pictures were in fact by Kirchner, the Kirchner Girl providing some of the 'cheesecake' of that period.

Young poets – indeed writers of all kinds and ages – who hope that distinguished literary confrères will buy their works would do well to ponder a letter reproduced here from Edmund Gosse to Siegfried Sassoon just after the latter's volume of poems *The Old Huntsman* had appeared:

> saw the Poet Laureate [Robert Bridges] . . . and he had seen your poems in a shop. He could not cut the leaves, but he read where he could. He is a rare and grudging praiser, and therefore I was much gratified at his warm commendation of several of your pieces.

Siegfried Sassoon Diaries, 1915–1918,   1983
edited and introduced by Rupert   *Daily Telegraph*
Hart-Davis, Faber.
The War Poems of Siegfried Sassoon,
arranged and introduced by
Rupert Hart-Davis, Faber.

III

This third volume of Sassoon Diaries resembles its immediate predecessor by beginning quietly, rather prosily, then slowly involving the
reader in Sassoon's life so that towards the close there is even a sense of
tension as to what will happen. The narrative is given shape by opening
with Sassoon lodging in the W. J. Turners' house in Tufton Street,
Westminster, ending with him leaving there and renting a flat of his
own in Campden Hill Square.

Sassoon made fair copies of most of these diaries. Hart-Davis says
that little seems to have been removed except entries that might have
pained the diarist's own family. Sassoon did, however, specifically
leave a note to the effect that he had taken out all references to love
affairs. As Sassoon's homosexuality was, he writes, 'the subject nearest
my heart', this often causes speculation as to relationships especially
when an entry is followed by a page being torn out: for example, in the
case of old 'Enrico' Festing-Jones (lifelong companion of Samuel
Butler) with whom Sassoon would from time to time dine.

The tone of the Diaries is conspicuously unhappy. After his gallant
and star-crossed war career Sassoon could not adapt himself to the
civilian life of a professional poet with an income of his own. He found
hunting people boring, was equally irritated by intellectuals, even more
by those who led a purely social life. He was perpetually complaining of
their smugness, and lack of moral backbone. It does not seem to have
occurred to Sassoon, or at least not often, that he himself might be
thought self-righteous, nor that his verse represented the backwoods of
poetry. He seems to have been, in general, hostile towards all that was
then looked on as 'modern'.

This extreme intellectual conservatism (combined with theoretical
socialism in politics) leads to several vignettes of writers and poets of an
older generation whom Sassoon tended to see more of than, say, his old
friend Robert Graves, or the Sitwells whose intermittent ragging he
took with desperate seriousness. He had always been a friend of
Thomas Hardy and Edmund Gosse. Here we are shown the then Poet
Laureate Robert Bridges, Ralph Hodgson, and suchlike figures of an
earlier date.

Gosse reported that when Bridges went to Buckingham Palace as
Poet Laureate, 'he said, hoity-toity-ish to Lord Stamfordham, "Under-
stand that I don't want any of your Stars and Garters." Lord
Stamfordham replied suavely, "His Majesty will not trouble you, Mr
Bridges."' Bridges could see nothing in Hardy's poetry, and thought
Scott, 'except for a few lyrics,' no better than Macaulay. Ralph
Hodgson looked forward to a time when Shakespeare would be
replaced in schools by Bernard Shaw and Ibsen.

That Sassoon's life was oddly organised at this period may be seen by an entry for 13 February 1924:

> In bed all day (as usual). Haddock and baked apple at 5.30 p.m. Soup, omelette, and stewed prunes at the Monico 10.45. Since then, reading Wycherley's *Plain Dealer*, and very dreary stuff it seemed. It is now 4 a.m. and I've just had some tea and bolted three sponge cakes.

Elsewhere in the Diaries he confesses to a weakness for sparkling burgundy. He was an occasional prison visitor (Pentonville), something which he seems to have enjoyed as little as did the incarcerated 'bigamist Yorkshire farmer' or the 'over-enthusiastic scoutmaster' whom he went to see.

The drama which slowly unfolds is Sassoon getting increasingly fed-up with W. J. Turner, an Australian literary and musical critic, in whose house he lived. He could not bring himself to quit, because he thought Turner unable to afford the house without his contribution. In point of fact Turner seems to have been earning considerably more money than Sassoon supposed, though he would touch Sassoon from time to time for relatively large sums, then complain that he was mean. This included being given a car by Sassoon. Turner later advised E. M. Forster, in Sassoon's presence, 'Never to get a car! It is the most exhausting and unpleasant form of recreation.' I have to admit that I got on well with Turner, just after the war, during the few months before his death when he was Literary Editor of the *Spectator*, but one could see that he might be difficult. Certainly he was a man of many rows.

While living at Tufton Street, Sassoon, as a friend of Delphine Turner, was particularly disturbed by her husband having an affair with a young 'Miss N', with whom Turner seemed to contemplate marriage, as she was the daughter of extremely rich parents. This was on top of musical differences with Turner which had resulted in Turner being free to play (allegedly badly) on Sassoon's piano, but not Sassoon himself. All sorts of extraneous people joined in this marital row of the Turners, including Lady Ottoline Morrell (an old friend of Sassoon's dating from his wartime pacifist demonstration), who entered the rumpus in Turner's interests. A book by Turner was, in fact, on the brink of appearing which lampooned Lady Ottoline so that ructions continued unabated on another front. All this has its entertaining side, apart from the picture of the period that is built up. Sassoon was undoubtedly a nice man, but without much humour. Notwithstanding, he prided himself on being a satirist.

Hart-Davis does his usual excellent job of telling you who everybody is, essentially and briefly. He slips up once. The George Villiers with

whom Sassoon supped at Painswick in September 1925, was not
'(1883–1969) son of the seventh Earl of Jersey', but (1891–1942),
grandson of the 7th Earl of Clarendon. The former, although George
was one of his names, was always called Arthur.

Siegfried Sassoon Diaries, 1923–1925,   1985
edited and introduced by Rupert   *Daily Telegraph*
Hart-Davis, Faber.

D. H. LAWRENCE

I

This book was well worth compiling, and its editor, Anthony Beal, is to be congratulated. It collects together over 400 pages of D. H. Lawrence's literary criticism, thereby forming a fairly coherent picture of what he thought about books and writers. I say 'fairly' because although it is not difficult to grasp what Lawrence did *not* like in life and letters, to agree about what he *did* like is not so easy. Two points, however, emerge with some clarity: the first, that he was a very 'clever' man – a writer with a really powerful brain. This is sometimes forgotten in the atmosphere of conflict and confusion that thrives round his name. The second point is that his whole approach seems largely inappropriate to the world of literature.

Lawrence was a frustrated politician or preacher. He wanted power: to force people to do his will. He was temperamentally unable to understand that different people by their nature may require to live different lives; and, accordingly, to find their expression in different forms of art. Everyone must be crammed into the Procrustean, or rather Laurentian, bed: stretched out or lopped off. It must be admitted that this method produces some amusing results, and a great deal of enjoyable vituperation. Lawrence regarded himself as essentially in revolt against such nineteenth-century writers as Flaubert, Ibsen, Thomas Hardy, 'the intellectual, hopeless people'; also, on the whole, against the Russian nineteenth-century writers about whom he has interesting things to say, especially Dostoevsky, 'like the rat, slithering along in hate, in the shadows, and, in order to belong to the light, professing love, all love'.

Rather unexpectedly he likes Petronius. With reservations, he is well disposed to Herman Melville; *In Our Time* by Ernest Hemingway receives some praise: and – in a moment of reviewing for *Vogue* – Lawrence enjoyed *The Station* by Robert Byron. But on the whole he is found in attack: attacks which, at their worst, are like endless and infinitely egotistical sermons.

The truth was that Lawrence's personal conceit, also, one cannot help feeling, his envy, were both unrestrained. By this I do not of course mean that proper reliance on self which must be the ultimate basis of all art. I mean the rage that possesses Lawrence when he comes in contact with any writer, indeed any person, who might be thought in competition with himself. Usually without humour (a rarity among English novelists) he also lacks the self-control necessary to a critic of the first rank; but this does not prevent much of his criticism from being acute and stimulating.

Perhaps the best section of this volume is that containing his *Studies in Classic American Literature*. Here the violence of Lawrence's manner seems to fit the subject in hand. He is fond of using the method (by which any book on earth can be made to sound silly) of recounting the plot in his own contemptuous words; but, when dealing with Fenimore Cooper, Poe, Whitman, a less knockabout approach might also have been less effective.

To read through this book is to be made painfully aware of the ups and downs of Lawrence's own health. From a clear statement of his critical point of view, when writing at his best, he will suddenly descend into a morass of apocalyptic denunciation (for example, the latter part of *Study of Thomas Hardy*) literally impossible to understand, while some of the passages that seek to describe, say, the behaviour of women ('the Female Principle') when their obscurity is unravelled strike one as of very doubtful psychological value.

Lawrence represents a form of neo-Romanticism perhaps not so different from that of many of his contemporaries against whom he felt himself so strongly in opposition – the old Bloomsbury doctrine that if you feel it you really ought to do it. He is often seen at his best when attacking behaviour of which he might be expected to approve, for example Bosinney and Irene in *The Forsyte Saga* ('the whole thing is doggy to a degree'); but there were no doubt simple-minded readers of Galsworthy and Lawrence who supposed that Bosinney and Irene were doing just what Lawrence recommended.

Lawrence was in a way too gifted; at least too lacking in self-discipline to control his gifts to their best advantage. Leaning heavily towards the state of being primarily a poet, he was chiefly, as it turned out, concerned with writing novels. As a novelist, with all his force, he is never wholly at ease with the medium. He himself is the only character who ever truly emerges. The style is often facetious and uneven. His short stories, where extended play of character is not required, are often more effective. He is perhaps best of all in remarkable descriptive passages like the evocative Australian opening of *Kangaroo*.

D. H. Lawrence: Selected Literary   1956
Criticism, edited by Anthony Beal,   *Punch*
Heinemann.

II

This first volume of the eight-volume Letters of D. H. Lawrence is impeccably edited by James T. Boulton (also General Editor). There is a full genealogical tree to explain relationships, and maps to illustrate Lawrence's surroundings in England and during his journeys on the Continent.

Though gifted poet and short-story writer, Lawrence's novels, notwithstanding brilliant passages, are marred by turgidity, ranting, sheer lack of reality, but he was scarcely capable of writing a dull letter, though his letters might sometimes be silly, occasionally unpleasant. All, even the most intimate, are signed 'D. H. Lawrence' or 'DHL', except one, written when depressed, which ends 'D. H. Gummidge'. The first letter applies for a job as book-keeper when he was sixteen, but for practical purposes the letters begin when he was twenty. They fall into roughly four groups: the period when Lawrence was still in Nottinghamshire; his time of teaching at Croydon; the moment when he falls ill with pneumonia in 1911; his meeting in the following year with Frieda (née von Richthofen), wife of Professor Ernest Weekley, and Lawrence's elopement with her.

All these groups have their own special interest. It is impossible not to be struck by the astonishingly good education Lawrence, as a miner's son, received as long ago as 1900, and, when he was twenty-three or twenty-four, the easy manner in which he was meeting all the literary world of London. Most of these earlier letters, half-flirtatious, half-intellectual, are written to a group of young school-teachers (much the ambience of the second Mrs Thomas Hardy) who all kept the correspondence, though few of them can be said to have been very well treated by Lawrence. Lawrence himself in this early period emerges as lively, gay (not in the sense sometimes so inappropriately used), and remarkably intelligent. At twenty he is pontificating on avoidance of adjectives and the importance of terseness in style (which he might have later remembered); at twenty-two he sees Sarah Bernhardt in *La Dame aux Camélias* at the Theatre Royal, Nottingham; a few months later takes a dislike to *A Shropshire Lad*. There are all sorts of interesting comments on books in the letters of this period.

At first Lawrence was tormented by loneliness in London, and, anyway in this volume, he continued to keep up with the friends of his home neighbourhood where his feelings were deeply rooted. At twenty-three he was writing to one of his female correspondents that he could never kiss a girl on the mouth on account of the 'life force', and two years later he analyses to another girl the intimacy of the bond between himself and his mother, then dying. Here is the beginning of what was to build up to an enormous and not very happy structure of Lawrentian information.

Would it have been better – anyway less bad – if people like Ford Madox Ford and Edward Garnett (a good influence on many writers) had not dinned into Lawrence that he was a 'genius'? The term, one of the burdens bequeathed by the late nineteenth century, is on the whole a handicap to serious writers and painters. Lawrence was by nature quite sufficiently unselfcritical to get along without a lot of hangers-on telling him that he was just how he should be. In the early stages his egocentricity, anyway so far as having manuscripts published was concerned, had been held within bounds. On 1 April 1910, for example, he wrote to Heinemann's regarding the novel that was to become *The White Peacock*: 'I am sorry also, that I could not compress it any further . . . if there is anything further I can do, I shall be very glad. I am the most docile, the most amenable of pens.' That was all much changed by 1912, a fateful year, when Lawrence came out of hospital, broke off his engagement of two years (which had itself, on impulse, taken the place of a previous betrothal) and resigned from his teaching post, hoping to earn a living by writing.

The meeting with Frieda in March was an explosion. Lawrence had been one of her husband Professor Weekley's pupils. The two went off together after six weeks, Frieda leaving her three children. They travelled to Metz, where Frieda's father, a colonel, was administrative officer of the German garrison. Lawrence was almost immediately arrested as a spy.

Frieda, about six years older than Lawrence, was well up to his weight. She had recently had two other lovers and was unfaithful to Lawrence himself within a few months of the elopement. Nevertheless, so far as it went, they suited each other. They roamed together through Germany, Austria, Italy with next to no money (regarding money, Lawrence was always immensely generous). This absorbing run of letters ends with Frieda's divorce going through.

Throughout his writing life Lawrence used his acquaintances as characters in novels, scarcely bothering to alter their names. There had been trouble about a girl called Alice Hall appearing as Alice Gall in *The White Peacock*. I was gratified that Lawrence should write (20 February 1911): 'I will contrive to have, in the next impression, the name changed to Margaret Undine Widmerpuddle.' Incidentally, when Lawrence wrote (11 April 1912) to Walter De La Mare (reader for Heinemann), 'And to call me C. E. Lawrence is – well! – ' this was not a mere misprint. C. E. Lawrence was a prolific novelist of the period (quite awful) and, as it happened, reader for John Murray, Professor Weekley's publisher.

The Letters of D. H. Lawrence. Vol. I: 1979
September 1901–May 1913, edited by   *Daily Telegraph*
James T. Boulton, Cambridge
University Press.

III

The second volume of D. H. Lawrence Letters, although covering only a few months more than three years, takes Lawrence from a world at peace into a world devoured by war. The letters demonstrate with extraordinary clearness how the First World War sent Lawrence off the rails. No doubt he would have gone off the rails in due course anyway, his tubercular conditions certainly playing a malign part in frenzies of nerves, but the war brought the first burst of apocalyptic denunciations that were to continue until the end of his life.

That Lawrence should have felt the war as a peculiar disaster to himself was not altogether unreasonable. He had not long before eloped with Frieda Weekley, née von Richthofen, who came of a German military family. Cousins of hers fell in action within the first few months. The mere fact of having a German wife was awkward enough. Not only that, but previously, in their frequent moments of financial crisis, Frieda could usually get money from Germany. As Lawrence's standards were entirely regulated by the extent to which he himself was able to live the life he wished to live, the war seemed merely an absurdity devised to inconvenience him. He was neither patriotic nor pacifist. Indeed he rather despised the Bloomsbury pacifists, at one moment saying he would like to kill two million Germans; at another, however, advocating surrender.

The real ravings can almost be dated as starting in January 1915, when Lawrence wrote letters to Lady Ottoline Morrell (beginning 'I have burnt your letter about Duncan Grant'); to E. M. Forster ('I am tired to death of the infant crying in the Night'), and to Lady Cynthia Asquith ('The War finished me: it was the spear through the side of all sorrows and hopes'). These wartime letters are on the whole a contrast to the period just before when he was living at Lerici, existing courageously on small amounts earned by poems and short stories, having rows with Frieda, but on the whole liking Italy.

The war brought on the crazy scheme of founding a community of twenty or thirty individuals sympathetic to each other, presided over by Lawrence. The constant application to his own position of a Spear in the Side, the Sepulchre, Judases, Resurrection and so forth, date from the same period. Of the individuals earmarked for the island-community there is not one candidate mentioned by name in this volume with whom Lawrence did not have a greater or lesser row during the period covered. Among them were Philip Heseltine (the composer Peter Warlock) and Michael Arlen (still Dikran Kouyoum-djian, an Armenian, not Jewish as described by Lady Ottoline), both of whom were to figure unfavourably in Lawrence novels.

It is only fair to say that even the greatest bosh – and some of it here is quite unmitigated – is written with an extreme liveliness. But during the period of cottages in Cornwall there are other letters, in quite another manner, to the painter Mark Gertler, giving instructions to send Lawrence's belongings to the country; to Lawrence's landlord on the subject of siting a second earth-closet, and to S. S. Koteliansky ('Kot'), trying to buy a typewriter ribbon, which are all in their own way very funny.

Kot, a Russian Jew who had come to England in 1911, seems to have been the person uniquely capable of handling Lawrence. He would stand no nonsense from him whatever and consequently is perhaps the only person with whom Lawrence never seems to have quarrelled. Lawrence wrote some wonderfully scathing letters to Bertrand Russell, describes his old friend Middleton Murry as a 'toad', and his letters to his patron Eddie Marsh are almost always of interest. It is to be noted that Lawrence uses the term 'the establishment', sometimes dated as a much later idiom, exactly as it is employed today.

His literary tastes are always entertaining. Colette was 'jolly good'; Belloc 'conceited, full of that French showing-off which goes down so well in England'; and 'one ought to be downright cruel to W. H. Davies and say "Davies, your work is getting like Birmingham tinware; Davies, you drop your Hs, and everybody is tempering the wind to you"'. Lawrence delighted in Petronius and Swinburne, but disliked Malory and Dostoevsky.

The Letters are extensively edited, but Lawrence, who was keen on correctness in such matters, would have been intensely irritated by ineptitudes in the Notes like 'Lady Mary St Helier' for Mary, Lady St Helier, or 'Lord Alfred Harmsworth Northcliffe' for Alfred Harmsworth, Lord Northcliffe. When (22 March 1914) Lawrence writes, 'it will be a kind of aesthetic qualification to know you, as it was to know Beardsley, and is rather now, to know Alastair', this is not Aleister Crowley, as editorially suggested, but H. H. von Voight, an illustrator feebly in the Beardsley manner, who signed himself 'Alastair'. In a letter (26 December 1913) to Ezra Pound 'I don't know who Preston is, or what is *The Egoist*,' the unidentified 'Preston' would have been E. Hayter Preston, a journalist concerned with Pound at that moment, and in the 1930s Literary Editor of the *Sunday Referee*.

The Letters of D. H. Lawrence. Vol. II: 1982
June 1913 to October 1916, edited by   *Daily Telegraph*
George J. Zytaruk and James T.
Boulton, Cambridge University
Press.

IV

These 700 pages of D. H. Lawrence's letters open with him still in Cornwall during the war, whence he was expelled by the authorities, retreating to London, Berkshire, and Derbyshire. Lawrence was generally speaking a lively, even brilliant, letter-writer, but one gets desperately sick of his complaints, and prophecies about the course of the war and public life, which were without exception incorrect, and continued to be so throughout this volume.

He made a great hard-luck story about being ordered out of Cornwall as a coastal area, saying it was only on account of his German wife. But the musician, Cecil Gray, who also had a Cornish cottage at that period and saw a good deal of the Lawrences, used to say that they had made themselves enormously unpopular in the neighbourhood, would sing German songs at night and took no trouble whatsoever about such regulations as shading lights – a wartime offence for which Gray himself was fined. The mood improves a great deal when the war is over and Lawrence gets out of England, first of all to Florence. Even at his worst in these letters there are sudden bursts of accomplished descriptive writing – snow in Derbyshire, or fields of corn in Sicily – which seem to flow spontaneously from his pen and make the landscape in front of him come alive. There are also plenty of literary opinions (for example, to Catherine Carswell, 27 November 1916):

> No, I don't like Turgenev very much: he seems so very critical, like Katherine Mansfield, and also a sort of male old maid. . . . They are all – Turgenev, Tolstoi, Dostoevsky, Maupassant, Flaubert – so very obvious and coarse, beside the lovely mature and sensitive art of Fennimore Cooper and Hardy. It seems to me that our English art, at its best, is by far the subtlest and loveliest and most perfect in the world. . . . Take even D'Annunzio and my Trespasser – how much cruder and stupider D'Annunzio is, really.

At the period covered by this volume Lawrence had written *The White Peacock* (1910), *The Trespasser* (1912), *Sons and Lovers* (1913), *The Rainbow* (1915), *The Prussian Officer* stories (1914), with various books of poems, essays, travel sketches, and a couple of plays. *The Rainbow* had been suppressed and he was having a certain amount of trouble with the manuscript of *Women in Love* (1920), both from the point of view of censorship and libel. To be Lawrence's publisher or literary agent was a most unenviable job, and in fairness to Lawrence he was the first to agree on this point. His affairs were first of all handled by Pinker, agent for quite a number of well-known writers, who certainly does not appear to have been very adroit in Lawrence's business. For a time Lawrence made his own contracts, with an American friend, a journalist called Robert Mountsier, dealing with rights in America, then he went to Curtis Brown, of whom he was critical almost before making the first arrangements.

It must be remembered that Lawrence was living on a shoe-string, book by book, all the time, and the Italian exchange rate (in which he took a keen interest) was always sliding.

Of personal relationships that with Kot – S. S. Koteliansky – remained by far the best. Kot was almost the only friend to whom Lawrence was always warm. A more surprising association was with Compton Mackenzie, whose humour, dash, theatrical manner of conducting life, certainly charmed Lawrence, though not always uncritically. One of Lawrence's fantasies was that he would take a steam-yacht to the South Seas with Compton Mackenzie, a project that never came off.

With Lady Cynthia Asquith, Lawrence is always a shade more circumspect than with most of his correspondents, but undoubtedly they got on well. On the other hand to Middleton Murry, once to be one of the chosen for the colony of ideal friends, Lawrence wrote (30 January 1920):

> But as a matter of fact, what it amounts to is that you are a dirty little worm, and you take the ways of a dirty little worm. But let me tell you at last that I know it – not that it's anything new: and let it be plainly understood between you and me that I consider you a dirty little worm; and so, deposit your dirty bit of venom where you like: at any rate we know what to expect.

One notes that Lawrence wrote to Kot from Derbyshire (14 March 1919):

> I am not going to be left to Frieda's tender mercies until I am well again. She really is a devil – and I feel as if I would part from her for ever – let her go to Germany, while I take another road.

In the same year he was writing to Eddie Marsh about fixing up a lecture tour in America, and, even more extraordinary, in 1920 talked of putting an advertisement in the *Nairobi Herald* to get a job on a farm in Kenya. Alas, a Lawrence novel about the Happy Valley was never given a chance to take shape. Among unidentified items, could not 'Jerusalem' (p. 34) mean Blake's 'Jerusalem', and 'Time for us to go – as the song is' (p. 87), surely Pew in the play of *Treasure Island*?

The Letters of D. H. Lawrence. Vol. III:				1984
October 1916–June 1921, edited by		*Daily Telegraph*
James T. Boulton and Andrew
Robertson, Cambridge University
Press.

V

This fourth volume of D. H. Lawrence's Letters contains 848 letters of which over 300 are hitherto unpublished; others are printed in full for the first time. Many deal with business matters involving publishers or agents, not necessarily less interesting for that reason. Lawrence's violent feelings did not prevent him from being on the whole businesslike, though his perpetual moving about and the comparatively small sums he earned make one wonder how at times he managed to keep going. No one who has been following the Letters, or read a certain amount about Lawrence, will need to be reminded of his chronic inconsistency of opinion, his rage against the world and his inability to consider any point of view but his own, something which was perpetually changing. He was, of course, a very sick man, always inveighing against neurotics, while being himself one of the most neurotic of writers.

For example, from Ceylon (March 1922) to Robert Pratt Barlow, an acquaintance in Sicily: 'I really think the most living clue of life in us Englishmen is England, and the great mistake we make is not uniting together in the strength of this real living clue.' Rather less than a year later he writes to Middleton Murry: 'And at the moment I can't come to England. Something inside me simply doesn't let me. I mistrust my country too much to identify myself with it any more.'

Incidentally, the 'Cunard' in the earlier letter was almost certainly Victor Cunard, living in Italy at that time, a very likely homosexual friend for Pratt Barlow.

During this period Lawrence published among other books and stories, *Women in Love, Sea and Sardinia, England, my England, The Ladybird, The Fox, The Captain's Doll, Kangaroo*; visited Ceylon, Australia, New Mexico, Mexico, England, France, Germany. At the end of this volume he is returning to New Mexico in 1924.

One of the few people with whom Lawrence remained on good terms was his mother-in-law, Baroness Anna von Richthofen, to whom he wrote fairly regularly (in German), always in affectionate terms. His extreme generosity about money should also be emphasised, which included re-paying debts of £5 to Eddie Marsh and £15 to Lady Ottoline Morrell, fifteen years after these had been incurred. He also wrote, as we can see in several examples printed here, accomplished letters of condolence.

Early in this volume comes the row with Philip Heseltine (Peter Warlock, the composer), who considered himself and his wife libelled in *Women in Love*. In one sense, it is true, the character Halliday is quite unlike Heseltine; in another, no one who knew Heseltine even as little as I did could suppose for a moment Heseltine was not intended. Lawrence was enraged by the libel-suit, inveighing against Heseltine's malice, shadiness, wish for publicity, but after all Lawrence knew Heseltine's characteristics before he devised the offensive portrait. The same was true of the portrayal of Lady Ottoline in the novel.

Lawrence was not always humourless. When his friend Koteliansky (Kot) was, with Lawrence's help, translating from the Russian Ivan Bunin's short story 'The Gentleman from San Francisco', Lawrence wanted him to leave uncorrected the phrase 'a little curved peeled-off dog' (it appeared, in the end, as 'a tiny, cringing, hairless little dog').

His rows with Mabel Dodge Lunan, the rich American lady, to some extent his patron in New Mexico, are very amusing, because Lawrence would be as rude to her as he knew how, while she was perfectly capable of standing up to him. One feels on Lawrence's side when he protested to her that the only way to 'help' the American Indians was to leave them alone. In the previous volumes Lawrence was about as uncivil to Middleton Murry as would be possible. Calling him a worm was one of the least damaging epithets. This did not prevent them making it up, and Murry nearly joined the Lawrences in New Mexico. Lawrence did go so far as admit he was glad that did not happen. The 'Mr Mortimer' (so described also in the index) attacked by Murry in the *Adelphi* was obviously Raymond Mortimer.

Turning to the 'definitive' edition of *Women in Love*, I was appalled. No lesser phrase can be used. All suggestion that a novel might be a book to read for entertainment, even if at a high level of entertainment, is abandoned. Here is purely a machine for the grinder out of theses and dissertations. The edition would be an elaborate affair for, say, the Dead Sea Scrolls; for a novel about the 1920s it seems altogether inappropriate. To begin with every page is marked off with a numeral in the margin at every fifth line. I can imagine nothing more off-putting. Lawrence made several versions before the final *Women in Love*, so there is an introduction of 60 pages. So be it. That settles the text, which was no doubt corrupt hitherto. At the end of the book are 58 pages of 'Explanatory Notes', 40 pages of 'textual Apparatus'. Do we really have to be told why Sodom was notorious; what was the Sword of Damocles; what are the Ritz and the Venus de Milo; who was Cassandra, etc? On top of everything the editors do not know the difference between a Baron and a Baronet (see page 531). Why does Lawrence provoke such extraordinary reactions?

The Letters of D. H. Lawrence. Vol. 4:   1987
1921–1924, edited by Warren Roberts,   *Daily Telegraph*
James T. Boulton and Elizabeth
Mansfield, Cambridge University
Press.
Women in Love, D. H. Lawrence,
edited by David Farmer, Lindeth
Vasey and John Worthen,
Cambridge University Press.

VI

This entertaining – at times slightly horrifying – book by the novelist Sean Hignett (who had a D. H. Lawrence Fellowship at the University of New Mexico and actually met Brett) offers all sorts of new points of interest about ground often covered. The two main features are the rebellion of an upper-class girl in Edwardian times, and the life with D. H. Lawrence, chiefly in New Mexico. It also illustrates the principle, which cannot be repeated too often, that what is thought of as 'The Twenties' really began, both in the arts and in social loosening up, before the outbreak of war in 1914.

The Hon. Dorothy Brett (1883–1977) was one of the daughters of the 2nd Viscount Esher. The Bretts had been raised to the Peerage (with a Master of the Rolls who married an Alsatian, in 1885), but it was Reginald, 2nd Lord Esher (married to a Belgian), who became a public figure of considerable influence. The family had no hereditary landed connection, and may be seen as one a little different from the characteristic House of Lords group of that period.

Esher's taste for power can be judged by the fact that he refused the Viceroyalty of India, preferring to be *éminence grise* as Governor and Constable of Windsor Castle. From there he exercised a powerful influence over Edward VII; a great many other people too. He was bisexual (with a distinct bias towards his own sex), astonishingly able, and of unattractive character, as may be seen from this book. Esher was passionately attached to his second son, but did not greatly care about his other children, who were brought up, the daughters especially, in a manner to leave them hopelessly immature.

This was Dorothy Brett's background. Her qualifications for life were not improved by being sexually assaulted, at the age of about fourteen or fifteen, by 'Loulou', 1st Viscount Harcourt. About twenty-five years later Harcourt, whose reputation in that field was to say the least dubious, made a similar attack on a boy, the late Edward James, an eccentric figure, who died very recently. Sean Hignett says James was twelve years old, but the story I have always heard was that Harcourt, anticipating trouble from the boy's mother, Mrs Willie James, took an overdose. That was in 1922, which would have made James fourteen, and at Eton.

Brett owed the fact that she was called by her surname to having been trained as a painter at the Slade school where girls were always so designated. With her it stuck, as with her contemporary Carrington. Brett had an undoubted touch of talent, though not a large one. In spite of her awkwardness, plainness, the deafness that overtook her early on, she fitted in pretty well to the bohemian life of an art student. Notwithstanding the disapproval of her father, with whom she had a complex relationship, she settled into this world, and she crops up in records of the territory stretching between Bloomsbury and Augustus John. Aldous Huxley, for example, rather unpleasantly one feels, introduces her in *Crome Yellow* as a deaf young woman staying at his caricature of Lady Ottoline's Garsington.

Despite the easy-going sexual mode of her contemporaries, Brett, owing to a natural timidity – the Loulou Harcourt incident and perhaps her obsession with her father – did not lose her virginity until her fortieth year, and then with the egregious John Middleton Murry as by that time she had drifted into that orbit, which of course included D. H. Lawrence.

The first meeting was at the Café Royal, when Lawrence vomited, after following up a good deal of drink with a glass of port. This was where Lawrence asked for recruits for his ideal community of friends, now to be situated in New Mexico (which Lawrence preferred to be spoken of simply as Mexico, rather a different thing). Several volunteered, but in the end the company boiled down to the two Lawrences and Brett. By that time Frieda Lawrence, too, had been having an affair with Middleton Murry, and at one moment it even seemed possible that Frieda might go off with Murry and Lawrence marry Brett.

Eventually the party arrived at Taos where Mabel Dodge Luhan, an American whose third husband was an Indian, had arranged for Lawrence to have accommodation. Taos had been an artists' colony since 1896, so locals, including Indians, were fairly conversant with the antics of writers and painters, though even there Brett's cowboy outfit, with a stiletto in her boot like a dart, caused apprehension.

Rows inconceivable now took place between Lawrence, Frieda, Brett, Mabel Dodge Luhan and anyone else who happened to have a taste for quarrelling. The ever-debated question – did Brett sleep with Lawrence? – is answered fairly definitely, allowing for Brett being a considerable fantasist, by a sealed account she left to be opened only after her death describing how on two nights running Lawrence entered her bed and was unable to show himself effective. Some still doubt the truth of this.

Brett lived until aged ninety-three, often in severe straits for money and having a wretched time. During other interludes, however, she did not do too badly. One of those roundings off of the story for which novelists are always castigated for 'contriving' was that Edward James, Loulou Harcourt's other victim, turned up in New Mexico, and was not wholly approved of by Brett. I think that when Brett (who couldn't spell) writes 'the "Nuts" at the Slade suddenly realised my existence,' this does not refer to Professor 'Nutty' Brown, head of the art school, but meant 'knuts', slang of the period for dandies or bloods – perhaps a double joke in the light of Professor Brown, and nut-brown ale.

Brett: From Bloomsbury to New Mexico.   1985
A Biography, Sean Hignett, Hodder.   *Daily Telegraph*

RABINDRINATH TAGORE

The name of Rabindranath Tagore sharply evokes the Edwardian mystic mood, bowls of pot-pourri, poems in limp bindings with a velvet marker, The-Wisdom-of-the-East-in-one-volume, withdrawn genius, a suggestion of incense . . . Perhaps this is unfair, but one should begin by stating one's own prejudices.

Tagore was born at Calcutta in 1861, of a rich, aristocratic, intelligent and enlightened family. His own gifts marked him out at an early age. He wrote poems, short stories, plays, mainly in Bengali, but also in English. He became the outstanding figure in Indian literary and semi-political life, dying in 1941. Krishna Kripalani, who writes this biography, married Tagore's grand-daughter and worked with him at Santiniketan, Tagore's school in Bengal, from 1933 until the founder's death. He has carried off what must have been a most difficult task with considerable distinction and some quiet humour.

To the reader in this country perhaps the most interesting side of the book is the picture it provides, as it were incidentally, of the relationship of an Indian of Tagore's standing to English life. Kripalani is particularly successful in conveying what might be called the Indian Love-Hate Lyric to England, sentiments which must be in some ways without parallel in the history of one race ruling another.

Tagore seems to have been extraordinarily skilful in making sympathetic British contacts, which he appears to have brought about, certainly later, by emphasising, rather than underplaying, his own 'orientalism'. More than once one feels that the Indian situation – Britain bringing unity and peace in the eighteenth century, the development and rise of Indian nationalism in the nineteenth, the inevitable sundering apart of the twentieth – was bedevilled by social rather than political considerations. The Mutiny may have been ruthlessly repressed: Mohandas Gandhi and Jawaharlal Nehru incarcerated from time to time to cool off; the trouble was really not there, but in an utterly different way of looking at life. Even Tagore, supposedly a liberal of liberals, often in trouble with the nationalists for 'un-Indian' conduct, married a girl of eleven, and set the Brahmin children apart at his own school.

It is now fashionable to blame the memsahibs for setting up a barrier between Indian and Briton, but Tagore's career, with its close contacts with English life and literature, show how near, and yet how far, things always were.

Tagore himself was, in theory, starkly opposed to much that has become associated with 'the East'. He detested the Indian philosophy – Maya – that the universe is an illusion.

Alas, my cheerless country [he wrote], dressed in worn-out rags, loaded with decrepit wisdom, you pride yourself on your subtlety in having seen through the fraud of creation. Sitting idly in your corner, all you do is to sharpen the edge of your metaphysical mumbo-jumbo and dismiss as unreal this boundless, star-studded sky and this great, big earth whose lap has nurtured a myriad forms of life, age after age. Millions of living beings make up the vast fair of this world, and you, unbelieving dotard, ignore it all as a child's play.

In rather the same way when, in 1921, Gandhi came to Calcutta to persuade Tagore to give active political support to his movement, and his supporters collected large bundles of foreign cloth from nearby shops and burnt them outside to show solidarity, Tagore said:

Come and look over the edge of my veranda, Gandhiji. Look down there and see what your non-violent followers are up to. They have stolen cloth from the shops in the Chitpore Road, they have lit that bonfire in my courtyard and are now howling round it like a lot of demented dervishes. Is that non-violence?

However, Krishna Kripalani does not conceal that Tagore was often inconsistent himself. As his fame grew he was treated with almost divine reverence by his admirers. When he posed for Epstein, the sculptor noted how two American women left Tagore's presence backwards, their hands raised in worship. Epstein felt this inappropriate in one who had written 'I am he that sitteth among the poorest, the loneliest, and the lost,' and sardonically recorded: 'It has been remarked that my bust of him rests upon the beard, an unconscious piece of symbolism.' Tagore annoyed D. H. Lawrence too, who wrote an angry letter about him to Lady Ottoline Morrell. The final judgment must rest with those who read Tagore's works in their own language. Against the background of modern Indian literature these may eventually have an important place, not so much for their own merits, but because they cleared the ground for later writers.

Rabindranath Tagore: A Biography,   1962
Krishna Kripalani, Oxford   *Daily Telegraph*
University Press.

THE LOVAT FRASERS,
THE BEGGAR'S OPERA,
JONATHAN WILD

I

Grace Lovat Fraser's memoirs recall her husband's brilliant designs for *The Beggar's Opera*, for which Claud Lovat Fraser's costumes and décor did so much to make Gay's opera one of the great theatrical successes of the 1920s. The Playfair production, effective as it was, could be called a shade lacking in the essential toughness of the theme, but Lovat Fraser's costumes hardly fell short of perfection in their combined historical correctness, sense of colour values, acceptance of suitably squalid trappings and a touch of very personal satire of his own.

Lovat Fraser, who died, as a consequence of being wounded and gassed in the war, in 1921 (when these memoirs end), was an artist of real originality and feeling. His gifts have been obscured by wholesale imitation, but work, for example, like the poster for John Drinkwater's play *Abraham Lincoln* shows his abilities in another field.

Grace Lovat Fraser was American by birth, going back to early America on both sides of her family. Her parents came to England and more or less settled here. The account of this is reminiscent of those Kipling stories – that strike one as rather too self-applauding – in which Americans fall in love with this country. However nothing less seems to have been the case in this instance. Written in a quiet, straightforward, capable manner, Grace Lovat Fraser's book is a real contribution to the history of a period that holds great fascination for those interested in the development of modern 'intellectual' life, the threads of which now seem so separated, but were then tangled together.

The author's family, the Crawfords, must have provided something of a centre for writers – in which their daughter's attractions obviously played a part, though she is modest about this aspect – Yeats, D. H. Lawrence, Ford Madox Hueffer (not yet Ford), Ezra Pound and others, all frequenting the house. Grace Lovat Fraser herself was training both to dance and to sing, contemplating a career in the world of opera and ballet. Her mother hoped that on this account she would not marry. This was the epoch of Diaghilev's Ballet Russe, and the author makes the good point that Nijinsky was not only an incomparable dancer, but that the whole idea of a male dancer, as such, was at this period of time – except in Russia – practically in eclipse.

What an Age of Innocence it was. The writers used to come to tea, and one gets an excellent idea of what they were like when at ease, not trying to show off in a rather grander, more self-conscious world, as one generally reads about them. This is particularly true of D. H. Lawrence, then about twenty-four. Several letters of his to Grace Lovat Fraser, before she was married, are reproduced. They present a far more sympathetic picture of Lawrence than was conveyed by the overheated, fractious style characteristic of so much of his later correspondence. On occasions Lawrence seems actually to have shared a bed with Pound, which must have creaked under the weight of such a burden of literary personality.

> Dear Miss Crawford [writes Lawrence] What a jolly girl you are! Do you know when Pound was asleep – I stayed with him last night – when he had hidden the glories of his head under the counterpane and was asleep, sighing like a child, I was watching you dancing all the time . . . We had been in bed two hours. Then you danced away and did not come back. Pound was quite oblivious. I was near to nudging him in the back and asking him if he could see anything.

Miss Crawford was obviously standing no nonsense from Lawrence, because she lent him Aleister Crowley's volume of poems *Ambergris* to read – an enjoyable incident.

When war broke out in 1914, Grace Lovat Fraser was in Germany with her family. Not bothering about the international situation they found themselves caught there. This must have been an exceedingly unpleasant interlude; especially when the American authorities refused to issue passports on the grounds that the Crawfords had lived too long out of the United States. Grace Lovat Fraser, in order to help her family make two ends meet, as money was running out, was forced to take part in a kind of German ENSA, a play to entertain the troops in which she played a French girl, at first anti-German, then charmed by the invaders' good qualities. This was acted in front of a Bavarian unit. At the words *Diese verdammte Preussen* ('These damned Prussians'), spoken before the heroine's change of heart, the Bavarian soldier audience held the whole play up by cheering for several minutes.

She met Lovat Fraser in connection with a fitting for a theatrical costume. They were introduced by that eccentric guardsman Hugo Rumbold (whose transvestite pranks surely deserve a small mention) and fell in love at once. There are quite a lot of amusing incidents, all characteristic of the age.

In the Days of My Youth, Grace Lovat   1970
Fraser, Cassell.   *Daily Telegraph*

II

Since *The Beggar's Opera* was founded on the career of Jonathan Wild (1683–1725), a word about him may not be amiss.

It is one of the many merits of Gerald Howson's *Thief-Taker General* that he faces squarely the unpleasantness of his hero. 'Wild had no sensitivity,' he writes, 'probably little creative imagination and, morally, was an oaf.' He possessed, on the other hand, ingenuity, cunning, resource, energy, and an undoubted taste for playing a double game. In fact Howson shows that there is good reason to suppose Wild gave the language the useful phrase to 'double-cross'. Starting in a modest way as a young buckle-maker from Wolverhampton, who became a ponce, then ran a brothel, Jonathan Wild worked his way up to be not only an immensely successful racketeer, but also one of the best-known public figures of his time. He did this by means that had been used for centuries – false witness, blackmail, protection, receiving – but brought to these methods improvements of his own, the most notable being his refusal to handle stolen goods himself.

In the eighteenth century there were no regular police. At the same time, the Law was tough. It may come as a surprise to some, for example, that in 1721 a woman was burnt alive for coining. Thieves were hanged for stealing a small sum, but the penalty varied according to the circumstances in which the theft took place, so that the operation of the Law (administered in dog Latin, even doggier French) was open to much manipulation.

Wild became assistant to the Under-City-Marshal, a thoroughly disreputable person called Charles Hitchen. This was not in fact an official post, though Wild behaved as if it were, carrying a silver baton, and making arrests as and when it suited him. Hitchens, incidentally, was homosexual, and the book contains a lively account of an eighteenth-century homosexual brothel.

Howson, whose research has been colossal, goes to the original documents, so that instead of having a lot of second-hand opinions, of little or no interest, so familiar in books about persons like Jonathan Wild, we are supplied with the real stuff; and fascinating it is. Much of Wild's labours were devoted to returning stolen goods to their owners for a price never less than half their value – a comparison can be made with modern art thefts – then arranging for the execution of the thieves when they became idle or awkward.

For supplying evidence that led to an execution the informer received £40. The value of money in the past is always hard to compute and Howson's workable but rough-and-ready system of multiplying by twenty can lead to apparent anomalies. At the same time it is on record, even if ironically, that a parson could be 'passing rich on forty pounds a year', so that it may be seen that informing could be a remunerative industry.

The most interesting aspect of Wild is certainly the manner in which he took hold of the imagination of contemporary writers. To supply a subject to Defoe, Fielding and Gay is not given to every criminal. The Fielding connection with the original is tenuous; *The Beggar's Opera*, on the other hand, very close to the mark.

Indeed, to reread *The Beggar's Opera* after Gerald Howson's book is not only to appreciate the extraordinary brilliance of Gay's work, but also to learn a lesson about the transmutation of life into art. That is to say Gay deals (literally) lock, stock and barrel with the material of Jonathan Wild's life: the thieving, receiving, murdering, executing – and, above all, the informing. Gay is absolutely true to life. He is witty, satirical, tender, moving – but he is never *sentimental*. The love affair with Polly momentarily out of the way, Macheath disports himself with tarts, who immediately betray him, and quarrel about the reward in high-flown language. Lucy asks nothing better than to poison her rival; Peachum and Lockit love their daughters in their own manner, but do not wish to see them united – above all, not married – to friends of the family so precariously placed in the world of crime as highwaymen.

In comparison with this, one can well imagine what sickly stuff would be dished out in a musical about, say, the 'Train Robbers', Kray brothers or 'Torture Gang'. Indeed, in a recent revival of *The Beggar's Opera*, although gangsters' and prostitutes' choruses were convincing, some of the humour of personal relationships was lost in a present-day inability to understand the amusement inherent in formal speech, and – what Gay so much appreciates – the enormous banality of the criminal mind. It was Wild's highest ambition to become a Freeman of the City of London, and he was genuinely surprised when he was himself arrested. Mystery remains about what happened to the considerable fortune he had piled up.

Thief-Taker General: The Rise and Fall of Jonathan Wild, Gerald Howson, Hutchinson.

1970
Daily Telegraph

GEOFFREY MADAN

What is sometimes called the Golden Generation of brilliant young men who lost their lives in the First World War extended so far as birth dates are concerned over the best part of two decades. Even so there always seems a unity about this final flowering of a particular sort of education – what the Editors here call 'English literary culture, based on intensive study of the Classics' – that binds them tragically together.

Geoffrey Madan (1895–1947) did not die but was wounded, and really broken for life by army service in Mesopotamia. He is a perfect specimen of a survivor from that civilisation which ended in 1914. Madan, son of Bodley's Librarian, took the top scholarship at Eton, where he experienced the legendary honour of being 'sent up for play', not what contemporary parlance suggests, but a phrase meaning that a boy had produced an exercise so brilliant that the entire School was given a whole day holiday.

At both Eton and Balliol (Michaelmas 1913) Madan was contemporary with Harold Macmillan (whose foreword is most deftly written), leaving Oxford within a year for a commission in the King's Own Royal Lancaster Regiment. He returned to the University after the war, but never took a degree. He married young, and went into the City. But his health had been gravely impaired, and after about half a dozen years he retired from work that had never been congenial. The Madans were not enormously rich, but had enough money for him to collect books, silver, and devote himself to seeing friends and compiling these notebooks, which are his contribution to English letters.

A note in the introduction, written by the Editors, J. A. Gere, Keeper of Prints and Drawings at the British Museum, and John Sparrow, late Warden of All Souls, says that Madan's essays on the two Eton headmasters, Edward Lyttelton and Cyril Alington (which I had the good fortune to read many years ago), have not been included. They felt, no doubt rightly, that these would throw the Selection out of balance. It is, however, to be hoped the essays will one day appear. Madan himself would send a small selection from what is now published to friends at Christmas.

This volume, unique in its way, would indeed make an admirable Christmas present.

From Cornelia Knight's Autobiography (1831) we are given: 'Boswell told the King that he had difficulty in deciding what to call the unfortunate grandson of James II whose adventures he proposed to narrate. "Why," replied the King, "call him the unfortunate grandson of James II".' And in a more modern vein: 'Two psychiatrists meeting: "You're pretty well, how am I?"'

Madan himself contributes some lively aphorisms, sometimes under a pseudonym, and surely one of his most profound comments is: 'Treachery is the very essence of snobbery.' How very true that is of Maclean, Burgess and the whole brood of traitors that have followed them in public exposure.

The editors make a point of indicating that although Madan had a very wide circle of acquaintance (another element that seems to mark him off from a modern, more specialised and fragmented world) – lawyers and dons, talkers and politicians, bankers and churchmen – not everybody found him easy to get on with. Those on his 'wavelength' found him excellent company, but he could be prickly and did not mind being disliked.

One of Lord Chesterfield's sayings has been splendidly misprinted here in a manner that would have earned it a place and delighted Madan himself, even had he not already decided to include the opinion: 'Women who are either indisputably beautiful, or indisputably Bugly, are best flattered upon the score of their understanding.'

Inevitably there are a few chestnuts; some generalisations by pundits of the time that have slightly lost their sparkle, but on the whole an immense amount of wit, and absurdity, that makes most enjoyable reading. One notices that among others Disraeli has held up pretty well; Jowett begins to sound a trifle laboured. Here too is an unpolished poem, convincingly attributed to Kipling.

A collection like this is not at all easy to review; a few quotes may suggest the variety:

Dean Westcott's letter of condolence to Charles Kingsley on a bereavement; 14 pages: only one phrase could be deciphered, apparently 'ungrateful devil'.

Sights of London: the church in Leicester Square where Mme Navarro, between the matinée and evening performance, used to pray to be delivered from the attentions of King Edward VII.

Several good entries come from Madan's friend A. C. Benson, Eton housemaster and keeper of a Diary, selections from which recently appeared. This, for example:

On Christmas Eve, 1869, in a lonely Derbyshire manor, two brothers dined together. Feelings ran high over a disputed inheritance, and the younger brother (after securing the connivance of the butler with a bribe) assaulted the elder, doing him grievous bodily harm. He was committed for trial but released on bail. On the advice of his solicitors, he jumped his bail and fled the country.

Mr Gladstone, who was much struck by the story, immediately remarked the following seven points as 'especially worthy of attention':

1. The sacredness of the season.
2. The close relationship of the parties.
3. The peculiar violence of the assault.
4. The subornation of the major-domo.
5. The assailant's singular ignorance of the gross illegality of his action.
6. The faulty advice tendered by his attorney.
7. The forfeiture of his recognizances by the Crown.

Geoffrey Madan's Notebooks: A Selection, edited by J. A. Gere and John Sparrow, foreword by the Rt. Hon. Harold Macmillan, OM, Oxford University Press.

1981
Daily Telegraph

JAMES JOYCE

I

A friend of mine who found himself at the end of the war on the staff of the Military Government of Trieste told me that his duties included extending help to Stanislaus Joyce, James Joyce's younger brother, who lived in that city, where he taught English. Asked what Professor Joyce was like, he replied: 'A nice old man, but a terrible nuisance.' After reading this book (Introduction by Richard Ellmann, Preface by T. S. Eliot) I can see that the description was probably a just one. All the same it is an admirable piece of work, one that can be recommended entirely on its own merits. Obviously the reader must in the first instance concede that James Joyce himself was a figure worth close consideration. Apart from that, the picture of the author's own character, the early life of the Joyce family in Dublin, make it alone well worth reading, indeed a literary tragedy that Stanislaus Joyce died before his narrative was completed. We are taken only to the year 1903.

John Joyce, father of James, Stanislaus and a string of other children, had started life as a medical student with a little money of his own, a fair share of good looks and social gifts. He had drifted from job to job, ending, as his son says here, as one of the deserving poor, in that he was one of those who richly deserved to be poor. Obviously there was an unusual strain in the family; a gift for music, a tendency to be disorderly and drunken; a rage against life that rose above even an accustomed Irish discontent.

James Joyce's brilliance as a boy was recognised from the first. Jesuit-educated, he was a great carrier-off of prizes. The picture of the hero of *Portrait of the Artist as a Young Man* as a shy, bullied, ineffectual schoolboy seems, autobiographically speaking, even wider of the mark than that of Beetle Kipling in *Stalky and Co*. So far from being bad at games there was a whole sideboard at home crowded with cups, and an electro-plated teapot and coffee pot, all won by James Joyce at hurdles or walking events. He was also a keen cricketer and great admirer of Ranji and Spofforth.

Stanislaus Joyce was always fated to play second string to this greatly talented, ferociously egotistical, at times cruel and cold-hearted elder brother. It is clear from this book that Stanislaus possessed considerable literary gifts of his own, and, although devoted to his brother, a

character in strong contrast. It is the clash of their different temperaments that gives such flavour to the story. Here we see James Joyce in
various unexpected contexts: playing the role of the Headmaster in an
amateur performance of Anstey's *Vice Versa*, writing book reviews for
the *Daily Express*; interviewing a French motorist taking part in the race
for the Gordon Bennett Cup to be run in Ireland. He found no difficulty
as a very young man in meeting relatively well-known figures like
Arthur Symons and W. B. Yeats, but it was one thing to have a
reputation as a promising writer, another to have settled on a way to
earn a living.

    More direct, better behaved, probably a better critic, Stanislaus
Joyce is at the same time more violent than James – or 'Jim', as he is
called here. James's agnostic obsession with the Roman Church
becomes in Stanislaus a really tremendous anti-clericalism. The reason
for the title of the book is in part an ironical reference to Cain, in part to
Stanislaus's efforts to make James drink less and lead a less irregular
life. This latter aspect of their relationship had not yet developed in the
period dealt with here. It was rightly felt by the editor that it should
remain in spite of that. The poverty and domestic misery in which the
Joyces lived, keeping up at the same time to some degree the standards
of a decidedly richer class (their father sometimes wore an eyeglass),
and also enjoying themselves with a modicum of boisterous behaviour,
is really astonishing. It explains much that took place in Bloomsday.

My Brother's Keeper, Stanislaus   1958
Joyce, Faber.   *Punch*

II

James Joyce had little or no imagination in the sense that Balzac or
Proust had imagination. No one who has read the unpublished Joyce
letters at Cornell University, with their harping emphasis on domestic
administration, hair-raising excretory obsessions, can fail to notice that
there was as much of the author of *Ulysses* in Bloom as in Stephen
Daedalus, if not more; while even Molly Bloom appears to be an
emanation of the relationship between the novelist and his wife. James
Joyce was not really capable of 'inventing' a character. The case of
Stanislaus Joyce emphasises, however, what an extraordinary family
the Joyces were. George Harris Healey, of Cornell, edits *The Dublin
Diary of Stanislaus Joyce*, written between 1903 and 1905. In it Stanislaus
frequently speaks of how much his brother despises him, but there are
indications that, on the contrary, James Joyce was exceedingly jealous
of his suppressed but acute younger brother. Certainly he borrowed
from him on numerous occasions ('Chamber Music' was a title

supplied by Stanislaus) and, by keeping him in intellectual subjection, not only picked his brain, but perhaps also hamstrung a formidable rival. Stanislaus Joyce, violent, undisciplined, was also absolutely unselfish so far as his elder brother was concerned.

> I envy Jim, for instance what Catholics would call 'the purity of his intentions'. His manner, his appearance, his talents, his reputation I do not envy him. When I do envy him anything – the strength of his emotions, the beauty of his mind at times, his sense of honour, his pride, his spontaneity – I do so impersonally. I do not really envy him, but his state of mind.

Stanislaus Joyce gives a picture of their father of a vividness that fails entirely to emerge from James Joyce's books. Stanislaus possessed a hearty detestation of his own countrymen:

> The Irish are morally a cowardly, chaos-loving people, quarrelsome and easily deceived, dissipated in will and intellect, and accustomed to masters, with a profitless knowledge of their own worthlessness, which causes them constantly to try and persuade themselves and others that they are what they are not.

In 1904, for a critic not yet twenty, it is remarkable to record:

> I have been reading lately some novels by Henry James and some George Meredith, and naturally constant comparison between the two men has been made in my mind. Meredith has the biggest name in English literature to-day, now that Swinburne has withdrawn, and James has practically no reputation. He is thought to be the writer of patient society novels.
> In my judgment a stupid injustice has been done to James in this. He is far and away the better novelist, but more than this his work is a much more important contribution to the modern consciousness than Meredith's.

The Dublin Diary of Stanislaus Joyce,   1960
edited by George Harris Healey,   *Daily Telegraph*
Faber.

III

Whatever reservations people may have about Ezra Pound's own poetry – and subsequent political role – there can be no doubt that where James Joyce was concerned he behaved with remarkable unselfishness, energy, on the whole, good sense. It all began in 1913 when Pound was helping Yeats compile the Imagist anthology. At the last moment Yeats remembered a young Irish poet named James

Joyce, who, he thought, ought to be represented; with the result that Joyce sent Pound the typescript of *Dubliners* and a chapter of *Portrait of the Artist as a Young Man*.

Forrest Read, who makes some sage comments in the portions of this book that weld together the letters and critical passages, remarks 'one may doubt whether Joyce could really understand the peculiarly native breed of American Pound represents.' Even allowing for a personal vitality and good nature that is always impossible to convey on paper, there must have been moments when all who came in contact with Pound grew heartily sick of his stylistic idiosyncrasies – for example, endlessly writing sentences like 'Wot I neverthurless suggess,' and in general corresponding in a jargon, not only strident but relentlessly unfunny. However, Wyndham Lewis well called Pound a 'Demon pantechnicon driver, busy with moving the old world into new quarters'. His tireless efforts with Joyce certainly seem to have been effective in circumstances where someone like him was probably required.

Read writes with justifiable severity: 'Joyce lived a quite unspartan life in Trieste and Zurich. His penury was largely self-inflicted: he was always willing, even eager, to be dependent, and despite his success at finding windfalls he always considered his plight deplorable.' Violent interest in himself, such as Pound showed, was just what Joyce wanted. In the end Pound drifted away into economic, rather than literary, theories – disastrous in the long run, and separating him from Joyce. However, he did a good job in that particular quarter. Pound made several ludicrously bad literary bets on other writers, but he retained a certain consistency of judgment in his three favourite works: Joyce's *Ulysses*, Wyndham Lewis's *Apes of God*, E. E. Cummings's *Eimi*.

H. G. Wells's reason for resigning from the Royal Literary Fund on account of a grant to 'Cressland' probably refers to T. W. H. Crosland, who would have certainly have provided adequate reason for resignation. 'Herbert J. Cape' (of Duckworth's) who gets a tremendous hammering for turning down the *Portrait*, is more easily recognised as the publisher Jonathan Cape – and surely the illustrator Jean de Bosschère was Belgian rather than French.

Anyone who has doubts about Joyce's abilities as a writer should read *Giacomo Joyce*, a brief but wonderfully taut fragment, describing an ineffective love affair he had in Trieste with a girl pupil, when he was teaching English there. Some of this was later incorporated into the *Portrait*, the alterations made being not, on the whole, an improvement. Richard Ellmann's introduction does all that is wanted in outlining the circumstances of this most interesting work. Ellmann rightly emphasises the vividness with which Trieste is recreated, without any factual description, thereby making a striking link with Italo Svevo's *Zeno* and his other books.

Pound/Joyce: The Letters of Ezra   1969
Pound to James Joyce, with Pound's   *Daily Telegraph*
Essays on Joyce, edited by Forrest
Read, Faber.
Giacomo Joyce, James Joyce, Faber.

IV

The symbolism of James Joyce's *Ulysses* rests – at times fairly tenuously – on the adventures of Ulysses, the Greek hero, as performed in parody by Leopold Bloom, a Jewish Irishman, wandering round Dublin on 16 June 1904.

These eighteen essays examine different facets of the Ulysses/Bloom story under the headings Joyce (writing each in a different style) gave them, beginning with Telemachus (Stephen Dedalus), and ending with Penelope (Molly Bloom).

T. S. Eliot called this 'manipulating a continuous parallel between contemporaneity and antiquity'. The essay 'Ithaca' (A. Walton Litz) brings up the reasonable question of whether *Ulysses* can be called a novel at all, and is not a kind of 'anatomy' or hybrid form of writing, not one to be considered in the same terms as, say, *David Copperfield* or *Madame Bovary*. The feature that seems to save Joyce's book from this non-admittance into the novel's enclosure is the vitality possessed by Bloom and Mrs Bloom especially, and a lot of lesser characters.

That *Ulysses* has not been shovelled off into some such obscure critical limbo is no fault of the critics; no fault either of Joyce himself, who, as pointed out in the essay 'Hades' (R. M. Adams) is never on record as 'taking out' anything in his book, which he once put in. If it is a virtue in an artist not to be afraid of being a bore, Joyce displayed that quality to an heroic degree.

So much for Joyce. If he delighted in obscurity, and carried pedantry to its furthest frontiers, at least he did produce a remarkable (in some ways very entertaining) book. To read some of these essays without having read *Ulysses* would be to run serious risk of supposing that there was nothing in Joyce's novel of a straightforward sort – moving, funny, told for the sake of being told, not because it 'meant' something quite different from what it appears to.

This point is worth making, because so many of the sequences in *Ulysses* are first-rate as pieces of naturalistic novel-writing, for example, the opening scene in the Martello Tower, the funeral, Bloom in the pub, to name only a few. This side of Joyce always seems the one critics try to play down, and treat in a manner that they would never use in reviewing a contemporary novel. For example, in these essays, the old woman selling milk is called 'ignorant and servile', and Mr Deasy (Stephen's employer) 'silly'. But surely this is like saying that Mr Micawber is silly, or Kipling's Soldiers Three ignorant.

This naturalistic side of Joyce is, of course, not by any means entirely ignored here. In 'Aeolus', M. J. C. Hodgart points out that Bloom actually does some work, a rare occurrence in the book. The chapter about the Winds has splendid visual qualities; it also evokes the transport systems of the Dublin of the period. In this last connection, one of the editors, Clive Hart, walked across Dublin, checking the journeys of various characters (including imitating the gait of the one-legged sailor and two hobbling old women), to confirm accuracy of time over distance, finding this approximately correct. A chart is supplied showing each character and his (or her) route – a useful adjunct for all *Ulysses* readers.

Much of Joyce's method in the interior monologue of his characters was used as far back as 1887 in *Les Lauriers sont Coupés*, a novel by Edouard Dujardin, a Frenchman whose name seems to give opportunity for a Joycean pun about gardens and laurels. Joyce, as pointed out here by Melvin J. Friedman in 'Lestrygonians', took the system much further. 'The novelist,' writes Friedman, 'as narrator of objective facts, is only intermittently visible in the eighth chapter of *Ulysses*, and even then his language is often caught up in syntax that belongs more to poetry than prose.'

J. S. Atherton, in 'The Oxen of the Sun', has some interesting things to say about the section of *Ulysses* written in a series of imitations of different sorts of prose that show the development of English. Atherton points out that this sequence owes a good deal to two anthologies, George Saintsbury's *History of English Prose Rhythms*, and W. Peacock's *English Prose: Manderville to Ruskin*. Perhaps for this reason the parody varies in skill – no doubt also affected by Joyce's own preferences in authors – his Bunyan being excellent, but Pepys and Evelyn scarcely recognisable.

As ever, when reading critical books about Joyce, one wonders just how far *Ulysses* was, in fact, planned from the start. It is apt to be assumed, when a novel has become famous, that the author knew from the beginning exactly what he was going to say. I do not suggest that Joyce had not a great deal of the plan and the parallels in his mind – after all *Ulysses* logically follows on *Portrait of the Artist* – but suspect all the same that much was improvised by the author as the narrative developed. There always seems a certain sense of conflict going on within Joyce himself in *Ulysses* (as opposed to what he wrote later) concerning how much the purely naturalistic narrative should be allowed to dominate the 'experimental'. In the latter, everything was permitted, everything 'put in'. It is obviously impossible to check this; but the introduction of Bloom is so late, so unattached, in the naturalistic narrative, that one wonders if Bloom as a character was thought of at a late stage.

James Joyce's Ulysses: Critical Essays,   1975
edited by Clive Hart and David   *Daily Telegraph*
Hayman, University of California
Press.

V

Many silly things have been written about James Joyce. It is therefore a relief to find this definitive biography excellently done. Richard Ellmann deals with the narrative at easy cruising speed, presenting in palatable form an enormous amount of material and research. If you want to read about Joyce at all, you want to know the details; because every word Joyce wrote was the direct outcome of something that had happened to himself or something he had been told about. He never invented.

The writer's great-grandfather had been a successful builder. Since then no one in the family had shown any capacity for making money, but there existed in the Joyce home an atmosphere of fallen greatness. The Joyces, so far as can be seen, had little claim, by even the least exacting Irish standards, to an aristocratic background, and this family pride, which Joyce shared with his father, is of interest – more interesting, indeed, than if there had been a mouldering Georgian mansion in the background. Ellmann smiles at Joyce's pretensions about coats-of-arms and such things, but perhaps does not sufficiently emphasise the paradox as an irritant in Joyce's early life.

To this sense of having come down in the world was added another pressure, Joyce's Jesuit education. He was a prize pupil, at one moment destined for the priesthood, and his later detestation of the Church was something very close to love. He developed sexually unusually early, so that the bottled-up emotions of his priestly schools seem to have been especially painful to him as a boy. Finally, there was Irish Nationalism. The Joyce family were Parnellite, but Joyce himself, in theory, renounced Nationalism. In practice, like his hate-love for the Roman Church, he never got it out of his system.

As a young man in Dublin, Joyce was a drunken, rackety figure. In 1904, when he was twenty-two, he went off with Norah Barnacle, a good-looking girl of peasant origin from Galway (who comes to life in this biography), taking a job teaching languages which, quite by chance, landed him in Trieste. Ellmann's description of Joyce's life in Trieste, where he lived for many years on and off, is of the greatest interest. There Joyce taught, among others, Ettore Schmitz, better known as Italo Svevo, author of *The Confessions of Zeno*. Genial and sardonic, Schmitz supplied much of the Jewish lore, and perhaps some of the character of Bloom in *Ulysses*.

Joyce's financial state was always catastrophic. The only conclusion one can come to is that he liked living in a permanent monetary crisis; for however hard it may have been to make two ends meet in his early days, he seems almost to have gone out of his way to inflame this condition later when circumstances were much easier. The fact is that Joyce cannot be regarded as a very nice man. He was egotistical, envious, disloyal, untrustworthy, quarrelsome and a great physical coward. (Moral courage he possessed in a high degree.) His drunkenness, and lack of scruple about money, somehow never lends him the charm those characteristics sometimes bring; just as his obscenity lacks all Rabelaisian joy in life.

By the time he was thirty-five and living in Paris in receipt of an allowance – another unbelievable example of generosity – from Miss Harriet Weaver, his conceit was overweening. He existed in a little court of sycophants. The fact remains that in *Ulysses* he wrote a monumental book. It was an extraordinary achievement, but was, so it seems to me, the only literary achievement he could have brought off with complete success. If you compare Joyce (as he liked to compare himself) with Picasso, it immediately becomes clear that Picasso could perfectly well have made a career as a brilliantly successful academic painter. His early drawings alone show that. Joyce, on the contrary, was the most minor of minor poets; his journalism is stiff and unwieldy; his realistic short stories – interesting at the period – are not of overwhelming merit; his powers as a dramatist were very limited – even his limericks (copiously quoted in the biography) are indifferent. He was committed to producing some eccentric version of his own life.

In *Portrait of the Artist as a Young Man* he began to find himself – for example, the wonderful quarrel about Parnell at the family table, or the Jesuit hell-fire sermons. In *Ulysses* his genius was suddenly able to express itself. *Ulysses* is by no means without longueurs but its highspots are splendid – the funeral, for example, or the return of Stephen and Bloom from Nighttown. The novel might almost be compared with Burton's *Anatomy of Melancholy* for its extraordinary accretion of incongruous material.

Like all cruel people, Joyce had in him a strong strain of sentimentality. There is plenty of evidence of both these characteristics in Ellmann's biography. For years an inward struggle had been waged between the Joyce of the early days, the writer of Swinburnian verse, and the Joyce dedicated to making a revolution in writing, the infinitely accomplished parodist, the etymologist obsessed with words. Finally, in *Finnegan's Wake*, the etymologist won, driving out the artist for his suspected sentimentality. As Constant Lambert wrote in *Music Ho!*, Joyce's ultimate works are like a man who is 'too shy to write a love letter except in the form of a cross-word puzzle'. Richard Ellmann shows how all this happened. He is admiring but not abject; he does not moralise, at the same time he does not evade all moral issues. He has, in short, written a fascinating book about an extraordinary man and a great writer – even if Joyce were not quite so great a writer as he himself liked to think.

James Joyce, Richard Ellmann,   1959
Oxford University Press.   *Daily Telegraph*

VI

Of all the great novelists – among whom, with his undoubted limitations, he must be numbered – James Joyce is the most pedantic and technique-bound. It is therefore appropriate that his work should have given rise to copious outpourings in the heavy industry of Eng. Lit. Joyce himself would have been delighted by this. He regarded himself (not entirely without reason) as a literary saint, and, in his own eyes, the corollary of that was that the parings of his literary toe-nails were sacred.

To those concerned with writing, the MSS of, say, *David Copperfield*, *Nostromo*, *The Great Gatsby*, *Decline and Fall*, *Lucky Jim*, might be of interest, but there is no real necessity to study these manuscripts to get the best out of the respective novels. Joyce threatens a different situation. These 810 pages (two volumes of the present edition, *Ulysses: A Facsimile of the Manuscripts*) show just what he wrote by hand. As each episode was finished, two copies of a typescript were sent off to Ezra Pound; one to the *Little Review*; one to Joyce's English patron, Harriet Weaver; the manuscript itself being sold to the New York lawyer and collector, John Quinn.

The third volume of the present edition reproduces in miniature the whole of the text of *Ulysses*, showing also in handwriting, though not Joyce's, alterations he made. Harry Levin and Clive Driver comment usefully on the difference between the manuscript and the printed version, Driver, with great clarity, doing the annotating in volume 3. For Joyce fans there is much more to excite. The plum is undoubtedly *Agenbite of inwit* (the middle English locution for remorse of conscience), often quoted as the key to Stephen's character in relation to his dead mother. *Agenbite of inwit*, added by Joyce in proof, does not occur in the MS, a silent exhortation to all authors to take trouble with their proofs.

Joyce's Letters, hitherto printed in three uncollated volumes, are now offered in a Selection by Richard Ellmann, who wrote the first-rate definitive biography. Ellmann's treatment of the Letters is equally capable and imaginative, providing the story of Joyce's life, in a sense, as told by the writer himself. The Letters show the important role played by Joyce's long-suffering and talented brother Stanislaus, whom he often treated abominably. Examples are given of Joyce's scatological letters written (for sexual excitement) to his wife (also long-suffering), Nora Barnacle. It seems right that these should be included, as they show that the similar passages in *Ulysses* were, so to speak, natural to Joyce, not written in for any ulterior pornographic motive.

Joyce's work falls into four well-defined sections: the *Dubliners* stories, breaking new ground in their ruthlessly naturalistic style, but (the author was only twenty-one) showing certain infelicities of construction; the autobiographical novel *A Portrait of the Artist as a Young Man*, which contains some of the best things Joyce wrote, but is not yet free from fruity Victorian romanticisms like 'Yes, those were noble names on the dusky flyleaf'; then *Ulysses*, an extraordinary *tour de force*, but one too often allowed to get out of hand, because of Joyce's inability to prevent himself from doing a good idea to death. Joyce needed the iron brace of his self-forged technique to hold him from falling back into the sentimentalities and romanticisms which were the other side of his implacable egotism; but those artists who live by technique always run a serious danger of perishing by technique. Joyce came close to doing that with his last work, *Finnegan's Wake*, a great unreadable, in which nuggets are certainly to be discovered, but of which the best to be said is that its existence might prevent any other writer attempting to do it again.

The Letters lay out Joyce's changing situation like a map. The early ones, before he was too much engulfed by his own literary mission, are the most engrossing. His problem was to get away from Ireland, but he did not want to earn a living in England, and he had run away with Nora Barnacle, to whom he was not married. This last factor obviously created a handicap for holding certain jobs. Joyce taught in English in Trieste, then worked in a bank in Rome. His hardships were appalling. After what was often not much short of a twelve-hour day in the bank, he would give English lessons when he got home in the evening.

Joyce's reputation was already sufficient in 1916, when thirty-four and living in Switzerland, for him to be given a Civil List grant of £100 a year; something for which the British Government deserves credit. Gradually his situation improved financially, the astonishing Miss Weaver paying out to him £25,000 or more, which Joyce had largely dissipated by the time he died. As in so many biographies, especially those surveyed through letters, there seems a kind of break in Joyce's.

All at once he is concerned only with the marketing of his work, his status, the fruits of success. He was one of the great heroes of the 1920s, in comparison with today an epoch with extraordinary enthusiasm for the arts – but his own inner creative brilliance needed no sustenance later than 1904.

Ulysses: A Facsimile of the   1976
Manuscript, 3 vols, introduction by   *Daily Telegraph*
Harry Levin, bibliographical
preface by Clive Driver, Faber.
Selected Letters of James Joyce, edited
by Richard Ellmann, Faber.

VII

By a singular piece of luck I was nearly at the close of a reread of *Ulysses*, when *Ulysses: The Corrected Text* came for review. My own copy (Shakespeare and Company, blue covers, May 1927, rebound with covers at end) was the ninth, smuggled back in the same year. I learn here that these earlier editions contain more than 5,000 mistakes, all of which are corrected so far as possible, sometimes with considerable ingenuity.

Joyce mythology has never raged in this country to the extent it did – to some extent still does – in America, the home of the thesis and critical investigation, but it is sufficiently strong to make even so moderate a Joycean as myself feel thwarted by a well-printed, well-bound volume, issued by a respectable London publisher. Somehow one needs the grey paper, the French compositors, the under-the-counter transaction. I am not sure that I could have got through again so sanitary a production as this one; certainly not with the same nostalgia for the period, if not exactly for Joyce himself.

The mistakes were predominantly errors like 'which' for 'with', together with the printer's habit of suddenly going into a different type-fount for a single word. This last eccentricity is disconcerting, because it sometimes looks as if the author wished to emphasise that particular word, which in several cases might make sense. In his preface, Richard Ellmann enlarges the more important corrections. For instance, he remarks:

> For purposes of interpretation, the most significant of the many small changes in Gabler's text has to do with the question that Stephen puts to his mother at the climax of the brothel scene, itself the climax of the novel ... Professor Gabler has been able to settle this matter by recovering a passage left out of the scene that takes place in the National Library. Whether Joyce omitted it or not is a matter of conjecture and debate.

The corrected edition of *Ulysses* takes up 643 pages as opposed to the 735 of the original publication by Sylvia Beach. It appeared this week of Bloomsday, 16 June, the date of the ramblings in Dublin which Leopold Bloom experienced sometimes in the company of Stephen Dedalus, eighty-two years ago in 1904.

About 250 pages at the beginning are occupied with the young Dubliners in the Martello Tower (including the wonderfully awful Liberal Englishman, Haines); the payments of Stephen's wages by Mr Deasy at the school where he is employed; Paddy Dignam's funeral, which Bloom attends. All this is absolutely first-rate in characterisation and movement, while presenting no difficulty to the modern reader. The narrative, if it can be so called, is then carried on by a series of pastiches of English writing from the earliest times, including popular journalese and novelettish styles. Here Joyce's pedantry begins to get the upper hand.

Bloom and Stephen now penetrate into Nighttown, the Red Light district of Dublin, and the method changes again to that of a play, with stage-directions as to scenes and characters. This is a perfectly feasible approach, indeed in many ways an excellent one for its purpose, but once more Joyce overdoes it. The scenes continue for too long. The play ends, and is briefly followed by comparatively straightforward narrative, rounding off the night that Bloom and Stephen have had together. Then comes about seventy pages of inspissated tedium, in the form of questions and answers. A certain amount of relevant information is conveyed in this manner, but it is too hard on the reader. Like so much of Joyce when he is being 'experimental', one feels that what is done is simply because he cannot keep up the comparatively straightforward narrative form, at which he can show himself so accomplished.

Finally, we have some forty pages of the ruminations of Molly Bloom. This is the main 'stream of consciousness' passage in *Ulysses*, though the novel is often spoken of as if it is all written in that convention. It is a part of the book that has won certain admirers – I have heard women say that it made them feel uncomfortable – but I am not sure that it is more than a remarkable *tour de force* on the author's part, rather than writing that carries conviction. Joyce departs here from his accustomed 'documentation', and relies on guesswork. Would Molly Bloom have mentally expressed herself like that? Is it not how Joyce thinks he would have expressed himself, had he been a woman? I remain unconvinced.

Ulysses: The Corrected Text, James
Joyce, edited by Hans Walter
Gabler with Wolfhard Steppe and
Claud Melchior, Bodley Head and
Penguin.

1986
Daily Telegraph

VIII

Mrs Ros stands alone. She cannot be altogether laughed off. She may be a long way from Shakespeare, but she partakes, in however infinitely minute a degree, of the Shakespearean power over language. If there be those who have never heard of Amanda M'Kittrick Ros, let us recall that she was author of *Irene Iddesleigh* and *Delina Delaney*, together with some poems. There exists also an unpublished work, *Helen Huddleson*. The first of these novels appeared in 1897 in Belfast. By 1911 both books were sufficiently well known to be the subject of an examination paper set in *Punch*, with questions and answers by F. Anstey, author of *Vice Versa*. In 1939, at an advanced age – to use her own expressive phraseology – Mrs Ros 'joined the boundless battalion of the breathless' and 'became a member of the missing majority'.

Irene Iddesleigh, the story of a baronet's wife who runs away with a tutor, was reissued by the Nonesuch Press in 1926, when it was reviewed by D. B. Wyndham Lewis in the *Daily Mail. St Scandalbags*, of which the editor, T. Stanley Mercer, who has done a service to literature in preserving this piece of vituperation, possesses no fewer than five variants, is the author's reply to this review.

D. B. Wyndham Lewis's notice, certainly a shade ponderous in treatment, received a terrific excoriation.

> Is there or could there be anything south of Heaven or north of Hell, more dishonourable, more degrading, more reptilic than to tarnish, with the filthiest compound a low vulgar mind is capable of inventing, the characters of the undeserving, years after they have resigned their right of existence, thus deprived of the option or power to defend themselves against such cruel calumny? These clay-crabs of corruption, nicknamed 'critics', know as well as life is a loan, that their lives are one crooked stream of dissimulation, dishonour, falsehood (with rare exceptions) and it is a wretched waif who would covet their 'jobbery'.

If anyone thinks such prose easy to write, let them observe the failure of Mr (now Sir) Francis Meynell's letter (quoted in the text) attempting to pastiche Mrs Ros's manner.

The fact is that Amanda M'Kittrick Ros, emotionally and stylistically, is a genuine native Irish writer. Again and again, for example, she reminds the reader of James Joyce.

> Heavily laden with the garb of disappointment did the wandering woman of wayward wrong retrace her footsteps from the door for ever, and leisurely walked down the artistic avenue of carpeted care,

never more to face the furrowed frowns of friends, who, in years gone by, bestowed on her the praise of poetic powers.

Irene Iddesleigh

Onward to the dead sea they tramp to drink, unslaked and with horrible gulpings, the salt somnolent inexhaustible flood. And the equine portent grows again, magnified in the deserted heavens, nay to heaven's own magnitude till it looms, vast, over the house of Virgo.

Ulysses

However, to return to *St Scandalbags*, the Critic, apropos of the book's illustrations, had referred to the trousers worn by a character in an illustration to one of Charlotte Yonge's novels.

It is in this connection that Mrs Ros wrote:

> Beaten down by a caustic tongue
>   Deploring the death of his pen
> He falls a victim to 'Charlotte Yonge'
>   And yearns for her 'trousers' again.
> Which don't resemble the age now dead
>   They're shorter by inches far
> And are closed all round with a pinky red
>   As a trade-mark of female war.

She had some right to be annoyed, for the pictures in her own book had been none of her own choosing, and had elsewhere aroused facetious critical comment.

Anstey's examination paper deals with some of the better known felicities of the novels. For example:

Question: How may we infer from a casual remark of Lord Gifford's that he had his doubts as to his cousin's claim to be addressed as 'Lady' Mattie?

Answer: 'Lady Mattie (Heaven knows who died, or if anyone died and legacied her the title).'

All who know Mrs Ros's work will welcome *St Scandalbags*. Others may be tempted by it to explore her haunting pages.

St Scandalbags, Amanda M. Ros,   1954
edited by T. Stanley Mercer, The   *Punch*
Merle Press.

Some Novels and Novelists

APHRA BEHN

There have been several books of late years about 'the unspeakable Mrs Behn' (1640–1689), none, so far as I know, contriving to sort out her origins (possibly illegitimate) at all satisfactorily. She is a striking figure in her way, mixed up with a lot of people who, if not in the top rank of history, played interesting or sinister roles in the life of the period. A really scholarly work based on informed examination of documents might illuminate some odd seventeenth-century corners.

Scholarship, alas, is not what we get from Angeline Goreau, who thinks that Shakespeare was educated at a 'very good public school' and seems unaware that King William III was as much grandson of Charles I as his Queen was granddaughter. Angeline Goreau, who is American, rambles on about what a rotten time women had in the seventeenth century, but with the best will in the world, Women's Lib cannot be made retroactive, and we do not have to be told on every page that Aphra Behn can claim to be the first woman in England to live by her pen. None the less I closed the book knowing considerably more about Mrs Behn.

I had supposed that she was née Aphra Amis, liking to think of her as a potential relation of the author of *Lucky Jim*, but although the year (1640) and place (Wye, Kent) fit in with available information, the twins 'Peter and Afera', children of John Amis, were both baptised and buried in that same year, according to the register. Nothing is more probable in the seventeenth century than that the next female child was given the same name, or the parson may have got muddled as to which child died. The name Aphra is not so rare as Angeline Goreau seems to think. She attributes it to a third-century martyred temple prostitute, but Withycombe's *English Christian Names* (1946) states that Aphra derives from a misunderstood text in the book of the Prophet Micah.

Anyway, the next thing we hear about Aphra, now in her early twenties, is as adopted daughter of one Johnson and foster-sister of Col. Thomas Culpeper. Johnson is described as relation of (5th) Lord Willoughby of Parham; Culpeper, an eccentric, came of a well-known Kentish family. Lord Willoughby, a magnate of some note, had changed from Cromwellian to Royalist in the Civil War and was much concerned with plots. He practically founded the South American colony of Surinam (later Dutch Guiana), of which he is said to have appointed Aphra's adoptive father, Johnson, Lieutenant General. There Aphra travelled in 1663.

Her adventures in Surinam were to be her stock-in-trade when she wrote her novel *Oronooko* (1688), among other things an early attack on the slave trade. She also had an affair in Surinam with William Scot, whose father had been Cromwell's head of MI5, so to speak, and one of the Regicides. When it is remembered that Aphra's foster-brother Culpeper was son and grandson of two fanatical anti-monetarists, both of whom had written a stream of books with titles like *Usury at Six per Cent Examined*, it will be seen that she was up to the eyes in the politics of the period. Angeline Goreau never seems quite to get the hang of this political involvement. On her return to England in 1664 Aphra married Mr Behn, of whom nothing is known except that he was of Netherlands extraction, possibly met through her lover Scot, who had Dutch associations. The marriage seems to have come apart almost immediately, and Aphra in 1666 was sent to Antwerp to spy on the war policies of the States General of Holland, a job for which her political affiliations must have well equipped her.

Aphra was thoroughly badly treated by the Intelligence authorities as to funds, and on coming home was imprisoned for debt. On release she settled down to her extraordinary career of writing plays, verse, and subsequently novels. In the last field she might quite reasonably be regarded, not merely as the first woman novelist but the first novelist in England. She got off the mark appreciably earlier than Defoe.

Angeline Goreau is rather scrappy about the literary world of the Caroline period, and a more expert examination of Aphra Behn's adventures in it might be rewarding. As in politics, Aphra seems to have found no difficulty in being at the centre of things, and was perfectly at ease in the *louche* circle of the bisexual Lord Rochester. She seems to have had an affair with Rochester himself who, I am sure, did not write 'ass' for the good Anglo-Saxon word 'arse' – a curious American misunderstanding of language, as if you wrote 'cat' for 'cart'.

Aphra was always hard up although she worked with enormous vigour. Her plays were regarded as outspoken for a woman. She seems to have had a lot of affairs, and regrettably she contracted the pox. Oddly enough, one of her lovers, John Hoyle, also bisexual was son of another of the Regicides, Thomas Hoyle, though Aphra herself was always an ardent Tory. Mrs Aphra Behn is credited with the phrase 'beauty unadorned'. She was a worthy forerunner of a host of enterprising later literary ladies.

Reconstructing Aphra: A Social Biography of Aphra Behn, Angeline Goreau, Oxford University Press.

1980
Daily Telegraph

LAURENCE STERNE

Judged by any standards, Laurence Sterne (1713–68) is a striking figure, though perhaps not a particularly attractive one. A new biography was required to put him into some sort of perspective. The prospect of having to reread *Tristram Shandy* would daunt me personally, but there can be no doubt that it is a remarkable experiment in technique, startlingly original at the time, and additionally interesting for its great contemporary success.

David Thomson rightly gives a good deal of attention to Sterne's parentage, about which comparatively little is known, but certainly key to much of his manner of facing life. Sterne himself sometimes went out of his way to lay false trails about his own career, and there are frequent gaps of material to make a biographer's job difficult. The Sternes were a land-owning, fairly prominent family, the writer's branch living for several generations on the Yorkshire/Nottinghamshire border. Sterne's father was the middle one of three brothers. The eldest inherited a small property, the youngest settled in a church living, but Roger, Sterne's father, enlisted in the army.

There are indications that Roger Sterne was not on the best of terms with the rest of the family, at the same time not a ne'er-do-well. He was given a commission after two years – one would have thought a comparatively rare occurrence at that date. Perhaps there was an understanding about it when he joined. In the navy serving as 'cabin-boy' or 'volunteer' was a common prelude to training for a naval commission, and Roger Sterne – though Thomson does not suggest this – might have done something similar as an educated man without money aiming at an army commission without purchase.

He remained an ensign in the 34th Foot (later The Border Regiment) until the age of thirty-nine. He was promoted lieutenant only a few months before he died. Admittedly his family never offered a halfpenny to buy him higher rank, but, since he served (apparently quite adequately) from the Low Countries to Jamaica, Ireland to Gibraltar, he seems to have had bad luck in never getting a 'step' from the unit's casualties, as apparently did some junior to himself. Roger Sterne married the widow of another officer (daughter or daughter-in-law of an Irish sutler, possibly of Huguenot origin) in slightly dubious

circumstances. From this upbringing in garrison towns emerges
Sterne's picture of Uncle Toby; as Thomson points out, the first of a
dynasty of good-hearted retired veterans as characters in novels.

Sterne himself seems to have been altogether unusual, marked out
for some sort of fame from boyhood. His character is evasive. Thomson
probably puts his finger on an essential trait when he says: 'Not one
human relationship in Sterne's life seems mature, lasting or to have
been experienced mutually.' He was a compulsive womaniser, falling
in love with every woman he met sentimentally, but not being
over-fastidious when it came to physical satisfaction. Even in the
eighteenth century, Sterne seems to have got away with a good deal
considering he was a parson.

All the portraits of him convey a very odd physical appearance, the
Nollekens bust (in the National Portrait Gallery) probably the best.
After his literary success, he was on the whole popular in society, both
with the *beau monde* and his fellow writers, though naturally there were
exceptions. One gets the impression of an amusing figure with whom it
was impossible to make anything like a personal contact.

Sterne's discovery was really 'instinctive writing'. He will always put
a dash or an asterisk, rather than allow the flow of interior monologue
to be held up, and continuity lost. In a sense he looks forward to Joyce,
even James, and is a complete contrast to Fielding or Smollett. 'Sterne,'
says David Thomson, 'is the first writer of fiction to believe that there is
no such happy thing as objective and universal reality.'

A Sentimental Journey shows one side of Sterne: his sermons under the
name of 'Mr Yorick', another. He liked travelling abroad by himself
and when he died had run through the fairly considerable sums his
writing had earned him. It seems highly probable that his body was
dug up and sold to the medical profession for dissection. A skull,
believed to be Sterne's, which accords with the Nollekens head, was
returned to the grave with its top sawn off, indication of the anatomists'
fright when they grasped the eminence of the corpse. This is a situation
which would have appealed to Sterne himself.

As a writer it might be suggested that Sterne's abilities were greater
than the seriousness with which he took writing. It was universally
agreed at the time that *Shandy* tailed off badly in the later instalments.
He seems to have filched the characters of Uncle Toby and Corporal
Trim, and the very name 'Tristram', in the most random way from
another book, yet his own originality is undeniable. It was Sterne's
view that 'it is not actions but opinions concerning actions, that disturb
men.'

Wild Excursions: The Life and Fiction   1972
of Laurence Sterne, David Thomson,   *Daily Telegraph*
Weidenfeld & Nicolson.

JAMES HOGG

Although objection can reasonably be taken to its awkward construction, *The Confessions of a Justified Sinner* remains a remarkably readable
and 'relevant' book. Its last edition was in 1947 with an Introduction by
André Gide. The present one reproduces the first edition of 1824 with
its occasional oddities of punctuation and spelling.

James Hogg (1770–1835), 'the Ettrick Shepherd', is one of those
unusual literary figures that the historical period and background – the
Lowlands of Scotland – seem to have been specially adapted to throw
up. Although he could claim the immense ramifications of relationship
characteristic of his country, he had little or no education except
reading the Bible, and earned his living as a shepherd. He began to
write verse in his early twenties and comparatively soon made some
sort of a name for himself. He became very much part of the local
literary scene, suffered a great many financial reverses of one kind and
another, and produced various works, of which the *Justified Sinner* is far
the most impressive.

The action of the novel takes place in the Lowlands between the last
decades of the seventeenth century and the first of the eighteenth. A
point worth noting is Hogg's originality in using real persons from time
to time in his narrative in the Proustian manner. Thus, for example, the
son of the (titular) Duke of Melford, who is falsely accused of killing the
Justified Sinner's brother, really did as a Jacobite enter the Austrian
service; James Watson, who flies into a rage on reading the Sinner's
pamphlet, really was the Queen's Printer in Scotland. The Sinner
himself is Robert Wringhim Colwan, younger son in name of the
easy-going laird of Dalcastle by his young, religiously bigoted wife, but
in fact – though we are never told this specifically – the child of her
lover, the equally bigoted Revd Mr Wringhim. He is brought up by his
mother and the minister in a separate part of the laird's house.

The story turns on the doctrine of predestination. There are the Elect
and the Damned, because God, knowing all, must know which is
which. Accordingly, it does not matter how the Elect behave, they are
safe, and, no matter what good works the Damned achieve, they are
still doomed to hell.

The catch is – or might seem to be – knowing which you are: but the

219

most rudimentary experience of human nature, on second thoughts, at once confirms that those who held the doctrine sufficiently strongly were subject to no doubts about being among the Elect. The Sinner himself suffered anxiety while growing up, but the moment he was informed that all was well by his mother and putative father, he never again felt serious cause to worry:

> Seeing that God had from all eternity decided the fate of every individual that was to be born of woman, how vain was it in man to endeavour to save those whom their Maker had, by an unchangeable decree, doomed to destruction.

Not only was that the case, so also was its corollary for those 'holding all the righteousness of man as filthy rags, and believing in the momentous and magnificent truth, that the more heavily loaden with transgressions, the more welcome was the believer at the throne of grace'. Does not the voice at this point become a trifle like Graham Greene's?

After a few rather amateurish evil deeds like getting a boy rival almost beaten to death for a caricature of their schoolmaster drawn by the Sinner himself, a young man called Gil-Martin appears in the Sinner's life, even more passionately convinced than himself of the necessity of carrying the doctrine of predestination to its logical conclusions. Gil-Martin, who, when he speaks of individuals at once begins to resemble them physically, is, in fact, the Devil. He spurs the Sinner on to commit several murders, including that of his brother and mother; finally abandoning him as an outcast enduring a life of terror in which demons fight for his possession above any hovel where he may take shelter.

Reflecting on *The Confessions of a Justified Sinner* one feels that its modern implications are not so much religious as political. The Communist party seems essentially, in Marxian terms, to take the place of the Elect who can do no wrong, whose very 'sins' – making a pact with the Nazis or invading Czechoslovakia – merely redound to the credit of what in itself must be the only 'good'.

In this connection attention should be drawn to an oddly appropriate detail in the novel. When the Sinner consorts with the Devil, he cannot at first imagine who this immensely distinguished, terrifyingly intelligent personage can be, who, by implication, seems powerful in the straightforward sense of ruling over many subjects. Then it dawns on him that he must be speaking with the Russian Tsar, Peter the Great, not long before visiting Great Britain incognito to study such things as shipbuilding.

The startling thing about the parallel of Communism is also how easily Gil-Martin's dialectic would fit into Dostoevsky's novel *The*

Devils (*The Possessed*). Much of his conversation could be satirically included by that great communist hater as it stands. *The Confessions of a Justified Sinner* would, incidentally, make a wonderful film, though one doubts whether we shall ever be lucky enough to see that done.

The Private Memoirs and Confessions
of a Justified Sinner, James Hogg,
with an introduction by John
Carey, Oxford University Press.

1969
Daily Telegraph

THOMAS LOVE PEACOCK

Thomas Love Peacock (1785–1866) possessed remarkable talents. His novels are, in their own way, quite original in form, and led to observable influence on later writers; if he is not a great poet, his verse is competent, some of it remembered; he was a considerable classical scholar; his work at East India House appears to have been useful and constructive. I own an 'omnibus' volume of Peacock's books, and tried to read it through some years ago. There are excellent patches, but in the end I broke down. Why, with so much to be said for him, does Peacock hold up less well than he should? His egotism is of the wrong sort. He thinks it sufficient to force all his views on the reader without consideration for his feelings, or trying to impose any pattern. He lacks discipline. He is not an 'artist'.

Surprisingly little is still known about Peacock's background. He was son of a London glass merchant, his mother, daughter of a naval officer. His latest biographer obviously feels there is more to be discovered, perhaps a mystery of some sort. One would agree. Peacock's father died (or disappeared?) when the author was a small child, and it seems possible he was taught to look on his grandfather as his father.

Another aspect of Peacock is his friendship with Shelley. Shelley, himself one of the most tiresome of men, seems to have found Peacock trying at times, but Peacock behaved well in various ways to the poet. (By the way, Mary Wollstonecraft's lover was Gilbert Imlay not Ismay.) There was a moment when Shelley, at the age of about twenty-nine, tried to get a job through Peacock as adviser to an Indian prince. It is greatly to be regretted that this project went no further. Peacock himself was thirty-four before he joined the Honourable East India Company's Service in London. One of his colleagues there, young at the time, but later of some distinction, said of Peacock that he 'enjoyed his company exceedingly', and that he was 'utterly unlike anybody I have ever seen before or since'.

One of Peacock's worst failings, so it seems to me, was that he thought the past *funny* in relation to the present. I find it hard to conceive a more detestable literary characteristic, but it was one from which many people suffered in the early nineteenth century, when it was to some degree understandable as a reaction from the Romantic Revival. Peacock wrote more than one facetious historical novel, and his sins in this direction are even less excusable because he was often well read in his subject. When quite a young man he went to Wales, fell in love with the country, and subsequently married the daughter of the Welsh clergyman with whom he had stayed. Wales and the idiosyncrasies of Welsh character and nomenclature play a great part in Peacock's works. For example, *The Misfortunes of Elphin* deals with Wales (more correctly Britain) in the Dark Ages. Peacock, uncommonly for the period, knew quite a lot about *The Triads* and the *Mabinogion* (not translated into English in his day), but he cannot prevent himself from finishing a chapter by saying that people have confused Cambria with Cumbria (a perfectly reasonable connecting of the two Celto-British realms), resulting in 'emboldening a northern antiquary to set about proving that King Arthur was a Scotchman'; a possibility, in historical fact, not at all to be ruled out.

On the other hand Peacock's 'War-Song of Dinas Vawr':

> The mountain sheep are sweeter,
> But the valley sheep are fatter

is a brilliant pastiche, in the best sense, of the poetry of the Bards.

Peacock's daughter married George Meredith, and Felix Felton has interesting things to say about the influence on Meredith of Peacock, a subject comparatively little explored. He might have included Norman Douglas as in some respects a Peacock derivative. The Meredith marriage was not a happy one. Meredith is, by tradition, the model for the *Death of Chatterton* by Henry Wallis, and the writer's wife subsequently ran away with the painter. This clouded Peacock's latter years, even though his son-in-law had got on his nerves, especially by going about the house humming, a habit Meredith attributed to his Welsh blood. There was a certain rough justice in this.

Reading Peacock, one is always coming across small items that have apparently been appropriated, or adapted, by other writers. In *Nightmare Abbey*, a character is described as being sent to a public school 'where a little learning was painfully beaten into him', and from thence to a university, where it was 'carefully taken out of him'. This seems likely to have inspired Max Beerbohm's comment that the 'nonsense' knocked out at school was quietly 'put back' at Oxford; in its way a good instance of Peacock's amusing, but usually rather unsubtle points, which can be improved upon.

Thomas Love Peacock, Felix Felton,   1977
Allen & Unwin.   *Daily Telegraph*

SHERIDAN LE FANU

When, in 1947, Elizabeth Bowen wrote an Introduction to a new edition of *Uncle Silas* – the novel which gives Sheridan Le Fanu (1814–73) a claim to be remembered – she pointed out that, although the story is set in Derbyshire, the book is plainly about an Irish country house, inhabited by Anglo-Irish characters. She expressed surprise at Le Fanu making this transposition, which inevitably resulted in certain incongruities. W. J. McCormack, Le Fanu's first full-length biographer, shows that the anglicisation of the story was simply the result of pressure from the London publisher.

The Le Fanus were a Huguenot family, one of whom had fought for William of Orange at the Boyne, another, of the following generation, settling in Ireland during the early part of the eighteenth century. Sheridan Le Fanu's grandfather was completely French by blood (the novelist's own portrait might well be that of a Frenchman), and had married a sister of Richard Brinsley Sheridan. This brought in a certain intellectual sparkle and some advantageous connections.

Le Fanu's father was a clergyman of the Church of Ireland, a man of considerable integrity, who, after a chaplaincy under viceregal patronage, had been appointed to a living in Limerick. An Irish parson's life was no sinecure. Apart from the Tithe War, Fenianism, agitations for Repeal of the Union, agrarian crimes, parishioners were accustomed to deciding even non-political local matters by methods that rejected any question of compromise. McCormack writes:

> The year of Catholic emancipation, 1829, was a disturbed one in Limerick and Tipperary. Between 11 April and 2 May four murders had been committed in the County Limerick (excluding the city) – according to the Limerick Chronicle, an average of one a week. On 3 August (a fair day) in Borrisokeane two factions arrived to fight by previous arrangement. Captain Dobbin (Sheridan Le Fanu's uncle cf. *Vanity Fair*), as the police officer in charge, tried to keep them apart: when one of his men had his skull fractured, he was obliged to read the Riot Act.
>
> He read the act three times in a futile attempt to disperse the rival mobs. Stones continued to pour down on his men, who returned fire

and shot a man dead. The police were now under siege and Dobbin read the act once more. The police fired: three men were killed, and a woman gathering stones was shot through the head. Finally the military arrived with a piece of cannon to restore order in the town. There was nothing exceptional about the incident except the pathos of Dobbin's oratory.

Le Fanu, educated at Trinity College, Dublin, became a barrister, but never seems to have been much of a hand at the Law. A Tory – though one prepared for radical changes – he tried at one moment to stand for Parliament. His candidature fell through more by chance than from what might be thought the unsuitability of his own temperament and the ramshackle nature of the family financial position. Le Fanu drifted into being an author and journalist, editing the *Dublin University Magazine*, a paper of some standing – a job he seems to have carried out adequately.

McCormack handles capably a lot of fairly intractable material including the contemporary Irish landscape, social and political; Le Fanu's character, one not at all easy to define; difficulties about shortage of information on aspects of the novelist's life. He freely admits that his subject wrote a good deal of poorish stuff (something Le Fanu himself would probably not have attempted to deny), and sets out the good points of *Uncle Silas* and some of the short stories. The literary criticism is inclined to fall back rather too often on the terms 'implosion' and 'hyperstasis' – to be avoided if practicable – but the final result is an interesting and intelligible picture.

Le Fanu, so far as that went, was happily married, though his wife suffered from religious disquiets (as to some extent he did himself), and died when her husband was in his forties. It seems a little hard to suggest that Le Fanu (who clearly liked flirting with his sister-in-law) 'may have been a latent homosexual' on the strength of his taste for telling his stories through a female narrator. However, he is undoubtedly a link, on one side, with the Gothic novelists of the 'Romantic Agony', on the other with the mystical excursions of Yeats and such.

Uncle Silas is about a girl whose father dies and in consequence she is sent to be brought up by a sinister uncle, believed by some to have committed a murder. An unusual element is added by the uncle being a Swedenborgian, a religious cult with which Le Fanu was familiar – a subject which opened up an extensive field of mysticism and symbolism. M. R. James, of ghost story fame, was an admirer of Le Fanu (some of whose writings he edited), and no doubt to some extent influenced by him.

Le Fanu tended to use his favourite situations and images more than once in his novels, and they are combined most effectively in *Uncle Silas*.

Some of the short stories contained in *Within a Glass Darkly* also have merit, among which 'Carmilla' deserves a mention, a tale of vampires and lesbianism.

McCormack draws attention to Le Fanu's habit of 'doubling' characters, showing that the 'good' brother in *Uncle Silas* is really another view of the same man as the 'bad' brother. He also points out that a legend seems to have grown up of a comparatively large school of Anglo-Irish writers in the nineteenth century, but in fact there were not many. Charles Lever (born in Dublin of wholly English descent) wrote breezy novels of military life, and was Le Fanu's contemporary and friend. Otherwise, there were few names until Wilde, Yeats, Synge, Shaw.

Like all the novelists of his generation Le Fanu would have benefited by more attention to form in his writing, but he was trying to make money, and could probably not have spared time, even had he wished. One feels that he might have told, had he chosen, a good deal about pre-Joycean Dublin.

Sheridan Le Fanu and Victorian Ireland,   1980
W. J. McCormack, Clarendon   *Daily Telegraph*
Press: Oxford University Press.

VERDANT GREEN AND VICTORIAN OXFORD

I feel pretty sure that I first read *The Adventures of Mr Verdant Green: An Oxford Freshman*, by Cuthbert Bede, BA, at the age of eleven or twelve in 1917, when, the war having brought my parents to Cambridge, we were living in what were normally out-of-college undergraduate rooms, where *Verdant Green* was among the few books. That was quite an appropriate background, though most of the Cambridge colleges were then accommodating army cadets. I did not understand a great deal of the story, but liked the illustrations drawn by the author himself, and, my sense of the past making me only dimly aware that Oxford must have altered a good deal since those days, accepted the picture as a realistic one. The vision never wholly faded, and notwithstanding the few vestigial traces that survived in the 1920s, undergraduates in the flesh turned out in many respects an anti-climax. From this initial reading I always retained the fact that scholars of Merton are known as postmasters.

Two points must be underlined: that the author of *Verdant Green* was never himself an Oxford undergraduate (nor even an Oxford don), and that his name was not Cuthbert Bede. He was called Edward Bradley, and fell in love with Oxford from the outside. This passion might be compared with Kipling's for the Army, both writers finding the same fascination in technical detail, and, Bradley especially, satirising as much as romanticising the institutions and types that had won their hearts.

Son of a surgeon from a Worcestershire family of long clerical (and perceptibly literary) tradition, the Revd Edward Bradley (1827–89) was educated at Kidderminster Grammar School and University College, Durham. Durham students in the Middle Ages had been associated with Trinity College, Oxford, since when several serious efforts had been made to establish a College in Durham itself, but these were unsuccessful until 1832. In short Durham University was new, but by no means 'redbrick'. Bradley graduated BA in 1848, Licentiate of Theology the following year. He was still too young to be ordained, and it was then that the Oxford experience took place. He seems to have studied at Oxford for about a year, and certainly made many undergraduate friends.

After he took orders there was a curacy at Glatton-with-Holme in

Huntingdonshire, the first of a procession of poetic names which were to be his incumbencies: Bobbington in Staffordshire; Detton-with-Caldecote in Huntingdonshire; Stretton in Rutland; finally Lenton-with-Hanby in Lincolnshire. Bradley was a hard-working, resourceful, popular clergyman, whose capabilities as a writer brought him into contact with a London world of books and journalism. He would sometimes raise quite large sums of money for his churches by lecturing on such subjects as 'Wit and Humour'. At a rather less gilded level there is perhaps a touch of a latter-day Sydney Smith.

Bradley wrote under the name Cuthbert Bede because the two patron saints of Durham are St Cuthbert and the Venerable Bede. He was not forgetful of his own *alma mater* in other respects either, calling his elder son by the former Christian name, and including a warmly reminiscent descriptive passage when Verdant Green passes through Durham to stay with friends in the North of England. The original *Verdant Green* drawings were based on Durham life, University College, Durham, possessing examples of his work. One regrets that Bradley never produced a novel about being a Durham undergraduate, which would have made an invaluable contribution to documenting the 'campus' life of a new university at that date.

Bradley wrote novels, verse, miscellaneous pieces for a great many periodicals, including *Punch, All the Year Round*, the *Illustrated London News*, the *Boy's Own Paper*, lots more. His occasional writings have gone the way of most journalism, and he had no gift as a poet, though he claims to have reintroduced into England the double-acrostic. As a novelist he was influenced no doubt by Dickens, Thackeray, Surtees, Marryat, and he contributed a few quite bright ideas of his own, but he is without much sense of construction or development of narrative. *Nearer and Dearer* (1857), for instance, opens with a promising situation. Two young men, bored by finding themselves snowbound in a country house, have a bet about persuading a hitherto unknown pupil at a neighbouring Academy for Young Ladies to grant a lock of her hair. One of the young men calls at the school, and asks for Miss Smith, saying he is her brother, taking a chance that there will be a girl of that surname; also risking (an embarrassment not emphasised) that Miss Smith might be revealed as less than ravishingly beautiful. It turns out that a pretty Miss Smith is indeed employed as a junior mistress. Her real brother has been in India since she was a small child, so that she at once embraces the impostor. All is going well, when the genuine brother arrives. Something might have been made out of this, but Bradley cannot sustain his story. All ends happily, but rather flatly.

Bradley may have seen *The Adventures of Oxymiel Classic, Esq.: Once an Oxford Scholar* (anon., 1768); otherwise *Verdant Green* seems to have inaugurated the subsequently proliferating 'Oxford novel' – T.

Hughes's *Tom Brown at Oxford* (1861), *The Hypocrite* (1898) by C. Ranger-Gull (the Oxford section wonderfully Ninetyish, the story ending in suicide), Beerbohm's *Zuleika Dobson* (1911), Book Three of *Sinister Street* (1914), by Compton Mackenzie, *Making Conversation* (1931), by Christine Longford (about a women's college), *Gaudy Night* (1935), by Dorothy L. Sayers – to mention only a few of a long line of Oxford novels, many of interest as period pieces.

Bradley's manuscript had considerable difficulty in finding a publisher. When this was done the work first appeared in three instalments: *Adventures* (1853); *Further Adventures* (1854); *Married and Done For* (1857). All were then bound up together in the last year, and sold in one volume. By 1870 *Verdant Green* had gone to 100,000 copies; sales doubled when the book was issued in sixpenny format. Bradley made only £350 out of the whole transaction, so that his publishers could congratulate themselves on their astuteness.

Twenty years later Bradley attempted a sequel in *Little Mr Bouncer, and His Friend, Verdant Green* (1878). This pendant to the earlier work usually gets rather a bad press. Certainly *Little Mr Bouncer* lacks the full impact of the original, but the author – curiously unchanged once back in his old element – has something to say in the Oxford sections (only about half the book), and these additional Verdant Green trimmings are worth a glance, especially for contemporary language.

Bradley was in the habit of illustrating his novels, and for *Verdant Green* the author's own pictures are beyond question a *sine qua non*. This fact is reinforced by the Boy's Holiday Library edition (1900), with four plates only, by M. Bede Hewerdine. The style suggests a hardened illustrator of school stories, who here felt it necessary to impose a faint touch of Pre-Raphaelitism via Walter Crane. The only conceivable reason for choosing Hewerdine (if not a pseudonym) must have been in his middle name. As a comic draughtsman Bradley might be defined as less professional than Thackeray but funnier, free of a self-conscious archness of comment that Thackeray's line so often conveys. Betjeman used many *Verdant Green* pictures with good effect throughout *An Oxford University Chest* (1938), something Bradley – and Verdant Green himself – would have appreciated from a future Poet Laureate.

The theme of *Verdant Green* is the classical one of the innocent young man who is taken in by everyone he meets; Oxford providing an ideal setting for hoaxes and swindles perpetrated on a novice. The hero, only son among several daughters of a Warwickshire squire, has on his mother's insistence not attended a public school. His father, never having been to a university, is not greatly drawn to them either, but is persuaded by the local parson, whose own son is already up at Oxford.

The next question to be decided was, to which of the three Universities should he go – to Oxford, Cambridge, or Durham. . . .

Mr Green at once put Durham aside, on account of its infancy, and its want of *prestige* that attaches to the names of the two great Universities.

Cambridge was next ruled out, Mr Green having heard that 'the great Newton' had been 'horsed' as a Cambridge undergraduate, and fearing such severe discipline might continue at that University. In fact very little is known about Newton's Cambridge days, Mr Green's misapprehension evidently referring to John Aubrey's note about Milton being whipped while at Christ's; interesting in the implication that Verdant Green's father had read, if incorrectly remembered, Malone's selection from the *Brief Lives* (1813).

Oxford therefore it had to be. The local parson arranged for entrance to Brazenface College, the name presumably designating Brasenose, though BNC is also mentioned quite often in the book; once as housing 'a very gentlemanly set'. This was before the period when Brasenose came to be thought of as a predominantly athletic college, its early-nineteenth-century reputation having more the sort of distinction Jowett was to achieve for Balliol; that was probably intended by Bradley to be also the Brazenface tone.

Going up at Easter (in what would come to be looked on as a 'by-term' now that the academic year begins in October) Verdant Green travels with his father in a stage-coach, thereby dating the moment to before September 1852, by which time the railway had taken over, coaches ceased to run. Fellow passengers include several undergraduates destined to play a part in Verdant Green's Oxford life, their behaviour heralding what he is in for. To the great alarm of Green *père* one of these young men, Four-in-hand Fosbrooke (a nickname borrowed without acknowledgement by Galsworthy for Four-in-hand Forsyte in *The Forsyte Saga*), for some miles of the journey takes over the reins from the coachman, causing the vehicle to rock ominously from side to side while (in a phrase from *Little Mr Bouncer*) Fosbrooke is 'tooling the tits'.

Verdant Green, matriculating with a minimum of formality, settles down to be an 'Oxford man'. The undergraduate generation portrayed is that of the late 1840s, early 1850s. Sweeping changes, institutional and social, were to take place in the University very soon, though still short of those to follow in the 1870s. The previous Oxford decade had undergone the heart-searchings of the Tractarian Movement; while Matthew Arnold (Balliol) had won the Newdigate with a poem on Cromwell; a few years later (about the date when the complete *Verdant Green* was published) Swinburne (Balliol) would be proclaiming rampant atheism to the Old Mortality Society. *Verdant Green* contains no hint of any such fierce intellectual life. The furthest anyone goes in that direction is for a 'Reading Man', anxious to earn a good degree, to object when the *cornet-à-pistons* or the drum are played too continuously under the window when he is attempting to work.

In *Little Mr Bouncer*, however, there does occur the expression 'aesthetical taste', one certainly current by the late 1870s, though perhaps questionable at the date of Verdant Green's Oxford residence. In any case aestheticism is not invoked in connection with what was later to be known as an 'aesthete'. On the contrary, the phrase is applied to the Hon. Blucher Boots, a raffish young man devoted to racing, who is found in the middle of the morning wearing a 'scarlet Turkish fez' with a crimson-and-blue striped dressing-gown. His rooms are decorated with Landseer prints, Parian statuettes, 'pretty feminine inanities', but horses rather than the arts preoccupy the owner, who tries to ensnare Verdant Green into 'making a book' on the Derby.

More in the ancestry of aesthetes-to-be – though O U D S aesthetes might be held to have fallen into a rather special category of their own – is the stage-struck Foote (St John's) in *Verdant Green*, known as 'Footelights' on account of his theatrical obsessions. Foote's rooms are hung with 'water-colour drawings by Cattermole, Cox, Fripp, Hunt, and Frederick Taylor' (all still holding their market reasonably well, especially Cox), making a background for suits of armour, Etruscan vases, a Gothic lectern. Foote was accustomed to give imitations of Keane and other famous actors; a trapdoor into the wine-cellar providing an aperture for representing Hamlet in Ophelia's grave. Another potential aesthete, this time of a gastronomic order, is promised by Towlinson, who always brings into Hall a bottle of *The King of Oude's Sauce* (doubtless a shrewdly named chutney, Oude then being in the news), but Towlinson, like Blucher Boots, turns out to be sporting in his tastes, belonging, in fact, to a 'bad set' that indulged in cock-fighting.

At this period St Mary's Hall (known as Skimmery) had not yet been absorbed into Oriel, and Worcester was referred to by more centrally situated colleges as Botany Bay. Noblemen still wore gold tassels on their mortar-board caps (a punishment for drunkenness, Verdant Green was told), hence the term tuft-hunter for a snob. When he speaks of the 'Oxford Snobocracy', however, Bradley means what he calls elsewhere the *profanum vulgus*, 'snob' (shoemaker) still denoting a person of lower social status, rather than one over-keen on associating with those of higher rank. All classes are derided equally by Bradley: rackety aristocrats; prosy dons; pilfering servants; rapacious tradesmen; shady loafers. Verdant Green's scout, Filcher, lives up to his surname, while Mrs Tester, the bedmaker (a female adjunct to become obsolete, then come into fashion again in recent times), is perpetually in need of lumps of sugar soaked in brandy to cure her spasms.

Owing to his spectacles Verdant Green is at once known as

Giglamps, possibly the earliest instance in print of this subsequently stereotyped nineteenth-century nickname for the bespectacled. Although prototype of all duffers at sport, and pitilessly ragged, he seems to have been generally popular. There is perhaps a slight ambiguity here, which the author never wholly resolves. If Verdant Green were quite so maladroit as represented, would he have gone down well with the 'hearties' in his college? In rather the same way, after abject failure as dog-owner, horseman, archer, cricketer, fencer, boxer, skater, oar, Verdant Green in the end manages to sit a horse reasonably well, and actually rows in the Brazenface Torpid (second College boat). Could he have so far adjusted himself? Perhaps he could, his innocence and doggedness exerting an invincible charm. His actual allowance is never mentioned, but it seems possible that he was fairly well off, which may have helped. At least his father supplied him with solid silver plate (with crest and motto *Semper virens*), most of which seems to have been 'mislaid' in due course by Filcher.

After his first 'wine' Verdant Green appears to have found no difficulty in joining in with his friends' drinking, and he at once took to smoking, a habit marred only by an occasion when he was lured into inhaling a giant cigar made up of cabbage leaves, brown paper, and refuse tobacco. The convincing account of a hangover suggests that Bradley himself was familiar with those dire symptoms. Much of Oxford undergraduate life of the period was for the not too fastidious. Over the river from Christ Church meadows lay a field where an itinerant hawker patrolled with a cage of live rats slung on his back. These could be released at sixpence a time for undergraduates to try out the sporting proclivities of their dogs. There were also the recurrent 'Town and Gown' scrimmages, which dated back to the Middle Ages, when medieval undergraduates had been known to lose their lives in these light-hearted rags.

Verdant Green takes part in the time-honoured Town and Gown brawl on the night of the Fifth of November – 'the Saturnalia of Guy-Fawkes' – when his undergraduate acquaintances engage the services of The Putney Pet, a London prize-fighter, to stiffen their ranks in what must have been at times fairly demanding encounters. On this particular evening hostilities are sparked off by a 'slang rhyme of peculiar offensiveness used to a Wadham gentleman'. We may safely assume that the verses in question included the word Sodom, but it is not clear how the townsmen knew that particular undergraduate came from Wadham College; the assumption perhaps causing trouble with someone who was in fact not a Wadhamite.

At the height of the battle we are told that 'a cowardly fellow was using his heavy-heeled boots on the body of a prostrate undergraduate', but 'to the credit of the Town, be it said, they discarded bludgeons and stones, and fought, in John Bull fashion, with their fists'. The Senior Proctor, felled in the mêlée, is rescued by The Pet. The prize-fighter had agreed to wear a mortar-board for the festivities, but could not be induced to assume a gown – even a short commoner's gown – for fear of cramping his pugilistic style. Accordingly the Proctor, once safe behind a College gate, immediately taxes his rescuer with failure to be in correct academic attire.

Muted in modern terms, the subject of sex is not altogether ignored. Indeed one feels that Bradley knew a great deal more than he was prepared to set down on paper. Incidentally his picture of Verdant Green kissing a maid on the stairs on his return from Oxford, which appears in some impressions of the book, was omitted from others. Had it caused disapproval? If so, from what quarter?

Verdant Green, walking one day down the High, is attracted by a girl who looks French; and French she turns out to be. Willing to try every sport at least once, 'he stalked this little deer to her lair.' The lair turns out to be a 'fancy hosiery warehouse'; and he spends the next fortnight buying odds and ends he does not in the least want in order to chat with her. One suspects that Mademoiselle Mouslin de Laine (like several of the dons, the waiter at the *Mitre* with a face 'like half a sliced muffin', Filthy Lucre, the dog-seller) may be drawn from life, if only because a French girl employed in an Oxford haberdasher's otherwise sounds so improbable.

The word 'deer' is used again by the author, possibly with a similar connotation in his mind. Verdant Green, on a walk one morning, 'strolled round the neatly-kept potato-gardens denominated the Parks, looking in vain for the deer that have never been there, and finding them represented only by nursery-maids – and others'. But who were the Others thus separated by a dash? Were they young men hoping to scrape acquaintance with the nursery-maids, or could tarts be picked up between the potato-gardens? There is a further hint of undercover sex, though only in reading-matter. Verdant Green falls into the habit of taking a punt out on to the Cherwell, where lounge other undergraduates 'with their legs up and a weed in their mouth, reading the latest novel, or some less immaculate work'. But, since novels in those days were apt to be denigrated as a 'waste of time', is an erotic book implied?

Verdant Green himself seems to have been strongly drawn to the opposite sex. On the occasion of the Northumberland visit to the country house of an Oxford friend's parents he immediately falls in love with one of the girls also staying there; and behaves with notable bravery when she is threatened by a dangerous bull. (Bulls seem to have been very much on Bradley's mind, because a similar incident with another bull takes place only a few pages later.) Unlike most novels of the period no difficulties whatever are raised by either family about the young couple becoming engaged.

Once again, since Verdant Green has no apparent job in prospect, we are led to wonder whether the Green family were not a great deal richer than generally indicated. It is agreed, reasonably enough, that the wedding should not be celebrated for two years. Even so, when Green formally takes his BA degree, he is a married man. That might well happen today, even more probably at an American college; but surely a married Oxford undergraduate would have been very unusual in the 1850s? Perhaps there were sides to Verdant Green underplayed by the author, and, from what they knew of their son, his parents were only too thankful to have him married and settled. Indeed the many stories about Verdant Green's vigorous sex life may have been the reason for his being found so acceptable by his more dissipated acquaintances.

The naturalist John George Wood (1827–89) has been put forward as a model for Verdant Green's Oxford friend Henry Bouncer (hero of the sequel). Wood, also a surgeon's son, was one of the undergraduate companions of Bradley's Oxford interlude, the friendship kept up all their lives, which occupied exactly the same span of years. Wood, well known in his day as a popular rather than rigorously scientific writer on his subject, had been at Oxford one of the Merton postmasters; became a clergyman; married; and throughout his life produced a flow of books on natural history, sometimes diverging to other matters like *The Boy's Own Treasury of Sports and Pastimes* (1866). This looks rather like one of those not uncommon occasions when a character in a novel is automatically identified with someone known to be associated with the author, the parallel drawn with little or no regard to actual resemblance. Wood is described as a 'weakly' child, devoted from his earliest years to natural history, a parson whose churches were noted for their choral services. He may well have been small and noisy, it is true, but one doubts whether even as an undergraduate he ever behaved quite like Bouncer, ceaselessly blowing a post-horn, two rampageous terriers always at his heels, almost illiterate, and cribbing in his exams to avoid being 'plucked'. Incidentally, Bouncer, whose mother, a widow, wished him to read for the bar, is represented on one page of the book as having been educated at Eton; on another, at Harrow. At first sight this duality might seem improbable, but it must be remembered that Matthew Arnold was at school both at Rugby and Winchester; Trollope at both Winchester and Harrow. Perhaps Bouncer was indeed that rare bird an Old Etonian Old Harrovian.

Bradley had an observant eye, and is well read. One must regret that he represents an early example of that only too common modern aberration of saying Frankenstein instead of Frankenstein's Monster, but against that he perceptively draws attention to the 'impossible gownsman' in Turner's *View of Oxford, from Ferry Hincksey*. When he quotes Tweedledum and Tweedledee they are from John Byrom ('Christians, awake! Salute the happy morn'), rather than Lewis Carroll's *Alice*. There are informative vignettes like Verdant Green's visit as a tourist to Blenheim, showing how far from recent is the Stately Home industry, and how much more exorbitant in the past; a servant taking the sightseer a short way, then handing him on to a series of other flunkies with the words: 'I don't go any further, sir; half-a-crown!'

In his *Notes sur l'Angleterre* (1872) the French philosopher and historian Hippolyte Taine employs *Aventures de M. Verdant Green, illustré par l'auteur* as one of the keys to English university life. Taine (whose investigations in England had taken place in the 1860s, when in some respects Oxford was already changed in tone from the Verdant Green period) records the hero's '*passion naissante pour une grisette*', concluding from all he had heard and read that in English universities drunkenness was more permissible than libertinism. Taine (incidentally, an admirer of Casanova's *Memoirs*) found the novel '*un petit roman assez gai*'; no doubt an excellent example of his own theories as to '*la race, le milieu et le moment*'.

When towards the end of the century Gladstone (Christ Church) visited Oxford after an interval of many years, the veteran Oxonian was appalled by the slovenly aspect of the bowler-hatted undergraduates. He himself had been up about twenty years before Verdant Green, in whose day there would still probably have been little to find fault with in the way of undergraduate turn-out. One wonders what either of them would think on returning to an Oxford where Town and Gown are indistinguishable; even male and female sometimes requiring a second look. An updated *Verdant Green* might achieve something amusing and penetrating in the way of satire.

Introduction to *The Adventures of Mr Verdant Green*, Cuthbert Bede, B A, Oxford University Press, 1982

I I

The social status of dons has probably never been higher than at the present time. Indeed, nowadays, their situation might almost be compared with that of Negroes in the 1920s, when no smart party could be considered complete unless at least one of them – and often two or three or even a whole company – were to be seen standing about conversing animatedly and sipping champagne, in immaculate evening dress. If C. B. Cochran were still alive he would probably be considering the production of an All-Don Revue, on the lines of *Blackbirds*; and very enjoyable it would no doubt also be. It is therefore of interest to trace the earlier stages of the don's emancipation from the obscurity of mere tuition and scholarship, into this more public – and perhaps in some ways more dangerously exposed – way of life.

Balliol Rhymes is a collection of poetical comment, nearly all in the same metre, written by seven undergraduates, on the contemporary Fellows, Scholars and Commoners of that college then at the peak of its fame. The Rhymes first appeared as a broadsheet in 1881, under the title *A Masque of B - ll - - l.* It was suppressed on publication. The High Table naturally predominates, though there are also many interesting portraits of undergraduates. The tone is set by what is, on the whole, the best known – and certainly often misquoted – lines on the Head of the House:

> First come I. My name is J - w - tt.
> There's no knowledge but I know it
> I am Master of this College.
> What I don't know isn't knowledge.

This was written by H. C. Beeching, who later became Dean of Norwich. Other contributors were J. W. Mackail, J. B. B. Nichols, Lord Sumner (formerly J. A. Hamilton), C. A. Spring-Rice, P. E. Matheson and L. F. Smith. After the verse on Jowett – and in strong competition with it for popularity, and inaccuracy of quotation – is that dealing with Lord Curzon:

> I am a most superior person, Mary,
> My name is G - - rge N - th - n - - l C - rz - n, Mary,
> I'll make a speech on any political question of the day, Mary,
> Provided you'll not say me nay, Mary.

The variant of the last two lines, which has acquired a certain undeniable orthodoxy, of course runs:

> My hair is soft, my face is sleek,
> I dine at Blenheim once a week.

It is of interest to note that even so late as 1925 the Bodleian authorities were unwilling to allow a photograph to be made of the original broadsheet, by that time unobtainable, because Curzon, then Chancellor of the University, had taken this definition of his character so hard. The explanation of the evocation to Mary is that

> there was a drawing, much circulated in the college, of Curzon – who had written in verse that he was joined to a supposititious Mary by a seal (*sigillum*) – standing with Mary in front of a seal (*phoca*), who joins their hands with his paws.

Spring-Rice, one of the undergraduate contributors, is thus depicted:

> Can story-telling be a vice
> When you've an uncle like Spr - ng-R - ce?
> My versatility is such
> None likes me little, or knows me much.

There is a variant of the first two lines:

> All things to all men, I'm Spr - ng-R - ce,
> I have not one redeeming vice.

From this gallery it is tempting to quote copiously, for the level is so high that first one, then another, seems to call for special mention. The severe discipline, exercised on technical grounds, may be judged by the fact that the following lines were excluded, because only a single couplet, while the rest of the collection were quatrains:

> I am ——; I care for nothing
> But my pink silk underclothing.

Paravicini, the Balliol don, is here, of whom many stories are told; perhaps the best known that, when a punt full of ladies passed accidentally through Parson's Pleasure, where he was bathing in a state of nature, he wrapped his towel round his head, hoping thus to avoid recognition. One of the ladies is alleged to have remarked: 'I think that must be Mr Paravicini. He is the only red-haired don in Balliol.'

> What an oddity am I,
> Little cynic P - r - vi,
> Virgil I can shrilly render
> Cock-a-hoop upon the fender.

There is much that is of interest, social and otherwise, in this volume, and W. G. Hiscock has done a service by putting these vignettes on record in a permanent manner. Reading the verses, it is hard not to feel that the glory has largely departed. There are twenty-two somewhat melancholy years from which the college must be reorientated: dregs of a mug of cocoa left on the table after a Fabian summer school. Let us hope the future will be more inspiring; perhaps more in the manner of these Rhymes. Collectors of rare items should look ahead and consider the possibilities of this little book.

Balliol Rhymes, edited by W. G.   1955
Hiscock, printed for the Editor,   *Punch*
18 Squitchey Lane, Oxford.

GEORGE MOORE

I

George Moore (1852–1933) is one of those figures who show up the inadequacy of normal descriptive methods. From one point of view he was a remarkable writer, perhaps even more remarkable critic of painting; from another it would hardly be going too far to say that in spite of these remarkable qualities he was a bore and rather an ass. At least many of his own contemporaries undeniably took the latter view. There seems really no way of reconciling such opposed aspects, less unusual among distinguished men than perhaps might be supposed.

Nancy Cunard is an admirable person to write about Moore, not only because she knew him since she herself was four years old, but also for her sparkling, spiky personality, riddled with the shot and shell of the Twenties, against which it is possible to contrast the special characteristics of her subject. How wonderfully wicked she looks, wearing a row of huge bangles on her arms, in a photograph taken by Cecil Beaton in 1930. It would not be exactly true to say that she writes well, but she puts across a lively picture of George Moore.

Moore is not, I should say, greatly read nowadays. For my own part I have never been able to get on with his books, except *Lewis Seymour and Some Women*, read at a very early age, and the *Hail and Farewell* trilogy, the volumes of which possess a quality of their own, and go a long way to explain Moore's fame. There is a coarseness of texture about his writing. One feels that he is on the right side but can never control his own personality. It is true, I think, to say that he won fame: because, read or not, he is certainly remembered for this powerful personality.

Soon after I was married we had the good fortune to acquire Moore's former cook, Clara Warville, who herself contributed a chapter to Joseph Hone's excellent *Life of George Moore*. She was a woman of mature age and great personal charm, although rather nervous after her Ebury Street days. 'Mr Moore said "I hope you will stay with me for the rest of my life, Clara,"' she told us, 'but it was only thirteen years . . .' She possessed a photograph of Moore taken standing beside Gosse, who was out of range of the camera. 'I had Sir Edmund Gosse's arm painted out,' she said. Her way of speaking of Moore and his tastes in food brought him immediately to life.

In the same way Nancy Cunard re-creates him against the background of Nevill Holt, the Cunard seat in Leicestershire, where, his duties as an MFH at an end for the day, her father used to spend his time – so she tells us – in the tower room carving coconuts to mount into cups. Moore was often a visitor, and used sometimes to read the Lesson in church.

Some of Moore's literary likes and dislikes appear here. He hated 'ideas' in novels. Certainly there are few in his own – therefore he detested the works of James and Conrad. He was induced to read a bit of Proust, but found it, naturally enough, unsympathetic. Hardy was anathema to him. On the other hand, he approved of Joyce – at least in the beginning – and was one of those who helped to obtain a Civil List pension for the author of *Ulysses*. Yeats, with whom Moore was, of course, closely associated, he described as 'looking like a large, rolled-up umbrella left behind by some picnic party'. He had wanted to be a painter in his early days, and the clue to Moore, both as a writer and a man, is perhaps this change of medium that was forced on him by his lack of proficiency with the brush. There must have been some very deep appreciation of painting born in him, for nothing in his background suggests any early encouragement or knowledge of the art. His connection with the Impressionists is perhaps his most interesting side. Nancy Cunard was fortunate enough to inherit from him Manet's beautiful *Étude pour 'Le Linge'*.

'I was a great dab at making love, you know,' he remarked once to Nancy Cunard, who writes a spirited defence of him against the accusation that it was a subject to which he was devoted chiefly theoretically. Certainly the way he wrote of love, and talked of it, must be admitted to suggest the reverse of 'a great dab', whatever the truth may in fact have been. 'Chabanel', by the way, should surely read 'Chabanais', the well-known Paris brothel.

GM: *Memories of George Moore,*   1956
Nancy Cunard, Hart-Davis.   *Punch*

II

George Moore possessed that peculiar form of self-absorption that makes a man interesting; although those who exist in this manner walk a tight-rope across an abyss of boredom into which they may not only fall themselves but also plunge many more or less innocent victims among those who have dealings with them. The fact is that in spite of doing, saying and writing many foolish things in the course of his life there was in him a hard core of intelligence and sensibility, most apparent in his approach to pictures, but cropping up at unexpected moments both in his books and in his life. Many of Moore's silly and unattractive pronouncements were made on the subject of his own love affairs. It is accordingly not unexpected that his correspondence has been received by certain reviewers with raised eyebrows and the suggestion that at least some of the letters were deliberately written with a view to eventual publication by a vain man incapable of deep feeling.

Such criticism immediately opens up a formidable consideration of who has a right to say whether or not another person is in love, and to what extent exhibitionism about a love affair may be held to add to or subtract from its seriousness. After reading these letters (admirably edited by Rupert Hart-Davis) my own feeling is that Moore was undoubtedly in love with Lady Cunard all his life; and I think that the oddness and unsatisfactoriness of the relationship is in its way more moving than many more streamlined passions.

Under 300 letters remain from what were probably several thousand. Whether the rest were destroyed deliberately or happened by chance not to be preserved we do not know. These here reproduced were bequeathed by their recipient to Sacheverell Sitwell, who released them for publication. We do not know how it all began, although it seems fairly certain that Maud Burke (1872–1948) met Moore before her marriage to Sir Bache Cunard – probably in 1894, when the photograph of the frontispiece shows her to have been a young woman of decided beauty and charm. Her parents were rich Americans from San Francisco and she spent much of her youth in Europe. Justly famous as a hostess, she was devoted to the arts – especially music – to which she brought an enthusiasm and intelligence that made themselves felt throughout the world that bothers about such matters; an enthusiasm, one might add, quite unknown in our epoch, absorbed in its own politics. She was, as might be expected, a woman of great toughness.

'Do not trouble about a fur-lined overcoat,' wrote Moore to Lady Cunard in 1906. 'You gave me a comb twelve years ago and I have the pieces still. I'd much sooner have a letter from you than all the fur in Canada.' She was apparently not much of a letter writer, as these complaints recur; but right up to the end he was assuring her that she alone made his life seem real and that their love affair in the first instance had come to him as a revelation.

In 1910 they were both nearly killed by a runaway motor car in Munich. The *Continental Daily Mail* gave an account of it, adding Moore's story in his own highly characteristic words:

The stopping of the motor seemed like a miracle, and the miracle did not seem less when, taking off my trousers at the hotel, I found the pattern of the nails of the tyre printed all along the torn cloth . . .

when I was pulled out and it was found that my legs were not broken and that I could stand on them I staggered off in search of Lady Cunard, attracted by the sight of men carrying women away.

Although nothing much is said, these letters give a curiously realistic picture of the last half of Moore's life; for he was already middle-aged when they met. Lady Cunard was commissioned in one of these letters to buy a commemorative brooch for his delightful and talented cook, Clara Warville, and a very nice brooch it turned out to be.

George Moore: Letters to Lady Cunard,   1957
1895–1933, edited by Rupert Hart-   *Punch*
Davis, Hart-Davis.

GEORGE GISSING

George Gissing (1857–1903) was – to employ Richard Cobb's useful term from the French – a miserabilist; in fact, probably the foremost miserabilist England has ever produced. His track-record has not been surpassed even by his fervent admirer George Orwell who loses points by being undeniably funny about Gem and Magnet Library school-stories or comic postcards. Gissing is never more of a miserabilist than when trying to be light-hearted. He established this overwhelming supremacy by blighting his own life early and irretrievably. The son of an intellectual chemist in Wakefield, he was a brilliant scholarship boy, set fair for a successful academic career. Then, when at Owen's College, Manchester, at the age of eighteen he fell in love with a prostitute a year younger than himself. In order to have money to reclaim her he stole from fellow students, was caught, and served a month's imprisonment.

Except as an irresistible need for personal disaster (a taste to haunt him throughout life) there seems no explanation of such conduct. Gissing appears to have been fairly highly sexed, romantic, but at the same time scrupulously honest in later dealings, never a young man to 'do a dare' while a moment's thought would have told him he was bound to be nabbed.

He went to the United States on release from prison, and managed to keep himself by teaching and, more surprisingly, writing short stories for newspapers. Then he suddenly gave up his teaching job, returned to England, and married the prostitute Nell with whom he had continued to correspond. As might be expected this was a ghastly failure. Nell was an alcoholic, showed no great wish to be reclaimed, went off from time to time on her former profession and finally, having parted from Gissing, died of syphilis in unspeakable squalor. The best to be said is that Gissing was not accused by the police of living on her earnings.

Gissing's story, anyway at its opening, is more adapted to Dostoevsky or Maupassant than any English writer, and greater freedom of expression would have suited Gissing himself in his novels. He managed to market his work but only on that edge of starvation, which he so ably depicts, and, in early days, through the medium of blood-sucking publishers like Smith, Elder. All this John Halperin describes well, putting forward the convincing theory that Gissing left

America because he had begun to fall in love, and felt that fate demanded he must return to suffer torment with Nell.

It was Gissing's conviction that a man with no money, no prospects, and a guilty secret could not marry an educated woman, though he might find a decent working-class girl who would take him on. This was not because he had any liking for the working classes. In fact, after a brief period of romantic Socialism, he detested them and thought they should not be bettered by education.

It is interesting that when Gissing lodged behind Madame Tussaud's, so strongly did he feel about social position that he was unwilling to carry a carton of sugar back to his flat in about 1888 when surely the worst to be encountered would have been a suspicious glance from Sherlock Holmes and Dr Watson.

Living an intensely lonely life, but somehow managing just to keep afloat through his books, Gissing finally succeeded in picking up and marrying a working-class girl, generally agreed to have neither looks nor notable intelligence. Her family, very sensibly, was not keen on the union. This, too, was a disaster. Gissing had two sons by his wife who – something not to be foreseen though perhaps to some extent provoked by a chilling streak in Gissing's personality – finally went mad, became violent, and, again after separation, had to be put under restraint.

Gissing, sometimes travelling abroad, lived for a time on his own, at one moment being attracted by a widow called Mrs Williams, who later remarried and became famed as Malcolm Muggeridge's mother-in-law. It was during this period that Gissing, now forty, met and fell in love with his French translator Gabrielle Fleury, a personable young woman with quite distinguished literary connections. Gissing could not marry as his wife was still alive, but Gabrielle agreed to live with him and pass as his wife. For a short time all was well, but circumstances forced Gissing to share a flat with Gabrielle's mother, whose French economy reduced him physically to a state that living for months in London on bread-and-dripping or German sausage had failed to do. He had to come back to England, stay with H. G. Wells (where he gained 7lb in a week) and enter a sanatorium. He pulled through, but death was not far off. Wells was present at Gissing's end, which he put to good use in *Tono-Bungay* (1908) in the picture of George Ponderevo's last days. Wells also did what he could after Gissing's demise to diminish his former friend's literary reputation.

Halperin is a keen Gissing enthusiast though not blind to faults. From knowledge limited to *New Grub Street*, *The Odd Women* and *The Private Papers of Henry Ryecroft* I would agree that the two former are remarkable novels if a trifle wooden. Gissing can convey none of the vitality to be found in, say, Conrad, born in the same year. At the same time there is no one quite like Gissing. *Henry Ryecroft*, a romantic vision of himself in retirement, has also a certain awful fascination.

John Halperin does not mention Joyce or D. H. Lawrence, but one feels *Dubliners* owed something to Gissing (whom Joyce did not find tough enough) while Joyce's Earwiker clearly derives from Gissing's Earwaker. Lawrence admitted to liking Gissing, and influences may be detected.

Gissing: A Life in Books, John   1978
Halperin, Oxford University Press.   *Daily Telegraph*

A. C. BENSON

Of the eighteen writers parodied in Max Beerbohm's *A Christmas Garland* (1912) the work of only three or four would probably be unknown to a reasonably literate young reader of the present day. Among those forgotten few A. C. Benson (1862–1925) would certainly figure; Beerbohm's quiet but devastating take-off of an A. C. Benson novel making clear why that should be so. Benson's most lasting literary monument – if one omits his editing of a selection from Queen Victoria's Letters – is *Land of Hope and Glory*. There is a certain irony in this particular memorial, because he was a man whose fears tended to swamp his hopes, and, although he appreciated glory in certain respects, he was inclined to mock its outward manifestations. He also kept a voluminous Journal, and – as the title of David Newsome's absorbing biography indicates – an unexpurgated version of this journal may prove very entertaing when published.

The largeish Benson family, children of an Archbishop of Canterbury, also included E. F. Benson who does not appear in Beerbohm's *Garland* but whose novels have not passed into such complete oblivion as his brother's. The ecclesiastical and intellectual background was fairly formidable, and in a sense A. C. Benson, in spite of a copious literary output, and becoming Master of Magdalene College, Cambridge, never quite adjusted himself to his own full life. He was neither a scholar nor an 'artist' but fell between these stools; nevertheless his personality and gift for description make him an extremely interesting man.

For eighteen years Benson was an assistant-master at Eton, during twelve of which he had a House (as it happens, handing on his boys to my own Housemaster there), and Benson's remained something of a legend, if a dim one, for civilised behaviour under the philistine headmastership of Warre. There was more than a possibility that A. C. Benson might himself have become headmaster of Eton but his desire to modernise combined with dislike for administration, would have made that position a burden to him.

Benson left Eton on the strength of earning enough money from his writing to live on; in due course became a don at Cambridge. Here one might cast an eye on the odd ups and downs of Benson's finances. Eton

245

was stingy about a pension, allotting him only the minimum, and Magdalene College, Cambridge, at first paid him nothing at all as a Fellow . On the other hand, for some years he made between three and four thousand out of Queen Victoria's Letters; soon about the same from his other books.

A. C. Benson's novels, which even he himself did not take too seriously, elicited passionate fan-letters from ladies. This was a great embarrassment to him reaching a peak when a very rich American lady wrote to say that she would like to make him a present of £40,000. (Speaking as a novelist myself I can confirm that this is unusual, even at a period of inflation.) Benson (like Caesar) refused the offer three times. Finally, however (like Caesar again), he accepted; ending his life with a capital of some £100,000.

Newsome's book naturally depends to a great extent on Benson's own diaries, from which many amusing quotations are made. One cannot fail to be struck by Benson's sharpness and wit in recording his own life, qualities he was quite unable to transfer to fiction.

Benson was not incapable of feeling attraction towards young women, but his life was ruled by romantic passions for boys. Newsome gives a full and balanced account of these, and one wholly believes that Benson never swerved in the smallest degree from a scrupulous correctness. None the less it is hard to accept his own claim to be all but sexless. Like others of his generation he disliked sexual matters being closely examined, and detested overt homosexuality. He was, indeed, extremely intolerant of friends and colleagues indulging in precisely the flirtations with young men which were the mainspring of his own emotional life.

On two occasions, each for a matter of several years, Benson suffered appalling nervous breakdowns. There was a strain of manic-depression in the family. Not always easy academic relationships, his impatience at being able to write only pot-boilers did not assist what was no doubt an hereditary disorder. David Newsome handles all this material with considerable agility, and his book is good reading from beginning to end.

In some respects Benson's world as represented here is as interesting for the people who are left out as for those who come in. Edith Wharton, for instance, is merely 'a rich invalid with a passion for literature separated from a tipsy husband'. There is a splendidly comic running row between Benson and Edmund Gosse, who, incidentally, found E. M. Forster's *Howard's End* to be 'vile, obscene and decadent'.

On the Edge of Paradise: A. C. Benson,
the Diarist, David Newsome,
Murray.

1980
Daily Telegraph

THE PRISONER OF ZENDA

Although they were originally published separately, *The Prisoner of Zenda* and *Rupert of Hentzau* together make up a complete story. Collected together for the first time in an Everyman volume, they may be thought of as one book. The rereading of this famous pair stirs all sorts of questions in the mind about the survival of this kind of romance. The first half, at least – Rudolph Rassendyll's exchange with the King of Ruritania – remains entirely readable. It has been suggested that R. L. Stevenson's *Prince Otto* (1885) was Anthony Hope's source of inspiration, with perhaps a touch added of the Feilding Earls of Denbigh's claim (demolished by the genealogist Horace Round) to be descended from the Hapsburgs. In any case Ruritania added a word to the language.

Anthony Hope (Hawkins) was born in 1863 and died in 1933. He was showing every sign of making a successful career at the Bar when he decided instead to devote himself to writing. Roger Lancelyn Green, in his Introduction, gives a good account of Hope's background and literary works, perhaps a trifle underrating *The Dolly Dialogues*. One would have liked to know something of sales, too, but otherwise Green places Hope neatly in his period.

The Prisoner of Zenda appeared in 1894. Obviously its story offers a strong surface appeal in the psychological self-identification fantasy of a man who becomes a king for a brief period, a very ancient theme in all literature. Rudolph Rassendyll is the younger brother of the Earl of Burlesdon. The surname is a strange one (we would suspect Netherlands origin if the title were not indicated as earlier than William III), and Rudolph has, rather inexplicably, received his education in Germany.

Because the Rassendylls are descended, on the wrong side of the blanket, from a Ruritarian prince, Rudolph is the living image of the contemporary monarch of Ruritania. This affair took place in the eighteenth century, thereby suggesting a Ruritania before the period of Balkan states – say, an independent Bohemia.

The extreme simplicity of Ruritanian internal administration, how ever, points rather to a country like Bulgaria. It is interesting to note also, that at the period this book was published, there is no indication of everyone being, internationally speaking, fed up with the Balkans as an area of perpetual disturbance. It should perhaps be remembered that the tragedy of Mayerling had taken place only four years before, in 1889. Rudolph, the name of both Rassendyll and the King, was also that of the unfortunate Austrian archduke, who shot himself and his mistress. The obscure hunting lodges, in which so much of the Zenda-Hentzau action takes place, may have owed something to the Mayerling story as also the Teutonic character of Ruritania and its inhabitants.

Hope, one feels, was quite unusually lacking in any grasp of the differences of behaviour and outlook between his own countrymen and other Europeans. There seem to be no politics in Ruritania, except Black Michael's rivalry with the King, and the reader is given no sense of a routine of government – even at the book's romantic level – with equally little ceremony or even normal formality. The court, indeed, seems more like a laxly-run country house. In this inability to indicate the court, Hope shows himself greatly inferior to, say, Molnar, in a play like *The Swan* (where a bachelor king falls in love with a lady-in-waiting he cannot marry), or Erich von Stroheim's film *Queen Kelly*, which is far more fantastic, yet at the same time more convincing.

Hope's style is certainly odd; it varies between a characteristically *fin de siècle* cynicism, faintly Wildean in tone, and the furthest extremes of Wardour Street English, both dialogue spoken by the characters and in the author's own descriptive passages – phrases like 'all lovers are wont', 'aye, and the Queen herself'. These mannerisms are hard to trace, possibly derived ultimately from Scott, with an occasional touch of Trollope.

There is the characteristic Victorian moral ambiguity – already getting a bit out of date – about Rassendyll's precise relationship with Queen Flavia.

'You must make love to her tonight, you know,' says Colonel Sapt (whose liking for addressing everyone as 'lad' hints at *disant* Lancashire origins), but although the Hentzau story turns on an indiscreet letter written to Rassendyll by the Queen, the reader is never certain whether her 'sin' is not simply in loving Rassendyll who is, on the other hand, represented earlier on as being rather a dog.

Rupert of Hentzau has the disadvantage of being told in the first person by the courtier-officer, von Tarlenheim, an inadequately realised character. It could not be narrated by Rassendyll, as he dies himself at the end of the book. Even this method at times collapses technically and facts about situations where Tarlenheim was not present are chronicled as if he had been there. All the same, in spite of grave flaws judged even by their own standards, this Ruritarian pair have by no means lost their vitality. It is sad to think of the place behind the Iron Curtain.

The Prisoner of Zenda and *Rupert of*   1968
Hentzau, Anthony Hope, Dent.   *Daily Telegraph*

ARTHUR MACHEN

Arthur Machen (1863–1947) came of a line of Welsh clergymen called Jones. His father hyphened his wife's name on to his own, and Machen always used the latter half for professional purposes. Oddly enough, although his mother was from Scotland, the name Machen, in one form or another, is also found in Wales. Wales, to be precise, Monmouthshire – the kingdom of Gwent – played a dominating role in Machen's imagination: his recurrent theme, a young man who comes from this quiet border country to a London world of sinister mystery.

When I was a boy I used sometimes to catch a glimpse of Arthur Machen in St John's Wood, with his longish white hair and Inverness cape, every inch a nineteenth-century literary man. Reading this account of him, one sees that was exactly what he was, a type, I think it would be true to say, now entirely extinct. It is impossible to imagine anyone these days having the career Machen had.

After giving up the idea of the medical profession, Machen supported himself by doing odd jobs of a literary sort, including a translation of the *Heptameron* of Margaret of Navarre. He was desperately poor. His father went bankrupt. It is hard to see how Machen himself survived at all. However, in 1894 he made some name for himself with *The Great God Pan* and published a new translation of Casanova's Memoirs, the following year producing another successful story, *The Three Impostors*.

Aidan Reynolds and William Charlton describe Machen's life unpretentiously, wisely making no excessive claims for him as a writer or scholar. It appears, for example, that his translation of Casanova leans heavily – indeed almost entirely – on one made earlier by a German. At the same time, it has to be admitted that Machen's to this day remains the main English translation, without which the Memoirs would scarcely be available in the language.

In rather the same way, Machen did much to propagate the importance of Rabelais as a writer. A High Anglican with Roman Catholic leanings, he was always greatly interested in the occultism so much the vogue at the turn of the century. A. E. Waite, translator of Eliphas Lévi's *Dogme et Rituel de la Haute Magie*, was his lifelong friend.

When he was twenty-five Machen married a woman some years older than himself. The marriage was happy but his wife died eleven years later. Then in his late thirties, Machen went on the stage with the

Benson company. He remained an actor for eight years. Aged forty, he married again satisfactorily.

It should be added that between his two marriages Machen fell in love with a lady who became Mrs Rosse and subsequently kept house for that remarkable figure, Maundy Gregory, notorious for his part in the 'sale of honours' scandal. Poor Mrs Rosse died in mysterious circumstances after changing her will in Maundy Gregory's favour, the latter going to great expense to have her buried in a place flooded every winter by the Thames.

After his second marriage Machen returned to writing as a profession in 1910, getting a regular job on the *Evening News*, at that time under the sway of Northcliffe. Machen described this employment as being like the case of a man 'captured by a malignant tribe of anthropoid apes'.

It was in the *Evening News*, on 29 September 1914, that Machen's short story 'The Bowmen' appeared. This characteristic example of his imaginative fantasy describes how British troops withdrawing before the German advance suddenly see and hear medieval archers in the sky directing their shafts against the enemy. Immediately was born the legend of the 'Angels of Mons'. By the following year the book containing an expanded version of this story, with two or three others, sold 100,000 copies; and there are probably still people who would go to the stake rather than deny the probability of a relation of theirs having shared that transcendental experience during the Mons retreat.

In the 1920s there was quite a boom in Machen, especially in America. A collected edition of his works was produced, and for a time he was in easy circumstances. Unfortunately this period of prosperity did not last, and his latter years were spent in a certain amount of financial embarrassment. However, he seems always to have been able to extract a good deal of enjoyment out of life, dying aged eighty-four in 1947.

Machen was one of the first writers to draw attention to the sinister horror that can be found in the banal; fiendish, inhuman faces peer from suburban windows, 'nameless' things are committed within. He was a brilliant pasticheur – too brilliant, perhaps, for his own good. He had no great invention, and his characters did not come alive as individuals, but there is an assurance in an autobiographical work like *Far Off Things* which is attractive, and in John Betjeman's favourite, *The Secret Glory*.

Arthur Machen: A Short Account of His Life and Work, Aidan Reynolds and William Charlton, with an introduction by D. B. Wyndham Lewis, John Baker for Richards Press.

1963
Daily Telegraph

J. M. BARRIE

I

We are told that there is too much sex about nowadays. If – in the manner of a Barriesque fantasy – some Good (or Bad) Fairy dismissed with a wave of the wand all physical expression of passion, but otherwise left things much as they are, something would remain substantially like what is described in this macabre, but absorbing biography. The American magazine *Outlook* wrote at the time about *Peter Pan*:

> After the indecencies of a Zaza and Sappho, the scarcely less veiled and more insidious indecencies of the plays presented by Mrs Patrick Campbell, the horror of *Ghosts*, the tropical passions of *Monna Vanna*, the sinister cynicism of *Man and Superman* and of *Mrs Warren's Profession*, Mr Barrie's *Peter Pan*, now being played at the Empire Theatre, is like a breath of fresh air.

But was it? We are not, however, here concerned with J. M. Barrie's work, but with his life, and a more extraordinary story could hardly be imagined.

To dispose of a few criticisms right away, Janet Dunbar's style is occasionally a shade arch. 'The little playwright', 'he told himself', 'Her Grace of Sutherland', 'pretty as a picture', are phrases that sometimes diminish what is in general effective handling of a mass of complicated and delicate material.

James Barrie was born in Scotland in 1860. His background was poverty, hard work, a determination to make good. All these things he was heir to with the utmost authenticity. Intended for the ministry, he was at a comparatively early age shrewdly recognised by his family as a potential writer, found a job on a provincial newspaper, and from that moment never ceased to flourish. Barrie's devotion to his mother would (to adapt Anita Loos) make D. H. Lawrence seem an ungrateful son. How this reacted on his own life is here made clear. The other recurrent and appalling theme is the manner in which he was visited again and again by the sudden death of those who were close to him. Many extraordinary threads run through the narrative, but the three main ones are Barrie's relations with his wife; his friendship with the Llewelyn Davies family; his connection with Lady Cynthia Asquith, who worked as his secretary.

When, at the age of thirty-two, he married a good-looking actress, Mary Ansell, two years younger than himself, Barrie was obviously set for success in the theatre. The indications are that, although he was much taken with her, it was she who was keen on marriage. Mary Barrie went off at the age of forty-seven with a man twenty years younger than herself. Barrie was exceedingly upset. Janet Dunbar, no doubt for excellent reasons, states categorically that the marriage had never been consummated owing to Barrie's chronic incapacity.

In the face of a mass of evidence that Janet Dunbar is absolutely right – there are just two sentences, both in Mary's letters to H. G. Wells, which suggest something different. The first, referring to Barrie offering to take her back, contains the words: 'give myself up to loving J. [Barrie] and accepting his loving advances': the second, 'It is seven years since we [she and Barrie] separated and that does not spell happiness until 18 months ago.' They had been married for fifteen years, so what does 'separated' mean?

Before this happened Barrie had made friends with some children in Kensington Gardens, as a consequence getting to know their mother, Mrs Llewelyn Davies, a daughter of George du Maurier, the *Punch* artist. What followed cannot be easily summarised. Dunbar's book must be read. Briefly, Barrie, in the face of considerable lack of enthusiasm from Llewelyn Davies, insinuated himself into the household, in due course taking over the five sons as a kind of second father. This might seem merely comic or whimsical had not both the Llewelyn Davies parents died within a few years in rather dreadful circumstances. The late Peter Davies ('Peter Pan') supplies notes to most of Barrie's letters in this volume. At times halting in style, these notes are also much to the point, neither minimising what Barrie did for the family (he virtually adopted them), nor pretending that the situation was not an awkward one. In fact the Davies sons are in some ways the people who come best out of the book.

With all his talent and ability to get on, Barrie remained incapable of transacting the petty administration of his life, literary and financial. As a consequence of this, and various other circumstances, in 1916 he took on Lady Cynthia Asquith as his secretary. Those who have read her Diaries published not long ago will have a picture in their minds of this beautiful, energetic, amusing, harassed, intelligent, at times rather silly woman. Something very like the Llewelyn Davies situation now took place over again. Lady Cynthia's husband 'Beb' (not, by the way, the only surviving son of the Prime Minister after Raymond's death, there were two more) was not at all keen on Barrie, but that made no difference whatever.

Barrie is a perfect example of that curious, philistine, Edwardian literary establishment. Except in the form in which he himself might be said to practise them, he seems to have had a real hatred for the arts. In the end one feels that only Dostoevsky could do justice to Barrie's life, the passionate sexless love affairs, the money (£44,000 in 1907 alone), the rows, the reiterated tragedies. It is all Dostoevsky's meat.

J. M. Barrie: The Man behind the   1970
Image, Janet Dunbar, Collins.   *Daily Telegraph*

I I

I tried Gilbert Cannan's name on one or two likely persons now in their thirties, with negative results. All I knew of him myself was that he had written a novel called *Mendel*, based on the life of the painter, Mark Gertler, and had run away with Sir James Barrie's wife. Nevertheless, in the fifteen years of his working life, Gilbert Cannan (1884–1955) wrote twenty-eight books, fourteen plays, countless poems, essays, columns of dramatic criticism. His painful story gives an engrossing picture of Edwardian and Georgian literary life, often sides that have not been too much worked over.

Diana Farr is a distant relation of Cannan's, and says in the foreword that her first draft was discarded as having 'become a saga of the Cannans'. One sees her point, but even so she has now gone rather to the other extreme – beginning with Cannan in the middle of a love affair – and the reader has some trouble in digging out Cannan's early circumstances, certain of which never come to light. A family tree would also have been a help, since Cannan was much involved with his own relations, many of whom he used as models in his novels.

His father was an unsuccessful shipping clerk in Manchester, but his two uncles were Oxford dons of some distinction, and one of them more or less adopted him. We require to have this information at the start. Possibly Diana Farr, accepting that Cannan is largely forgotten, felt she must immediately establish a sex interest in her subject. It also seems likely that Cannan suffered from epilepsy, an important aspect that openly emerges towards the end of the book. Cannan, a bright boy, from a board school, won a scholarship to Manchester Grammar School, then to Cambridge. His Uncle Edwin (an economist, authority on Adam Smith) gave him an allowance to read for the Bar.

This is where Diana Farr's biography opens: Cannan, aged twenty-two, competing for the love of a beautiful sculptress, Kathleen Bruce, with the man she subsequently married, Captain Scott, the famous explorer of the Antarctic. Cannan is apparently on familiar terms with older writers like Galsworthy and Shaw (getting on well with the former, badly with the latter). We might have been told a bit more

about his Cambridge life, and how he made such an opportune début in
literary London. Perhaps evidence is simply not available.

Once she has Cannan under way Diane Farr produces a very
readable narrative of that extraordinary – as it now seems – Edwardian
and Georgian world, in which writers were so much less 'sorted out'
than they subsequently became. Thomas Hardy, Ezra Pound, Compton Mackenzie, A. E. W. Mason, Henry James, Jerome K. Jerome,
dozens more, all seem to be elbowing people like Captain Scott himself,
or H. H. Asquith, from quite other spheres. Cannan, through becoming
honorary secretary for the Society for the Abolition of Censorship, met
J. M. Barrie, became friends, and started an affair with Barrie's actress
wife. Mary Barrie, twice Cannan's age, seems to have been to some
extent the instigator of this relationship, though Cannan always acted
(and wrote) as a man rushing headlong into anything he did.

Mary Barrie used to go down to their country cottage without her
husband for weekends, where Cannan (suitably chaperoned by several
ladies more or less in the know) would come as a guest. For some
inexplicable reason Cannan, instead of using the door, always entered
his mistress's bedroom window by a ladder. One morning the
gardener, probably needing the ladder, took it away. This would not
have greatly mattered, as Cannan could always return to his own room
by the passage, but Mary Barrie later got the wrong side of the gardener
over some horticultural matter, and he told Barrie about the ladder.

The row, a tremendous one, broke in 1909. Barrie was thought to
take little physical interest in his wife, but was not at all pleased when
she left him. Cannan and Mary Barrie married and set up house
together, a ménage round which writers congregated, including D. H.
Lawrence, who for a time got on with Cannan pretty well. When war
came in 1914 Cannan declared himself a 'conscientious objector', but a
medical board found him below the required category and there was no
trouble on this score. By this time Cannan's erratic temperament was
showing itself as something more ominous than a mere state of being
highly strung. He put his wife's 'jewel' of a maid in the family way, and
then left with a pretty blonde (who subsequently established herself in
quite a different world) met by chance in a bookshop. Finally, in 1926,
after many breakdowns, Cannan had to be put under restraint, a state
in which he remained for the next thirty years until his death.

His novels, characteristic of their period in England, pour out in an
irrepressible style, the dialogue largely made up of remembered
conversations, the tone by no means entirely dissimilar to that of D. H.
Lawrence. I remember finding *Mendel* heavy going, but it is generally
agreed to give a very realistic picture of Gertler. Cannan's plays were
put on, and sometimes received excellent notices. He knew several
languages and was an accomplished translator. His story is essentially

a tragic one, but full of interest as displaying the varied intellectual life of its period and a sort of novel-writing that was really swept away by the good American writers of the 1920s, who were interested in technique.

Gilbert Cannan: A Georgian Prodigy, 1978
Diana Farr, Chatto. *Daily Telegraph*

III

Lady Cynthia Charteris (1887–1960) was daughter of the 11th Earl of Wemyss (who spent most of his life styled by the second title, Lord Elcho, because his father lived to be ninety-six). She married Herbert (Beb) Asquith, younger son of the Prime Minister H. H. Asquith, later created Earl of Oxford and Asquith. Her early background was Stanway, the Elchos' house in Gloucestershire, centre of the group in smart society nicknamed The Souls, of whom a great deal has been written in the last few years.

Nicola Beauman well describes this biography as aimed at showing 'how the child of the English aristocracy, hothouse reared in the schoolroom for a great marriage, became a South Kensington literary lady living in relatively modest circumstances'. This is an excellent definition of the sad, at times even macabre, story of the life of a woman who was not only a beauty, but unusually gifted.

Cynthia Asquith had wanted to be an actress. That would probably have suited her entirely self-centred nature, love of public display and immensely retentive memory. She had three outstanding opportunities to do this, later often regretting her decisions not to take them up. Only in the closing years of her life did she manage to give expression to this flair for making practical use of a theatrical personality. Her husband, Beb Asquith, inclined to drink a shade more than was prudent, began as a not very successful barrister, served bravely in the First World War (which his wife inclined to regard as merely a nuisance), then settled down to write untalented poems and novels. Permanently hard up, they remained attached to each other, though Lady Cynthia (what the French call an *allumeuse*, not to use a coarser term) had a great many admirers, few of whom seem to have converted their try, even after rough work in the scrum, of which she often complains in her diaries.

The two relationships in Cynthia Asquith's life of most interest are those with D. H. Lawrence and J. M. Barrie. Both are tied up with her own particular circumstances. They could, in fact, never have taken the form they did if she had not been the comparatively impoverished daughter of an earl and married to a husband whose earning capacity, and general approach to life, had been undermined by war service.

When the Asquiths were staying near Broadstairs in 1913 the indefatigable Eddie Marsh introduced them to D. H. Lawrence, then in Broadstairs for a month to provide evidence for the divorce of Frieda Weekley, with whom Lawrence had recently eloped. The meeting was an immediate success. Many of Lawrence's subsequent letters were to be written to Cynthia Asquith. Lawrence is always at his least silly when writing to her. He was by no means indifferent to social position, well aware that if he tried on too much nonsense Cynthia Asquith would merely make fun of him. In fact, as Nicola Beauman points out, Lawrence's advice about the unhappy case of the Asquiths' eldest son (who declined into insanity) was certainly sounder than their own approaches to the problem.

Lawrence not only used facets of Cynthia Asquith in several of his stories (in one of which the character's father is given the not altogether fortunate title of 'Earl Beveridge'), the prelude of the two girls visiting Germany having some bearing also in *Lady Chatterley*, but he outlined Cynthia Asquith's features on one of the slightly Picassoesque naked figures in one of his paintings which were seized by the police for obscenity. When passing Lawrence's letters to Aldous Huxley for publication Cynthia Asquith appears somewhat to have bowdlerised them.

This association with Lawrence was pleasant enough. That with the Dracula-like figure of J. M. Barrie was far more sinister. The fact that in the end she became more or less obsessed by Barrie by no means decreased this aspect. Poor Beb Asquith felt fed up to the last degree with having to trail round *à trois* with Barrie, but, as this little impotent vampire provided most of their means of livelihood by employing Cynthia as a secretary, he had to put up with it. Desmond MacCarthy (another of Cynthia Asquith's admirers) depicted Barrie as 'part mother, part hero-worshipping maiden, part grandfather, and part pixie with no man in him at all'. The Llewelyn Davies boys (from whom Barrie had wrought Peter Pan) were now growing up. He was looking about for some other family to get his claws into. The Asquiths provided just the job.

I had not been aware that Barrie was so extremely moody and bad-tempered. In between beginning a letter to Cynthia Asquith as 'My darling Puss', ending 'Such an adorable baby, and how proud I am of her, and how I revere her', or 'Dearest downy . . . I shall go on being dreary till my lamb comes back again, Your loving Master', he was kicking up frightful rows. For those with strong stomach, all this is fascinating to read about.

Cynthia Asquith, Nicola Beauman,   1987
Hamish Hamilton.   *Daily Telegraph*

THE LANCHESTER TRADITION

It is a common complaint of foreigners that the English are too fond of writing novels about school life; and there can be no doubt that in this country, at one time or another, a great many books of that sort have appeared; often good of their kind, if not necessarily first class. The implication of Continental critics is that we are more obsessed than they by that period of life; but, if the matter is closely examined, the few countries that have ever had enough literary vitality to produce serious novelists in considerable numbers – they are very few – seem to show at least an equal interest in adolescence. Where they differ is in not possessing the boarding school as an institution, with its inherent limitations of daily life, so peculiarly convenient to the novelist's art.

On the whole novels about schools have dealt principally with the boys, but from time to time the masters take the foreground. *The Lanchester Tradition* belongs to the latter sort. Its name is undoubtedly known to many people who have never read it. To republish it was a good idea.

G. F. Bradby, the author, was a housemaster at Rugby and son of a headmaster of Haileybury. He was a Balliol man with a first in Mods, a second in Greats, and a Rugby blue. He died in 1947 at the age of eighty-four, obviously a schoolmaster to the core of his being. The school he depicts may be assumed to have something in common with Rugby, with its much propagated 'Arnold Tradition'. Bradby wrote other novels, but this is his best-known work. *The Lanchester Tradition* appeared in 1914, and its manner, self-confident and humorous, brings with it a great whiff of the pre-war period. For example, 'the titled plutocracy' is a phrase recalling happier days. Bradby has marked skill as a writer in expressing the essentials of characters in a few sentences, but he is not always able to refrain from descending into the masters' meetings he depicts, and joining in the mêlée with his imaginary colleagues.

The central situation is the appointment to the headmastership of a school called Chiltern of an unknown candidate, Mr Flaggon, who gets the post quite unexpectedly owing to a disagreement on the part of the governing board. Flaggon has ideas of his own about the 'Lanchester Tradition' – in his eyes a radical tradition, instead of the intensely conservative policy of *laissez-faire* to which the years have transformed it – and this attitude brings him in conflict with his staff, especially Mr Chowlder. All this is well done, and often very funny. The book might be compared at one end of the scale with Hugh Walpole's *Mr Perrin and Mr Traill* (1911) and at the other with William Cooper's *The Ever-Interesting Topic* (1953). Indeed, the latter novel poses a very similar central situation to that of *The Lanchester Tradition*, even including the threat by a headmaster at the end of the book to call in the police in connection with a moral offence among the boys.

Bradby adopts a somewhat godlike attitude towards the problems his schoolmasters are called upon to solve; an attitude that attempts to strike a mean between too much conservatism and an unwise taste for new methods. Sometimes the satire recoils a bit, as in the case of Mr Tipham, a young master appointed by Flaggon. Tipham is untidy, conceited and grubby, and he admires the Post-Impressionist painters. Some rather heavy fun is poked at this taste, and it is Time's revenge that nowadays Van Gogh's Sunflower is almost a *sine qua non* of any schoolroom. Indeed, it is probable that Mr Tipham is now headmaster of some famous public school, if he is not a prominent BBC personality.

In rather the same way, the scandal that occurs in the school towards the end of the book is treated simply as if there were 'good' boys and 'bad' boys, and that a schoolmaster's chief duty was to find out who were 'bad' boys and expel them. Perhaps, after all, that is the easiest method; but considering how much misunderstanding of human nature is shown on certain planes of the book, this particular problem seems to be treated not so much without understanding as without any grasp that there is anything to be understood. Possibly this is to take *The Lanchester Tradition* too seriously, rather than concentrating on its lighter side. But it is, in a sense, a serious public-school novel, in certain respects the first of its kind. The author hints on the last page that there might be a sequel, but it is doubtful whether a sequel could ever have been written, although the story is plainly unfinished. In any case, it remains an undeniably entertaining piece of work for those who enjoy reading about schoolmasters and their idiosyncrasies.

The Lanchester Tradition, G. F. Bradby,　　　　　　　　　　　　1954
Richards Press.　　　　　　　　　　　　　　　　　　　　　　　*Punch*

Q (ARTHUR QUILLER-COUCH)

The most interesting aspect of Q – as Sir Arthur Quiller-Couch (1863–1944) was always known from the pseudonym he used – is his editing in 1900, 1910 and 1939, *The Oxford Book of English Verse*. He thereby set an indelible mark on at least two, probably three, generations of poetry readers, wartime readers at that, when poetry is particularly in demand. He also founded the School of English at Cambridge. His entry in the *Dictionary of National Biography* does not really convey much idea of him. This study by A. L. Rowse provides the personal touch necessary for an essentially eccentric figure, whose books are largely forgotten. Rowse's own idiosyncrasies sharply highlight those of Q, nothing if not an idiosyncratic man, bringing him to life in a way mere biographical chronicling fails to do. Above all, both are Cornishmen, and Cornwall is part of their lives.

Q was very kind. He helped at a critical moment in Rowse's early career, for which the latter is affectionate and grateful. At the same time he is not blind to the fact that Q was a colossal egotist, who represented a manner of writing that was on the way out. None the less, Q's somewhat primitive approach to Eng. Lit. probably did more good in the long run than the crochety puritanical dialectics of F. R. Leavis, who followed him at Cambridge, who was chiefly interested in handing out good and bad marks and whose own prose was usually less than coherent.

By chance I was reading Thomas Hardy's letters to his smart friend, Mrs Henniker, when Rowse's book turned up for review. Hardy (on Christmas Eve 1900) refers to Q's *Oxford Book of Verse*:

> much disappointed: the selected names are a good and fairly exhaustive list, but the specimens chosen show a narrow judgement and a bias in favour of particular views of life which make the book second-rate of its class.

This severe criticism anticipates much later opinion. One would agree with Rowse that the 1900 volume was better, for its time, than the 1939 one.

Q was not at ease where sex was in question. He had married happily at an early age and never seems to have known any problems whatever in that field, accepting a totally romantic approach to love. 'He did not like the sad or the satirical,' says Rowse. In short, he was as Rowse finds himself bound to admit, a 'high-minded Victorian prig'.

Q was prolific in producing books of all kinds, especially novels and occasional verse. The novels are written in an arch, over-ornamented style, everything a more modern school of novelists was determined to get away from. Q's poem on Oxford which begins:

> Know you her secret none can utter?
> Hers of the Book, the tripled Crown?

was regarded by Betjeman as 'still unsurpassed', but I must say most of the light verse quoted here seems at best fairly run-of-the-mill stuff. The literary movement of the 1890s was naturally unsympathetic to Q, so much so that he even omitted from his anthology his fellow-Cornish-man Arthur Symons.

Although Q was hard up for much of his early life (he had unproductive relations whom he helped financially most of the time), one is struck by the way that a young classical scholar could immediately earn some sort of living by his pen on coming down from Trinity, Oxford. Q also fitted perfectly into what was required at that period of a man of letters, one of the reasons why later he was to fall so drastically out of date. Q had a strong taste for public life, although Rowse insists that at heart he was a shy man. Rowse himself is not unaware of a certain humour in his championing of an older friend who could once say to him: 'If anything goes wrong, er, in regard to sex . . . it is – you know – the end.'

The tragedy of Q's life was that his only son, after joining the Army in 1914 and winning an M C and D S O, died (presumably of Spanish flu from the speed of the illness) while serving with the Army of Occupation in Germany in 1919. His father threw himself more than ever into work, athletics, dramatic societies, political speeches (old-fashioned Liberal), for a time officiating as Mayor of Fowey, the town represented in his books.

Decidedly exhibitionistic in dress, Q did not make an immediately good impression when appointed King Edward V I I Professor of English Literature in 1912. A. C. Benson, another Cambridge don (who would not have minded the job himself) thought he dressed like a 'racing tout', though later became better disposed to his Cornish colleague. Rowse points out that although Q may have been stuffy in some of his tastes, he looked ahead in certain others. For example, Trollope, now widely read, was recommended by him when the Trollope novels were utterly in the doldrums; he had a good word to say for Crabbe, a remarkable poet in his way; and he rightly regarded Byron's *Don Juan* as the second of English epics.

On an Army course at Cambridge during the war, I was invited to dine with Jesus dons and sat next to Q. He was amiable, if profoundly conscious of being a 'character'. He told me Marie Stopes (the apostle of birth control) had recently written to him to raise money for Lord Alfred Douglas (whose poetry Q admired).

Quiller-Couch: A Portrait of 'Q', A. L. Rowse, Methuen.

1988
Daily Telegraph

THREE MEN IN A BOAT

Slowly the golden memory of the dead sun fades from the hearts of the cold, sad clouds. Silent, like sorrowing children, the birds have ceased their song, and only the moorhen's plaintive cry and the harsh croak of the corncrake stirs the awed hush around the couch of the waters, where the dying day breathes out her last . . . and Night, upon her sombre throne, folds her black wings above the darkened world, and from her phantom palace, lit by the pale stars, reigns in stillness.

It is always difficult to get away from the writers of one's own youth. *Three Men in a Boat* first appeared in 1889, the year Jerome was thirty: *Studies in the History of the Renaissance* in 1873. The passage quoted above shows how a Fourth Man – Walter Pater – managed to get into the boat, on and off, for some of the trip. He kept fairly quiet on the whole, unnoticed by the other three, and his place was sometimes taken by another extraneous figure (perhaps the author's father, a lay preacher), who will suddenly sermonise with violence, as in the extraordinary incident where they find the corpse of a woman floating down stream.

All the same, it is a remarkable book. The sales in England exceeded a million and a half; while over a million were pirated in America. Translations appeared in every known tongue, Russia finding this jaunt up the Thames particularly sympathetic. That is easy to understand. Harris (who was, incidentally, a Pole) lost in the maze at Hampton Court, could easily be transferred to Chekhov; while the episode of the Cheese could be well imagined in Gogol. The Cheese remains intensely funny. When I read the book as a child I thought 'the black gentleman' was a coloured visitor to this country, but I find that he was, in fact, an undertaker. There seems a possibility that A. Frederics (whose original illustrations are, happily, here included) was under the same misapprehension. It is true that an undertaker-like figure is also shown among the passengers in the railway carriage, but he seems to be feeling the disturbing effects of the Cheese; while the only complacent traveller – apart from the author himself – is a bowler-hatted person of decidedly Negroid cast of countenance.

Some of the other famous passages no longer made me laugh – though still overwhelming in their effect on the young. The aspect of the

262

book that remains most impressive is the way in which the discursive method of narrative, comparable with *Tristram Shandy*, is throughout successfully maintained. That this is a matter of skill, and not chance, may be seen from *Three Men on the Bummel* (illustrations by Raven Hill), written a dozen years later, which has become ponderous and dated. It is not surprising that *On the Bummel* was popular in Germany, as it is full of praise for the quiet domestic virtues of the Germans.

Jerome K. Jerome (1859–1927), after a hardish start in life, made a successful career as a writer. His middle name, 'Klapka', was given (so D. C. Browning informs us in his introduction) after a Hungarian general who was a friend of the family. In the home, he was usually called 'Luther', to prevent confusion with his father, Jerome Clapp Jerome. One gets the impression of an unusual family background.

Like other books about that period – *Trilby*, for example – there is a sense of contrasting the pleasures of male companionship and rough fun with the boredom of having to be bothered with women. In *On the Bummel*, Harris and the author are married, and the book opens with some account of the sex-war, approached without much subtlety or perception. The individual psychology of George and Harris is hard to disentangle (cf. *Trilby*, Taffy and the Laird), but in general it may be said that Harris appears to have been the more extraverted of the two, always inclined to heartiness and practical jokes, while George liked philosophising and had musical leanings that caused him to buy a banjo, though never to learn to play that instrument.

There can be no doubt melancholy broods over the high spirits of *Three Men in a Boat*, even apart from the consciously sombre passages. Some found the book vulgar; and at times it certainly possesses a rich, unselfconscious absence of any attempt at social pretension for which one can find nothing but praise. The style brings back the epoch in a very different manner, but with the same pungency as Sherlock Holmes. It is unquestionably a classic.

Three Men in a Boat and *Three Men on the Bummel*, Jerome K. Jerome, with an introduction by D. C. Browning, Everyman.

1957
Punch

SHERLOCK HOLMES

S. C. Roberts presents here the fruits of long study of the Sherlock Holmes–Doctor Watson cycle. The chronology is scientifically examined, and many psychological points investigated. Roberts rightly insists that the methods of Holmes himself must be applied to Holmesian researches, and that mere speculation is not in itself appropriate, unless backed with evidence. We begin with Holmes's family origins, described by himself as 'a long line of country squires', varied by a grandmother who was sister to the French painter of battle-pieces, Horace Vernet. The name 'Holmes' is found too generally for any local conclusions to be drawn. Roberts toys with the Isle of Wight, but East Anglian or Yorkshire stock would be equally probable. He does not probe the question of the names 'Sherlock' and 'Mycroft'; the former with distinctly Irish associations, the latter, found sparsely in the London telephone book, but hinting at the north.

Like all experts Roberts is at times a shade pontifical. When Guy Warrack (in his interesting monograph, *Sherlock Holmes and Music*) suggests that Holmes's fondness for Mendelssohn, Meyerbeer, and Offenbach indicates Jewish blood, Roberts dismisses this perfectly legitimate conjecture as 'a piece of ill-judged pleasantry'. However, Watson sold his Kensington practice to a young doctor called Verner, a distant relation of Holmes. Roberts adds a note to the effect that 'Verner' may be a corruption of 'Vernet'. But 'Verner' might equally well be a slip for 'Wernher': though it would perhaps be going too far to suppose that 'Sherlock' was a form of 'Shylock', a name retained in the family for sentimental reasons to recall an ancient Jewish-Venetian descent. Holmes's temperament – and some of the extant pictures of him – make a Jewish strain at least a credible hypothesis.

On his own statement Holmes went to the university. Roberts produces good negative evidence to rule out Cambridge. He believes that Holmes's character prevented him from being sent to a public school, but that his brother Mycroft's 'unique and pivotal position in the Foreign Office' could not have been achieved 'without an expensive public school and university behind him'. But are we certain Mycroft *was* permanently in the Foreign Office? He 'audited the books in some of the Government departments' (*Greek Interpreter*), and would give information to a Minister which involved 'the Navy, India, Canada and the bimetallic question' (*Bruce-Partington Plans*). He was only earning £450 when at least fifty years of age. Does this not rather indicate a man who had worked his way up from small beginnings, possibly in some obscure branch of the Treasury?

Nor can we entirely agree with Roberts that Holmes 'did not betray the slightest self-consciousness in dealing with such clients as the Duke of Holderness or the illustrious Lord Bellenger'. On the contrary, Holmes almost invariably comments to Watson with what might be regarded as 'self-consciousness' wherever great names are concerned; and he refers to 'exalted circles' in connection with a decidedly job-lot list of country notables (*John Scott Eccles*). There is also the question of his intermittent references to Lord Robert St Simon (*Noble Bachelor*) as 'Lord St Simon': a solecism Roberts rather unworthily attributes to Watson's 'carelessness'. Holmes, by the way, must have been guilty of serious inaccuracy when he read aloud the description of the St Simon arms from 'the red-covered volume'; not only is the heraldry gibberish, but even had some word or words dropped out, such charges would be exceeding improbable as the presumably medieval coat of a family of 'direct Plantagenet descent'.

It is clear that Holmes did some hard reading between 1880, when Watson records he had never heard of Thomas Carlyle, and 1886–7 when he refers to Carlyle as leading to Jean Paul Richter. Even in retirement Holmes was still trying to improve himself, studying philosophy for which, in his first scathing summing-up, Watson had awarded him '*nil*'. Is it conceivable that Holmes's background was not all he put forward to Watson, and that much of his life was a feverish struggle to educate himself up to his friend?

Yet when we turn to Watson (admirably documented by Roberts) further mysteries face us. There *is* one explanation of Watson's Australian boyhood which delicacy may have prevented Roberts from mentioning. *Was Watson's father transported?* Would this explain the fifty-guinea watch inherited from Watson's dissipated elder brother? The watch might even have been the cause of Watson Senior's antipodean interlude; hidden, perhaps, to be recovered later like the Agra treasure. That would at least explain the Doctor's reticence about his parents.

Many further points tempt discussion. S. C. Roberts lists a formidable series of remarks by Holmes to show that women were by no means anathema to him as has sometimes been suggested. But surely Holmes's fundamental sentimentality about the opposite sex is typical of a man who had never had much to do with it? Moriarty – one brother a Colonel, another a station-master in the west of England – would also repay study. Finally, Wiggins, leader of the Baker Street Irregulars for seven years (*Study in Scarlet* to *Sign of Four*), must have grown almost to manhood in the great detective's service.

Holmes and Watson: A Miscellany,   1953
S. C. Roberts, Geoffrey   *Punch*
Cumberlege: Oxford University
Press.

RAFFLES

Although it is fairly common to meet people who have never read about Raffles, to come across anyone who had never heard of him, or to whom the name did not suggest a man about town who was also a burglar, would be unexpected. Written merely to entertain, the stories, combining as they do a touch of the philosophies of both Kipling and Wilde, embody *fin-de-siècle* sentiment in more than one of its protean forms. Their spirit at once revolts against respectability, and chants a paean in respectability's praise. Perhaps this closeness to their period's inconsistencies has caused their survival; because, after the passing of fifty years, they have lost none of their flavour. If anything, they have gained by becoming, as it were, a costume piece.

In his essay, *Raffles and Miss Blandish*, George Orwell examined with much acuteness the contrast between the moral standards of the 'amateur cracksman' and the gangster of today, pointing out that Raffles was content with a haul of a few hundred pounds-worth of jewellery, that he never willingly committed murder, and that he possessed a healthy, athletic approach to crime. Indeed, his only recorded sadism – apart from savage handshakes – is mental torture inflicted on his accomplice, Bunny, so often reduced to ignominious self-abasement before being cheered with some such commendation as 'you dear little brick'.

The relationship between Raffles and Bunny inevitably invites comparison with the association of Sherlock Holmes and Dr Watson: though – endemic professional antagonism apart – there can be no doubt that mutual dislike between the two pairs of partners would have been profound, had they met. The uncorrupted natures of Holmes and Watson, older men reared in a more austere tradition, would have recoiled from an atmosphere of baccarat parties in the Albany and smart country-house cricket, so indispensable socially and financially to Raffles and his friend.

Hornung and Doyle, creators of Raffles and Holmes, were, in fact, brothers-in-law. Ernest William Hornung was born at Middlesbrough in Yorkshire on 7 June 1866. He was educated at Uppingham ('The Field of Philippi' to which Raffles and Bunny repair on Founder's Day and rob a bank), which he entered in 1881: a year before the arrival there of the author of *South Wind*. Norman Douglas (so he tells me) cannot recollect Hornung at school, though he 'met him later, on the Posillipo, near Naples, round about 1900–1903' (in other words close to the vineyard where Raffles was employed for eight months, meeting Faustina and falling foul of the Camorra, after stealing the German Emperor's pearl on the Norddeutscher Lloyd's s.s. *Uhlan*) and found him 'good company', a judgment borne out by others.

As a young man, between 1884 and 1888, Hornung was in Australia (visited by Raffles on a cricket tour, where *le premier pas* in theft took place), and Australian life is often referred to in the stories. On his return to England he worked as novelist and journalist, his first book, *A Bride from the Bush*, appearing in 1890. He married Constance Doyle, sister of Arthur Conan Doyle, in 1893. In 1907 he was elected a member of the M C C, and – since clubs played a large part in the lives of Raffles and Bunny – it is of interest to know that he belonged at different times to the Reform, the Savile, the Authors', and the Royal Automobile. When war broke out in 1914 he joined an anti-aircraft unit. His only son, a subaltern in the Essex Regiment, was killed at Ypres. He himself went to France with the Y M C A in 1916, and was present in 1918 at the German bombardment of Arras, experiencing at a mature age warfare already described in imagination. He died on 27 March 1921, at St Jean de Luz, in his fifty-fifth year.

Hornung wrote nearly thirty books, of which, apart from the Raffles series, *Stingaree* is perhaps the best known. None of them comes up to the Raffles standard for liveliness and originality, though the writing is never less than competent. Social distinctions and crime exercised a strong hold on his imagination as an author, and he was attracted by the personal qualities exemplified in Raffles's 'lazy insolence' and 'his natural charm and humour and touch of sadness'. This melancholy, and regret for schooldays and boyhood, is rarely far from the surface. Considered in antithesis, *Raffles* never rises to the almost poetic implications of the best *Sherlock Holmes* – the haunting descriptions of the outer suburbs of London in the late nineteenth century, or the arresting, quasi-necromantic figure of Holmes himself – but for construction and sustained excitement Hornung is often as good as Doyle, if not better.

Raffles has not left behind him any very notable progeny of upper-middle-class burglars. An occasional figure, like Captain Dancey in Galsworthy's *Loyalties*, makes a bungling and amateurish effort to steal: an impulse possibly prompted by some dim memory of having read one of the Raffles books in his youth. More significant was a case of robbery with violence from a jeweller that actually took place some years ago, written up in the press as the affair of the 'Mayfair Men'. The earlier intentions of the participants in this episode – before the more violent element was introduced – seem to have owed something to the Raffles story *No Sinecure*, in which the jeweller was spun a yarn about a marriage engagement, and an empty box substituted for a full one.

Social adjustments of recent years have done much to elevate the status of criminals as a class; and, if Raffles were to return among us, he would notice this, especially in current literature. The development would probably be distasteful, and one can imagine him deploring to Bunny (had the latter been permitted to accompany his hero) the intrusion into so much of contemporary fiction of the idiom of the thieves' kitchen; or commenting that memoirs written by convicts now rival in number – and in dullness – the reminiscences of public men who have avoided gaol.

He would find that characteristics not considered criminal in his day – a hedonistic approach to life, a somewhat aggressive patriotism, an ostentatious desire to 'play the game', coupled with traces of what can only be described as snobbishness – are now regarded in some quarters with graver disfavour than mere legal offences. He would also encounter a tendency to look upon the law-breaker as an invalid rather than a delinquent, and discover that his sins, though of scarlet, had been washed by the psychiatrists as white as cocaine – a situation that could only be wounding to his *amour propre*, and unpredictable in its awful effects on Bunny. He could, however, congratulate himself with the thought that the name of Raffles has passed into the English language. There he would be well advised to leave matters, withdrawing once more to some elysium of fast living and slow bowling, to rest on past laurels. and – with Bunny at his feet – watch the smoke of a Sullivan curling over the asphodel; while he 'murmured of Whistler and Arthur Severn' and recalled in the celestial landscape the tints of Melrose sapphires and Kirkleatham diamonds.

Introduction to *Raffles: The Amateur*   1950
Cracksman, E. W. Hornung, Eyre &
Spottiswoode.

NORMAN DOUGLAS

I

It was a good idea to reproduce these sixteen photographs of Norman Douglas (1868–1952) at various stages of his life, together with Max Beerbohm's imaginary picture of him, plying an uneasy priest with Bombarolina, 'bent on winning an admission that the rites of the Church are a survival of Paganism, pure and simple'. Constantine FitzGibbon, a relation, introduces these plates with a biographical essay, on the whole informative and sensible; though it is hard to see why his family should be blamed for sending Douglas to Uppingham, for which his near contemporary at school, E. W. Hornung, creator of Raffles, retained infinitely sentimental memories. The remarkable thing is that Douglas was taken away from the school because he was unhappy, completing his education in Germany, his mother being of Teutonic origin.

Since this is primarily a book of photographs, Norman Douglas, about whom there is an immense amount that could be said, should perhaps be approached here primarily through his portraits. The early pictures bear a strange resemblance to those of Winston Churchill, and even the 21-year-old young man in the grey bowler, posed in 1890, is by no means unlike representations of the Prime Minister at that age. However, by the time Douglas was Third Secretary at the British Embassy, St Petersburg, a moustache had changed and conventionalised his appearance. No likenesses are included between this one, aged twenty-five, and a snapshot taken on Ischia at thirty-nine: the latter, just about the time when he lost most of his money, and 'his career as an amateur scholar and scientist came to an end. From then until his death he was to live by his pen.'

This was also the moment, FitzGibbon indicates, when Douglas threw discretion to the winds as regards his private life. There is certainly an extraordinary change in the next photograph, taken in 1912, aged forty-three, just before he went to work on the *English Review*. From then the pictures proceed, as it were, logically, terminating with Douglas as he looked in London during the war, and afterwards on his return to Italy: the prominent nose and chin, the intelligence, the humour, the dissipation, the good nature, the touch of cruelty.

Norman Douglas is in the front rank of the writers of his period. His books, although treated as bibliographical rarities, are not generally appreciated at their true value. This is perhaps due to certain

270

conflicting aspects of his own nature which, in spite of brilliant gifts, somehow adversely affected his work when considered as a whole. He possessed an odd mixture of seriousness and frivolity, characteristics that were at times to the fore at the wrong moments. His own strong will and 'logical' point of view caused him to ride his hobby-horses unduly hard, for example, in the pseudo-historical *longueurs* of *South Wind*, which remains at the same time one of the most remarkable novels of the last fifty years. He was really at his best in travel books such as *Fountains in the Sand* or *Old Calabria*, in which erudition and a reckless attitude towards life could be combined with pure imagination, occasionally assisted (as he tells us) by *kiff*-smoking or such other local stimulants as he might feel appropriate.

Constance FitzGibbon comments on Douglas with acuteness:

He was gradually put in a position which was essentially a false one. For though he might flout the morality of his society, he was never anti-social, and though a hedonist, his hedonism was that of the Victorian gentleman, not of the eighteenth-century diabolist or of the twentieth-century experimenter. He suffered for his hedonism, as much perhaps from his admirers as from anybody else.

This could not be better expressed. Douglas was one of those strong personalities – really intended, it was impossible not to feel, for the world of action – who are prepared to forgo nothing of what momentarily appeals to them. Modest and forthright to a fault about his own writing, he was prepared, at the period of the war when food was at its worst, to kick up a terrible row in a restaurant because the spaghetti happened not to be exactly to his liking. On that particular occasion there was good reason to suppose that if we did not eat the spaghetti provided (which, by standards then prevailing, might have been much worse) we should none of us get any food at all that evening. I mention this only because it serves to illustrate Douglas's unwilling-ness ever to trim his sails in the smallest degree, a failing that led him into literary by-paths which were sometimes mistaken.

He is a masterly writer of prose, and possesses that gift, so horrible when abused by second-rate writers, of giving the reader a feeling of intimacy. *Siren Land*, *Alone*, and *Together* should be recalled with the volumes mentioned above; and *Late Harvest*, the survey of his own work, which appeared in 1946, is also extraordinarily interesting and enjoyable, a notable achievement at the age he wrote it.

Norman Douglas: A Pictorial Record,   1952
with a Critical and Biographical Study,   *Punch*
Constantine FitzGibbon,
Richards Press.

II

Since his death in 1952, there have been several projected biographies of Norman Douglas. None of these was ever completed, largely owing to the formidable difficulties that writing about Douglas presents. Indeed only comparatively recently could his sexual side be treated in a straightforward manner – quite apart from the problem of charting so deliberately unsystematised a career.

The Douglases, lairds of Tilquhillie in Kincardineshire, were also prosperous businessmen (cotton) in Austria. Norman Douglas's father married an aristocratic Austro-Bavarian lady (herself, as it happened, half a Forbes), and was killed mountaineering in his middle thirties. His widow immediately married an artist, whose own father, also an artist, had for a time become perforce a house-painter. Both the Douglases and her own Teutonic relations were thoroughly disagreeable about what was in their eyes a *mésalliance*, which turned out to be perfectly happy.

Norman Douglas never mentions his mother's remarriage in any of his writings, but there can be no doubt, from the details Mark Holloway gives, that family disruptions took place which must have been exceedingly painful to the Douglas children. At an early age Douglas showed a taste for natural science (butterflies, snakes, fossils), and by the time he was eighteen was contributing pieces to papers about zoology. He decided to go into the Diplomatic Service, passed the examination, and was sent to the British Embassy in Russia. At this time the Austrian cotton factory was still doing well, and he seems to have possessed an income of about £2,000 a year.

The importance of a writer is in what he writes, not his other doings, but it is hard altogether to separate Douglas's writing personality from his sexual adventures. This also causes difficulty for a biographer in deciding what tone to adopt towards the subject's often uncommendable behaviour, or in knowing just how much to believe of what Douglas records about himself. Holloway is, one would guess, a man of ordered life, not altogether at ease with goings-on of the Douglas sort; at the same time rightly determined not to be shocked.

Douglas (whose 'hopping it' often irresistibly reminds the reader of Evelyn Waugh's Captain Grimes) continued to put himself within range of police action until his eighties, and Holloway is forced to admit that he would have kept his own children away from him. Until he was about forty Norman Douglas was in principle heterosexual. In St Petersburg he had a mistress called Anyuta Ponomarev and another, unnamed, on account of whom he had to flee the country, and ultimately leave the Diplomatic Service. He married a cousin, settled in Naples, had two children. His marriage broke up; he took to boys –

sometimes little girls – and gradually found himself with less and less money.

Douglas's novel *South Wind* (published 1917, pirated in the USA) derived from Peacock and W. H. Mallock, but spoke with a new voice in a scene dominated by Bennett, Wells, Galsworthy. *South Wind* (which greatly influenced Aldous Huxley) has its *longueurs*, the cocksure tone is not today's, but it remains a remarkable book, full of amusing things.

The rest of Douglas's output has in general worn less well. *Old Calabria* has its supporters – Cyril Connolly thought it might be the book through which Douglas's name could survive – but, as Holloway remarks: 'It would never do as a work of reference, and will not quite do as a work of art.' The former is certainly true, if anyone hopes to use *Old Calabria* as guidebook to that part of Italy.

Douglas was anti-poetry, anti-pictures, anti-Proust, had musical abilities and a natural gift for writing. His point of view is essentially that found in scientists among whom he always liked to consider himself – an absolute certainty that he was right, and there were to be no arguments about what he himself had proved by experience.

Lytton Strachey, charmed by *South Wind*, sent Douglas a fan letter. They corresponded. Douglas suggested they might collaborate on 'the private journal of the Emperor Claudius' – so *I, Claudius* might have been forestalled. When they met, Strachey thought Douglas 'had a touch of Sickert', which one can see, both in appearance and demeanour.

Douglas's friendship with Conrad has been sometimes mentioned, but never highlighted as in Mark Holloway's book. That these two should have been close friends (the Conrads looked after Douglas when he was nearly dying) is of particular interest, because Conrad believed implicitly in duty and honour, concepts Douglas held in the greatest contempt.

D. H. Lawrence caricatured Douglas in *Aaron's Rod*, one of his worst novels. On the other hand Lawrence's Introduction (as good as anything he wrote) to Maurice Magnus's *Memoirs of the Foreign Legion* gives an excellent account of the life Douglas and Lawrence shared in Florence. They made up the row that took place over this Introduction, but on leaving Florence, Lawrence asked Douglas to luncheon and arranged to catch a train, so Douglas had to pay. In the 1940s, when Douglas was in London, I used to meet him occasionally. He had great charm, was without the smallest pomposity regarding his fame as a writer.

Norman Douglas: A Biography, Mark
Holloway, Secker & Warburg.

1977
Daily Telegraph

M. R. JAMES

When Montague Rhodes James (1864–1936) was in his early thirties, the already celebrated historian Lord Acton spoke of him as among three or four first scholars of Europe in knowledge of manuscripts. He was a medievalist rather than a classicist, but all obscure branches of learning attracted him, most especially 'any document that has claimed to be a Book of the Bible, and is not'.

Monty James – as one always heard him called – in due course became Provost of King's College, Cambridge, and Provost of Eton. Unlike many considerable scholars he was a big man of striking presence. When you took off your hat to him passing in Eton High Street, you were immediately aware of something powerful and unusual. James's reputation remains secure in certain esoteric fields; the general public remembers him for his ghost stories.

A little more information about Michael Cox, author of this compact, informative, but unadventurous and rather prim biography, would have been acceptable, simply to enlighten the reader as to the point of view from which it is written. Here, in one sense, is no doubt all that needs to be known of James; in another, a chance has no doubt been missed of writing a book that might have spread itself on some of the minor characters concerned, and the general implications of James's life.

James was one of those always interesting figures, a weak man with a strong personality. He represented the peak of one kind of civilisation, and to read about him is to see how inevitable was that intellectual revolution loosely known as the Modern Movement. From earliest boyhood James was marked out as a scholar, always with a taste for the most obscure byways of history and letters, together with a distinctly sadomasochist preoccupation with martyrdoms. Is it a mere chance that he was himself involved in mild rows about bullying both at his prep school and at Eton? Is there a touch of cruelty about his mouth? Probably no more than to indicate the thoughtless insensitiveness of the clever boy of about twelve years old, with a love for ragging and horseplay, something which, according to more than one witness here, James always remained. Certainly he appears to have been generally popular as a man.

One need not be a professional psychoanalyst to see the ghost stories as some release from feelings held in check with a rigour remarkable even for the Victorian James so often declared himself to be. Cox writes:

I may as well state here, as a personal opinion only, that I do not believe Monty's sexuality (whatever its precise characteristics were) ever became problematic in his life in the way that it did for his friend Arthur Benson. Unlike Benson, Monty could live on easy affectionate terms with young men, even handsome young men, without agonising over them.

I myself have heard it suggested that James's (of course platonic) love affairs were in fact fascinating to watch. There are signs of that here.

His intense conservatism, dislike for any form of speculation, abhorrence of rows, were combined with a natural timidity in undertaking the duties of high academic office both at Cambridge and Eton. In consequence, he prepared the way for violent deluges after him, of the kind he most feared and hated. Much of this course of events may be followed in the brilliant but pitiless diaries of A. C. Benson, James's too candid lifelong friend. Benson, a far more constructive figure in education, wrote of James: 'He has no sense of beauty or decorum, only interest.' That truth could not be better demonstrated than by James's removal from Eton College Chapel of the neogothic canopied stalls to display the scraps of medieval painting behind them. No doubt the frescos should have been made available when discovered in 1848, but that could have been done (as suggested at the time by the Prince Consort) by putting the stalls on a hinge. As it was James's historically defensible but aesthetically barbarous act was turning the chapel into a 'palaeolithic cave'.

Among the actors in these scenes, as well as A. C. Benson, were that sanctimonious old stick H. E. Luxmoore (who had been James's tutor at Eton), always ready to improve the occasion with some piety, that engagingly comic figure Oscar Browning, and many others with whom more might have been done in dramatising the picture. It should be noted that Benson himself also wrote some good ghost stories as did the two other Benson brothers.

Some of James's ghost stories – notably 'Oh, whistle and I'll come to you, my lad' – hold up well, and possess a real originality. James had a very professional way of telling a story, and perhaps his horror of sex in life, or even 'matrimonial complication' in a novel was a help in concentrating in his own writing other forms of emotional pressure.

Michael Cox does not mention that the magician in the story 'Casting of the Runes' seems to some extent to be based on Aleister Crowley, which implicitly suggests James as following the career of a not very desirable modern who would certainly have attracted him explicitly had Crowley been a sorcerer of the Middle Ages.

James's method of building up a sinister atmosphere seems to me well illustrated in 'The Residence at Whitminster' in *A Thin Ghost* (1920):

> It was on the same day that Dr Ashton, looking out of an upper window, saw the two boys playing in the corner of the garden at a game he did not understand. Frank was looking earnestly at something in the palm of his hand. Saul stood behind him and seemed to be listening. After some minutes he very gently laid his hand on Frank's head, and almost instantly thereupon Frank suddenly dropped whatever he was holding, clapped his hand to his eyes and sank down on the grass.
>
> Saul, whose face expressed great anger, hastily picked the object up, of which it could only be seen that it was glittering, put it in his pocket, and turned away, leaving Frank huddled on the grass. Dr Ashton rapped on the window to attract their attention, and Saul looked up as if in alarm, and then springing to Frank, pulled him up by the arm and led him away.

M. R. James: An Informal Portrait,
Michael Cox, Oxford University
Press.

1983
Daily Telegraph

ELINOR GLYN

As recently as 1932 a Mickey Mouse cartoon was banned in the state of Ohio because it showed a cow reclining in a field reading *Three Weeks*. Quite why, on its publication in 1907, Elinor Glyn's story of a young Englishman's love affair with a Balkan Queen (staying incognita in Lucerne on a tiger-skin) should have electrified the reading public of Europe and the Americas is now hard to see. Even the countries which found nothing shocking in the novel devoured it voraciously. Dr Edward Lyttelton (beginning his letter 'Madam') informed the author that her book would be forbidden at Eton, of which school he was then Head Master. He had to admit, in reply to her spirited challenge, that he had not read the story himself. After doing so he wrote again to say that he had enjoyed *Three Weeks*. Anthony Glyn has produced a lively and entertaining life of his grandmother; unpretentious, yet full of interest. He brings off the difficult achievement of treating her life seriously and her work lightly. Here is much for the psychologist and social historian. It was a most unusual career.

If one had to hazard a reason for the extraordinary popularity of the novels of Elinor Glyn (1864–1943) it might be suggested that their power lies in their exploration of those ever fascinating subjects, Sex and Class. Incredibly crude the books may be, yet, in their day, they had a certain originality. In the former field she presents always as hero the passionate, masterful man, brought to his knees in the last resort by the mysterious, beautiful woman. The psychological background is unvaryingly class-conscious; displaying through the characters the author's idea of the 'aristocratic' virtues – high birth, generosity, recklessness, discipline and self-sacrifice.

In general there are many resemblances to Ouida. Elinor Glyn was far more fortunate in her looks, and also in her family circumstances. These deserve a glance, as they indicate to some extent why the themes referred to above held a foremost place in her mind.

A red-haired woman of striking beauty, she had been brought up to think her personal appearance a handicap. Her father, Douglas Sutherland, was a civil engineer, son of a Captain Sutherland who had settled in Nova Scotia. The Sutherlands were, by tradition, distant kinsmen of Lord Duffus. Douglas Sutherland married Elinor Saunders of Ontario, who was a connection of the Admiral Saunders who sailed Wolfe's ships up the St Lawrence, and whose grandmother belonged to the French *noblesse*.

This was certainly no background of which to be ashamed, but it was similar to that of literally thousands of other people, and Elinor Glyn worked it rather hard as being 'aristocratic'. The facts are worth looking into, because she does seem always to have put on tremendous social airs which appear a trifle unjustified within their own terms of reference. No doubt an admirable sense of what they owed to their family origins carried her immediate forebears through exceedingly uncomfortable and often penurious circumstances; but one really cannot agree with Anthony Glyn in drawing a parallel with Lord Curzon's childhood and family, even though both of them may have taken moral strength from the *mystique* of aristocracy. Incidentally, Curzon's relationship with Elinor Glyn (he gave her one of her several tiger-skins) is one of the most interesting things in this book.

So far from being infinitely exclusive, as she was always fond of representing it, one is surprised by this picture of how easy to penetrate – for those with good looks and firm wills – late Victorian Society must have been; even though it seems to have been decidedly the raffish end of it into which she found her way. During her first two seasons several men proposed to her, including, so she stated, the then Duke of Newcastle. The Duke was, however, so 'absorbingly [*sic*] interested in the details of ecclesiastical apparel' that, no doubt wisely, she refused him. She was not married until the age of twenty-seven, when she became the wife of Clayton Glyn, an Essex squire, descended from a Lord Mayor of Welsh extraction.

Clayton Glyn, in the end, behaved rather badly, and his wife exceedingly well; but there will be those to find a sneaking sympathy for him. When Elinor told him that Lord Warwick, showing her round his new rose-garden, had told her that she was the fairest rose there and had kissed her, and hinted further, Clayton, who was trying to tie his white tie in front of the looking glass, simply said 'Good old Brookie!'

Elinor Glyn did not like other authors. She felt, perhaps not without reason,

> that literary people were not people one invited to one's house or cared to be familiar with . . . When Elinor wished for intellectual company, as she often did, she preferred to find it with university professors, a class to which she was much attached.

Elinor Glyn: A Biography, Anthony   1955
Glyn, Hutchinson.   *Punch*

JOHN GALSWORTHY

I

John Galsworthy was born in 1867, the same year as Arnold Bennett, a year after H. G. Wells, two years after Kipling. Even towards the end of his life, when he was receiving his OM and Nobel Prize, his literary reputation, fiercely attacked by the more go-ahead critics, was beginning to curl at the edges. Since his death it has slumped worse than that of any of his contemporaries. All the same, *The Forsyte Saga* is not forgotten. This immense chronicle remains, in its way, an extraordinary production. It cannot hold a candle to *Vanity Fair*, with which Dudley Barker, author of the present study, compares it. Indeed, in his portraits of old Mr Osborne and old Mr Sedley, Thackeray says just as much *qua* Forsytism – the worship of property by the rising middle-class businessman – as Galsworthy, but in a hundredth part of the space.

The treatment of character is not very subtle in either book. Thackeray reaps a positive advantage by his rough and ready methods. Galsworthy – humourless, yet sardonic, passionate, yet inhibited – forbids himself the often trite machinery that animates Thackeray's puppets, while he lacks also the pitiless knowledge of human nature to be found in, say, Proust or James.

However, the point of Dudley Barker's book, which manages to be at the same time unpretentious and informative, is to show how Galsworthy's life interacted on his writing, rather than to deal at any great length with the writing as such. To continue the analogy, it may be fascinating to those studying Thackeray's life to speculate just how far his love for Mrs Brookfield went; but that question, whatever the answer, could not be said to play any but the most oblique part in Thackeray's novels.

In the case of Galsworthy, on the other hand, his adultery and subsequent marriage provided not only the whole foundation of the work which gives him a claim to be remembered as a writer – also the theme of many of his other novels and plays – but actually seems in itself to have galvanised him into authorship. The story Barker has to tell is therefore far more relevant to the subject than the mere dredging up of a forgotten scandal.

After a markedly conventional, wholly unintellectual career at

Harrow and New College, Oxford, Galsworthy read for the Bar. He was supported by his father, model for Old Jolyon in *The Forsyte Saga*, one of a string of brothers most of whom had themselves amassed considerable fortunes. Galsworthy's allowance was adequate, but not abundant, and it is notable that no particular parental pressure seems to have been put on him to earn a living, although his interest in the Law was far from profound. In his late twenties he met Ada Galsworthy, wife of a cousin, Arthur Galsworthy, and fell in love. Galsworthy's life never seems to have possessed any real impetus until this happened. It was Ada who suggested he should try to write.

Whatever may be thought of the literary value of Galsworthy's work, as a true-story romance of How-I-made-my-pile, it is hard to beat. Trollope is nothing to it. Galsworthy's early efforts were feeble to a degree. He seems to have been curiously lacking in those purely imaginative gifts possessed by most novelists. Everything was observed directly from life, sentimentalised perhaps, but – with the exception of Soames Forsyte – never 'developed' in the manner of greater novelists.

It is sometimes forgotten that Galsworthy was nearly forty before success came to him. When that success did arrive, the cornucopias were abundant in the extreme, but the will-power that kept him slogging along must have been immense, colossal, for a man with, in one sense, comparatively lean natural gifts. No novelist has more than a few stories to tell. They are the myths of life which each novelist creates for himself. In Galsworthy's case, the myth that absorbs all others is the story of the sensitive wife, married to the brutal husband, who leaves him for a lover who dies – in *The Forsyte Saga*, Irene, Soames Forsyte, Bosinney.

It is here that Galsworthy's own story comes in. Having read H. V. Marrot's *Life and Letters of John Galsworthy* (1935), I had accepted the marriage triangle of *The Forsyte Saga* as describing, anyway more or less, the story of John, Ada and Arthur Galsworthy. Barker sets the picture in a somewhat different light. The circumstances, in fact, were that John and Ada Galsworthy lived together as lovers for nine years. Arthur Galsworthy, so far from being a man of strong will and cold-blooded brutality, was shy and reserved, easily rebuffed in sexual matters. From that aspect his married life with Ada had not been a success. He was not rich, living on a modest allowance from his father. After the divorce, Arthur Galsworthy remarried, had two children, and lived happily ever after. His worst crimes appear to have been an inferiority complex, an abiding interest in the Territorial Army and a lack of enthusiasm for music. He fought in the South African war and, at the age of fifty-four, managed to be commissioned again during the First World War and to get out to France.

Although they had not been 'on terms' for some time, Arthur

Galsworthy was deeply upset when he returned from South Africa to find that his wife had left him, set up on her own, and was 'carrying on' with his cousin. He was quite unaware that she had been going for weeks at a time on continental trips with John Galsworthy for half a dozen years. The divorce, however, did not take place for another three years. The reason given by Galsworthy for keeping the affair clandestine was that it would have upset his old father. It seems far more probable that, as he was still entirely dependent on his father, Galsworthy feared financial pressure to make him drop Ada – and additionally that his prospects of inheritance would be imperilled. The same reason – that it would upset his own father – is given for Arthur Galsworthy's forbearance from seeking a divorce at once. John and Ada Galsworthy were not living under the same roof, which they did not do until 'Old Jolyon' died. They then joined up together and Arthur's father (who survived till ninety) had to be upset, whether he liked it or not. It is permissible to wonder whether Arthur Galsworthy was not somehow 'squared' to hold his hand. It would no doubt have been imprudent, indeed utterly feckless, to have followed any other course; that adopted was a typically Forsytean one in its regard for the pennies. At the same time, it is not easy to see how Ada Galsworthy's case differed from that of any other woman who finds her marriage unsatisfactory and goes off with someone else. She may have had a reason for dissatisfaction, but that is all there was to it.

In considering the manner in which the facts were finally dished out, the word 'humbug' inevitably comes to mind. Perhaps Galsworthy felt that a little himself under all the layers and layers of high-mindedness which enclosed the myth. Certainly he behaved throughout his life as a man who had to atone for something. He did many very kind acts, gave away quantities of money, pressed for all sorts of reforms in prisons and elsewhere.

All the same, John Galsworthy, like Soames, remains a trifle unsympathetic. Worse men, certainly worse writers, exert a more genial spell.

The Man of Principle: A View of John   1963
Galsworthy, Dudley Barker,   *Daily Telegraph*
Heinemann.

II

The Forsyte Saga, in spite of its many absurdities – emphasised rather than modified by the TV production – somehow transcends Galsworthy's own view of life. At least it does in the early part of the narrative. That view, repeated over and over again in his other books and plays, is not, it might be felt, particularly interesting. What is the reason for this survival? One has often heard the opinion put forward, when *The Forsyte Saga* is under discussion, that Soames was a misjudged and maltreated husband, Irene a tiresome, selfish, neurotic wife, and Bosinney, not only professionally incompetent, also an irresponsible and half-baked lover. Indeed, the dramatisation of the book would have been more gripping had some such alternative version been at least implicit in the background.

The notable thing is that Galsworthy was himself to some extent aware of all this. More than once in letters and remarks quoted in Rudolf Sauter's book *Galsworthy the Man* he expresses satisfaction that Soames should be judged to have his tragic side, and says that he himself is worried by the way in which Bosinney does not come to life.

There is always a certain unfairness in praising a given character in a novel or play, and then adding that the author himself was unaware what he was doing in achieving that character. In this respect, one does not want to be unjust to Galsworthy, an immensely industrious writer. All the same, his view of himself as a novelist (expressed to his sister, Rudolf Sauter's mother, in 1905) seems far different from what most critics would find in him:

> I feel more like a sort of chemist, more cold, more dissective, always riding a philosophic idea, and perverting, if you like, my values to fit in. I start out from the thesis that property is not exactly a Christian, decent idea; I perhaps expect people to see this; in any case I deal always negatively, destructively, I can't bear the idea of the beautiful character, it seems to me obvious, commonplace, and disgusting, above all eminently unphilosophical.

But if you are 'a chemist riding a philosophic' idea, you surely become like Lysenko, primarily a Marxian propagandist (as, in his perpetual nagging against property, Galsworthy threatens to become), but not a true man of science. It might also be thought that Galsworthy does go in for 'beautiful characters' – for example, Irene or Young Jolyon.

We have only to think of *Anna Karenina* for a second to see how far short Galsworthy falls of examining adultery in anything like a detached manner. He was not, of course, in the least a detached man, even apart from his 'philosophic' approach. What sort of man he was is indicated in Margaret Morris's unusual and, in its way, striking memoir, *My Galsworthy Story*.

Margaret Morris, later well known as the head of the Margaret Morris School of Dancing, met Galsworthy in 1910, when she was nineteen and he was forty-three. It was on the stage of the Savoy Theatre after the first night of the Marie Brema production of Gluck's

Orpheus and Eurydice. Galsworthy seems to have taken an immediate interest in the younger dancer. She was invited to Galsworthy's house (he had married Ada about five years before), and in due course money was contributed to found Margaret Morris's school.

. It is not surprising that Margaret Morris fell in love with Galsworthy, and he with her. The book, which contains about seventy letters from him, documents an innocent association that lasted about three years. It is not uncommon for the 'affairs' of the celebrated to be put on record, with a collection of letters. Equally, in biographies, one reads of some passing, inconclusive relationship. To have the latter described in detail in the way Margaret Morris does is rare, and possesses a peculiar interest for that reason. Galsworthy was unable to conceal from Ada what was taking place. Although she sent Margaret Morris what one feels was a characteristic letter in the high-mindedness of its approach, it is clear that she also took strong action, bringing into play the hypochondria to which Dudley Barker's book refers. Incidentally she survived to her ninetieth year.

Margaret Morris implies that everything would have been much simpler and less wearing for all concerned, if she and Galsworthy had briefly allowed their feelings free rein. It is impossible to adjudicate on such cases, but certainly a great deal of stress resulted from the alternative situation, from which one does not feel that Galsworthy himself emerges very sympathetically.

The fact remains that Margaret Morris herself was devoted to him, and to his memory. The same applies to his nephew, Rudolf Sauter, who was more or less his adopted son. Nevertheless, Rudolf Sauter's picture also raises doubts. He, one feels, is the agreeable personality, rather than the uncle. Sauter's father was a German subject, and both he and his son were interned during the First World War, Sauter himself only when he reached the age of eighteen. He is very good natured about this. It must be admitted that when the British censorship refused to allow him his uncle's novels, because they were too 'social', even that famous branch achieved something of a record.

Rudolf Sauter writes with affection and complete simplicity:

Dressed in russet jacket (much patched by Ada with soft leather to match – a particular skill of hers), in buff breeches and mahogany riding boots, if he were riding the chestnut – and in equally ancient green jacket and breeches, if riding the silver roan.

Galsworthy the Man: An Intimate Portrait, Rudolf Sauter, Owen.
My Galsworthy Story, Margaret Morris, Owen.

1967
Daily Telegraph

SAKI (H. H. MUNRO)

H. H. Munro (1870–1916), who used the pseudonym Saki (the cup-bearer in the *Rubaíyát* of Omar Khayyám), belongs to an easily recognisable tradition of English light comedy writing. His approach had been preceded by, say, Kipling's *The Gadsbys* or Anthony Hope's *The Dolly Dialogues*, and it looked ahead to P. G. Wodehouse, also in a sense to Ronald Firbank. Munro has nevertheless a distinct touch of his own, harsh, ruthless, which in spite of a debt to Wilde has little else of the 1890s about it, and is equally untouched by more modern influences then coming up. In short, there is something essentially Edwardian about Saki's world.

A. J. Langguth tries to rebut this label of Edwardianism, insisting that Munro chiefly produced his work during the reign of George V; thereby missing the point that it is where an author's feelings lie which colours the books, not the date when they are published. Indeed it must be faced that Langguth, an American, does not write at all well, has scarcely a glimmering of what English social life was like in Munro's day, and is much given to inept comments of his own. None the less, with his many failings, Langguth does try to provide some sort of a connected narrative of Munro's life, including an effort to throw more light on the homosexual and sadistic preoccupations that the most cursory reading of Saki's stories reveal; the brown-limbed fauns, and savage beasts devouring tiresome women, the latter aspect of the Saki picture often very funny.

Munro's father was in the Burma Police, his mother died young, so that with his brother and sister he was brought up in England by a couple of horrible aunts – a parallel with Kipling's childhood, one which in both cases may well have encouraged sadistic fantasies. His sister never married, adored him relentlessly, burnt every scrap of paper about Munro after his death, making biography difficult and not decreasing the likelihood that she felt there was something to hide.

Munro himself began life (like Orwell) in the Burma Police, but had to abandon that career from ill health. Did he just resign or was he invalided? Was there any question of a pension? Langguth does not go into such things. Although Munro liked the cheap polo available, in general seems to have been able to cope with a Burma policeman's lot with less distaste than Orwell, there are indications in his books that he felt unpleasantly cut off out there. On coming home he seems to have established himself as a journalist without too much difficulty (he got on well with his father, by then retired). He picked up languages easily and became a successful war-correspondent in the Balkans. It is interesting that during his period of convalescence on returning from the East, Munro went with his family to Switzerland, where at Davos he saw a good deal of the Renaissance historian John Addington Symonds, not only the first considerable literary figure encountered, but also an early crusader in the cause of homosexuality.

Munro was a newspaper correspondent in Russia during the abortive insurrection of 1905, and always retained a strong interest in Russia and Russian affairs. When Diaghilev's Ballet came to London in 1911, a season that did not at first achieve the wild success the company was later to enjoy, Munro and a friend gave a studio party for the company, Nijinsky among them.

Meanwhile Munro was pouring out political parodies and short stories. The six stories included in this volume are far from his best, but they would give some idea of the Saki style. At no stage does he appear to have experienced any trouble in turning out stories or articles. When war came in 1914 Munro joined the army at once in the ranks. He was by then forty-four. Almost immediately efforts were made to persuade him to take a commission, but he was determined not to do so. He had seen a certain amount of action, been promoted to Lance-Sergeant when he was killed by a sniper in 1916. By then he had decided he could never go back to his pre-war London life, and talked of having a farm in, of all places, Siberia.

Munro's stories abound in house-parties and duchesses, a convention of the period not to be taken too seriously. In fact his social life when in London was probably fairly seedy. His hostesses like Mrs Packletide and Loona Bimberton are certainly funnier and more convincing than the grander settings, which lack the touch of Max Beerbohm, two years younger. The Saki stories also have a strong line in animals, notably the talking cat Tobermory, something of a classic in that genre.

A. J. Langguth states that gossip about Munro's homosexuality was current in the office of his publisher John Lane, and mentions that Munro's wish to hasten publication of his German invasion novel *When William Came* was supported by 'Robert Ross, a literary columnist for the *Bystander* and Oscar Wilde's editor and steadfast friend'. Munro's friendship with Ross might have been a trail worth pursuing. The Saki stories here are themselves in fact incontrovertible evidence of Munro's tastes. They are supported by a gold locket. Instead of two portrait photographs, one side of the interior is inscribed '8th May 1908'; the other 'Hector With best love Cyril'.

Saki: A Life of Hector Hugh Munro. With Six Short Stories Never Before Collected, A. J. Langguth, Hamish Hamilton.

1981
Daily Telegraph

FORD MADOX FORD

The title of Arthur Mizener's biography of Ford Madox Ford (1873–1939) was that first given by Ford himself to a novel of his own which finally appeared as *The Good Soldier*. The phrase is apt. Ford's story is a sad one. In a long and absorbing book, which covers a great deal of ground needing exploration, Mizener shows why that was so. Although in certain respects nothing could be further than Ford from Scott Fitzgerald, there is also a basic romanticism that brings them together, accordingly something apposite in Ford's examination by Fitzgerald's first and best biographer.

Ford's life was not sad because he was chronically short of money, in a perpetual tangle about sex, nor because his books never received the recognition he himself felt they deserved. He had quite a good time in his way, achieving a reasonable reputation as a writer, associating with many remarkable people, living the sort of life that suited him, enjoying an emotional status once summarised to me by the novelist Mary Butts in the remark: 'It's extraordinary what a fuss is always going on about who's to get into bed with old Ford.'

He came of a long established family of German printers. His father had anglicised the name as Hueffer, and married the daughter of the pre-Raphaelite painter Ford Madox Brown. This gave an odd heredity, which had odd effects. On the one hand, Ford was always passionately anxious to be an English gentleman; on the other, he was attracted to continental life and standards. Although he eventually changed Hueffer into Ford, there was a moment when he very nearly took German nationality just before war broke out in 1914. This well expresses Ford's perpetual dilemma, his tendency to say one thing and do another. After that near-miss (one wonders what on earth would have happened had he become a German citizen), he served in France as a subaltern in The Welch Regiment, performing tedious regimental duties and earning the detestation of his Commanding Officer. This again was typical of Ford. Well into his forties, he could almost certainly have avoided army service, but he stuck it out rather nobly – then had to invent an imaginary war career for himself as the real one was not sufficiently glamorous.

Vain and unreliable, Ford had a besetting vice, both as a man and writer: his self-pity. This addiction to self-pity comes over with overwhelming force in *The Good Soldier*, a novel much praised, among others, by Graham Greene, here quoted. I cannot agree that it is a masterpiece. The obvious facility seems to me vitiated by stagey dialogue and a lush social unreality that has something of Michael Arlen about it, without Arlen's wit and obvious familiarity with the smart, rackety world of which he writes.

Mizener, calm, thorough, sympathetic but just, makes no extravagant claims for Ford, beyond being well disposed to an ability, even an originality, that somehow never managed to be adequately expressed.

If Ford had these grave faults, what were his merits? Why is he worth reading about? He also had unusual virtues. He was remarkably generous. He was not only free with money, when he could put his hand on any; he was without professional jealousy. He had a flair for recognising talent. When he edited the *English Review* in London the magazine was a centre of lively writing; in Paris, when he edited the *Transatlantic Review*, a host of young American writers owed much to his encouragement. Ford has some claims to have discovered D. H. Lawrence. He immediately recognised the powers of Joyce. He was an early admirer of Hemingway; who behaved thoroughly badly to him in return. In short Ford was the link – almost the sole one possible to call to mind – between the world of young Americans who largely set the tone of writing in the 1920s and early 1930s and the literary circles in which he had been brought up, bridging the gap between James and Joyce.

One of the best things in Mizener's book is the account of Ford's relationship with Conrad. Ford collaborated with Conrad, later making claims, not always to be substantiated, of the great help he had given. Mizener thinks Conrad never liked Ford. The picture of Conrad himself that emerges from Arthur Mizener's book is one of the most convincing and interesting that I have come across. There are plenty of other vignettes of literary life: Wells, trouble-making and touchy; Arnold Bennett objecting to Ford propagating his own peace terms at the Ministry of Information; Pound writing his incredible letters to Ford, whom he admired.

Ford wrote over eighty books. His four war novels, subsequently collected in one volume as *Parade's End*, seem to me his highest claim as a writer. They come near to effecting that fusion suggested above between what writing had been and what it was to become. They could have made a literary stepping-stone in handling of dialogue and freedom from conventional characterisation. *Parade's End* never quite rises to that, remaining rather a muddle, though perhaps a stimulating one.

The firm for which I was then working published Ford's war novels, and I met him in Paris about 1928. He gave me luncheon at Lipp's. He seemed a ponderous old buffer. Like Mary Butts, I could not imagine why so many ladies seemed to be fighting to go to bed with him. I was quite unaware that he was very hard up at the time, and to pay for my meal was a generous and kindly act. I have no recollection of feeling particularly grateful. I think he probably signed the bill.

The Saddest Story: A Biography of Ford Madox Ford, Arthur Mizener, Bodley Head.

1972
Daily Telegraph

SOMERSET MAUGHAM

I

Somerset Maugham has already taken a certain amount of punishment regarding this book, sections of which appeared recently in a newspaper, provoking some fairly heated correspondence. Here, it is true, the ten novels are no longer presented as the ten 'best' novels in the world – as if novels could be graded like apples or razor-blades – but, even so, things remain which are likely to cause disagreement, even perhaps a little regret; not least that so distinguished a writer should seem to advocate the 'compression' of great novels.

The study surveys Fielding and *Tom Jones*, Jane Austen and *Pride and Prejudice*, Stendhal and *Le Rouge et le Noir*, Balzac and *Le Père Goriot*, Dickens and *David Copperfield*, Flaubert and *Madame Bovary*, Melville and *Moby Dick*, Emily Brontë and *Wuthering Heights*, Dostoevsky and *The Brothers Karamazov*, Tolstoy and *War and Peace*.

Maugham writes: 'A sensible person does not read a novel as a task. He reads it as a diversion'; and again: 'You read a novel for its entertainment, and, I repeat, if it does not give you that, it has nothing to give you at all.' In different forms he repeats this opinion many times; but he also remarks: 'Unless a reader is able to give something of himself, he cannot get from a novel the best it has to give. And if he isn't able to do that, he had better not read it at all.'

But this word 'entertainment' takes us no farther. Some people's idea of entertainment is to exchange dubious limericks; others, to discuss the nature of the Higher Good. Besides, the statements quoted above can only alarm a nervous reader by their peremptory manner and lack of clear instruction. If a novel shows signs of being 'a task' he must cast it aside in order to show himself 'a sensible person'; but, at the same time, he must 'give something of himself' or 'he had better not read it at all'. The margin between these two courses seems a distinctly narrow one. Surely the latter piece of advice comes nearer the truth than the former. I wonder how many people could honestly say that they would be prepared to embark on – and get through – all these ten novels without an effort. And yet that effort might be well worth making. The point is that it would be 'a task'.

The various novels here considered are each prefaced with a brief account of the author. These biographical notes are uneven in quality.

Dickens, for example, fits in well with Maugham's approach, and the result is sympathetic, though unwhitewashed. Many of us will support Maugham in his dislike for Little Em'ly, and his view that she only got what was coming to her. Fielding, on the other hand, is less successfully described. Admittedly, it is hard to know much of the personal life of a man of his comparatively distant period, but Maugham's picture of a weary figure, no longer able to afford to hunt and frequenting the bar of the golf club, to say the least, leaves out a good deal. It is hardly likely, one might think, that a man who wrote, in a sense, the first English novel – still perfectly readable after two hundred years – was not, at least within himself, a bit more interesting than this vignette. In the same way we never get to grips with Stendhal's complexities.

He shows himself greatly concerned with Jane Austen's social position, almost determined to prove that the Austen family were considered no great shakes locally. This may well have been true, but it is not easy to know from precisely what point of view Maugham himself writes. On the one hand he seems to decry snobbery, while on the other his own rather slapdash social history seems to risk the imputation of that very failing, in spite of the fun made of it. He is more at ease with Emily Brontë and Herman Melville; Flaubert is presented much as usual; Balzac, Dostoevsky and Tolstoy crowd any brief biography with their goings-on to a degree that makes a clear-cut picture difficult. In the concluding chapter all the authors meet at an imaginary party. This is literary Wardour Street – costumes or films – at its worst.

Somerset Maugham has a dogged manner of writing that carries him through thick and thin. Sometimes he is illuminating; sometimes a little unworthy of his own good qualities. Occasionally he surprises us with general comments such as 'Blondes don't wear well,' which seem to belong to some quite different sort of book.

Ten Novels and Their Authors,   1954
W. Somerset Maugham,   *Punch*
Heinemann.

II

In his earlier book, *Somerset and All the Maughams* (1966), Robin Maugham gave an interesting account of the genealogical origins of his family, as well as their contemporary goings-on. One of the stories in *Conversations with Willie* suggests that the former subject is always worth attention. When Somerset Maugham was in New York about 1907 an unknown Maugham cousin, descendant of a branch that had emigrated to the United States a century before, called at his hotel. The young American bore not only a striking likeness to himself, but also had a pronounced stutter. 'We are the product of our genes and chromosomes,' remarked Maugham to his nephew, author of this book. 'And there is nothing whatever we can do about it.'

Robin Maugham, son of Somerset Maugham's elder brother (a former Lord Chancellor), is peculiarly well placed to write of his uncle. Himself a talented writer, also bisexual with a strong bias towards his own sex, he knows the international society in which his uncle lived. At the same time he has knocked about the world a good deal, and was wounded in the Second World War. Somerset Maugham made no secret of detesting his brother, the first Viscount Maugham, who in his turn disapproved of his only son's association with his uncle. Nevertheless, if Robin Maugham was more of a son to Somerset Maugham than to his own father, that did not prevent a great deal of bad temper.

Somerset Maugham wanted his biography written by his nephew, but one feels that Robin Maugham's gifts are much more appropriate to the impressionistic sketch given here – in some way brilliantly done – than to the work an official biography requires. Indeed, several assertions are made that seem doubtful in accuracy, but, as most of these occur in the reported speech of persons visiting Somerset Maugham's house in the south of France, the Villa Mauresque, they at least show what was thought at the time. These debatable points have mostly to do with Somerset Maugham's marriage, which broke up mainly on account of his connection with Gerald Haxton, a young American he met in the First World War. Haxton, a good-looking drunken extravert, used to travel with Somerset Maugham on his journeys to the Far East, where, sitting up in the bar after his ungregarious employer had retired to rest, he would collect anecdotes which eventually appeared in Somerset Maugham's books. By no means all writers would be able to make use of this particular method. Maugham was a tortured man. Quite why his torments were so appalling Robin Maugham admits he cannot explain. Even Gerald Haxton seems seriously to have pondered whether his employer had not bartered his soul to the Devil in return for material success. Material success Somerset Maugham certainly achieved, his books sold in millions; his plays were ceaselessly performed. He was on familiar terms with the famous, royalty was nothing exceptional at the Villa Mauresque. Robin Maugham gives a painful account of his uncle's old age, and some of the photographs freeze the blood.

The horrors (as here displayed) from which Somerset Maugham suffered seem to have taken two main shapes: first, he could never forget the disaster of his marriage; secondly, he felt that, although in one sense the most successful writer in the world, in another he was not regarded as a 'great' writer. Why the former of these two vexations continued to gnaw at him quite so much is hard to see; the matter had been cleared up years before. He himself admitted he was unsuited to marriage. He had settled down to quite another sort of life, as had his former wife.

The second affliction is more understandable. All writers have occasional doubts about their own writing, and in certain moods Somerset Maugham would take the line that he wrote only to entertain. This is a perfectly tenable approach (in which a great many big names could be included), but Somerset Maugham did not always stick to that. It is clear from his critical writings that he aimed at something higher. One is not required to pass judgment here except in so far as these torments are concerned. It seems to me that Somerset Maugham did write some first-rate short stories (an excellent novel in *Cakes and Ale*), though he was not much of a critic and never achieved a distinguished style.

The recurrent epithet that occurs in *Conversations with Willie* is the word 'haunted', something everyone seems to have felt who stayed at the Villa Mauresque. It could not exactly be said, in Wilde's phrase (Maugham himself was somewhat given to Wildean epigram), that he knew the price of everything and the value of nothing, because he did appreciate the value of much that he missed. Nevertheless, in spite of all his worldliness, there was a great deal in human relationships, also in books, that he never came to terms with.

Conversations with Willie: 1978
Recollections of W. Somerset Maugham,   *Daily Telegraph*
Robin Maugham, W. H. Allen.

III

Persons of eminence who want to make sure that plenty of books – probably quite gamy ones at that – will be published about them after death cannot do better than direct that a biography must not appear. W. Somerset Maugham (1874–1965) was no exception to this rule. In the end his literary executor, and his daughter (Lady Glendevon), both agreed that it was better to give assistance to Ted Morgan rather than turn their faces away, and the truth, so far as truth goes, was no doubt best served by this capitulation.

If the subject is interesting – and one cannot agree with Rebecca West that Maugham was an uninteresting man – I am all for hearing everything, however trivial. But Morgan does make a long book even longer by inserting from time to time wordy pen-pictures of the epoch at a given moment, and detailed accounts of such episodes as the Wilde case, of which we have all heard plenty already. Nevertheless this biography is absorbing. Even those familiar with the Maugham picture will find new things.

The story begins with the unhappy lonely childhood, leading up to Maugham's early hard-worked medical days, which are well presented. Then came publication of *Liza of Lambeth* (1897), after which Maugham may have had ups and downs but never really looked back. With regard to *Liza*, it is surprising that Kipling's *The Record of Badalia Herodsfoot* (1893), surely an obvious influence, never seems to get mentioned.

By his middle thirties Maugham was doing exceedingly well as a dramatist. In some ways he is a typical Edwardian product: the wit not quite so elegant as that of the Nineties; the sexual daring still untinged with Freud. Then came the First World War. Maugham, now forty, served honourably with an ambulance unit, was then in demand by the Secret Service. Out of his spying experiences he wrote the 'Ashenden' stories from which all subsequent fiction about the Secret Service derives. The war period was also something of a showdown as regards Maugham's homosexuality, an aspect Morgan treats fully. One gets the impression that, in the first instance, Maugham was bisexual in a manner that might have developed either way. Certainly that was what he himself thought. As he grew older he moved more definitely towards his own sex, specifically in the person of Gerald Haxton, his lifelong love, a thorough-going bad lot from San Francisco. Haxton was barred from Britain not only for what were then homosexual offences, but also for an alleged crime still unrevealed. This was one of the reasons why Maugham himself settled in France.

Maugham was an extraordinary mixture of materialistic cynicism and abject sentimentality. Both made him profoundly unhappy. In *The Painted Veil*, one of his characters defines marriage as a man wanting to sleep with a woman so much that he is prepared to pay her board and lodging for the rest of her life. This genuinely seems to have been Maugham's view of marriage.

In the end, as he wished, Maugham became the bestseller of the age – of any age – money pouring in. The Villa Mauresque, his house in the south of France, was filled with the famous and the notorious. It was also the scene of rows, embarrassments, uncomfortable sexual relationships, to which the pen of Dostoevsky could scarcely have done justice. At least Dostoevsky would have had to hand over to Swift when Maugham took rejuvenation injections which prolonged his life to ninety-one, by which time his mind had long since gone. On the other hand the problems regarding his will, relating to Maugham's family and his secretary Alan Searle (who presided over his declining years), would probably have been best chronicled by Balzac.

And so we are left with a full-length picture of a talented and tragic figure, whose enormous vitality produced many good, several first-class, short stories, and at least one excellent novel. It is hard not to feel that even by his own standards, Maugham was anything but a rather awful man. Certain that he was always right, he was accordingly incapable of understanding that he might sometimes have had his leg pulled. If (the source of the story does not seem impeccable) Winston Churchill really told Maugham that, from curiosity, he, Churchill, went to bed with Ivor Novello, I am much inclined to think that the ancient statesman was pulling the ancient author's leg.

To find his brother the Lord Chancellor referred to here as Lord Frederick Maugham, rather than Lord Maugham, would have been painful to Maugham himself; as would the hostess Lady Juliet Duff being called Lady Duff. Patrick Kinross was a Scot, not Irish. The incident of Julian Maclaren-Ross seeing Cyril Connolly turn down a piece written by Maugham for *Horizon* took place in 1940, not 1936. Morgan has been misled about the Companionship of Honour. Maugham's pleasure at receiving the decoration was not unreasonable. It ranks well *above* a knighthood and is not normally given to 'retired generals'. Still, all in all, Ted Morgan's book is a good read, partly owing to his dissenting from the judge's view that what the soldier said is not evidence.

Somerset Maugham, Ted Morgan,   1980
Cape.   *Daily Telegraph*

P. G. WODEHOUSE

I

There are three main aspects of P. G. Wodehouse as a writer: first, the journeyman author-journalist, determined to make a living by his pen, instead of having to work in a bank; second, the immensely accomplished purveyor of the light novel in the manner of *Ice in the Bedroom*, his newest book; third, the artist and brilliant manipulator of words and images.

Writing about 'humour' is such a subjective matter that it is best that I put my own cards on the table. I enjoy what I have called the journeyman Wodehouse books – the skilfully put together school stories with improbable plots, that represent at its best a certain English tradition of writing for boys. At the other end of the scale, I enormously admire Wodehouse as a creator of phrases that bring an individual or a situation dazzlingly to life. It would hardly be going too far to speak of this as Wodehouse the poet. In this aspect, I include such themes of melancholy beauty as the relationship of Wooster and Jeeves, regarding which Richard Usborne has some penetrating things to say. On the other hand, I have to confess that the routine Wodehouse novel, as such, does not consistently hold my attention. I recognise the ingenuity, the finish, but there is something there I find for some reason not wholly sympathetic, in spite of the bursts of high spirits and comic feeling. *Ice in the Bedroom*, for example, written with not an ounce less vitality and punch than its author would have infused thirty or forty years ago, I would heartily recommend to any Wodehouse fan; for myself it falls somehow between two stools.

This is, of course, purely a matter of taste, reflecting, I like to think, adverse criticism of neither Wodehouse nor myself. Wodehouse insists on the necessity in his books of his own particular sort of unreality. Awareness of this need is, in itself, a mark of self-assurance as an artist. Ronald Firbank is another case of that kind adrift when he approaches naturalism.

Trying to analyse what I find amiss in some of the Wodehouse *mystique*, I came to the conclusion that it is the constantly reiterated doctrine that nice men are ill at ease with the opposite sex. It is an interesting question when this teaching – later to spread through the country like wildfire – arose in the nineteenth century. An equally brilliant comic writer like Surtees – with whom Wodehouse might reasonably be compared – would have found it preposterous. Kipling, of course, played a malign part in the game.

In saying this, I do not, of course, mean that the embarrassments of love and sex are not admirable subjects for comedy, or that every Englishman is a Don Juan. It is just the fact that this point of view became in late Victorian writers, and Edwardian ones like Ian Hay, almost a matter of social propaganda. As Usborne comments on an incident in one of the Wodehouse novels: 'There is no suggestion that either clubman or girl would recognise a double bed except as so much extra sweat to make an apple-pie of.'

Usborne also remarks with great truth that Wodehouse is a peculiarly unsnobbish writer, even though much preoccupied, on the one hand, with the nobility, and, on the other, with domestic servants. Here again, we must note Wodehouse's emphasis on the artificial nature of his world. We are nowadays perpetually told, in print, that snobberies deal with unreal, imaginary differences; but, of course, the really painful thing about snobberies is that they are, in their particular context, only too real. If they were not, everyone would laugh them off. This Wodehouse does by, as it were, accepting them.

In this connection, Usborne is guilty of one omission in his otherwise excellent sketch of the Wodehouse background. He does not tell the reader that Wodehouse himself belongs to a cadet branch of an unusually ancient family, holding one of the oldest baronetcies extant (of which he could, in theory, be the heir), later submerged in an earldom. In other words, the nostalgia for an aristocratic world of fantasy has some obvious basis in circumstances to encourage that personal myth. It seems to me as interesting to know this as to know that Wodehouse's brother fell in with Mrs Besant and became a key figure among the Theosophists of India.

George Orwell wrote an essay on Wodehouse, and was not only interested in him as a writer, but also, I think, in certain ways influenced by what might be called the Wodehouse view of life. Orwell as a man with very set views which no power on earth would change was a characteristic figure to whom the Wodehouse stories make a specially strong appeal. They are essentially stories for those who do not want to question the conclusions they themselves – the readers – have already arrived at. They do not deal in those subtleties of feeling anathema to the doctrinaire of all philosophies.

Having spoken perhaps rather pompously of Wodehouse's qualities and caprices, let us glance at some of his *jeux d'esprit*. If any proof were necessary of genius, it is sufficient to say that in one of the school stories published in the 1900s, the rival captains of two cricket teams were called Burgess and Maclaine. Who can fail to be charmed by clubs

called The Six Jolly Stretcher Cases and (for photographers) The
Negative and Solution? What could delight more than the following
vignette:

> 'I've got to take Mother to the flat,' says Rosie on the platform. 'She's
> not at all well.'
>   'No, I noticed she seemed to be looking a bit down among the
> wines and spirits,' said Bingo, casting a gratified glance at the old
> object, who was now propping herself up against a passing porter.

Lord Ickenham was not at Eton, by the way, because fives-bats are
not employed there.

Wodehouse at Work, Richard   1961
Usborne, Jenkins.   *Daily Telegraph*
Ice in the Bedroom, P. G. Wodehouse,
Jenkins.

II

This is P. G. Wodehouse's last and unfinished novel. Here are sixteen
chapters out of a projected twenty-two, a perfectly coherent start to the
story, with elaborate notes by the author, indicating how it would, or at
least how it might, have ended. Richard Usborne, High Priest of the
Wodehouse Cult, writes with insight about these authorial comments,
snatches of dialogue, doubts about characters (all fascinating to anyone
engaged in the novelist's trade), and speaks knowledgeably of Wodehouse himself. There is also a panorama by Ionicus of Blandings Castle
and estate, with an appendix on the train timetables from London to
Market Blandings in Shropshire.

The plot is not unlike other books belonging to the Blandings cycle. A
niece of Lord Emsworth is incarcerated in the castle because she has
fallen in love with a penniless young man. At first the solution seems to
be that the young man, architect turned drawing-master, will paint
Lord Emsworth's prize pig, but as usual difficulties of every kind,
notably Lord Emsworth's fearsome sisters, obstruct the path of love.
The trouble Wodehouse took in his narratives is emphasised by the
notes, sometimes in his own hand, sometimes set out on an ancient
typewriter, of which facsimiles are provided.

Not being an addict, I rely on gems recounted by Wodehouse fans,
always finding them immensely funny. For example, in *Sunset at
Blandings* I laughed uncontrollably when the hero, accidentally locked
out, climbs through a bedroom window into a burglar-trap set by an
acquaintance also staying in the castle; had I not been reviewing the
book, I would never have reached that point in the story. One of the
best points about Wodehouse, both as writer and man, is that he

accurately accepted his limitations. He did not intend to write naturistically. He was aware he had no talent for treating sex except altogether superficially. This appeals especially to persons of set views, who do not want any threat to have these convictions influenced or altered by subtleties of feeling or psychological investigation. Belloc and Waugh, whose warmly expressed admiration for Wodehouse is quoted on the jacket of this book, are typical examples who find repose in an extreme simplicity of convention when reading for entertainment.

From time to time the Pelican Club (believed to have contributed something to the Drones Club) is mentioned in this, and other Wodehouse novels. One learns from Usborne's notes that the Pelican really existed in Denman Street, Soho, in 1887–92, and was frequented by the gang of sporting journalists who wrote for *The Pink 'Un*, a periodical which certainly did not share Wodehouse's tendency to sheer off sex. Indeed too broad a joke about 'six inches of snow in May' (a play upon surnames) led to the suppression of the paper in the 1920s. The dates of the Pelican's survival suggest that the middle-aged characters in *Sunset at Blandings* were born in the 1860s or perhaps early 1870s, thereby setting the scene at a period before 1914, but all sorts of things are mentioned that were pretty well current at the time when Wodehouse himself was writing. It is only occasionally that something like 'raised pies' has to be explained in a note.

It might be argued that Wodehouse does no more than employ an age-old convention of boy-meets-girl, boy is impeded by one sort of older person, aided by another. In these perfectly legitimate vehicles of comedy Wodehouse is apt to avoid any touch of too much reality by putting aunts or uncles in the place of fathers and mothers. There is an unwillingness to be truly satirical, which I somehow find a shade unsympathetic. None the less, to be able to write a book like *Sunset at Blandings* within a month or so of his death at the age of ninety-three in 1975, is remarkable enough even if by severely Wodehousian standards the action may seem a shade repetitive.

Sunset at Blandings, P. G.   1989
Wodehouse, with notes and   *Daily Telegraph*
appendices by Richard Usborne,
Hutchinson.

III

As an admirer, rather than worshipper, of P. G. Wodehouse (1881–1975), my recommendation of his Letters is not the indiscriminate adoration of a fanatic. These Letters perfectly illustrate what a strange personality he was, a merging of extreme simplicity with extreme complication of character. From time to time one laughs aloud, yet an uneasy melancholy hangs over the picture, one I do not pretend to be able to explain. The technical difficulties of sorting out the Letters themselves must have been enormous. As well as writing nearly a hundred books (some untraceable because under pseudonyms), more than 300 short stories, collaborating in innumerable theatrical productions of one kind and another, Wodehouse was also an inveterate letter-writer. Naturally, a great many of these Letters were about business matters, others, say, reports on sport at Dulwich (where he had been a cloudlessly happy schoolboy), or similar trivialities, but a lot remain that throw light on the likes, dislikes, general oddities of a very odd figure.

Frances Donaldson has chosen to make what she calls a kind of anthology, Wodehouse Letters arranged under various headings, which disregard chronology. One sees her point, and demur might well be answered with the words: 'All right, you edit them.' It must have been a Herculean labour. All the same, sometimes the anthology method seems successful; at other times one wants to know the different matters taking up Wodehouse's attention at a given moment. For example, to put together all the material about the Wodehouse animals seems a mistake – glimpses of pekinese behaviour would have lightened subjects like rows about showbiz. Let me temper this criticism by adding that one certainly hopes for a further selection.

The anthology method is undoubtedly successful where the Letters are to Leonora, Wodehouse's adored stepdaughter (at school with Frances Donaldson). Leonora (who died tragically at the age of forty) satisfied Wodehouse's need to be a parent (regretting her drinking wine at nineteen, etc), desire for a candid young critic of his works, taste for a link (after marriage with Peter Cazalet) with the English racing world that did not at the same time make too onerous social demands.

In an interview (1975) Wodehouse was reported as saying: 'Sex, of course, can be awfully funny, but you have to know how to handle it. And I don't think I can handle it properly.' This is a signally clear statement, and it seems permissible to infer that an unusually successful marriage was scarcely, if at all, based on that side of life. Wodehouse's wife, Ethel, comes into the Letters here comparatively little, though there can be no doubt she played an immensely important part in his life. Frances Donaldson refers in passing to 'one of Ethel's followers . . . whom Plum did not seem to mind', so that a separate compartment in that field may also be supposed.

Without any real resemblance to Max Beerbohm (whom Wodehouse did not care for, though liking *Seven Men*), Beerbohm's specifically sexless marriage (indicated in a letter to his future wife) comes to mind, opening up the question of Wodehouse's literary tastes at the same time. Wodehouse was a compulsive reader, always complaining that he could not find enough readable books: liking, for example, *The Constant Nymph* and *Dusty Answer*, but not the works that followed by their authors. He was a great Shakespeare reader (perhaps only after the disaster about the broadcasts from Germany, that is not altogether clear). He could not, however, in general summon up the necessary effort to read a writer who required it, such as Balzac.

When he was in America in the autumn of 1923 he writes (to Leonora):

> Oh yes, I was forgetting. I have also met Scott Fitzgerald. In fact I met him again this morning. He was off to New York with Truex, who is doing his play *The Vegetable*. I believe those stories you hear about his drinking are exaggerated. He seems quite normal, and a very nice chap indeed. You would like him. The thing is he goes to New York with a scrubby chin, looking foul. I suppose he gets a shave when he arrives, but it doesn't show him at his best in Great Neck. I would like to see more of him.

This is of some interest. Ernest Truex was the actor playing the lead in Fitzgerald's play *The Vegetable*, which was a flop, but *The Great Gatsby* was to be published in less than eighteen months, and Great Neck, Long Island, was the intrinsic Gatsby background. It also illustrated Fitzgerald's ability to conceal his alcoholic side, because biographers date his steady drinking (as opposed to drunken parties) from this period. I have quite a collection of books about Fitzgerald, none of which mentions a meeting with Wodehouse.

Wodehouse was immensely generous with close friends, this done through a private account containing his racing winnings, etc, kept secret from Ethel, who seems to have arranged all general financial affairs. She did not, however, act for Wodehouse in business matters, at which he appears to have been extremely capable; for instance, an amusing row with Ziegfeld being chronicled.

Wodehouse was one of those authors who always thought his own books good when he had finished them (Evelyn Waugh was another). He was far more sensitive to criticism than might be expected, though often critical of other writers. Of Waugh's *A Handful of Dust* he writes (to Leonora):

> Excellent in spots, but he ought to have read over his stuff before he published it. You would have told him (a) that he couldn't have a sort of *Mr Mulliner* farce chapter about a man going to Brighton if he wanted the story to be taken seriously and (b) for goodness sake keep away from Brazil. What a snare this travelling business is to the young writer. He goes to some blasted jungle or other and imagines everybody will be interested in it. Also that Dickens stuff. Marvellous as a short story, but much too much dragged in.

He laughs at American editors, who, while liking a story about a clergyman swindler, do not dare to print it. He found the film star Ronald Colman 'the most difficult man to talk to I ever met'. Of the several clubs to which he had belonged, Wodehouse says: 'I think I hated the Garrick more than any of them. All those hearty barristers! I did resign from the Garrick.' One is surprised by his interest in the occult and planchette, then remembers Wodehouse's Theosophist brother.

In regard to the trouble about the German broadcasts, Wodehouse writes (15 February 1945):

> It's fine if the papers are beginning to change their attitude. But I am afraid there is a long way to go before things come right, but I haven't a twinge of self-pity. I made an ass of myself and paid the penalty.

All the same, one regrets that this acceptance of having slipped up went so far as to fraternise later with the odious William Connor (Cassandra), so largely responsible for the unjust attack on Wodehouse in the first instance.

In June 1953 Wodehouse refers to a 'brilliant parody of Jeeves in *Punch* 20 May'. This, by Julian Maclaren-Ross, appears in the Appendix of the Letters, and is, indeed, splendid, an appropriate footnote to a collection of Letters, the fascination of which might easily be missed if their writer's nonchalance is taken too much at face value.

Yours, Plum: The Letters of P. G. Wodehouse, edited with an introduction by Frances Donaldson, Hutchinson.

1990
Spectator

COMPTON MACKENZIE

When, at the age of twelve or thirteen, I was taken out for the day from my prep school, we used to lunch at a country hotel which had a bookcase containing the first volume of *Sinister Street* (1913). I managed to get through quite a bit of it, especially enjoying Meats, who, as Brother Aloysius, seized the hero's hand, cursing him for bringing to mind a girl in Seven Sisters Road. Cyril Connolly and George Orwell, two years older, were equally revelling in Compton Mackenzie's novel at Eton, which, read in adolescence, has a quality that never quite blurs in memory. When I met Mackenzie, then in his seventies, I told him this. He said: 'Not so many years ago a man touched my arm in the street. I could not place him. "Meats," he said very softly.' Mackenzie's rendering of the surname was exceedingly funny.

Later, Connolly chose a passage from one of Mackenzie's books to illustrate Georgian prose at its most tired and over-ornamental. Connolly's other example was by Rupert Brooke. There is no doubt, had Compton Mackenzie been killed in the First World War, he would have been mourned, like Brooke as poet, as a disastrous loss to the English novel. Henry James himself declared that Mackenzie was the most promising of the young writers.

The ancestors of Compton Mackenzie (1883–1972) had come to London from Cromarty in the first half of the eighteenth century. They owned a wharf on the Thames, like the poet Dowson's immediate forebears. His grandfather and father had broken away to become actors of some distinction, under the name of Compton; his American mother's family was also wholly of the theatre. This heredity had a profound effect on their eldest son's personality.

Andro Linklater has written an excellent biography, clear, thorough, affectionate, not in the least blind to its subject's many failings. An immense amount of ground is covered, all done skilfully, so far as possible, succinctly. The only demur (applicable to almost every biography that comes my way) is that the reader is often uncertain of the year he is in.

Compton Mackenzie was overwhelmed with gifts. He possessed looks which a touch of the saturnine kept from insipidity. At St Paul's School the High Master was disappointed in him only because more

industry would have made him a classical scholar to rival Porson. He
was good at games, had great charm, got on with everybody, was
dowered with a formidable ambition, finally – the Bad Fairy's gift at the
christening to help him become a writer – there was just the right
element of moderate unhappiness in childhood. Mackenzie's picture of
Oxford (Magdalen) must have decided many schoolboys that here was
the university of their choice; the measure of his general success there
that, as an undergraduate taking the part of Gratiano in *The Merchant of
Venice*, he was offered by Arthur Bourchier, actor-manager of the
Garrick Theatre, a seven-year contract at £500 a year rising to £2,000.
This Mackenzie turned down.

There followed the period in London which represents Mackenzie's
most characteristic world as a novelist: sleazy rooms, cafés round
Leicester Square, the Empire Music-hall, the varying degrees of
prostitution, from the chorus-girl kept fairly steadily, to the nightly
streetwalker. Linklater says, with complete grasp of what was wrong,
that Mackenzie 'had almost every gift that a great writer required
except the belief that writing is of supreme importance'. Had he been
able to claim the last, this picture of seedy London life of the early 1900s
would have given the twentieth-century novel a superb start.

Mackenzie's years until thirty are by far the most interesting, it
seems to me, but for those who like action the liveliness begins with the
outbreak of war in 1914. Mackenzie (oddly enough like Evelyn Waugh)
managed to be commissioned into the Royal Marines through Winston
Churchill. There he soon became, as a captain, more or less in charge of
the Secret Service in the Aegean. To what extent victory was advanced
by his exertions seems doubtful, but it must all have been great fun. He
found his feet as a man of action (inevitably but a pity), from which in a
sense he never looked back, even though he wrote more than a hundred
books, some at incredible speed.

The moral basis of *Sinister Street* had been a deep sense of evil,
countered by the hero's Anglo-Catholicism. In 1914 Mackenzie was
received into the Roman Catholic Church, but, characteristically, 'He
made it clear to the priest who instructed him that he could not alter his
schoolboy conviction that the orders of the Anglican priesthood were
genuine Catholic and in the apostolic succession.'

Mackenzie died a few weeks short of ninety. Before that he managed
to pack in a great deal: prosecution under the Official Secrets Act for
writing about his Greek adventure (the case no less excruciatingly
boring to read about than those we suffer today); championship of
Scottish Nationalism (later shelved); promotion of gramophone
records, for which he ran a paper; enthusiasm for Siamese cats (whose
now universal popularity he did much to forward); a radio and
television broadcaster of the first rank.

There has been no space here to touch on Compton Mackenzie's three marriages, his love affairs and much else. One small point: John Hope-Johnstone (the Hope J., Hopey, of innumerable anecdotes), who was at one moment Mackenzie's closest friend, was not in the very least a 'hippie'. He was meticulously neat in mind and dress. Impecunious, eccentric, maybe, but always keen to know the smartest place to buy shirts.

Compton Mackenzie: A Life, Andro
Linklater, Chatto.

1987
Daily Telegraph

HUGH WALPOLE

In this admirably executed life of Hugh Walpole, Rupert Hart-Davis, perhaps wisely, avoids much specific consideration of his subject from the angle of purely literary criticism. He has certainly proved that an extremely entertaining, even deeply understanding, book can be written about an author without probing far below that particular surface, and it is doubtful whether a detailed examination of Walpole's books, as such, would have added greatly to the fascinating picture that emerges from this narrative of the making of a literary man. In that respect, however, the critic is in a more vulnerable position than the biographer. To some extent, at least, he must put his cards on the table, commenting on outstanding aspects of the biography: a process which almost inevitably commits him to an expression of views regarding Walpole's place as a novelist.

In his capacity for setting down words on paper Walpole was remarkable. Rising at 4.30 a.m. he could watch the coronation of King George VI, exactly twelve hours later, drenched to the skin and sitting in his underclothes, write 3,000 words in two hours at the *Daily Mail* office, describing the ceremony in an account which delighted both the editor and America. That was a power not to be despised. He brought the same energy and flow of phrase to novel-writing, but the requirements of art are not the same as those of journalism. Critics on the whole, even in his lifetime, although prepared to admit that he could 'tell a story', were rarely inclined to accord the unstinted praise to which Walpole's coarser self felt entitled. There was, however, a more discriminating side, which appears from time to time in his diaries and recorded conversations, a side well aware of his weaknesses as a writer, surprisingly modest in its assessment of his own capacity. In 1935, when almost at the height of his success, he could, for example, note down:

> I have undoubtedly considerable gifts as a novelist but I *cannot* learn the reality of *The Old Wives' Tale*, *Of Human Bondage*, *Esther Waters*, nor have I anything new in technique or style to offer. . . . None of this matters. One does one's best, but as each book appears I realize once more that the essential thing has escaped me.

He was at the same time unusually sensitive to adverse criticism; although, instead of savaging in return his assailants – some of whom, both male and female, have become by now a trifle tarnished by time – he would accept humbly the nagging of even the most third-rate pundit as the voice of true authority. There was, perhaps, a certain justice in this humility, because he himself finally took a prominent place in that strange middlebrow world that owed not a little to the existence and activities of the kind of person most in the habit of attacking him, a region where the by-products of literature rather than literature itself supplied many of the landmarks. He himself wrote nearly sixty books, of which *Mr Perrin and Mr Traill* is possibly the only one to be regarded by fairly general agreement as containing seeds of some genuine strength and originality; although such works as *The Old Ladies* and *The Cathedral*, or in another manner *Above the Dark Circus*, were, at their own level, far from negligible in achievement. All the same there was, almost always, a kind of unreality and woolliness about his manner which prevented him from using his gifts to full effect, leading to the rather wearisome outpourings of the *Herries* series; nor was Robert Ross's criticism, 'Mr Walpole is not as wholesome as he thinks,' entirely beside the point as a critical comment. There was a fundamental lack of grasp of what human beings are really like, an inherent failing suggested again and again by innumerable incidents set down in the biography.

In short, as Hart-Davis unfolds his story and we are shown a kind of chart of how a career could be made by the pen in the first quarter of this century, the reader inclines more and more to find Walpole interesting as a human being rather than as an author. He was so essentially a product of his time. A man of the fan letter: of the Book Society: of Hollywood: of the lecture tour: of the literary club. A man who found women too exacting, social life almost intoxicating, and 'the perfect friend' – whom he was always seeking – among the possessors of those stolid masculine virtues which he so much admired, but could not himself attain. Pushing, timid, egotistical, kind-hearted, short-tempered, affectionate, stingy in small matters, open-handed in large ones, commonplace in his ambitions, yet not without some taste and some wit, he provided an amalgam almost bound to succeed in the world he set out to conquer. Around him, in the chronicle, swim the great and lesser literary fish of his epoch, with most of whom he had some contact or other that remains of material interest to the reader of today.

His own background should not be ignored. Son, grandson and great-grandson of clergymen, he belonged to an ancient family that had produced one of England's most notable statesmen, also her most distinguished dilettante. It is remarkable – and strongly in contrast with what might be commonly supposed in such a connection – how little effect these aristocratic origins had in influencing the general tenor of Walpole's career. His early life and education seem to have been on the whole disordered, uneasy, not very enjoyable, largely owing to the fact that his father's hard-worked vocation led him, rather unwillingly, all over the world; and, even if there may have been a certain family tradition of grandeur, long past, some of the ordinary amenities of a middle-class home were frequently at a discount. There was also, perhaps, a lack of zest on his mother's part in her relationship with her own family; at such things, at least, the book hints.

Walpole, who was born in New Zealand in 1884, disliked his various schools (for a time he was at King's School, Canterbury, like Somerset Maugham), and took a Third at Cambridge. Naturally enough, he too was intended for the Church, and his physical appearance, as the illustrations of this book show, indicated – indeed, almost insisted on – an ecclesiastical career. However, he himself had doubts about his own suitability as a minister of religion, and, after a spell of working at a seamen's club in Liverpool, he decided to make the attempt to become a professional writer. It was a decision that required courage, but, in spite of haunting fears in some directions, he possessed plenty of enterprise in others; also a curious instinctive knowledge of how to make his way. His technique in this last respect is worth considering. The method was based mainly on writing innumerable letters to his favourite authors: the replies he received showing that he himself was, in the first place, no ordinary letter-writer.

No one with any experience of the literary world can fail to be struck by the fact that when he came to London as a young man in 1909 Walpole was able to obtain a room in Glebe Place, Chelsea, for 4s. a week, and, soon after this, a job reviewing novels at £3 a week. The former would now cost some present-day literary aspirant perhaps eight times as much, while the latter would bring in – perhaps the same sum. In other words, the potentialities, in the circumstances, were in those days decidedly more favourable for embarking upon a career of letters; although it could perhaps be argued on the other side that the particular spheres in which Walpole excelled, some of them ancillary to the literary world proper, have in our own day, on the whole, whether BBC, British Council or the like, tended to increase in number.

Among the writers approached by him was the author of *Elizabeth and Her German Garden*. Their correspondence resulted in his appointment as tutor, at the age of twenty-two, in the house of the Gräfin Arnim (as she then was) of whom the book supplies a somewhat devastating picture. Few young men could stand more than six months of the battery of mingled baiting and flirtation that fell to their lot in the Countess's house; and Walpole, although they became friends in later life, was almost at the end of his tether after a few weeks. Within a couple of years, however, he made a far more important foray than this one, and, by way of an introduction from A. C. Benson, he became a friend of Henry James.

Walpole won James's heart as few, if any, had done before, but affection was never allowed to fall into critical indiscretions when faced time and again with his protégé's latest novel. They corresponded frequently, and when James presented the young author with a desk for his cottage in the country he wrote:

> I hope the thing will seem to you of an adequate shape and aspect, and that when you lean your inspired elbows on its extended table you will feel a little as if resting them on your poor old friend's still sufficiently broad and sturdy and all-patient back.

That was in 1913, the year of James's seventieth birthday, to which a period touch is given by the recollection that his portrait by Sargent was slashed at Burlington House by a suffragette.

The outbreak of war involved Walpole in various activities in Russia. His eyesight was bad and his part did him nothing but credit, although his absence from England was made the subject of criticism in some circles. He was in Russia at the time of the Revolution in 1917, of which his official account, forwarded to Mr Balfour by the Ambassador, Sir George Buchanan, is included in the appendix. Described in Buchanan's dispatch as of an 'extremely interesting and picturesque character' and 'this admirable document', the paper speaks of Kerensky as 'the strongest, ablest and most far-seeing of them all in this crisis', and, in its general sentimentality, incoherence and lack of grasp, provides what might be looked upon as a melancholy monument of both professional and amateur incomprehension. It is interesting to speculate whether it was ever read by Walpole's close friend Conrad; and, if so, what were the comments of the author of *Under Western Eyes*.

Hart-Davis calls the section of his book that follows the Armistice 'The Pursuit of Happiness', and from here onwards Walpole's success steadily increased, his personal characteristics settling down to a pattern they were to retain until the end of his life. It was during this period that he saw a good deal of Conrad. Some tantalising glimpses are given here. He was, it appears, a great admirer of Proust's writings, an enthusiasm he shared with Walpole. Arnold Bennett, a friend first encountered in 1910, also belongs chiefly to these years following the war. They carried on a bantering correspondence ('My sweet Hughie' – 'Darling Arnold') largely devoted to questions of literary style. We are shown Kipling remarking to P. G. Wodehouse: 'But tell me, Wodehouse, how do you finish your stories? I can never think how to end mine.' Quotations from Walpole's diary provide some piquant sidelights on authors' behaviour when together; for example, at a house-party at the Galsworthys':

> J. G. was beaten at croquet, which he couldn't bear. He has no sense of fun about games. They are battles for Galsworthian justice, and when he was beaten it was as though we had acted *Justice* all over again, there on the lawn in front of his eyes.
>
> But he is a *dear* – gentle, honest, just, trying not to be self-conscious about his terrific present success. It was hard for Arnold to hear at dinner that a first *Man of Property* had just fetched £138 at Hodgson's, but he bore it well – only made a brief allusion to *The Old Wives' Tale* and told me my tie was the wrong colour for my suit.
>
> We were all very happy together.

Publication of *Cakes and Ale* took place in 1930. Somerset Maugham's letter, denying that Alroy Kear, a character in the novel, was a portrait of Walpole, is here reproduced. The incident, a painful one to Walpole, is of interest for other reasons than the obvious pungency of its personal implications, because it brings out so clearly the essential difference, not only between two writers, but between two schools. Walpole – although he, too, had caused offence of a somewhat similar kind in *Mr Perrin and Mr Traill* – could never have attained the complete naturalism of his own prototype: and in this connection it is not out of place to mention his friendship with Virginia Woolf, a writer whose work was regarded by Walpole almost with veneration. Although he considered himself far below her as an author, her 'inner looking' approach can be found surprisingly to resemble some of Walpole's own romantic writing (compare, for example, the dialogue of *The Years* and *Wintersmoon*, both of them in severe contrast with the clear-cut exteriors of Maugham and other writers of a more exact style).

The story ends with the last war. Although Walpole could have retired to his house in Cumberland – or, like others, gone to America to lecture, an undertaking no doubt easily to have been arranged in the light of his former successes there – he preferred to find employment in London, and identify himself with events of the time, however unpleasant they might be. He had been suffering for a number of years from a diabetic complaint, and his general health breaking down under the nervous strain, he died on 1 June 1941. His life was not quite the one he had planned for himself, though its record provides a kind of window looking on to many things that are of absorbing interest. By refusing to disregard his faults, his biographer has most successfully suggested his virtues.

Hugh Walpole: A Biography, Rupert Hart-Davis, Macmillan.

1952
Times Literary Supplement

RONALD FIRBANK

In Terry Coleman's enjoyable study of the birth of railways in England, *The Railway Navvies*, he mentions a certain Joseph Firbank, who began life at the age of seven in a Cumberland coal mine, and ended as a rich railway contractor and High Sheriff of Monmouthshire. This nineteenth-century ideal of the self-made man was the grandfather of Ronald Firbank, the novelist. His father was a Liberal M P, eventually knighted; his mother, daughter of an Anglo-Irish protestant clergyman. The novelist himself was the second of three sons, the youngest of the Firbank children being a daughter, who left the nation a collection of dresses of the fashions of her day.

Ronald Firbank (1886–1926) has two claims to fame: first, his interest in writing dialogue effectively influenced, for example, Evelyn Waugh, I. Compton-Burnett, possibly Ernest Hemingway, and left a mark on subsequent novel writing; second, he was, in his day, one of those fabulous social figures whose eccentric goings-on were endlessly talked about and whose remarks were repeated. Consequently, as a late child of the 1890s, the *décadence*, he is one of the bridges between that movement and contemporary novel writing.

Miriam J. Benkovitz has been collecting material for a Ronald Firbank biography for many years, and there are indications that it has not always been easy to establish facts or use material, as, for example, the 450 postcards in existence which Firbank sent to his sister. It would be nice to record that, in spite of difficulties, a satisfactory account of Firbank has been compiled. Alas, Miriam Benkovitz writes without a glimmer of humour.

There are details here Firbank fans will be glad to know (Lady Firbank in a letter to Ronald about his brother: 'Tomorrow will be Joey's 17th birthday; poor boy he has seen as much as a man of 40! but I trust and pray he means now to turn over a new leaf'), but little that is substantial is added to Ifan Kyrle Fletcher's *Memoir* (1930), with its excellent contributions by Lord Berners, Augustus John, Vyvyan Holland and Osbert Sitwell. Indeed, something is lost, because one would scarcely guess from Miriam Benkovitz's work that Firbank was in his way a considerable wit.

To be fair to the author, her avowed intention is to present a 'serious'

311

Ronald Firbank. She writes 'They [the Firbank papers she examined] denuded him of a part of his amusing eccentricity, but he took on a greater humanity.' It is, of course, true that the life of a talented, painfully shy, lonely, tipsy, ailing homosexual makes at times sad reading, as he wanders from continental hotel to continental hotel. However, that is no reason to omit many of the best stories, which, after all, show the courage with which Firbank faced his often depressing circumstances, still less to wreck anecdotes about him. For example:

> This dependency [on his mother] endured and had a lasting effect on his other relationships. He liked to be protected and looked after. The truth of that statement is obvious in an incident of the early twenties. As Osbert Sitwell told it, one day at 'luncheon in the Café Royal', Firbank asked a friend, Gabriel Atkin, a young painter, to give him lunch. Atkin replied that he could not, because he had no money. According to Sitwell, Firbank promptly 'took a pound note out of his pocket, pressed it into the hand of his friend and, sinking at the same time into the seat opposite, exclaimed, "How wonderful to be a guest!"'

But this was something Miriam Benkovitz seems never to have heard of – a joke. Firbank, although it appears he had no more than £700 or £800 a year, was, in the bohemian circles in which he moved, a relatively rich man. He was always expected to pay. No one was more aware of this than Firbank himself. He was not demonstrating his Oedipus Complex in the Café Royal, he was making one of those comic public gestures that caused people to laugh.

When Miriam Benkovitz talks about *Valmouth* balancing 'a natural and primitive love of beauty against the love of Catholic discipline and form without Christianity', and *Sorrow in the Sunlight* expressing 'the moral vacuum of the times and society he knew', she manifests an inept, not to say fatuous form of contemporary criticism to which Americans are peculiarly subject. This lack of contact derives from an inability to distinguish between comedy and satire. When a comedian imitates a drunk man, he is not miming a tract against alcoholism. He is being funny. Mr Micawber is not a 'satire' against improvident retired officers of Marines. He is a great comic figure. Thus with Firbank. He was being funny about priests, and – dare one hint it? – about Negroes.

'Ragland Somerset' should be Raglan Somerset, 'Lady Douglas', Lady Alfred Douglas, 'Frank Rewitt', Frank Prewitt, 'Alistair Crowley', Aleister Crowley, and the High Street at Oxford is, for some reason, quaintly known as The High, rather than 'High'. One wonders

whether Firbank might not have had some fun sketching Miriam
Benkovitz's prototype writing a dedicated biography of Harvester, the
name he gives himself in his own novel *Vainglory*.

Ronald Firbank: A Biography,
Miriam J. Benkovitz, Weidenfeld
& Nicolson.

1970
Daily Telegraph

ALDOUS HUXLEY

I

This essay describes the effect on the author of taking mescalin, the active principle of peyotl, a drug derived from the cactus. Mexican Indians have used peyotl for centuries. This drug is said to change the consciousness powerfully, but at the same time to have no poisonous effects, and to form no habit in the taker. It is now suggested that there is a close chemical similarity between mescalin and adrenalin: accordingly, to quote Aldoux Huxley, 'each one of us may be capable of manufacturing a chemical, minute doses of which are known to cause profound changes in consciousness.'

Before going further, it is perhaps worth remarking – a point not mentioned by Huxley – that, at a much lower level, the characteristics attributed to mescalin are also to some extent true of the Mexican drink, tequila, itself a product of the cactus. Tequila is drunk as an aperitif, to the accompaniment of a taste of salt and lemon. It gives a lift of somewhat limited duration without later intoxication: just the thing for starting a luncheon party, for example. Tequila is, of course, often mixed with other ingredients to make a stronger drink, and no doubt excessive potations of tequila alone might have bad results. It does, however, serve as an illustration of the curious properties of the cactus.

Huxley points out that it is not only important to see ourselves as others see us but also to see others as they see themselves. It seems virtually certain, he says, that he will never feel like Sir John Falstaff or Joe Louis, the famous boxer. Would some form of hypnosis make this change in him possible? It is an attractive idea, and we follow the experiment with excitement. Those who feel that something rather risky is going to be attempted should remember that Aldous Huxley himself is essentially a puritan. He has some severe things to say about drinking and smoking, for example, in this essay. The reader can therefore feel perfectly safe in the assumption that no guilty pleasure will be involved. The worst that can happen is that Huxley may derive a little intellectual excitement; and he is, after all, well equipped to keep even that dissipation within reasonable bounds.

Most takers of mescalin experience only the heavenly part of schizophrenia. The drug brings hell and purgatory only to those who

314

have had a recent case of jaundice, or who are suffering from periodical depressions or a chronic anxiety. If, like the other drugs of remotely comparable power, mescalin was notoriously toxic, the taking of it would be enough, of itself, to cause anxiety. But the reasonably healthy person knows in advance that, so far as he is concerned, mescalin is completely innocuous, that its effects will pass off after eight or ten hours, leaving no hangover and consequently no craving for a renewal of the dose. Fortified by this knowledge, he embarks on the experiment without fear – in other words, without any predisposition to convert an unprecedentedly strange and other than human experience into something appalling, something actually diabolical.

To find out what happened to the maker of this experiment the book must, of course, be read. It would be unfair to pick out its conclusions, separating them from the running commentary. One thing, however, seems quite clear. Huxley did *not* become Sir John Falstaff or Joe Louis; he remained, very essentially, Huxley. What, for example, could be more like himself than to remark, when shown, under the influence of the drug, a reproduction of Cézanne's self-portrait, wearing a large straw hat: 'It's like Arnold Bennett in the Dolomites.' His other reactions were equally characteristic. The colours around him were heightened in their range; such designs as the folds of material in pictures gained an infinite subtlety. Yet, at the same time, he writes:

Art, I suppose, is only for beginners, or else for those resolute dead-enders who have made up their minds to be content with the *ersatz* of Suchness, with symbols rather than with what they signify, with the elegantly composed recipe in lieu of actual dinner.

Speaking as a dead-ender of the most resolute sort, it seems to me that Huxley, after his shot of mescalin, ran tremendously fast only to find himself standing in the same place. In fact, perhaps Alice was really in Mescalinland, or Through the Cactus. Certainly the manner of looking at life, here analysed, is apparent from almost the earliest of Huxley's writing. Unfortunately Messrs Chatto and Windus do not enclose a mescalin sample (at least not in review copies), so that it is not at present possible to make further comment from personal experience.

The Doors of Perception, Aldous   1954
Huxley, Chatto and Windus.   *Punch*

I I

It is difficult now to express the prestige attached to the name of Aldous Huxley in the 1920s. Its very sound had an intellectual ring, but one

that seemed also free from the pretensions and pedantry of Bloomsbury. Huxley was still under thirty when his second novel, *Antic Hay*,
appeared in 1923 (during my first term at Oxford), and how well I
remember being bowled over by its originality, daring and brilliance.

Huxley's story is an interesting one, and Sybille Bedford tells it well.
His grandfather was Thomas Henry Huxley, the man of evolutionary
science; his mother descended from Dr Arnold of Rugby fame;
Matthew Arnold and Mrs Humphry Ward were close relations. This
was a powerful heredity, loaded with Victorian intelligence, doubt, and
– one cannot help feeling – a fair amount of self-satisfaction.

Aldos Huxley won a scholarhsip to Eton, where he was happy,
though (contrary to popular myth) overworked. That state of being
overworked was one from which he really never emerged. He left Eton
after two-and-a-half years because of serious trouble with his eyes. This
eye complaint was always with him – at times it seemed he might go
blind – and, of his many qualities, Huxley's courage and endurance in
overcoming this handicap are perhaps his most remarkable achievements.

He went up to Balliol in 1913. Here, in Bedford's narrative, one
becomes aware of Huxley's less solemn side, his gaiety (in the true
sense), enterprise, taste for social life. In the following year the war
came. Huxley was, of course, totally unfit for the army. In due course he
found himself living at the Morrells' house, Garsington, among the
pacifist elements who had taken refuge there. Lady Ottoline Morrell's
household was to play a great part in Huxley's life, not least in
providing him with a wife, Maria Nys, then a Belgian refugee. If Aldous
Huxley is the hero of this book, Maria Huxley is decidedly the heroine.
The couple were married in 1919, a few years before his twenty-sixth
birthday. Neither had any money. Huxley kept things together by
literary jobs of the most fragmentary kind. It is something of a revelation to learn – if by no means for the first time – how exceedingly hard
up a writer can be, even while his name, as in Huxley's case, is well
known.

By the time *Point Counter Point* was published in 1928, Huxley had
been receiving for some years a small but regular income (as advance
royalties) from a publisher. He had to produce *two* books a year, a novel
and some lesser work. The strain of doing so was appalling. Although
his first three novels – *Crome Yellow, Antic Hay, Those Barren Leaves* – do
not retain quite the glamour of their earliest impact, they remain full of
wit and sparkle. It was natural for him to attempt something wider and
deeper. He wrote *Point Counter Point*, which put him, comparatively
speaking, into the big money. Although a vigorous attempt, it is a
lifeless novel, commonly held to derive to some extent from Gide's *Les
Faux-Monnayeurs*, but one would guess Dostoevsky's *The Devils* was also
an influence.

Sybille Bedford does not mention Wyndham Lewis's savage attack on *Point Counter Point* for its sentimentality and cheap writing. It has to be admitted that Lewis's strictures were not unjust. Here we have one of several paradoxes in Huxley's life and work. Considered the prototype of all highbrows, a dedicated intellectual, this was by no means wholly his position; especially when it came to writing a novel. He was, in fact, a capable literary journalist, who had indeed – as Lewis implied – more than a touch of vulgarity. Much of his 'brutal' writing, for example, is a sort of inverted sentimentality.

In this connection, Sybille Bedford reasonably points out that Huxley himself was, so far as his own status as a writer was concerned, in many ways a modest man, laying no claim to being a 'great artist'. It is no doubt also true that, had he written in a less popular style, he might well have starved.

But, in spite of stimulating ideas in essays, which continued until the end of his life, one cannot help seeing in Huxley something of a Lost Leader. He possessed inventiveness of one kind, but not of another. It is perhaps fallacious to suppose that, even had he controlled a sometimes shoddy style, he would ever have produced in subsequent novels anything much better than, say, the verbal ingenuities of *Brave New World*. He was that rare thing in a novelist, a frustrated man of science, which comes out over and over again in his books. In about 1935 a side of Huxley, no doubt always latent, seems to have taken over: a crankiness that expressed itself in diets, systems of life, all that might come under the general heading of 'guru-mindedness' – some sort of an answer to life must be found. By now the Huxleys were in the south of France, not doing too badly financially, but living an oddly rootless, cut-off existence in certain respects.

It was here that Sybille Bedford first knew them. Her book has the great advantage of being written by a biographer who can not only handle with skill this sort of material (not at all easy), making the narrative both factual and entertaining, but, by her own personal experiences, subtly convey the tone of Huxley's daily life. If one has a criticism it is that the toughness of intellectuals' give-and-take among themselves is allowed a shade too much amelioration of sweetness and light.

Aldous Huxley: A Biography. Vol. I: 1973
1894–1939, Sybille Bedford, Chatto   *Daily Telegraph*
with Collins.

ERIC LINKLATER

Eric Linklater (1899–1974) was a picturesque, complicated, talented figure, who had a huge success with his early novels (*Juan in America*, 1931, sold between 50,000 between spring and autumn of publication year), then gradually lessened in public esteem though always remaining a thoroughly competent and successful professional writer, broadcaster, to some extent public personality, and what generally comes under the heading of man of action. All this did not prevent him living exuberantly, having a lot of friends, and showing himself – to use an old-fashioned phrase – the backbone of the country. He forged his age as a year older in order to get out to active service in France in 1917, undertook a lot of useful but often boring army jobs in the second war and, in his fifties, went out to Korea (which he didn't particularly want to do) as an official observer with the rank of lieutenant-colonel.

Linklater is thought of essentially as an Orcadian but, like so many persons with passionate feelings about a country or locality, he was only partly of the Orkneys. He was born in Glamorgan, and lived in South Wales until the age of twelve. His mother was half-English half-Swedish; his father, a master mariner, son of an Orkney crofter. The Linklaters had long been in the Orkneys; a village bears their name, and (Orkney and Shetland becoming part of Scotland only in 1468) Linklater traced his descent in a fifteenth-century Norwegian document to one Cristi Aelingaklaet ('A stone in the heather'). Linklater attended Aberdeen Grammar School, but could claim to be only the second most distinguished literary alumnus, as Byron had preceded him. That no doubt caused a certain Byronic preoccupation.

Opportunity to place his modern Don Juan in the United States came from a Commonwealth Fellowship to Cornell University in up-state New York. By then, having abandoned medical studies (fortunately for all concerned, one feels), he had already been a journalist in India.

Parnell emphasises that under a self-assured, even at times aggressive, exterior, Linklater was uncertain of himself and of what he thought. He never ceased to view life from a romantic angle, trying to correct that with hard work and a fairly earthy approach to many things, but his feelings were often at war. He was persuaded to stand as a Scottish Nationalist candidate although the last thing he wished was to enter Parliament – in any case the Orkneys preferred a certain sense of identity separate from Scotland – while Linklater himself always remained an entirely unrepentant advocate of the British Empire 'to whose creation Scotland has so lavishly contributed'. He also declared in his manifesto: 'I am unwilling to bargain for your support with an easy promise of attention to local amenities and zeal in the support of local industries.' Not surprisingly, Linklater was bottom of a poll of five.

After marriage (happy, but not without storms) Linklater lived for a time in Italy, at Lerici, where Lady Sybil Lubbock, wife of Percy Lubbock, held court and linked up with much literary life past and present. When the Linklaters' first child was about to be born she persuaded them to move into a cottage which really belonged to her daughter, Marchesa Iris Origo, though Iris Origo was rarely there. This turned out by no means cheap and Linklater was tempted to write a thank-you letter beginning: 'Dear Lady Sybil, owing to your very great kindness, we are now almost entirely destitute.'

Long residence in Orkney followed. Then, after the war, to facilitate the children's education, a move was made to Pitcalzean House in Ross-shire, an attractive place though characteristically much too big for the family. All the while Linklater travelled a great deal and was involved not only with books but in films and the theatre. The whole biography gives a very good idea of what can constitute an energetic writer's career.

Linklater speaks of one of his own books as 'opulent, empurpled', and as a writer he is impelled by almost too much intoxication with words, combined with personal taste for a romp. He was erudite, felt strongly about things, could be very funny (the scene in the Suez Canal which he witnessed when an Italian troopship, on the way to Ethiopia, passed a British troopship returning from India should not be missed) but surprisingly, considering his time in the United States, he never felt drawn to the discipline of Hemingway and the American writers of that period.

I met Eric Linklater several times in London but saw most of him on a National Trust of Scotland cruise in 1968, on which he had a semi-official position. He and his wife Marjorie were ideal *compagnons de voyage*. She was always telling him he must go and talk to so-and-so; he preferred to have another scotch and more gossip. By that time there was perhaps a touch of melancholy. He would still come out with remarks like: 'Lady Macbeth and Gertrude, Queen of Denmark, were typical North British matrons – and that goes for Iceland and the Faroes too.'

Eric Linklater: A Critical Biography,   1984
Michael Parnell, with a foreword   *Daily Telegraph*
by Andro Linklater, Murray.

WILLIAM GERHARDIE

The family of William Gerhardie (1895–1977) belonged to a little known but specific category, British subjects who had lived for several generations in pre-Revolutionary Russia. To his particular case was added a rather unusually complicated racial background, and business connections with Manchester. Then the war came in 1914. At the age of twenty, already set on writing as a career, he joined the Scots Greys as a trooper. Later he served as a captain in the campaign undertaken by the Allies against the Bolsheviks during the Russian civil war.

The hero of *The Polyglots* is a young officer on the staff of the British Far Eastern Command, who spends most of his time between Vladivostok and Harbin. Many of his relations have taken refuge in Siberia. He has a love affair with a girl cousin, seems about to marry her, then loses her, but sails back in her company – and that of their relations – to England.

It is reasonable to consider a good deal of *The Polyglots* autobiographical. *Of Mortal Love*, written a decade later, has something of the same air, though in a very different manner. It is the story of a love affair with a married woman, a divorce, the dissolution of love, final disaster. The narrator is a comparatively well-known, but impecunious, composer. It is an odd book, which no one else could have written. One is aware in it of the presence and influence of Gerhardie's old friend Hugh Kingsmill, who occurs as 'Max Fisher' here and elsewhere in Gerhardie novels. The material of the novel sometimes seems to be not quite sufficiently digested by the author; that is by the high standard set by *The Polyglots*.

The extraordinary burst of praise on the part of Arnold Bennett, H. G. Wells, and a row of other pundits, that greeted *The Polyglots* when it appeared put me off as such pontifical recommendations do when you are young – and I did not read it until about 1928; then for business reasons, as the publishing firm for which I worked was taking the novel over.

On first reading, *The Polyglots* seemed immensely enjoyable. Since then I have returned to it many times. Now, just reread in this new edition, the book has lost none of its freshness. Only to be regretted is the replacement, 'allergic to waiters', for 'nervous of waiters'. This introduces a much later, not particularly respectable epithet.

The Polyglots is a 'war book', even though a peculiar kind of war book. There is some parallel with *The Enormous Room*. E. E. Cummings was born in 1894, the year before Gerhardie. His book is not a novel, but an account of being immured for some months by the French authorities for 'careless talk', while serving with an American ambulance unit. It appeared in 1922. Practically the only things the two men have in common are age, talent, and the war. Nevertheless these supply a link of extraordinary strength. The hero of *The Polyglots* reflects that the lunatics and eccentrics who surround him in Harbin are no madder than the people who run the world: Cummings, surrounded by the equally astonishing rag-tag-and-bobtail the French security officials have incarcerated, makes the almost identical comment.

In both the mood of the period is exactly reproduced. The unusual circumstances of the two books provide a kind of sermon against those critics who preach that only 'ordinary' people should be written about, if the general principles of human life are to be illustrated. There is also perhaps a warning againt being too politically 'committed' – at least a warning of Time's revenges in the passages, admittedly jocular, where Winston Churchill is treated as a mere buffoon, and Russian *émigrés* derided for insisting that an odious tyranny would be established by the revolution in their country.

William Gerhardie, before writing *The Polyglots*, had made something of a trial-run with his first book *Futility*, similar in subject. *The Polyglots* – whatever Edith Wharton may have thought to the contrary – is fuller, more deeply felt, infinitely better. The author is particularly at home with the pains, contradictions and disappointments of love. *The Polyglots* has another unusual characteristic. A lot of quite young children come into it, all characterised with astonishing skill. I can think of no other novel where children are handled in the same way. If the author rather lets himself go at the death of nine-year-old Natasha in the last pages, it is, so to speak, as an equal. The grief is passionate, not at all sentimental.

The Polyglots, William Gerhardie;   1970
Of Mortal Love, William Gerhardie,   *Daily Telegraph*
revised definitive edition with
prefaces by Michael Holroyd,
Macdonald.

MICHAEL ARLEN

I only met Michael Arlen once, not so very long before his death, when by an odd chance we lunched tête-à-tête. Small, neat, immensely at ease, he possessed the attractive gift of being able to plunge at once into conversational intimacy.

Arlen, who came of an Armenian family of Manchester businessmen, was born in 1895. His first novel, *The London Venture*, appeared in 1920. It was a success. Noel Coward, in his foreword to the paperback, describes how he borrowed £250 from the author on the strength of it, which made possible the staging of *The Vortex* – an extraordinarily appropriate incident. Slight, much influenced by George Moore, *The London Venture* is, in its way, a remarkable book to be written by so young a man. All the elements of Arlen's later writing are there. It is also notable, at this early date, for its references to D. H. Lawrence, James Joyce and Wyndham Lewis. The then less familiar vocation of 'shop steward' is also mentioned.

Arlen's short stories built up his reputation. The real bestseller came in 1924 with *The Green Hat* which, so he told A. S. Frere, earned him £120,000. That was in days when writers could keep some of the money they earned. One would have liked Frere's Introduction to have been longer (Arlen was educated at Malvern, by the way, rather than Clifton), as it whets the appetite for information about the undertones of an always interesting period, and decidedly mysterious personality.

Arlen, one feels, was essentially a melancholy man under the protective sophistication, but it is hard to assess his own approach to writing, particularly as he refused to have his books republished in his lifetime. The charge of vulgarity was aimed at him, not without reason – indeed he refers to this side of novel writing in *The London Venture* – but, if vulgarity puts a novel out of court, quite a lot of famous works would have to be withdrawn.

If he were simply 'writing for money', why not make some more with republication of what does not matter anyway? If – and one suspects the latter – the books never rose to his own critical standard, it is strange that this inner fastidiousness did not impose a stronger discipline on a lively talent. No doubt if he had been more severe with himself, Arlen would not have made a fortune. It was the silliness that sold the books in such quantities. Yet even the silliness is certainly no worse than, say, *Lady Chatterley's Lover*, in which a disobliging picture of Arlen occurs as a small return for his recommendation of Lawrence.

Arlen's strength and weakness can perhaps be pinpointed in the sequence towards the end of *The London Venture*, where the old French nobleman, guardian of the English girl, proposes to her. The essential improbability of their whole situation is redeemed by the author's awareness that the Marquis's proposal is partly a genuine wish to do his duty and save her financial situation, partly the desire of an old man for a young girl. This recurring appreciation of the complex and contradictory strain in human behaviour made Arlen an innovator, anyway to the wide public for which he wrote. Where he fails is not in his paradoxes and exotic situations, so much as the sentimentalised descriptions and flamboyant dialogue.

All the same, he still conveys an extraordinarily potent whiff of the period. He supplied his generation with their particular version of what is said to be one of the formulae for a never-failing bestseller, the 'shameless, shameful lady' – the woman who still feels chaste after a thousand lovers. Brett, of *The Sun Also Rises*, was to make her literary début two years later. Hemingway's version of the type was more down to earth than Arlen's, but the myth is the same. To be just, quite a few ladies of that sort were then about.

The opening of *The Green Hat* remains strikingly readable, in spite of affectations of style. The narrator is spending his last night in his Shepherd Market flat, from which he is moving the following day. Above lives Gerald March, an alcoholic who has once written a good novel. March's sister, Iris, calls late at night. She finds her brother passed out. She talks of books with the narrator. They go to bed. All this is alive. The novel's tragedy is not so much Iris deliberately driving her Hispano-Suiza into a tree, as the dreadfully unconvincing confrontation of English Gentlemen that precedes it.

Twice, speaking of himself in the course of our 'luncheon' (the form for which he expressed preference), Arlen said: 'I, Dikran Kouyoumdjian, an Armenian.' This national awareness I am sure never left him, his imagination for ever straying to an ancestral past:

The lake upon which the great queen Semiramis (who was the first in the world to discover that men could be conveniently changed into eunuchs) built the city Semiramerkert, which is now called Van, and where later, when she was pursued by the swordsmen of her son, she threw a magic bracelet into the lake and turned herself into a rock, which still stands there covered with the triumphant script of the Assyrians.

The triumphant script of the Assyrians was perhaps what Arlen really ought to have been writing.

The Green Hat, Michael Arlen,   1968
Cassell.   *Daily Telegraph*
The London Venture, Michael Arlen,
Cassell: First Novel Library.

PAUL SCOTT

Paul Scott's reputation as a novelist rests on the four volumes of *The Raj Quartet* (1975), and *Staying On* (1977), a shorter sequel, written in a slightly different tone. Both made good television, the former sequence (called *The Jewel in the Crown*) particularly memorable for the haunting character of Merrick, District Police Officer, a homosexual sadist, played with great attack by Tim Piggott-Smith.

Paul Scott (1920–78) was the son of a rather unsuccessful commercial artist, who at fifty had married a girl regarded in the North London suburb where they lived as socially beneath him. The Scott family, from Yorkshire, had been richer, there was a professional background on the mother's side of designing Christmas cards of hunting and coaching scenes and such like. Scott himself could make amusing drawings.

He was the favourite of two sons, getting on well with his brother and strong-willed, possessive mother, not with his inarticulate father, in later life extremely deaf. Scott remains a somewhat enigmatic figure, notwithstanding the detailed and subtle examination Hilary Spurling has devoted to him. He possessed the contradictory traits of an inner self-dramatising egotism combined with a reserved exterior, usually goodnatured, though varied by sulks, vile temper, even violence. The family was wholly inward-looking; Scott thought of himself as a poet, read everything he could lay hands on, did the best he could to be intellectual in a surrounding unintellectual world. Hilary Spurling thinks that all his life he felt an outsider. He also judged himself homosexual. It is hard to estimate to what extent this was merely a schoolboy/undergraduate condition, trying to get to grips with sex, or an engrained bisexuality.

This sense of not belonging was far from being due to any lack of ability. On the contrary, Scott was unusually good (especially for a novelist) at turning his hand to anything. Much against his will he was forced to go into an accountant's office at fourteen or fifteen. At seventeen, without any special training, he won a silver medal from the Royal Society of Accountants. He proved an excellent Army officer. When he became a literary agent his clients were all greatly upset that he left the profession for his own writing.

325

Scott was conscripted in 1940. He thought he would be granted a commission at once, but was turned down by the first selection board, supposedly because he said he wrote poetry, more probably because he showed signs of being in the midst of enthusiasm for *Dorian Gray* and all which that state implied. His second try was obstructed for eighteen months. There was some sort of homosexual row. This might have been serious. It has even been suggested that Scott was to some extent drawing on himself for the picture of Merrick, in this case, so to speak, in reverse, Merrick's persecution of the homosexual Corporal Pinker possibly owing something to this awkward incident.

While Scott was still in the ranks he married a nurse, Penny Avery, whom he met at a soldiers' dance. This could have been partly to establish his own heterosexual respectability, but there is no doubt that it became a very genuine marriage. Penny Avery herself, too, came from an uneasy home. She seems to have behaved with the greatest forbearance in what was often a difficult situation, leaving her husband at last, though returning during his final days.

A week after Scott became an officer cadet, the squad was formed up, a sergeant major inserted his pace stick between Scott and the next file, dismissing the remainder, Scott's section being earmarked for India. He was extremely fed up at the posting, which was to the Indian Army Service Corps. Although Scott was eventually to fall in love with India, the immediate impression was not favourable. That was in 1942, when the Congress leaders had been imprisoned, the Quit India riots in full swing, the atmosphere far from pleasant. Scott held strong anti-imperialist views, of a somewhat simplistic order, as he himself found. By 1944, promoted captain, he was serving with an Indian Air Supply Company, sending *matériel* to Slim's Army during the battles of Imphal and Kohima. He showed himself an efficient, conscientious officer, who got on particularly well with Indian subordinates. One is struck by the number of people Scott met during the war, who were to turn up later in his civilian life.

When Scott was at last demobilised he took a job in a small publishing concern, the combined Falcon Press and Grey Walls Press, the former run by Peter Baker. Baker, after a dashing war career, found a similar recklessness not adapted to publishing; in fact he ended up with a sentence of seven years for fraud and forgery. None the less, Scott, who managed to clear out before the final explosion, met some useful contacts during this employment, notably Roland Gant. Gant was to turn up again as Scott's editor at Heinemann, not to mention introducing him to a doctor who cured the disease, amoebiansis, from which he was suffering.

Scott now became a literary agent with David Higham. There I met him in about 1959, when standing in for Higham himself. Scott was quiet, understanding, well up in whatever matter was to be discussed. It never occurred to me that he was a phenomenal drinker, at that moment suffering all sorts of acute worries, about to give up a regular job for making a living through his own books.

Scott was to return to India to polish up his own knowledge of the subcontinent, visits from which several of the characters in his novels may be easily recognised. There was also a disastrous fortnight's stay in the village of his former *havildar* (sergeant), to which romanticism led him in the face of stern warnings against from Indian friends. Hilary Spurling's biography brilliantly covers all this, and lots more. She seems equally at home everywhere: accountancy; the Army; India; literary life. The story is of absorbing interest. In an interesting critique of *The Raj Quartet*, John Bayley suggests that Scott, a theorist, relied too much on documentation to create a 'world of his own'. It is certainly true that the anglicised Indian, Hari Kumar, and the Rajput lady, Lady Chatterjee, to mention only two characters of the sequence, come straight from the account of Scott's later Indian trips. Merrick, on the other hand, perhaps merely a phantasm of Scott's own private horrors, leaps from the page, yet more from the screen. Bayley thinks that, owing to Scott's method, reliance on 'real people' rather than creative fantasy, the saga could only be fully realised in another medium, that is to say television, in order to fall into place. He says that no one watching *The Jewel in the Crown* will object an actor is 'not my idea' of Daphne, Barbie, Tusker Smalley, because television does not require a world of the author's own, but a literal world, easily adaptable.

One would certainly agree that Hari Kumar never quite comes to life in the way Merrick does. Scott's writing, like Maugham's, is sometimes pedestrian, but the construction of *The Raj Quartet* is masterly. Whatever reservations may be held about the narrative method it succeeds in what Maugham thought the most difficult achievement of a novelist, that is to stick to the point. The point, in Scott's case, was to express his own views on the birth of Indian Independence.

Paul Scott: A Life, Hilary Spurling,   1990
Hutchinson.   *The Spectator*
Paul Scott's Raj, Robin Moore,
Heinemann.

The Europeans

THE GREEK ANTHOLOGY

The two original editors of the collection of epigrams usually known as *The Greek Anthology* were Kephalas, a tenth-century Greek, and Maximus Planudes, a Byzantine scholar, who died in 1305. For a long time the Kephalas manuscript was lost. It was rediscovered in 1606 in the Count Palatine's library at Heidelberg. The Greek idea of an 'epigram' was primarily an 'inscription', rather than a pithy saying, the wayside tombstone a characteristic place for an epigram to appear. Greek epigrams usually take the form of an elegiac couplet, and date back as early as the seventh century BC. There were about 4,000 epigrams in *The Greek Anthology*, upon which much groundwork was done by A. S. F. Gow, an authority on A. E. Housman and, incidentally, George Orwell's classical tutor at Eton. Peter Jay, editor of the present selection, says in his Introduction interesting things about translating poetry. He feels, no doubt with good reason, that 'traditional English metres with rhyme tread heavily over any semblance of the Greek style'. On the other hand, the severe discipline of the Greek rhythm is hard to convey otherwise on account of the unfettered nature of English.

Jay suggests that the contemporary way of writing poetry and, indeed, of looking at things in general, is more amenable to translating what is to be found in *The Greek Anthology* than was a somewhat earlier standpoint. Certainly, so far as subject matter goes, the considerable proportion of erotic and homosexual matter is no longer the treat both were to the Victorians. For examining method, one cannot do better than compare some of the verse here with that in the *Oxford Book of Greek Verse in Translation*, edited in 1938 by Higham and Bowra.

To begin with an old favourite, by Kallimachos (c. 270 BC) translated by W. J. Cory: 'They told me, Hêraclîtus, they told me you were dead.' This is Jay's own version:

> Someone spoke of your death, Herakleitos. It brought me
> Tears, and I remembered how often together
> We ran the sun down with talk . . . somewhere
> You've long been dust, my Halikarnassian friend.
> But your *Nightingales* live on. Though the Death-world
> Claws at everything, it will not touch them.

331

Nightingales is almost certainly the title of Heracleitus's collection of poems, of which only one example (reproduced here, translated by Edwin Morgan) remains, making us regret their loss.

Turning from friends to courtesans, we find Asklepiades (c. 270 BC), translated by R. A. Furness, in the Oxford volume:

> Archeanassa lieth here,
>   The courtesan from Colophôn,
> Whose wrinkled cheeks and sere
>   Were still sweet Erôs' throne.
> Ah! lovers who in bygone time
>   Gathered the buds unfolding fast
> Of that fresh vernal prime,
>   Through what a fire you passed!

Again to quote Peter Jay himself:

> Here lies Arkheanassa of Kolophon,
> Courtesan with sweet love scored on her face.
> Lovers who had the pick of her youth's garden
> In its first spring, through what a furnace you passed!

Moving a couple of centuries on to Philodemos of Gadara (c. 70 BC), translated by Walter Headlam:

> Shine out, O hornéd Moon,
>   O festal night's befriender,
> Shine through the latticed
>   windows with thy silver light;
> My golden fair illume, gaze
>   forth in all this splendour, –
> Immortal eyes are free to look
>   on love's delight: –

William Moebius here trims Headlam considerably:

> Double-horned, nocturnal Moon fancier of all-night activities,
> shine, penetrate the window slits,
> train your beam on golden Kallistion.

The subjects tend to be the horrors of old age and poverty, sailors lost at sea, bad hosts, the unreliability of women, the attraction of boys. There are some amusing inscriptions on altars of mischievous demi-gods like Priapus and Pan; for example, that by Niarchos (translated by Peter Porter) saying what Pan did to you if you defiled his spring by washing your feet – and, if you happened to have a taste for that, what he did as an alternative. Girls come in for a good deal of denigration. For instance, Maccius (of the Roman period), translated by W. G. Shepherd, comments:

Philistion's a hard bitch:
in her book 'penniless lover'
is a mere contradiction in terms.
She seems more bearable now? She
   mellows? One may die from the bite
   of a less than totally hostile snake.

From the early Byzantine period, Paulos, translated by Andrew Miller, shows that rhyme can sometimes work well:

Gold undid Danaë. Take note
   Lovers whom Beauty's ways abash:
Worship her not with hollow words
but full and faithful hearts. And cash.

or, by the same poet and translator:

Soft are Sappho's kisses,
   soft under silken skin,
   those snowy arms – but hard
   as stone what lies within.

The Greek Anthology: A Selection in Modern Verse Translations, edited and introduced by Peter Jay, Allen Lane.

1973
Daily Telegraph

THE SATYRICON OF PETRONIUS

Certain books possess a magic not altogether explicable in merely critical terms. The Satyricon is one of these. Why is it such a favourite? For example, Scott Fitzgerald toyed with the idea of calling *The Great Gatsby* by the title *Trimalchio* from the pages of Petronius, while Cyril Connolly has recorded that at school he had a copy bound as a prayer-book to read in chapel. I came late to Petronius. Having often heard of him, I was well into my thirties before I bought, quite by chance, a rather dilapidated reprint of the seventeenth-century translation, 'made English by Mr Burnaby of the Middle-Temple, and another Hand'. After a few pages, I was caught for ever in the Petronian net.

The Satyricon is now available in paperback. Those not already familiar with it should read it before approaching J. P. Sullivan's excellent and scholarly study, full of interesting points, but naturally addressed to those who know something of this great classic already. It has many odd features. The length of the original work is uncertain, as is the exact order in which the incidents that have come down to us occur. Sullivan suggests the original might have been 400,000 words, say two-thirds the length of *War and Peace*. The fragment that remains is 35,000 words, half the length of an average detective story.

To this radical incompleteness is added a lack of absolute certainty as to the identity of the author. It has been traditionally accepted – on evidence not earlier than AD 200 – that he was Petronius Arbiter, courtier and literary Beau Brummell of Nero, who, finding himself likely to be put under arrest, through the jealousy of another of the Emperor's favourites, committed elegant suicide in AD 66. Some scholars have demurred at this identification, but Sullivan assembles a lot of evidence – notably the ragging in the Satyricon of the contemporary writers Seneca and Lucan – which seems to establish Petronius Arbiter as author.

The narrator of this picaresque novel – the Satyricon has real claims to be the first 'modern' novel ever written – is Encolpius, an 'anti-hero', youngish, sexually ambivalent, well educated, cowardly, full of *angst*. It seems he has in some way offended Priapus, the Roman god of Sexual Relationship (and of Gardens), whose pursuing wrath is the apparent theme of the narrative. It is not clear what Encolpius did in the first instance to bring this trouble on himself. He may have desecrated a Priapian temple or shrine, for which his bouts of impotence are one of many punishments. On the other hand, impotence and homosexuality would in themselves be displeasing to a god of fruitfulness, so that Encolpius may be being punished for these as much as by them.

Some have thought the rough time Encolpius suffers to be a parody of the Odyssey (another claimant to be the first novel, but not a 'modern' one), the anger of Priapus against Encolpius taking the place of that of Poseidon against Odysseus. In general, it is no longer held, as was thought at one time, that the characters are recognisable personages from Nero's entourage, to whom the work was probably designed to be read aloud.

Far the most notable figure in the Satyricon is Trimalchio, the ageing *nouveau-riche* tycoon, obsessed by his own wealth and the approach of death. Trimalchio gives a big dinner to which Encolpius is invited, a sequence of extraordinary characterisation, wit and power. This famous set-piece, rediscovered in a monastery in what is now Jugoslavia, was only printed first in 1664. There have been endless arguments as to what the Satyricon is 'about'. In this connection its title can be misleading, *Satura* not meaning precisely the modern 'satire'. It is part of Sullivan's argument – with which one cannot too heartily agree – that the Satyricon is much more than satire, and not in principle intended to moralise.

Petronius, who seems to have been temperamentally a literary conservative, possessed at the same time an immense originality and appreciation of the possibilities in writing of evolvement and expansion. He was bound by certain rules of Roman literary tradition – comparable perhaps with those of the French today. As the Satyricon is, to say the least, outspoken in its language and incidents, critics have found it necessary to excuse its lubricities by saying that Petronius was only showing how immoral Roman life was.

> Petronius [says J. P. Sullivan] whatever his deficiencies, is an artist and not a moralist . . . the Satyricon is a work of literature and not an Epicurean tract, a political pamphlet, or an elaborate parody. And there is more to the Satyricon than this. Those who wish to assimilate him to de Sade as a wicked, if sophisticated, pornographer, amorally overturning accepted values; those who try to see him as a Swiftian satirist, vividly describing what he condemns; and those who regard him as a Neronian T. S. Eliot, sketching the sterility, barbarism and futility of the waste land about him, are not without some justification of their views.

The point is, however, that here, probably for the first time, is the pure, imaginative vision of the novelist, directed towards the life around him that may have seemed grotesque enough, but was all the same accepted – and in many ways not all that different from our own day.

The Satyricon of Petronius: A Literary Study, J. P. Sullivan, Faber.

1968
Daily Telegraph

HÉLOÏSE AND ABÉLARD

The lives of Héloïse and Abélard provide one of the world's most famous love stories – deservedly so – but what actually happened is, as usual, a little different from the legend. It is not for that reason any the worse. In certain respects it is rather better. Peter Abélard (1079–1142), eldest son of a Breton landowner, might have made a normal career as a knight, but he deliberately chose an intellectual vocation, forgoing his patrimony, and becoming a 'clerk'. This did not necessarily imply taking Holy Orders, although the philosophic matters with which he concerned himself were chiefly of a religious nature.

There seems no doubt that Abélard was not only unusually able, but also unusually aggressive and pleased with himself. By the time he was about forty he was looked upon as a famous philosopher, but one who had made many enemies, and whose views, especially regarding the Trinity, were individual to the point of risking being thought heretical. According to Abélard's own account, he had never suffered serious temptations of a sexual nature until this relatively advanced age (regarded then as more venerable than today), but now, obsessed with sex, he combined a conviction that 'I never need fear rejection from any woman' with uncertainty where best to strike. 'The lewd dealings of debauchery repelled me; the hard work for preparing lessons left me little time for associating with women of noble birth, and I was almost entirely unacquainted with those of the burgher class.'

The answer turned out to be Héloïse (1101–64). Nothing whatever is known of her background except that she lodged with her uncle, Canon Fulbert, in Paris, was seventeen or eighteen, a girl of exceptional intellectual attainments, and (no one contradicts) very good-looking. Her circumstances in Paris were such as to make it reasonable to compare her with, say, the 'first girl' to go to Oxford, Cambridge or the Ecole Polytechnique. Abélard, knowing Canon Fulbert liked money, suggested himself as a lodger. He did this with the deliberate object of seducing Héloïse. The Canon jumped at the idea, and went even further. Abélard should not only join their household, but also instruct his niece. With such a master and such a pupil big things might be expected. Even Abélard himself was staggered. 'He entrusted Héloïse

to my entire control, asked me to devote all my free time to her
education, night and day, and said I should not hesitate to chastise her
when she was at fault.'

It really was not surprising that in due course the Canon blundered
in on them one day in circumstances that allowed no doubt as to their
relationship. Abélard found other rooms in Paris while keeping in
touch with Héloïse. Before long (she was having a baby) he abducted
her. He then went to Fulbert and offered to marry Héloïse, provided the
marriage remained secret, so that it did not harmfully affect his own
professional activities. Here we come up against habits of the time
which are almost impossible to assess in modern terms. There seems no
particular reason why Abélard should not be married. Celibacy was by
no means universal, even for the clergy, a matter (especially in
England) which was giving the Vatican constant trouble. On the other
hand, even in the late nineteenth century dons were not allowed to
marry and keep their job. It may well be that Abélard was not behaving
unreasonably.

Fulbert agreed to these conditions, but Héloïse herself said that she
did not wish to marry, and risk prejudicing her lover's career. She
would be prepared to be 'his whore'. In spite of that the marriage took
place. Fulbert then not merely failed to fulfil his part of the bargain by
keeping silence, but arranged for a gang of relations and hired ruffians
to break into Abélard's room and castrate him. This might well have
been the end of the story, but Abélard, with incredible toughness, not
only survived this assault, but, professionally speaking, experienced
some of the most important incidents of his career after it. He went into
a monastery, before he did so, arranging that Héloïse should take the
veil. For this – not trusting her to do so in any case – he has been
criticised.

Héloïse became head of a religious house, which was liquidated on
grounds of scandalous behaviour. There is no reason to suppose she
was to blame for this, and the closure may even have been a
consequence of her own representations. Abélard's experiences with
disorderly monks were equally unfortunate. The two lovers – indeed
the married couple – kept in touch, both surviving into their sixties, and
a surprising amount is known about them and their problems.

All this is well told by Régine Pernoud, who, though rather fond of
moralising, handles a great many immensely complicated questions
clearly and vividly. The fastidious should not be put off by her opening
sentence: ' "Paris at last!" the young student thought eagerly as the
bend of the river came into view.'

Héloïse and Abélard, Régine Pernoud,
translated by Peter Wiles, Collins.

1973
Daily Telegraph

CHARLES OF ORLÉANS

Charles of Orléans (1394–1465), nephew of Charles VI of France, father of Louis XII, and husband of Isabella (his cousin, widow of Richard II of England) was also a poet. Captured at Agincourt in 1415, he spent twenty-five years as prisoner-of-war in this country. When he returned to France he lived mostly at Blois, where he continued to write the poetry that had supported him in captivity, and his court became a noted literary centre. Enid McLeod, author of the definitive biography of Héloïse and well known for her translations of Colette and Supervielle, is obviously fascinated by her subject, and has produced a most distinguished historical study. As Charles of Orléans is unusually well documented for a figure of his period, the book is packed with interesting material, throwing light on all sorts of different sides of life in the late Middle Ages.

Enid McLeod's argument, broadly speaking, is that Charles was prepared to do what was expected of him as a royal personage of the time, but that, in truth, he was, unlike most of his contemporaries, opposed to war, wanting to live a life devoted to the arts against the background of a country landowner. At first sight this might seem a rather romantic view of an era when the struggle for personal power was never more savage (Charles's own father had been assassinated), and, reading the book, one awaits the moment of crisis when Charles turns out to be just as prepared to be murderous as any of his fellows. It has to be admitted that the moment does not come. Enid McLeod makes her case. We are left with a decidedly Proustian figure, or perhaps – allowing for the action taking place at a much more exalted level – a character not altogether unlike Lampedusa's prince in *The Leopard*, or even Lampedusa himself.

The canvas is so wide that only a few of its aspects can be considered here. A word should, however, be said of Agincourt, if only because it is at the moment fashionable to explain away English successes in war as far less considerable than nationalistic history has pretended; battles we claim to have won, it is sometimes nowadays suggested, were really won – anyway morally – as often as not by the other side.

The English army at Agincourt consisted of 5,000 men-at-arms and 1,000 archers – say two brigades; the French had a force of 50,000 to

60,000 – say three to four divisions. Any doubts as to who won were set at rest by the capture of half the French nobility. Henry V may have been priggish; the massacre of prisoners when the battle seemed likely to turn in the French favour was undoubtedly horrible, but the result was beyond argument.

One cannot help feeling that the character of Charles of Orléans was not so much shaped by his years of English captivity, as that Fate demanded such a tribute of a man of his particular character. There is something extraordinarily appropriate in a poet of just his sort having that particular affliction visited on him which he was so capable of celebrating in his melancholy, sometimes humorous, verse.

By the time Charles was captured, his first wife had died and he had married Bonne of Armagnac. The majority of the poems he wrote in England are believed to have been addressed to her, but there is evidence that some sort of a love affair took place with an English lady called Anne Moleyns, possibly the young widow of Sir William (sometimes styled Lord) Moleyns who had been killed in the French wars. One of the poems, written in English, spells the name 'ANNE MOLINS', who, if rightly identified (Enid McLeod does not mention that) was Cornish.

Another of Charles's poems looks like a forerunner of Villon's 'Ballade des dames du temps jadis':

> Ou vieil temps grant renom couroit
> De Creseide, Yseud, Elaine
> Et maintes autres qu'on nommoit
> Parfaites en beaute haultaine.

There were, indeed, contacts later with Villon himself (b. 1431), who may even have been a pensioner at Blois for a short time. In any case he took part in poetry competitions there, and, when Charles's two-and-half-year-old daughter made a state entry into Orléans in 1460, Villon happened to be in prison in that city, and was let out to celebrate the occasion in verse.

Charles's marriages deserve a glance because they show the wide sweep in time that medieval families could achieve, sometimes seeming so incredible in recorded pedigrees of the period. When he married Isabella in 1406, Charles was eleven, his bride sixteen – in tears because she had so much enjoyed being Queen of England, and thought this a come-down. Isabella died giving birth to a daughter in 1409. Bonne of Armagnac was eleven in 1410, by which time Charles was sixteen. Bonne died in 1432, while Charles was still a prisoner in England. Finally, in 1440, Charles married Mary of Cleves, aged fourteen, himself forty-six. When, at the age of seventy-one, Charles of Orléans died in 1465, Mary had just given birth to a daughter. If his first daughter had lived, she would have been fifty-six years older than her half-sister.

Charles of Orléans: Prince and Poet,   1969
Enid McLeod, Chatto.   *Daily Telegraph*

FRANÇOIS I

In the foreword to his lively, informative, admirably illustrated biography of François I (1494–1547), Desmond Seward emphasises that no study of this remarkable king has appeared for forty years in Great Britain, and no cult for him exists in France comparable with those of Henri IV or Louis XIV. In fact, François I has in recent times taken a back place. Without denying that, I find it surprising, because in what was taught about French history in the past, François I always seemed one of the main characters. It is, of course, perfectly true that the Field of Cloth of Gold's colossal impact accounts for a good deal of François's 'image', with his defeat and capture at Pavia as a suitable pendant contrasting failure with success. One thing is quite certain, what François himself looked like is clearly fixed in the mind; the countenance Seward calls 'mocking and enigmatic'.

The book begins with an account of the political scene into which François was born, the royal relationships that decided the destiny of nations. Seward makes the good point that a 'king over the water' existed in the opening years of the sixteenth century, 'Richard IV', the Yorkist Pretender, whom the French called 'Duc de Suffolk *dit* Blanc Rose'. This first cousin of Henry VIII was taken just as seriously as any Stuart.

François I succeeded his cousin, Louis XII, as King of France: Louis XII, just before he died, had married, as his second much younger wife, Henry VIII's sister Mary Tudor. The legend one was brought up on was that this beautiful, enormously wilful lady agreed to marry the elderly King of France, provided she could marry whom she liked when he died. This seems to have been by no means what her relations understood, but her own strong will brought her Charles Brandon as second husband (who thought he would have his head cut off for it). Stepmother of François I, she was also grandmother of Lady Jane Grey.

François I and Henry VIII do genuinely seem to have liked each other whenever they met, in the way that inordinately egotistical persons often get on well together. The manner in which their characters can be contrasted, by the details about François which Seward gives, is of great interest. Henry had none of the sweep of

342

François's cultural interests (though perhaps not less personally talented in certain respects), but above all the paradox that emerges from Henry's Bluebeard side is that, emotionally speaking, he cared to whom he was married, while François did not.

The Venetian ambassador (as Seward says, 'the inevitable recording Venetian') thought François 'resembled the Devil' when he saw him at the late King's funeral. There is, indeed, something a shade diabolical about François I, his enormous energy and a kind of inner coldness, expressed in an unrelenting desire for changes in his mistresses. In the restless movements of the court over France, a select group of prostitutes (regarded as no security risk) were part of the royal establishment, every first of January François giving these ladies gifts, each May Day they presenting him with a bouquet of flowers.

The violent extremes of François I's life, although they came to him as a king, would have been remarkable in forming the character of any man. He was only twenty-one when he defeated the supposedly invincible Swiss pikemen at Marignano; at Pavia he was nearly killed, before his assailants grasped that the knight whose armour they were tearing off was the King of France. A dreary imprisonment in a Madrid prison cell followed that disastrous day.

François appears to have enjoyed an extraordinary resilience. Once he was free, in spite of humiliations, in spite of religious disputes making government difficult, in spite of the usual shortages of money for immensely ambitious architectural schemes, in spite of syphilis, his activities never abated. The only persons he seems deeply to have loved were his own relations, especially his mother and sister.

Seward, I think rightly, is insistent that people are unaware of how much François did for the arts in France. He was a patron in the grand manner at a level which Henry VIII could not hope to approach. Among his court painters were Leonardo da Vinci and Andrea del Sarto. Leonardo died in France at the little château François presented to him. The King tried to get Michelangelo, too, but the invitation was refused. Benvenuto Cellini was his jeweller, and for François was made Cellini's famous salt-cellar (oddly 'modern' in look), now in Vienna. François's collection of books formed the basis of the Bibliothèque Nationale. He founded the Collège de France. Among many other magnificent buildings he constructed the Châteaux of Fontainebleau and Chambord. Cosimo de' Medici specially commissioned for him Bronzino's 'Venus, Cupid, Folly and Time' (now in the National Gallery), which Seward justly calls 'perhaps the greatest of all Mannerist painting'.

In short, François I found France a gothic medieval kingdom, left it a Renaissance realm, in which the potentialities of a future huge French contribution in matters of art and letters had been given solid foundation. He also, by his absolutism, prepared the way for a great deal of constitutional trouble. There is, perhaps, something peculiarly French in François's combination of splendid victories and disastrous defeats, his flourish, wit, recklessness, cynicism. Desmond Seward says Clouet's portrait of François's son, the Dauphin, has 'the air of a Proustian Duke in fancy dress'. François himself could easily be imagined in just that role.

Prince of the Renaissance: The Life of   1973
François I, Desmond Seward,   *Daily Telegraph*
Constable.

MICHEL DE MONTAIGNE

Montaigne invented the word 'essay' for a particular form of writing. He remains, on the whole, the essay's supreme exponent. There was, however, the special aspect of his own essays that they were intended to paint a picture of their writer. He was a Gascon country gentleman (a quarter Jewish by descent), born in 1533; a Roman Catholic, though one of his brothers and two of his sisters became Protestant.

Montaigne himself was of the entourage of Henry of Navarre before that king decided that 'Paris was worth a mass'. Indeed, Montaigne is not only an extraordinary personal example of tolerance in a world that was just emerging from the ideas of the Middle Ages to those of the modern national State; he also lived at a time when France was peculiarly faced with the choice of how her future government was to be carried on. All kind of things had not yet been decided.

It is impossible to read Donald M. Frame's biography without feeling this sense of Montaigne being set against the most appropriate background imaginable. No doubt he was to some extent the product of that background, but equally he would have been quite a different phenomenon had he written in the same sort of way 100 years later.

Frame translated the *Complete Works of Montaigne*, which appeared in 1958. The present book embodies the most recent researches about Montaigne, with the aim of setting him in an up-to-date light. This is done in a scholarly way, and a volume of what is at times rather complicated material is well, if a trifle repetitively, handled. One of the points that has emerged in recent years is that Montaigne was, politically speaking, a distinctly more important figure than was supposed in the past. He was an early example of the French tradition of writer-diplomatist – a well-known author, equally well known in public affairs.

Another matter that Frame makes clear is that Montaigne's wife was no cypher in the home. Montaigne is almost caustic about marriage – Frame perhaps rather underplays recorded extramarital interests – and he says little in his writings about his own matrimonial situation. There are matters related here, enigmatic certainly, but suggesting that there might have been reasons, quite early in his married life, for

Montaigne to be dissatisfied with his wife, apparently good-looking, intelligent and wanting her own way.

It is natural that a work so original, objective and acute as Montaigne's should present a different face to different generations. Although the Vatican did not object to the first appearance of the Essays (beyond reprehending Montaigne's distaste for the use of judicial torture), the next century thought differently. Montaigne's writings were put on the Papal Index, where they have remained. The reader sometimes wonders whether one of the aims of Frame's book is to extract them from this limbo. He is at pains to emphasise Montaigne's orthodoxy, and usually has a kindly word for the Jesuits, who might be expected to lend a hand.

It is hard not to feel that had Montaigne and his ideas become more generally acceptable, many painful interludes of French history – no doubt European history, too – might have been avoided. He lived at a thoroughly dangerous time when his country house could easily have been occupied and sacked by marauding elements, Catholic or Protestant; so that his tolerance had nothing theoretical about it.

Brantôme, a comparatively near neighbour, a retired soldier who had taken to writing, made spiteful remarks suggesting that Montaigne's military record was not an adequate one. Brantôme, undeniably a swashbuckler himself, is chiefly known for his *Dames Galantes*, usually presented as a near pornographic work, but in reality a kind of early attempt at collating sexual behaviour in something like psychological terms. It is interesting to note that he obviously felt such a burning jealousy for Montaigne's success in the literary field. There seems no reason to suppose that Montaigne was, in fact, backward in showing courage, though his innate scepticism about human behaviour would certainly not have allowed him to become involved in danger for danger's sake.

He was prepared to accept the fashions of his time, though sometimes without 100 per cent seriousness. For example, writing on education, he said that if a pupil should prefer dancing or playing with ball to jousting, 'I see no other remedy than for his tutor to strangle him early, if there are no witnesses, or apprentice him to a good pastry cook in some good town, even though he were the son of a duke.' Quite a number of Montaigne's editors took this comment in deadly earnest, some apologising and insisting that he would have changed his mind on reflection, others leaving this incitement to murder out of their edition. In short, to his other qualities, Montaigne adds the requirement that he must be read by those prepared for humour.

Montaigne: A Biography, Donald M.   1966
Frame, Hamish Hamilton.   *Daily Telegraph*

MADAME DE SÉVIGNÉ

To attempt to write objectively of Madame de Sévigné (1626–96) would be, at this stage, absurd. As Somerset Maugham points out here, in his preface, everything that could be said about her was already thought to have been said even a century ago. Sainte-Beuve himself stated that fact. There remains only to give one's own opinion, and, speaking for myself, I am immune to Madame de Sévigné's charm. I can see that she wrote with extraordinary fluency, that she took a cool, somewhat humorous view of the world, that in an age when there was no limit to what someone in her position might have allowed herself in the way of bad behaviour, she conducted her life with good sense and dignity. The fact remains that I do not like her. Indeed, it comes as no surprise to me that her husband, before his death in a duel in 1651, lived a life of profligacy with Ninon de l'Enclos and not a few others.

In fairness to Madame de Sévigné I must admit to possessing a similar distaste for the letters of her English contemporary, Dorothy Osborne (1627–95). Here, too, in Miss Osborne, we find the same ghastly literary facility, the same rather professional gaiety, the same correctness of personal behaviour. One feels that if either lady had lived in our own day, each would have written enormously successful middlebrow novels. Yet Dorothy Osborne, from Macaulay onwards, has been ceaselessly lauded to the skies for the charm of her writing. It is very rare to find anyone she irritates.

Neither of these two letter-writing ladies seems to me to possess the good points of the seventeenth century as exemplified, in one manner, in France, for example, by La Rochefoucauld and Saint-Simon, or, in quite another, in England by Aubrey and Pepys – a general approach which might perhaps be summarised, though inadequately, by saying that they all appreciate the discovery of the individual. No doubt it would be unfair to Madame de Sévigné and Miss Osborne to say that they have no eyes beyond their own prejudices. This, in itself, would not be a valid objection to their writing. It would at least be attractively feminine. It is something of the cold fish about both of them that repels. The good humour, the well-bred cynicism, the interest in life, fashionable or local, all comes pouring out like a torrent of metallic-tasting claret cup, and all expressed in the best possible manner. Yet at the end of it all one feels depressed. Did either of them really have any grasp of what individual life was about? Perhaps this view is merely the consequence of some innate prejudice in myself against the writings of the opposite sex. I record it only to make my position plain.

Pepys, oddly enough, notes in his diary that he dipped in to *Histoire Amoureuse des Gaules*, in which Madame de Sévigné's witty cousin, Bussy de Rabutin, somewhat improperly lampooned her and other of his friends and relations; but, so far as I am aware, there is no evidence that the diarist knew anything of Madame de Sévigné herself. It is interesting to speculate what his entry about her in his journal might have been.

Most of the Sévigné letters were written to her daughter, married to Comte de Grignan, who, as Governor of Provence, had under his charge the Man in the Iron Mask. For her daughter, Madame de Sévigné cherished an uncomfortable, indeed morbid passion, writing to her as she might have written to a husband or lover. The terms in which she addressed Madame de Grignan suggest some maladjustment in the mother's nature that can hardly be explained by reference to Monsieur de Sévigné's goings-on. Her son ended in a monastery after a rakish life (with episodes of which he used to regale his mother), but a career apparently without much enjoyment owing to chilliness of temperament inherited from her. The Letters, in their fullest extent, are 'voluminous'. They have passed through various vicissitudes both in France and England. Violet Hammersley's translation is admirably readable, conveying a sense of the historical period, while at the same time avoiding any suggestion of conscious archaism. The selection is also a wise one, taking the reader neatly over the jumps in something under 400 pages.

Letters from Madame de Sévigné,   1956
selected and translated by Violet   *Punch*
Hammersley, with a preface by
W. Somerset Maugham, Secker
and Warburg.

GIACOMO CASANOVA

Although Havelock Ellis put him in the top class as a serious and talented writer, Casanova has never been much of a favourite in this country. Between the puritanism of one kind of British critic and the envy of another, he is usually treated either with shocked disapproval, or a kind of facetious scepticism, both of which mark our innate lack of ease where autobiography is approached without hypocrisy. The fact that Casanova is so universally regarded here as a seducer, who also had a lot of other adventures, rather than an adventurer, who performed a certain number of seductions, is symptomatic of this national self-consciousness about sex in dealing with a man of his type.

Given the life Casanova lived, it is not surprising that he had a great many love affairs. The fact that some people think he ought to have had fewer, others that they themselves (or their acquaintances) have had even more, is beside the point; which is, in short, that Casanova's Memoirs arc, in themselves, a work of genius.

J. Rives Childs, a retired American diplomatist, has devoted many years to the bibliography and critical examination of Casanova material. *Casanova* is the summary of his researches. It is a book of the greatest interest to Casanova fans, one that by its careful documentation should persuade others to read the Memoirs, not for their tall stories but for their veracity.

The great merit of Rives Childs's book, the style of which at times falls short of complete flexibility, is this keen attention to proof. I am at a loss to understand why some critics have expressed lack of interest as to whether or not Casanova can be shown to have spoken the truth about some minor romp. This suggests insensitiveness to the aims of literature. It is not the romp that is important; it is the light the stories throw – if they are indeed true, but not otherwise – on what human beings are really like, the way they live. In case I myself appear too enthusiastic, let me say that Rives Childs seems to me to overemphasise the view that Casanova, so far from being all he is painted, was honest, sober and an early riser.

To insist too much on Casanova's finer qualities is, in a sense, to detract from his own extraordinary powers of self-examination and self-expression. For example, having quoted the passage in which

349

Casanova says: 'My heart bled when I found myself compelled to spend any money that I had not won at the gaming table,' Rives Childs immediately remarks: 'Whatever the popular conception, Casanova was never a professional gambler who derived a substantial part of his resources from cards.' It is certainly true that Casanova frequently shows himself as losing at the tables; just as quite often – a fact that is almost invariably overlooked – he shows himself as unsuccessful at seduction. No doubt he had many other financial interests, but his gambling, especially when he 'corrected fortune', was surely of a kind to prejudice his amateur status.

The picture that emerges is that Giacomo Casanova (1725–98), self-styled 'de Seingalt', was the illegitimate son of a Venetian noble, rather than the actors supposedly his parents. He was a man of remarkable energy and natural gifts, that, above all, he was an enormously talented writer. Even his supporters never seem to make sufficient of this fact. Casanova's handling of narrative is masterly.

The Memoirs must run to something in the neighbourhood of a million words. Occasionally, when in poor form in his old age, there will be perhaps a line or two of too much philosophising, or a story that creaks a bit in its joints. But of how many writers who write at that length can that be said? Usually the plums must be picked from vast tracts of boredom, an extremely rare failing in Casanova.

The fact is that very few people in this country have read the *whole* of Casanova's Memoirs. They have dipped into some of the well-known stories, perhaps read in a separate volume his account of his escape from the prison in Venice called the Leads – to be seen to this day for those who doubt that it was an extraordinary feat. I speak with authority, having finished a complete rereading within the last year. I cannot recommend the Memoirs too strongly, but you must read them all. Their strength is in their entirety.

Some of the verifications given by Rives Childs of Casanova's stories – like the discovery of the advertisement he put in the London paper saying that he had rooms to let in Pall Mall – are astonishing; while other accumulations of evidence, not completely authenticated, but pointing to the amplification of some of the other episodes, are scarcely less interesting.

We still do not know what exactly caused Casanova's perpetual movements about Europe from capital to capital; his equally perpetual expulsions for comparatively small misdemeanours. It has been suggested that he was a spy. For whom? The Freemasons? The Jesuits? What would such organisations have been prepared to pay him? Did he manage on basic income from some such quarter – and a little from Bragadin and those two other rather sinister old gentlemen who lived in Venice and took an interest in him – while he derived his luxuries from such business as he could pick up, and from the gaming tables?

After all, to be given the organisation of the French lottery was no small achievement. Plenty of other people in Paris must have wanted to take the job on. There can be no doubt that Casanova impressed persons in authority by his administrative efficiency. The extraordinary thing is that he should have combined powers of this sort, not only with an insatiable love of pleasure and capacity for getting money by unconventional means (e.g. extracting it from Mme d'Urfé by pretending to be a magician), but also with the talent to write about all these experiences in an objective manner. One is staggered by the unexpected assortment of his characteristics.

The last twenty years of Casanova's life were depressing. He returned to Venice, lived with obscure mistresses, became a police spy. Then, at the end of his tether, he was offered by Count Waldstein the job of librarian at the Castle of Dux in what is now Czechoslovakia. It was desperately tedious there and the other retainers did not take him seriously. All the same, there is a certain poetic justice in this end which, if not so deeply involved, Casanova would himself have certainly appreciated. He died in 1798 at the age of seventy-three.

Casanova: A Biography Based on   1961
New Documents, J. Rives Childs,   *Daily Telegraph*
Allen & Unwin.

RESTIF DE LA BRETONNE

However much one may admire Valéry's critical judgment, it is hard to agree with his pronouncement, quoted in the preface to this edition of *Monsieur Nicolas*, that 'I place Restif far above Rousseau.' Nevertheless, Rousseau and Casanova are the names that suggest themselves against which to measure the work of Restif de la Bretonne.

Nicolas-Edmé Restif or Retif (he adopted the first form himself) was the son of a peasant vine-grower who lived at a farm called la Bretonne on the borders of Burgundy and Champagne. He was born in 1734, one of the children of a second marriage, and worked for a time as a printer in Auxerre. Then he came to Paris, where he wrote about 240 volumes, most of them realistic stories of lower-middle-class life that pointed a moral. He died in 1806.

Monsieur Nicolas is Restif's autobiography, though intended, he himself said, not as 'confessions', but to lay bare 'the springs of the human heart'. The distinction Restif makes on this point is worth noting, because it to some extent absolves him from the charge of giving an inadequate account of his own character. In point of fact he does describe himself in great detail, and obviously was not – except sexually speaking – in the least interested in anyone else. The sub-title is of importance, however, as suggesting that he realised the writing of 'confessions' was a difficult thing to take on.

This fact is perhaps not, in general, sufficiently appreciated. The art of autobiography is a special one, like poetry or keeping a diary. Mere intelligence, as such, is not sufficient to make it successful. The chief need is a hard-outlined picture – true or not – possessed by the writer of him or her self. This Restif never arrives at. He is fond of telling the reader how good-looking he was a young man, but most of time he divided between vanity and self-pity. The fact is that he is not nearly as intelligent as Rousseau, in one way, or Casanova, in another.

On the other hand, if he is to be believed at all, Restif was not only unusually highly sexed, but also exceptionally sexually precocious. He claims to have achieved puberty at ten and a half. Even allowing for the fact that seducer's stories, like those of fishermen and golfers, are apt to need scaling down, there seems no reason to suppose that he did not have a lot of adventures, even though they may not have taken the precise shape, or involved the ornamental speeches, that Restif himself records.

One of the aspects *Monsieur Nicolas* successfully puts over is its author's uncontrollable randiness. In his earlier days the village girls were his aim. Later, in Paris, he seems to have become deeply involved with prostitutes and near-prostitutes, from whom his health in due course suffered severely.

Restif has many obsessions. Of these, the most extraordinary are that he supposed that any liaison always resulted in a child; that this child was a daughter; and that this daughter was herself his mistress when sufficiently mature. He was also a shoe-fetishist, and appears to have had a sadistic strain that took the form of playing practical jokes on prostitutes.

At this stage of describing Restif's point of view and activities, many will feel they need trouble no more about him. That would be not altogether just. He is all the time making an effort to record the oddness of human beings through himself, but his own defects as a writer – one of which, rare in France, is a total lack of humour – prevent him from doing this, so it seems to me, with the genius with which he is sometimes credited.

He was, it is not surprising to find, unsatisfactorily married. Throughout his life he dreamed of a woman with whom he was romantically in love and had never possessed. He hoped to marry her when, after the Revolution, he obtained a divorce, only to find that she had died not long before. His not very happy life was spent in poverty, and, without rich patrons, he would at the end have starved to death.

Robert Baldick has made a lively translation and presents a fighting defence of Restif in his preface. Without going all the way with him, it must be admitted that the period atmosphere, especially of the provincial life, is conveyed with a curious pungency. Baldick points out the odd vicissitudes of Restif's reputation. Although never financially successful – nor, so it appears, penetrating into a particularly interesting or attractive social world, so often in France the compensation for literary indigence – he enjoyed in his own day a fair reputation as a writer.

In the nineteenth century, he was remembered, if at all, as a pornographer. That, one feels, Restif certainly is not. He may be boring, romantic, sentimental, vain, even rather mad, but in spite of the frankness with which an unending series of physical encounters are recorded – one in which a friend who was an ex-priest, played an unworthy assistant role – the reader never feels that all this is being written down with a pornographic end in view.

Probably Restif's main claim to importance is the influence he exerted on other writers. Among these, it is possible to observe distinct marks left on Stendhal – particularly Stendhal's trick of giving a fairly lengthy description of some incident, then italicising the point of what he, or some character who had played a part in the narration, felt about it. Balzac, too, may be suspected of taking a few hints. He could have been interested, in connection with *Illusions Perdues*, in the fact that Restif was a printer. Restif himself was sometimes so impoverished that he set his own books straight up into type, without making a manuscript of them – a thought that must cause most writers to feel faint, in the light of the typesetting of those days. It is no surprise to learn from Robert Baldick that Restif was keen on the idea of a communist society, collective farms, communal refectories, organised leisure, and so on. Among other things, *Monsieur Nicolas* brings out that element in French life so often forgotten – its innately puritanical side is one aspect, from which so much that we regard as 'French' is a violent reaction.

Monsieur Nicolas, or the Human Heart Laid Bare, Restif de la Bretonne, translated and edited by Robert Baldick, Barrie & Rockliff.

1966
Daily Telegraph

SADE

'An excess of fantasy, Sire, resulted in a sort of misdemeanour' wrote the Marquis de Sade's wife to the King of Sardinia, who had incarcerated her husband at the request of the French authorities. This was in 1773, after Sade's high jinks at Marseilles, that had included giving a party of prostitutes doctored sweets, which had later seriously upset their digestions.

Gilbert Lély's book gives a good account of Sade. At times the narrative lacks smoothness, but the facts are there, together with an enormous amount of information and interesting comment. The translation is at times a trifle eccentric, among other things rendering French titles and forms of address as 'Lord' and 'Lady', which strikes an odd note. Donatien-Alphonse-François de Sade, Marquis (in fact latterly Comte) de Sade, an uncomfortable figure when alive, is almost equally difficult to handle dead. Was he a criminal lunatic or rather a great man?

The Sade family was one of considerable antiquity and distinction. They came from Avignon, where they had been magnates since the twelfth century. Petrarch's Laura has been long thought to have been a Sade by blood (the Marquis was very proud of this ancestress), but Lély's researches suggest that she was only a Sade by marriage. The Marquis's father was Colonel of the Pope's Light Cavalry and French Ambassador to Russia. Through his mother, Sade was distantly connected with the Royal House of Bourbon.

Owing to his father's diplomatic missions, Sade was largely brought up by his grandmother. It is characteristic of his psychological acuteness that he says 'her blind affection for me fostered all the defects I have just confessed.' The Sade family was, in any case, not straitlaced. The Marquis's uncle, the Abbé de Sade, Abbot of the monastery of Ebreuil, was imprisoned for debauchery at the age of fifty, much to the amusement of his friend Voltaire.

Sade, 5ft 2in in height, entered the cavalry, where he seems to have been a difficult customer from the start. Indeed, most of Sade's troubles stem not so much from the things he did, as the utter intractability of his own nature. The manner in which he set about his goings-on, the way he behaved when people objected or restrained him, could only lead to trouble, although, as Lély points out, there were no doubt other persons behaving just as perversely on the quiet.

In 1763, a few weeks before his twenty-third birthday, Sade married Renée de Montreuil. The bride's family were of minor and recent *noblesse*. She was not particularly rich, but there were good prospects. Sade's wife, as may be imagined, had a consistently difficult time. She seems to have behaved admirably, accommodating herself to his whims during their early years of marriage, working ceaselessly for his release during his long years of imprisonment. Rather understandably, she obtained a separation from her husband when he was finally released, by that time in his fifties, after which he settled down, apparently happily, with a mistress.

Sade cannot be said to have earned this consideration from his wife, although there seems to have been a genuine tie of affection between them. He seduced her sister, not without scandal, and was perpetually grumbling (a form of snobbish sadism) about her family's middle-class origins and behaviour. It should be said in extenuation that marriage had brought him a really appalling mother-in-law. Mme de Montreuil's vindictiveness pursued Sade through life, stripped him of his fortune, kept him in prison for his best years.

The effect of confinement on a person of Sade's uncertain balance and sexual ebullience, who possessed at the same time a keen interest in literature and philosophy, was the production of a vast series of works from his pen, some of which have been found disturbing in their nature. However, it is by these that he stands or falls.

The pro-Sade party, who number among them many distinguished names, present him as a writer of the highest originality, foreshadowing the Nietzschean superman – the disciple of pure power – while at the same time tearing aside the curtain that had hitherto concealed all the anomalies of sexual psychology. Sade, they say, prepared the way for Freud and Jung. This last claim seems to me to ignore writers like, for example, Brantôme, who, in his *Vies des Dames Galantes*, a hundred years earlier, conceals a good deal of acute sexual psychology under a show of bluff heartiness.

Sade, although his descriptive passages are in the fullest sense unrestrained, must also be considered, on the one hand, as a branch of the Gothic novel; on the other as an example of the traditional French eighteenth-century novel of ideas, of which Choderlos de Laclos's *Les Liaisons Dangereuses* is the most brilliant specimen. Lély points out that Sade and Laclos almost certainly met when both were under arrest in 1794. Although one is reminded of Laclos when reading Sade, the latter's works never rise to the literary heights of *Les Liaisons Dangereuses*. One of his critics complains that Sade 'lacked poetry'. That is perhaps the point. There is much that is of interest about him, but he was not an artist. He could not command the required discipline and restraint.

However, if he is at times wearisome as a novelist, Sade must certainly be granted extraordinary insight into the causes of his own difficulties. He writes in *Justine* (1791) a century before psychoanalysis was thought of:

> It is in the mother's womb that are formed those organs which are to make us responsive to this or that fancy; the first object it comes in contact with and the first speech it hears complete the work of formation; tastes are now there, and nothing in the world can destroy them.

He notes a natural trend in the infant towards incest and cruelty. He even foretells the hormone theory and physio-pathological anatomy:

> When the science of anatomy is perfected it will easily make clear the relationship of a man's structure and the tastes which govern his emotions. Pedants, executioners, functionaries, legislators, all you of the tonsured rabble, what will you do when we get so far?
>
> What will become of your laws, your morals, your religion, your gallows, your heavens, your gods, your hells, when it is proved that this or that flow of juices, this or that sort of tissue, this or that degree of strength of the blood or other animal essences is enough to turn men into victims of your trials or your rewards?

In short, Sade cannot be dismissed as a thinker. His diagnosis has proved only too near the mark. Live women he may have flogged, but not dead horses.

The Marquis de Sade: A Biography,   1962
Gilbert Lély, translated by Alec   *Daily Telegraph*
Brown, Elek.

FRANÇOIS DE CHATEAUBRIAND

I

Chateaubriand is probably best known in this country from the dish named after him, a thick slice from the thickest part of a fillet of beef. For some reason, as a man, he lacks what is needed for export. In France, a greatly renowned figure, here he is likely to be at once recognisable as a historical personage, but one hard to supply any details about. He is perhaps the best example on the market of the man, only happy in the turmoil of love and politics, always saying that all he wants is to go into a monastery or live on a desert island. His considerable gifts and gigantic egotism were not lightened by a ray of humour – a rare thing for a Frenchman, whatever may be popularly thought to the contrary – so that throughout his life he managed to maintain this theoretical position to his own satisfaction. Even his biographers tend to take his word for this longing for solitude more than might be expected. One searches for a modern equivalent of Chateaubriand; perhaps André Malraux comes somewhere near – adventurer, novelist, art-historian, finally Minister in the Government.

Chateaubriand came from an ancient Breton family (two or three Celtic generations before the time of surnames) which, like many Breton families of that sort, had little money available. He was a younger son, his background perhaps to be thought of in terms of the long pedigrees and short purses of Wales in the past, a less feudalised, but somewhat similar Celtic community where sons – as Chateaubriand remarks of Brittany in these Memoirs – might easily return to tilling the soil if they did not succeed in making a career for themselves.

His father, ambitious to re-establish his branch of the family, became a merchant skipper, making many voyages to Nova Scotia and elsewhere, eventually achieving reasonable profits in the slave-trade. He did not trap slaves, but purchased them from African kings. With the proceeds he bought a castle in Brittany, which had been much associated with the Chateaubriands in the past, though never actually owned by them. He inhabited only a small corner, living by his own choice like an owner crippled by death duties, of an unmanageable stately home today. Chateaubriand was furnished with a commission in the army, not much else. He certainly cannot be described as having been born with a silver spoon in his mouth.

The *Mémoires d'outre-tombe*, of which Robert Baldick here gives a selection, is a work of vast length. Like all long books that are any good, it should really be read in its entirety to be fully appreciated. All the same, we must be grateful for Baldick's excellent selection, although the translation of Chateaubriand's highly decorated prose poses some stiff problems for the translator.

Born in 1768, Chateaubriand actually hunted with Louis XVI as a young man. He went to America to avoid the Revolution, about which he had mixed feelings, and managed to meet Washington. As a disciple of Rousseau, he was horrified to experience his first sight of Red Indians in the form of a group of almost naked savages, wearing feathers and taking dancing lessons from a Frenchman in a wig. He failed to find, as he had hoped, the North-West Passage, returned to France, fought against the Revolutionaries with the Army of the Emigration, was wounded, came to England. There he remained in exile for seven years. Meanwhile, Chateaubriand was writing hard. He returned to France with the advent of Bonaparte, and was fortunate in publishing his *Le Génie du Christianisme*, a book of Christian apologetics, just at the moment when the First Consul decided to re-establish religion as part of his policy of government. Chateaubriand was sent as ambassador to Rome as a reward. He resigned at once after the kidnapping and shooting, by Bonaparte's orders, of the Duc d'Enghien.

Whatever one may think of Chateaubriand's posturing and personal conceit, there can be no doubt that he was a man of honour where such matters as the Duc d'Enghien's semi-judicial murder were concerned. More than once in his life he put himself in physical danger, not to mention the most acute financial difficulties by his refusal to accept what he regarded as dishonourable behaviour on the part of the authorities on whom his job depended. Indeed, unlike so many people of his kind, he could almost be said to have behaved better in practice than in theory, because, although he is always telling the reader how splendid his conduct was, it is extremely difficult to extract from the Memoirs any consistent view of history and politics. At one moment he is dazzled by Bonaparte; at another outraged by his crimes and the odiousness of his personal character; at a third, resentful of the English for taking the finally effective security measure of interning the Corsican at St Helena.

In this inability to commit himself, we see the innately political and opportunist tendency of Chateaubriand's mind. He was basically a man of action, not of theory, but he happened at the same time to be gifted, unlike most politicians, with an extraordinary felicity of literary style.

Chateaubriand's overpowering egotism prevents him from describing individuals with any skill. His relations, his friends, his enemies, the

women he loved – none of them comes to life in his pages. Yet his
account of the Retreat from Moscow and his life in Rome are absorbing.
His mind was concerned with events and impressions, not with
persons. He had, there can be no doubt, a streak of plain vulgarity that
stood him in good stead in dealing with the callous men and
governments with whom he sought office. An example of this vulgarity
can be found in the contrast he draws between his life in England as a
penniless exile, and that as a powerful ambassador: his meeting with
the girl he had formerly loved, after the lapse of years, in his moment of
eminence. The colours are laid on with the relish of Hollywood. Again,
such phrases as 'at Smyrna, in the evening, nature sleeps like a
courtesan wearied by love,' opens up the style of Pater and Wilde.

The Memoirs of Chateaubriand, edited   1961
and translated by Robert Baldick,   *Daily Telegraph*
Hamish Hamilton.

II

The first volume of George Painter's biography deals with Chateaubriand's early life: his passion for his sister, Lucile; the journey to
America; the return to France; enlistment in the Army of the Princes,
the Royalist force mustered in Germany to fight the Revolution; the
defeat of the Royalist army, and Chateaubriand's escape to the
Channel Islands where this volume ends.

There is always a certain difficulty in retelling the story of someone
who has already told it in great detail himself. How far is that person's
own narrative to be followed and believed, how far to be reassessed and
criticised? This is particularly difficult in the case of Chateaubriand,
enormous egotist, overwhelmingly romantic, full of the pride that apes
humility.

I think Painter sometimes accepts Chateaubriand's version of his
own doings and feelings rather too easily, but it is difficult to know
where to draw the line in retailing adventures that were extraordinary
enough however you look at them. It may well be that Chateaubriand's
romantic approach occasionally does himself less than justice. The
question also arises of how much a writer about Chateaubriand's life at
this period should become involved in the complicated course of the
revolution. Painter does give a fair amount of detail, again one hesitates
to criticise what may have been unavoidable in telling a story that
depended largely on day-to-day changes of the political scene.

Some of the incidents of Chateaubriand's life would be more
believable if he had taken himself rather less seriously. Painter draws
attention to the seduction, at the age of eighteen, of a spinster lady

thirteen years older than himself, whom Chateaubriand described as an 'agreeable frump'. He may have behaved less than chivalrously in making this remark, but retribution followed – the lady never married, spoke of the incident with unfading resentment, and lived to the age of 102.

The highspots of this volume are the travels in America and service with the Army of the Emigration. In America journeying in a great sweep from Baltimore, Philadelphia, New York, round by the Lakes, down to the mouth of the Ohio River, Chateaubriand came back to his starting point through the southern States. There were a great many shocks for a disciple of Rousseau and the Simple Life, but he was relieved to find that General Washington's front door was opened by a parlourmaid rather than a butler.

How Chateaubriand managed to survive the defeat of the Royalist army and eventually get to Jersey is an amazing story. He had not only been wounded in the thigh, but was suffering from dysentery and an unknown rash (everyone thought it was smallpox but it appears to have been a recurrent form of chickenpox).

Chateaubriand has been called 'a French Byron', and he himself felt there was a certain rivalry between the two of them for being regarded as the Great Romantic of the age. It is hard to feel that they were much alike. Byron certainly had his worldly side, but it is impossible to imagine him devoting himself to the humdrum aspects of politics which were, in many ways, the breath of life to Chateaubriand. Nor do Byron's love affairs at all resemble Chateaubriand's. Although opinions differ on this point, it seems probable – as Robert Baldick assumes – that Mme Recamier, having held off so many other lovers, gave herself to 'the Magician', as Chateaubriand was called.

'I have no liking for wit, which is well-nigh repugnant to me,' Chateaubriand wrote. At the same time, he was capable of shrewd observations, such as his remark that 'equality and tyranny have secret connections'.

Chateaubriand: A Biography. Vol. I: 1977
The Longed-for Tempest, 1768–93,   *Daily Telegraph*
George D. Painter, Chatto.

MADAME DE STAËL

Germaine de Staël is one of those larger-than-life personalities to whom it seems impossible to apply ordinary standards of measurement. From one point of view she was, both in private and public life, among the most dreadful women who have ever lived; from another, she was brave, intelligent, witty, passionate, and – in politics – both capable and moderate. J. Christopher Herold has written an excellent book about her. In the earlier pages his irony leans a trifle towards the heavy side, but he shakes free of this, and deals with an immensely complicated narrative deftly and with the right admixture of seriousness and humour.

Madame de Staël was the daughter of Necker, the Swiss banker, and her father comes an easy top of the men she loved. To estimate Necker's position just before the French Revolution, a being might be envisaged with the combined qualities of, let us say, Lord Keynes, Lord Beveridge and Montagu Norman, no less sure of himself than any of these, and just about to bring the rabbit out of the hat and save the country from a truly desperate situation. Unfortunately, in Necker's case, no rabbit materialised, the Revolution took place, and he went into retirement at Coppet, his country estate near Geneva.

Herold rightly devotes a generous portion of his introductory chapters to explaining this background, which meant that Mme de Staël herself, from her earliest years, was brought up in the very centre of the political and social world of France; and in a home where both her parents thought that they knew all the answers.

'It is not your fault that you are ugly,' wrote the Left-wing *Journal des Hommes Libres*, in one of the many abusive newspaper attacks on Mme de Staël, 'but it is your fault that you are an intriguer.'

It was true that she had no looks. One of the illustrations to this book shows a *jolie-laide* of thirteen with a high powdered hair-do and a certain nymphet charm; the more mature portraits all emphasise the miracle of her power to make men fall in love with her unaided by the smallest outward physical attraction.

She was married to Baron de Staël, a Swede, in 1786. Staël, a young man of good but impoverished family, by his personable appearance and behaviour had brought himself to the notice of his own King, and later, when attaché to the Swedish Embassy in Paris, to that of Marie-Antoinette. According to the utilitarian ideas then in vogue, it was arranged that if Staël allied himself to Mlle Necker's large fortune he should be appointed Sweden's Ambassador to France.

Even so, Catherine the Great – such was the level at which she was gossiped about – thought Mlle Necker had 'made a very disadvantageous marriage'. It is interesting to note that Mme de Staël's father had begun life as a bank clerk, her mother as a governess; and that it is not only in modern times, as is sometimes implied, that careers could be forged by talent and industry.

Catherine the Great turned out to be quite right, at least so far as poor Staël was concerned. He got his embassy but proved quite unequal to his wife; or even his in-laws. Talleyrand is generally supposed to have been her first lover (at the period when he was Bishop of Autun), and, although later she put an uncomplimentary portrait of him into one of her novels (as a female character called 'Madame de Vernon'), she always ranked him in the first three, emotionally.

By the time Bonaparte appeared on the scene Mme de Staël was already a force to be reckoned with. At first she was determined to make a conquest of the victor of the French invasion of Italy. When she called on him the butler explained that the Citizen General was in his bath. 'No matter,' she replied. 'Genius has no sex.' Bonaparte disliked that sort of remark. He always went out of his way to be disagreeable to Mme de Staël, and, in justice to him, he was one of the few people who could put her out of countenance. In return, she presided in Paris over a salon of clever people from all political parties who discussed, and severely criticised, his administration. Finally he stood it no longer and exiled her. Again one is impressed by that age in relation to our own, in that even so arbitrary a ruler as Bonaparte – always deporting political undesirables to French Guiana – was slow in taking action against this famous woman from fear of the moral effect.

Her love affair with Benjamin Constant, one of the outstanding episodes of her life, is nowhere better described than in Constant's own novel, *Adolphe*. Constant deliberately confused the circumstances by introducing into his story elements of what had happened during his entanglements with other women, especially a Mrs Lindsay. But the essence of the theme – a man's inability to extricate himself from the clutches of a woman he no longer loves, but who still exercises an emotional domination over him – describes principally the author's relationship with Mme de Staël. Of no great length, it is one of the best novels of its kind ever written.

And Mme de Staël herself? There was a superbly comic side to her. She thought the Irish were Germans; she had an affair, during a boring interlude, with two jealous Scots called Robertson and MacCulloch;

she learnt to play the mouth organ on the way to visit Goethe; she experienced one of her books being anonymously reviewed by Bonaparte. . . .

Mistress to an Age: The Life of Madame de Staël, J. Christopher Herold, Hamish Hamilton.
Adolphe, Benjamin Constant, with an introduction by Harold Nicolson, Hamish Hamilton.

1969
Daily Telegraph

NAPOLEON BONAPARTE

I remember, during the war, lunching with a French officer in the now defunct Junior United Services Club, where a bust of Napoleon used to stand on the half-landing. As we came up the stairs he dryly remarked 'You will not find a statue of Wellington in any of the military clubs of my country,' adding, 'that man and his nephew were the ruin of France.'

It must be admitted that, certainly during the nineteenth century, English sentimentality about Bonaparte often took a particularly ludicrous form. He might reasonably be regarded as the subject of marvel on account of his absolute disregard for all moral feeling and humanity, or for his consistent egocentricity and pursuit of power for its own sake. Indeed his will and consistency make him one of the most remarkable men who ever lived. He was always true to form. But to suppose that he was bent on creating a better world, interested in justice or the common man, devoted to the arts and sciences, or indeed bore any resemblance to the picture of him so dear to the near-quisling British Whigs of his own time is to make a very big mistake.

Anyone who still doubts this should read Jean Savant's enthralling book, which takes Napoleon Bonaparte (1769–1821) from schooldays to death entirely from *contemporary* accounts. Only a brief note is given regarding each writer and chronological circumstance. The result is extraordinarily successful, sometimes even uproariously funny, so vividly does Napoleon come to life, seen from a thousand different angles.

His personal habits were abominable, from drinking his coffee out of the saucer, to having an incestuous relationship with his sisters and stepdaughter. He cheated at all games, and after dinner would collect the napkins and table cloth, in which he would dress up and give long and wearisome imitations. If he heard anyone open a snuff-box in the council of state he would send an usher to bring it to him, use the snuff, and then throw the box in a drawer whence the owner never recovered it. When reflecting, he would take a pen-knife from his pocket and (using it only for this purpose) jab it continually into the arm of his chair.

Nothing was too large or too small to avoid the impact of his pathological egotism. The remarkable thing is how often men who had everything to lose by their integrity stood up to him, for example, Admiral Bruix, who refused point-blank to order his ships into open sea for review when a storm impended, with disastrous results to his own career; or the unnamed notary (obviously a splendidly 'logical' French figure) who had registered Lucien Bonaparte's marriage to the widow of a Paris stockbroker, when his brother had plans for some much more ambitious union.

The rest of the Bonapartes were on the whole far from being nonentities, and the rows, intrigues and general vulgarity of their family life make enormously comic reading. The line the Bonaparte family took was that Napoleon had 'done' his eldest brother, Joseph, out of his patrimony by becoming Emperor himself – when he was really only the fourth son.

Intensely envious of his own commanders, none of whom he would willingly praise, Bonaparte always preferred to have a third party present if he were going to blackguard a subordinate. This habit, his love of teasing, and his offensive manners suggest an innate sadism. For example, Josephine had a great fear of driving fast. He therefore forced her, when suffering from one of her habitual migraines, to sit in a chaise (subsequently wrecked by the impact) and drive at full gallop over a deep gully.

All this private behaviour was, of course, reflected in his public life, from the murder of the Duke d'Enghien to the invasion of Spain, and the imprisonment of the Pope to his method of distributing awards to his army. He was heartless, petty and common, and there seems no reason whatever to suppose that if he had imposed his sway over Europe the result would have been in the least beneficial. However, where dictatorship is concerned such failings count not at all with people who wish for dictators. Just as Hitler or Stalin was credited with superhuman gifts, it was alleged in his own time that Bonaparte had invented double-entry bookkeeping. It is the Will people who like dictators want; the Legend can be supplied later. 'My mistress is power,' said Bonaparte. Jean Savant, Chancellor of l'Académie d'Histoire and author of more than twenty books about Napoleon, has composed a volume of the greatest interest, showing the history of this, his only passionate love, and the one to which he was always faithful.

Napoleon in his Time, Jean Savant,   1958
translated from the French by   *Punch*
Katherine John, Putnam.

STENDHAL

I

Stendhal's *De l'Amour* is not one of his most popular books, either among his fans or in that much wider circle where he is merely read as a famous French author. All the same it contains a mass of good things. It was first published in 1822, when he had just returned to Paris after the years in Italy, where he had fallen in love with Métilde Viscontini. This love was not returned, and Stendhal, then thirty-nine, wrote the book – or rather collected together these impressions and reflections on all kind of subjects – in a mood of considerable dejection. This edition is a great improvement on the English translation which appeared about forty or fifty years ago.

Stendhal (real name Henri Beyle) is so strange and contradictory a figure that it is hard to make any simple statement about his gifts; but he had some claim to be considered the first writer to apply what are now called 'psychological' methods. Although he regarded himself as a 'romantic' – and certainly much of his approach to life was of a romantic kind – he also tried to write down how people actually behaved, not some conventional picture of stylised human conduct as employed in the novels of the time. He is particularly interesting on the subject of love, because he thoroughly appreciated both the tender and ruthless aspects of that passion. He was on the side of the Man of Feeling against the Don Juan; but he realised that Don Juan scored up most of the points on the board, even if those points were not always wholly valid ones.

'Possession is nothing,' he writes, 'only enjoyment matters'; and later, 'A woman's power lies only in the degree of unhappiness with which she can punish her lover.'

His comments must of course be read against the background of the society in which he was accustomed to move: soldiers, bureaucrats, adventurers, meeting together in not outstandingly smart *salons*; Europe convulsed by the Napoleonic upheaval; France defeated, under a government coloured by unenlightened clericalism. It was a water-shed, political, moral, even emotional.

Let us remember that *beauty* is the visible expression of character, of the moral make-up of a person; it has nothing to do with passion.

Now *passion* is what we must have, and beauty can only suggest *probabilities* about a woman and about her self-possession. But the eyes of your pock-marked mistress are a wonderful reality which makes nonsense of all possible probabilities.

That is one side of the picture (*cf.* Shakespeare), certainly, but a few chapters later we are given yet another angle on this inexhaustible subject:

That charming fellow Donézan said yesterday: 'In my young days, and indeed until quite late in my life (for I was fifty in '89), women used to powder their hair. I confess to you that a woman without powder is repugnant to me and always gives the impression of being a chambermaid who has not had time to finish her toilet.

To this last remark Stendhal adds a most typically Stendhalian – and infinitely shrewd – comment: 'This is the only argument against Shakespeare and in favour of the unities.'

On the subject of Modesty he writes: 'A woman in Madagascar thinks nothing of showing what is most carefully hidden here, but would die of shame rather than exhibit an arm.' He adds a note on Jealousy: 'An academy should be established in Philadelphia for the exclusive purpose of gathering material for the study of man in the state of nature. This should be done now, before these strange tribes become extinct.'

Where Stendhal shows less than his usual grasp is in a lack of understanding of the fundamental nature of much of the material with which he deals. Nineteenth-century optimism infected even his sceptical view of human nature. 'Nothing will be so beautiful, just or happy as the moral atmosphere of France in about 1900.' He believed that a more liberal attitude towards marriage would put everything right; so much so that he even suggests (perhaps not very seriously) that a woman who had freely chosen a husband, and then committed adultery, should be sent to prison for life.

Stendhal's *Love* can be opened on any page and read with pleasure. There is always something unexpected. 'The more a man has the gifts of a great artist, the more he should aspire to titles and decorations as a protective rampart against the world.' How different from what is usually said on the subject. It must have been enjoyable to have gone to get a passport from him when he was French consul at Civitavecchia – enjoyable, that is, provided one had been tipped off that he was a man of letters, and it was not one of those innumerable occasions when he had slipped away on leave without meticulously reporting the matter.

Love, Stendhal, translated by   1958
Gilbert and Suzanne Sale, Merlin   *Punch*
Press.

II

It was an excellent idea to make a selection from Stendhal's journalism, which, as it happens, largely appeared in England. We are surprised to find him, under different pseudonyms in various magazines, side by side with Lamb, Hazlitt, de Quincey, Landor, and John Clare. In the first instance the articles were crudely translated into English Regency journalism. Later, they were run to earth and turned back into French by the great Stendhalian authority, the late Henri Martineau. Now they are transformed once more into English by Geoffrey Strickland. Strickland has done the job well, catching on the whole the authentic Stendhal note; although one may demur at the verb 'to enthuse', and suppress a cry of pain at 'horse-riding' for riding.

Some remarks of Henry James are quoted at the beginning of this edition, defending Stendhal from the charge of being a 'light writer'. James perfectly hits off a definition of Stendhal's manner – 'a kind of painful tension of feeling under the disguise of the coolest and easiest style'. If you like Stendhal you have to put up with his failings. He does not always adhere strictly to the simple truth. He was at times, for example, inclined to claim that he had been present at battles which had taken place several hundred miles from where he was himself operating. He says in one of the articles reproduced here that he remembered having seen Mirabeau, who died in 1791, when Stendhal was eight and had not yet left his native Auvergne. I regret to add that Stendhal is also to be found reviewing his own books under another name – as Strickland mildly puts it – 'with a warm feeling for their true merits'. These are small things compared with the more general truth of much that Stendhal has to say, the way in which he shows us life from a new angle.

Strickland provides an excellent introduction, perhaps a shade too serious in its determination to show that Stendhal's 'aristocratic' prejudices have been exaggerated, that he was not the prophet of modern 'realist' totalitarianism, and that above all the French must not be allowed to get away with quoting Stendhal today as an excuse for dubious behaviour in North Africa. It is a mistake to be too portentous about Stendhal. He was well aware of his own political inconsistencies, at times even drawing attention to them himself. Fastidious as an individual, he liked the idea of democracy at a distance. Temperamentally (and economically) drawn to Bonaparte, he was also well aware of Bonaparte's many odious characteristics. One must accept such contradictions as different sides of Stendhal he never managed to fuse. They add to his interest as a writer, but they supply one of the reasons why he failed to gratify his own wish to make a career in the world of action.

At times Stendhal gives his political views their head in his literary criticism. We find him praising an indifferent poet like Béranger in what must be one of his worst poems. On the other hand, he attacks Benjamin Constant's *Adolphe*, one of the most accomplished short novels ever written, which deals with the psychology of love in just the manner in which Stendhal himself was supposedly interested.

These articles were written in the 1820s, just after Stendhal had returned from his seven years in Milan. There he had met Byron. His description of the poet is perhaps the best thing in this book. Stendhal gives two slightly varying accounts. In one, at a box at the opera, Byron asked Stendhal, as the only person present who spoke English, how best to get back to his inn, which was on the outskirts of the town, and showed haughtiness when Stendhal suggested taking a cab. In the other, there was a misunderstanding because Byron had been told that he was to meet a veteran of the Retreat from Moscow, and assumed that it must be a man in the group with moustaches. Stendhal was clean-shaven. However, they saw something of each other in the end, and were both involved in a row one night at the Scala because an officer of the guard wore his bearskin cap in the stalls, which prevented a friend of theirs, an Italian poet, from seeing the stage from the pit. The Italian poet was taken to the guard-room, and Byron and Stendhal were among those who went round there to make a fuss. The incident is described with all Stendhal's extraordinary power of bringing a story of that kind to life. Incidentally, Byron subsequently wrote Stendhal a letter, defending Sir Walter Scott, so that their meeting certainly took place.

There is good stuff here about Rossini, Talleyrand, Chateaubriand, Talma, Scott, Mme de Staël, Harriet Wilson, and dozens of others. Sometimes the writing is obviously hurried, sometimes Stendhal mounts too high on one or other of his hobbyhorses. He is never a bore. He is always champion of that school of thought – occasionally under fire from modern pedants – that a work of art is something to be enjoyed.

Selected Journalism from the English   1969
Reviews, Stendhal, with translations   *Daily Telegraph*
of other critical writings, Geoffrey
Strickland, ed., Calder.

III

Robert M. Adams's long essay has the merit of making the reader want to argue with him. Aware that there has been too much uncritical Stendhal admiration, he tries to adjust the balance, although at the same time an admirer himself. As a result he sometimes sounds patronising and does not always rise above the besetting sin of American criticism, an attitude that seems to suggest that all sorts of questions about Love, Social Life, and Government have been satisfactorily and finally settled long ago. All the same, Stendhal is not easy to investigate without seeming to take him either too seriously, or not seriously enough:

> None of the books of Stendhal is very much like any of the others (says Adams), yet, paradoxically, each of them is pervaded by his personality, and none of them could conceivably have been written by anyone else. A politically minded critic has cleverly suggested that among the devotees of Beyle [Stendhal's real name] one can distinguish a right wing of Fabrizians, a centre of Julienites, a Brulardist left wing (I should prefer to call it Lucienist), and far out on the frantic left flank, a fringe of Octaviasts.

This means, I take it, that Stendhal's least fanatical readers choose *The Charterhouse of Parma*, also those probably less interested in the man himself: then come the people who prefer an intelligible story with Stendhalian overtones, represented by *The Scarlet and the Black*: then (myself among them) those who like best *The Life of Henry Brulard*, Stendhal's autobiography to the age of seventeen, together with *Lucien Leuwen*, the unfinished novel, dealing with Army life and political intrigue. Adams chides Gide for liking *Lucien Leuwen* best – so it seems to me, unjustly – although I admit that the Octaviasts, the people who put first *Armance*, the novel with an impotent hero, are well to the left of my own critical position.

Rome, Naples and Florence and *A Roman Journal* are best taken as books about Italy in general, the former representing that country in 1817, the latter in 1827. *A Roman Journal*, mostly about Rome, has many digressions on the subject of other Italian towns. *Rome, Naples and Florence* contains a long account of life in Milan, where Stendhal spent probably his happiest years, until he was evicted by the Austrian police. Stendhal's theory was that in Italy life had remained simple, untouched by artificiality and vanity, violent and tragic, owing not only to the temperament of the people, but also to the political oppressions – Austrian, Papal, Bourbon – under which the Italians suffered. Accordingly, love existed here in an unselfconscious, unspoilt form, and the arts – at least music – flourished against a background of lawlessness and death by the dagger.

It is one of the charms of Stendhal that he is completely inconsistent and well aware of his own inconsistency. As a liberal he wanted to bring 'bi-cameral government' to Italy, but also saw the reforms for which he hoped as the enemy of the life which he loved. The picture he paints of the Italy of his day recalls the Iron Curtain States of our own time: endless difficulties on the part of petty officials about passports; police spies openly following tourists on their expeditions and grateful for a bottle of wine sent across to them by those whom they watched. It was a government under which a butcher could be sent to the galleys for selling meat on a Friday, and where all books were regarded with suspicion.

Richard N. Coe's translation of *Rome, Naples and Florence* takes you along at an excellent pace, and conveys the true Stendhalian flavour. Perhaps words like 'brash', 'moron', 'bird-witted', 'travelogue', 'subconscious' might have been avoided, simply because they recall too much contemporary life, even when otherwise perfectly expressing the meaning.

Haakon Chevalier is less successful with *A Roman Journal*. 'Battalion chiefs' is inadequate for 'chefs de bataillon' and 'curate' in English has quite a different meaning from 'curé', in French. It is interesting to note in *A Roman Journal* that Stendhal had read Casanova's Memoirs, published for the first time in relatively complete form only about a year before he wrote this book. He does not say much about them, although at the period it was suspected by some that Casanova himself was one of Stendhal's own inventions.

In *Rome, Naples and Florence* Stendhal describes a meeting with Shelley. Without corroborative evidence we cannot be certain this took place, as Stendhal sometimes embroidered his autobiographical experiences. Adams, who – I repeat – has written an amusing and provocative study, supplies two pages of Stendhal's howlers in the appendix. It is therefore impossible to resist pointing out that Vittoria Accoramboni is familiar to us from Webster's *The White Devil*, rather than from his *The Duchess of Malfi*, as Adams suggests.

Stendhal: Notes on a Novelist, Robert   1960
M. Adams, Merlin Press.   *Daily Telegraph*
Rome, Naples and Florence, Stendhal,
translated by Richard N. Coe,
Calder.
A Roman Journal, Stendhal,
translated by Haakon Chevalier,
Orion Press.

IV

Jean Dutourd's method is to take Mérimée's vivid essay on Stendhal, split it up into its component parts, and make chapter headings of these. He then investigates the particular Stendhalian characteristics dealt with by Mérimée in each section. Mérimée, who was twenty years younger than Stendhal, gives a first-rate account of him. One is made to feel all the energy, eccentricity, charm, boisterousness, pleasure in social life, yet, at the same time, all Stendhal's innate awkwardness and melancholy. We see his love of women, yet comparative lack of success with them; his passion for the arts, yet ingrained preference for a life of action; the strength of his political views, and their extraordinary contradictions; his delight in elegance of behaviour, coupled with his reverence for Bonaparte, one of the most inelegant men (Hitler always excepted as an easy first) who have ever lived.

All this comes out in Mérimée's essay and is amplified by Dutourd. Now Dutourd is a Frenchman, and therefore must know, roughly speaking, what it would be like to meet Stendhal as another Frenchman; just as one knows, roughly speaking, what it would have been like to meet Byron, Keats, Scott. He implies, with the greatest modesty, that the sympathy he feels for Stendhal is because he himself somewhat resembles him.

If I may say so without seeming impertinent, it seems to me that he admires Stendhal because he is so different. Dutourd may have been bored in his childhood; we know him to be a good writer and a brave man in the Resistance. At the same time, one cannot help suspecting from his writing that he has plenty of common sense and leads a well-ordered life. These are, I know, dangerous accusations to make.

The point is that if Dutourd possessed more of Stendhal's weaknesses himself, I feel sure he would not be so indulgent to them. Let us imagine Stendhal on Stendhal. Indeed, we need not imagine it. We have almost the whole of Stendhal's own works treating that subject. If we are too tolerant of Stendhal's bad habits, for example, saying that he had been present at battles when he was, in fact, hundreds of miles away, his plagiarism, his writing reviews of his own works under assumed names, his pretence that he knew Byron well when he had hardly met him, and a hundred other peccadilloes of that kind, we are losing much of the man himself. Dutourd's praise sometimes threatens the emergence of a kind of literary Bayard. I agree with him in dismissing with impatience the theory recently put forward that Stendhal was perhaps homosexual – as Dutourd truly says, if Stendhal had been, he would have told us so – but if all his failings are too lightly passed over, we lose a great deal of his strangeness, even of his greatness.

Where Dutourd seems anxious to build up Stendhal is just the place where he must essentially remain tumble-down; that is to say as a socially unassimilable character. Stendhal was a kind of soldier-cum-civil-servant bohemian, who was also a genius. Passionately interested in politics and administration, he was not – he cannot really have been – very satisfactory in official life. Goodness knows what would have happened had he succeeded in being appointed *Préfet* of Le Mans. I agree that it nearly happened; so perhaps I am wrong about his capabilities.

In the same way, one cannot in any circumstances imagine Stendhal, like Dutourd, married, with a family. He looks at life essentially as a bachelor, and a bohemian one at that.

Dutourd illustrates his commentary with some background from his own life and contemporary literature. It would have been enjoyable to have had more of this. For example, he contrasts Stendhal's utterly unselfconscious diary-writing, with Gide's, designed all the time for publication to a contemporary public. We learn, too (not without some guilty sympathy) that Dutourd detests *Le Grand Meaulnes*.

There is one obscure matter upon which Dutourd throws welcome light. Mérimée relates that Stendhal, denying that great speeches are made on the battlefield, told him that 'one of our bravest cavalry generals [Murat] harangued his troops, who were close to breaking rank, in these terms: "Forward, you swine! my arse is as round as an apple! my arse is as round as an apple!"' Many must have wondered why this statement was calculated to put heart into his men. Dutourd points out that there are traditional words for all bugle and trumpet calls. This was probably the phrase applicable to the musical notes of the Charge. Prosper Mérimée, as Jean Dutourd remarks, would have greatly appreciated this point, but never having been a soldier, was probably unaware of it.

The Man of Sensibility, Jean   1961
Dutourd, translated by Robin   *Daily Telegraph*
Chancellor, Macmillan.

V

It is rare – in my own experience unknown – for a woman to write about Stendhal. Although very interested in the opposite sex himself, he was the first to agree that he was not a riotous success with it in person. This comparative indifference of women to Stendhal seems hitherto to have applied even more to his published works. Margaret Tillett's brief study, accordingly, has a certain initial interest attached to it on this account. It considers Stendhal's works in a detached, unpedantic manner – though a fair knowledge of them is required to appreciate what is said – the result being a most interesting and intelligent commentary. To say something fresh about Stendhal at this stage is not easy. Margaret Tillett, applying a feminine sensibility, does set a lot of his work in a new perspective. Her book is recommended to all old Stendhal-hands. She shows an admirable understanding of the principle that men, especially authors, can behave in a tiresome manner without necessarily prejudicing the importance of what they do, or, in Stendhal's case, what they write. She is not at all blind to his faults, freely admitting that he can be prolix, boring, rather dishonest, but she manages to make light of these failings without ever becoming a counsel for the defence.

One of Stendhal's trickiest standpoints is the political one. An ardent

Bonapartist – which in his time, odd as it may now seem, meant having 'liberal' convictions – he was also well aware that Bonaparte was a power-maniac, quite uninterested in 'democracy'. As Margaret Tillett points out, Stendhal's own middle-aged view is to some extent expressed by the character of Count Mosca in *La Chartreuse de Parme*. Mosca hopes to hold down his job, is anxious to alleviate the injustices of petty absolutist government, yet sees even worse would befall if the fanatical revolutionaries triumphed. 'In the end the value of *La Chartreuse* is that it asks innumerable questions that are of enduring importance, and gives no answer to any of them.' She points out that Stendhal – who had none of Balzac's capacity for creating scores of living human beings in his novels – did possess 'inexhaustible resources' for playing the variations on four types. These characters are a young hero, an older man of experience and wit, two women, one gentle and reflective, the other lively and brilliant. With all his gifts, Stendhal was not in one sense an artist, admitting himself that he was inclined to write only when he had nothing better to do, starting and never finishing, often regardless of form. At the same time he could achieve extraordinary beauties in style and presentation. This preference for a life of action certainly makes Stendhal no less interesting when he does write. What would be his modern equivalent? An officer of the Army Service Corps, who had had a fairly gruelling 1914–18 war; then lived on very little money in Spain between the wars; to return to a reasonably important post in the Ministry of Food in the Second World War; ending up with a distant job in the British Council? That is roughly what it might be.

Margaret Tillett rightly emphasises Stendhal's passion for giving himself different names. She puts forward the ingenious theory that he called himself 'Henry Brulard' when he wrote about childhood, recognising that 'the child seen through the eyes of the mature man is a fictitious character'. The other pseudonyms to some extent indicate, she says, that Stendhal was aware that he was being supposedly autobiographical. He inferred, she suggests, things happened to 'Stendhal' that he would not have claimed as 'Beyle'. There is a validity in this. The keystone of Stendhal's own philosophy was the *âme généreuse*. It is not at all easy to define what he meant by this phrase, but it implied a sort of 'niceness' that appreciated there were other things in life than 'getting on'; that found the concomitant of love was not necessarily sexual relations; that was devoted to magnanimity and beauty.

Stendhal himself was aware that he was not always a shining example of his own creed, indeed often goes out of his way to show how far he veered from it. He might be said to complete the circle, and become an *âme généreuse* by his honesty about himself and grasp of what was really required. He believed in an élite, one that was privileged, but not by birth, wealth nor intellect, some of whom might seek power, others remain contentedly obscure.

On the whole, Stendhal's life was one of a series of disappointments, and, as Margaret Tillett remarks, 'the retreat from Moscow was surely enough to mark for life anyone who survived it.' He comes out of his tribulations remarkably well, an odd mixture of frankness and reticence, a Romantic to whom 'the Romantic conception of the Artist is completely alien'. He would like to have been a Prefect, but have time to write while he administered his Department. His views are endlessly worth reading, though I can never make out quite what happens in the latter part of *La Chartreuse*.

Stendhal: The Background to the Novels,　　　　　　　　　　　1971
Margaret Tillett, Oxford　　　　　　　　　　　　　　　　*Daily Telegraph*
University Press.

VI

'Every time you discuss Stendhal, you are left with the impression that you have said nothing at all, that he has eluded you, and that everything remains to be said. In the end you have to resign yourself and restore him to his unpredictable and miraculous utterance.' F. W. J. Hemmings quotes these words of an earlier critic (J. P. Richard in *Littérature et Sensation*), and few of those who have themselves at one time or another attempted to approach the subject would disagree. It should be added at once that Hemmings has written a very good book indeed; as good as anything about Stendhal that I have read.

His object is to communicate to his reader something of the delicate poetry which is, or which can and should be, woven into the fabric of the individual life, not so much in order that the reader should admire the clarity and power of the communication, as that he should pursue on his own, the book being closed, that tender meditation that *rêverie*, which is '*le vrai plaisir du roman*' . . . Stendhal seeks neither to edify nor to instruct, neither to denounce, nor simply to entertain: he wants more than to beguile an idle hour, less than to alter the social order.

This approach to writing was, of course, largely dictated by Stendhal's own character. If he was in some ways the least professional of all great writers, he was at the same time the least practical of men, who quite seriously nourished hopes of being a worldly success. This poetry which refused to come to life in him as poet or dramatist, both roles he attempted, found expression as novelist; although here again he experienced the greatest difficulty in inventing plots.

He is one of a distinguished though heterogeneous band of major French writers which, even if one leaves aside the poets, includes

Montaigne, Rousseau and Proust; such men as constructed their best work out of nothing more substantial than their own endless self-questioning self-analysis, self-communing.

This was certainly a side of Stendhal, but as Hemmings goes on to show, not the only side. He was far less sure about what he was himself like than were Montaigne, Rousseau and Proust. That is clear from the autobiographical material he left behind him; also from the novels dealt with here. The period covered by Stendhal's life was, of course, one of colossal social change. In this it resembled our own. Stendhal himself was fully conscious of the necessity of altering the novelist's approach, though he deplored the fact that the audience for the sort of play he would have liked to write had disappeared with the *Ancien Régime*.

In examining this situation Hemmings remarks: 'There had been realists in the previous century; but the great watershed of the Revolution had rendered their portrayal of society outdated, though their observations on mankind were, of course, eternally valid.' This last statement should be obvious enough, though there probably exist contemporary critics who, observing the social background of, say, *Les Liaisons Dangereuses* is somewhat different from their own – or indeed, anyone else's nowadays – assume that the portrait of human nature is therefore at fault. Stendhal's two most famous novels are interesting in this respect because *Le Rouge et le Noir* could be fitted into the frame of 'social significance', while *La Chartreuse de Parme* would be relatively difficult to treat in the same manner.

F. W. J. Hemmings points out that Julien, hero of the former, represents the ambitious 'poor boy' in whom Bonapartism – the desire for power – takes what turns out to be a fatal form. Fabrice, on the other hand, hero of *La Chartreuse*, is born with a silver spoon in his mouth, and, although he too comes to a bad end, he really represents the unselfconscious, and therefore totally opposite, type of hero. *Lucien Leuwen*, some people's favourite Stendhal novel, was never completed by its author. Here again we are shown a rich young man, with – unique in Stendhal's writings – an indulgent father. Lucien first of all tries life as an officer in a Lancer regiment to prove to himself that he can make some sort of a career, then becomes a politician's secretary. Lucien is in some ways the hero who is most like Stendhal himself, though the former had no vocation as a writer, the latter not nearly so much money. It was perhaps its too autobiographical nature that made the novel difficult to complete.

Stendhal: A Study of His Novels,
F. W. J. Hemmings, Clarendon
Press: Oxford University Press.

1964
Daily Telegraph

THE BROTHERS GRIMM

Grimm's Fairy Tales first appeared in England in 1823 under the title *German Popular Stories*. I happen to possess a copy. They are illustrated by the incomparable George Cruikshank, whose work delighted the authors, as well it might. Ruth Michaelis-Jena makes some interesting comments on the pictures that have accompanied the stories at different times and in different countries. The rather bleak English title fitted in with the Grimms' view of their work, because, although the book had been called in German *Kinder und Haus Märchen*, the emphasis was intended to be on the folklore side of the collection, rather than on entertainment for young people.

The brothers Jakob and Wilhelm Grimm were born at Hanau in Hesse, in 1785 and 1786 respectively, the sons of the Town Clerk, of stock long settled there. It was a large family, and another brother was a competent painter. From their earliest days Jakob and Wilhelm seem to have been set on their folklore interests.

The story of the brothers themselves is chiefly that of trying to obtain tolerable employment as librarians, or the like, which left sufficient time for their researches. They lived in disturbed days, but they were themselves, in a sense, all part of that disturbance, representing as much as Bonaparte the reaction from an eighteenth-century manner of looking at things. Jakob Grimm was briefly librarian to Jerome Bonaparte, when King of Westphalia. Jerome gets a bad press on the whole, but he left Jakob alone, the only instruction being: '*Vous ferrez mettre en grands caractères sur la porte: Bibliothèque particulière du Roi.*' The petty German rulers the Grimms had to deal with were uncooperative and on the whole more of a nuisance. Not for the first time one marvels that there exist people who say they would have liked to live at a small German court.

Ruth Michaelis-Jena has brought together a considerable amount of information about the brothers, but she never quite masters her narrative, nor gets a firm hold of them as characters. To achieve that is probably difficult, as scholars and students of research are not always easy to define. One gets an impression of an intense 'Germanness', of the kind that – before Bismarck – made people think of Germans as quiet, peaceful, home-loving, more than a trifle dull. All the violence, hysteria, kinkiness, that now seem such an essential aspect of one side of Teutonic make-up has been documented for not much more than a century.

This is one of the reasons why it is hard not to feel that more might be discovered about the Grimms' personal characters. There seems to have been elements of childishness. To leave their native Cassel for Göttingen, about fifty miles away, was an appalling exile. They ended up in Berlin, quite famous.

Ruth Michaelis-Jena does mention that 'the brothers' unique relationship' has suggested 'an "unnatural" fraternal attachment', and certainly her disposal of such psychological speculations is entirely acceptable. At the same time, it is surprising to find Jakob Grimm elected a member of the Frankfurt Parliament, when such emphasis has been laid on the brothers as retiring scholars. Again the unexpected-ness of this outbreak into public life may be less if the background is more fully studied. There was a meeting with Hans Andersen in 1845, at which Andersen, at the first attempt, made a characteristic bungle, getting hold of the Grimm brother who had never heard of him or his work. However, this was righted in the end. Scott was an early admirer of Grimm's Tales.

If the stories themselves are examined, the number that are unfamiliar may well come as a surprise to many people. For 'The Fisherman and his Wife', 'Tom Thumb', 'Snow-drop', 'The Golden Goose', 'Hansel and Gretel', 'Rumpelstiltskin', 'Ashputtel' (Cinder-ella), to name a few well-known ones, there are scores of relatively forgotten tales. A re-translated edition, illustrated by that brilliant artist, Arthur Rackham (for whom it should be remembered Picasso has an admiration), appeared in 1909. The Rackham illustrations have always been popular in Spain and Finland. They are perhaps a shade too romantic, lacking the enormous enjoyment Cruikshank takes in the horrors and grotesqueness of the narrative, which makes his drawing so perfectly suit the stories.

The Grimms have been translated into seventy or more languages, from Afrikaans to Yiddish, taking in Ibo and Korean on the way. On the whole I feel them to be an excellent introduction to life, and that people who are not told or read aloud fairy stories as children miss something.

Ruth Michaelis-Jena quotes: 'Lady-bird! lady-bird, fly and begone! Your house is a-fire and your children at home!' Personally, I should have said: 'Lady-bird! lady-bird, fly away home, your house is on fire and your children are gone.' However, the 1823 edition of Grimm says: 'Lady-bird! lady-bird fly away home, thy house is a-fire, thy children will roam.' This shows what difficulties 'The Folklore Fellows' (as Finland's society is called) encounter when collating material.

The Brothers Grimm, Ruth Michaelis-   1970
Jena, Routledge.   *Daily Telegraph*

ALFRED DE VIGNY

There can be few subjects upon which so much rubbish has been written at one time or another as life in the Army. At one end of the scale the duties of a soldier are represented as purely romantic or facetious; at the other, considered solely in terms of persecution and self-pity. The latter approach probably reached its highest point in this country in some of the books deriving from the First World War. American novels about the last war tend, in rather the same manner, to be hard-luck stories of the kind published in England during the early Twenties, of which scarcely any examples reappeared over here.

Why should books about soldiers often be so uninspired? Is it because the whole basis of a soldier's life is rarely understood, especially by the kind of person with some ability to put things down on paper? Alfred de Vigny's *Servitude et Grandeur Militaires*, translated here as *The Military Necessity*, sheds light on this question. It is a work of absorbing interest; most of all to those with some experiences of the Army, or, indeed, any of the Services. Humphrey Hare has produced a first-rate translation, and his introduction is full of good points.

Vigny's thesis is briefly this: that it is not so much a soldier's courage on the field of battle that makes him a person of a special sort, but the tedious life he has to endure to make him a fit person for his courage to be used. After all, a civilian can be just as courageous in a variety of ways. The nobility and saintliness of a soldier's life, if properly lived – so Vigny indicates – is in his capacity to submit to the dullness, futility and servitude which are the unavoidable accompaniments of military routine. The soldier's uniform, music and drill are, as Hare well says, 'all means to an arcane ideal, the state of military grace. They set him apart, mark him as a member of a dedicated sect and thereby exact the tribute of emotion.' This theme is illustrated in three short stories, linked autobiographically together. The method recalls Lermontov's *A Hero of Our Time* (1840), a book that *The Military Necessity* (1835) oddly resembles in manner. Perhaps this is because the old captain, Maxim Maxemich, might so well have appeared as one of the Frenchman's examples. The stories show the hard and often paradoxical régime imposed by the sentiments of Duty, Loyalty and Honour.

Vigny knew what he was talking about. Born in 1797, a younger son of the *noblesse*, he was brought up to hate Bonaparte. All the same it was the era of the Napoleonic victories, which, with his family's military tradition, made him long for a life of action – to which mentally and physically he was quite unsuited. However, at the Restoration he was enrolled in the Corps des Mousquetaires of the Royal Bodyguard. Almost his first important duty, in his scarlet uniform, was to escort the carriage of Louis XVIII to Ghent at the start of the Hundred Days.

He remained in the Army for thirteen years. When the Mousquetaires were disbanded he exchanged into the Infantry of the Guard. Towards the end of his service he was promoted captain in a regiment of the line. He was involved in civil disturbances, experienced the explosion at Vincennes (vividly described in this book), and was moved to the frontier when war was declared with Spain. But he never saw 'action'. It was a depressing period for any professional officer. What must it have been for a man whom some consider France's greatest poet?

Incredible as it may seem, this book was at first considered an attack on the Army. Apart from its narrative brilliance, its depth and clarity of thought, the pages provide a new picture of this period of French history, seen through such different eyes from those of Stendhal and Balzac who have made the period so familiar. Vigny (who died in 1863) was a leader of the Romantic Movement. His few female characters are charming but unreal. He is at his best describing an elderly sentry patrolling a rampart, or the conversation of an officer in charge of a platoon patrolling the boulevards during the July Revolution:

> 'Will you forgive me,' he said, 'if I ask you to lend me your gorget of the Royal Guard, if you have preserved it? I left mine at home, and I can't send for it or go myself, because they're killing us in the streets like mad dogs: but perhaps, after the three or four years that have elapsed since you left the Army, you no longer possess it. I, too, sent in my papers a fortnight ago, for I'm thoroughly bored with the Army: but yesterday, when I saw the Orders in Council, I said to myself: They will be fighting. I made a parcel of my uniform, my epaulettes and my bearskin, and I went to the barracks to join those good fellows who are going to be killed at every street corner.'

Vigny is a writer who knows about Resignation and Self-Sacrifice; and also how appallingly boring Army life can be. *The Military Necessity* is a book that should not be missed.

The Military Necessity, Alfred de   1953
Vigny, translated with an   *Punch*
introduction by Humphrey Hare,
Cresset Press.

HONORÉ DE BALZAC

I

Balzac is in every sense an indigestible figure. 'The vulgarity of his mind,' says Proust, 'was so massive that a lifetime could not leaven it'; and, after a terrific excoriation of Sainte-Beuve for missing the point about Balzac's style, Proust goes on to demonstrate how this vulgarity, and his unselfconsciousness about it, is one of Balzac's many strengths as a novelist. He was utterly untroubled by attempts to conceal what he himself thought; and, although the fastidious reader has a lot to swallow in the way of improbability and unattractive standards of value, the fact remains that the *Comédie Humaine* is a work of terrifying vitality and power.

For letting you know what you are in for, if you decide to tackle its 100 volumes and 2,500 named characters, Herbert J. Hunt's analysis could hardly be bettered. He takes the books in the order in which they were written, at the same time casting an eye at the categories in which Balzac himself arranged them. He firmly outlines the plot of each volume, explaining its connection with incidents and characters of the great work as a whole. By 1834 Balzac had conceived the idea of linking all his novels together, so that they become occasionally rather muddled in their time sequences.

Power, money, and sex are Balzac's subjects; especially the manner in which the pursuit of any of those aims past a certain point may turn a human being into a monomaniac. Hunt is prepared to grant the first two as strongly motivating forces, but sometimes shows impatience with Balzac's unrestrained interest and belief in the third as an overwhelming influence. Indeed, Hunt sometimes speaks almost as if uncontrolled sexual motives had been devised by the French as an imaginary subject useful for heightening the dramatic side of a story.

Balzac – who, unlike most of his fellow writers of that date, was a great admirer of his contemporary psychological novelist, Stendhal – was himself one of the first novelists to deal in psychology; so much so that a critic of his own day, said of him: '*C'est M de Balzac qui a inventé les femmes.*' He also believed in the straightforward conflict between virtue and vice, and at times has to pay for the simplicity of this approach by the sentimental nature of some of his virtuous characters. In this last respect he does not, in general, go so far as Dickens; but, against that, Balzac has not the humour of Dickens, nor his bursts of descriptive poetry. Dickens never has the foggiest idea of how people earn a living; Balzac knows this very well. Indeed, he will almost drive the reader mad with detailed descriptions of the method in which some obscure trade or profession is conducted.

An interesting example of Balzac's ability to understand the ways of his own countrymen is shown in Hunt's account of *Les Employés,* a *Comédie Humaine* novel about civil servants. Rabourdin (prototype of the author) is an Office Director in the Treasury Department, who has been working on a scheme of administrative and fiscal reform, which involves a drastic reduction both in the number of ministries and the number of civil servants – where have we heard all this before?

> The plan for fiscal reform (writes Hunt) is less easy to follow, but it involves the suppression of land-tax and all indirect taxation in favour of a curiously conceived personal tax based on the scale of living indicated by expenditure on such things as house-rent, furniture, servants, equipages, etc.; a rational device, according to Balzac-Rabourdin, making for an equitable assessment since standard of living is a reliable guide for estimating capacity to pay.

But is not this the very system that General de Gaulle's administration has put into practice, or proposes to put into practice, for the payment of Income Tax in France? No doubt some Balzacian has been at work in the General's Cabinet.

Balzac has not much to say about working-class life, but, from the lower middle-class to rich and fashionable circles, he covers the ground with extraordinary thoroughness. It has been urged, with some truth, that he did not possess sufficient first-hand experience of the high society of which it was his joy to write.

All the same, his capacity for simplifying situations and putting life into them makes it hard to bring definite accusations of going badly wrong, except on some minor point. Proust derived an enormous amount from Balzac, although, of course, Proust also brought a brilliance and subtlety of his own that elaborates and expands the Balzac tradition. Henry James wrote a characteristic appreciation of the situation:

> Balzac carried the uppermost class of his comedy, from the princes, dukes and unspeakable duchesses down to his poor *barons de province*, about in his pocket as he might have carried a tolerably befingered pack of cards, to deal them about with a flourish of the highest authority whenever there was a chance of a game.

Balzac's Comédie Humaine,
Herbert J. Hunt, University of
London: The Athlone Press.

1959
Daily Telegraph

II

Honoré de Balzac (1799–1850) was son of a peasant, who could have become an agricultural labourer, but in fact raised himself to a relatively important official position. Admittedly, this was a moment in history when energy and talent were suddenly offered the glittering prizes of an immensely expanding society. Even so, Balzac's father was an unusual man. At eighty-three there was still trouble about the village girls, and he was not without imagination and humour. Balzac's mother, thirty-three years younger than her husband, was also a remarkable personality, evidently good-looking in her youth, tough to a degree. She quarrelled with her family, dominating them while they furiously fought back. She was determined they should be well brought up. Her own youngest child, it is accepted, was by a lover.

At the age of eight Balzac himself was sent to an Oratorian school, a kind of clerical Dotheboys Hall (no holidays) which sounds just as disagreeable as any English public school of the period. After six years (during which his mother visited him only twice) he was withdrawn, pretty well at the end of his tether.

The interesting thing is that when the time came for Balzac to choose a profession, his parents recognised his literary gifts sufficiently to offer him a small allowance for two years, while he settled down in Paris to make a living as a writer. This does them much credit. They kept the awful secret from their acquaintances. They also, rather naturally, soft-pedalled the fact that the novelist's uncle was executed for the murder of a farm girl he had seduced – it is indeed possible that he was innocent – but the immediate proximity of such violent circumstances show what a short way Balzac had to look to find highly coloured material for his novels.

Balzac emerged as a young man with his two often quoted ambitions 'to be famous and to be loved'. On these two commandments, so far as he was concerned both as a writer and as a man, hung all the Law and the prophets. One has only to compare these ambitions with those of other great novelists – almost without exception complicated by moral ideas or personal inhibitions – to see how well placed was one prepared to accept wholeheartedly this simple formula, and at the same time gifted as few have been with energy and intelligence.

Over and over again, reading André Maurois's book, one is struck by this extraordinary combination in Balzac – his simplicity and his intelligence. To the end of his life he was making plans for a great political career (total failure in business never shook his belief in his own commercial abilities) and the fact that he polled only twenty votes against Lamartine's 259,800 merely convinced him of the public's essential wrong-headedness. In rather the same way, his desire to be loved was – and remained – curiously straightforward, and in a sense, undemanding. At the age of twenty-two he went as tutor in the family of a lady of forty-five, and at once fell in love with her. She seems to have been a woman of great qualities, who for ten years was the chief influence in his life and work.

There were, of course, many other ladies, including the Countess Guidoboni-Visconti, English by birth, who used to call him 'Bally', a name he signed in his letters to her. Sooner or later, those who had a love affair with Balzac were expected to help him out financially, as no amount of money earned by his books ever put him on a really firm foundation owing to his hopeless extravagance.

He would write, normally for twelve or fourteen hours on end, sometimes as much as eighteen or twenty. He did this by retiring to bed, 'like the hens', at six o'clock in the evening, then rising for work at one in the morning. When Mme Hanska (whom he finally married) reproached him with infidelity, he pointed out that the amount of words he produced and the hours he kept provided an unimpeachable alibi.

It is hard to deny this, and there is no doubt that the affairs he had can, on the whole, have borne little resemblance to what usually passes for the day-by-day texture of such relationships. Eveline Hanska herself is an extraordinary example of dreams coming true. She was a Polish lady with family connections of a kind to dazzle Balzac. She wrote him a fan letter. That was their introduction. Writers were accepted in her circle, since her sister had been mistress to Pushkin.

A meeting was arranged and at once Balzac and Mme Hanska fell into each other's arms. It was agreed they should marry when her husband – considerably older than herself and relatively easygoing – died. The interesting thing about the Balzac-Hanska association, which covered nearly twenty years, closed by marriage and Balzac's death, is that he does seem to have loved her deeply; and, although doubts have been cast on her own feelings being equally strong, there can be no question that she was very much attached to and emotionally involved with him. Meanwhile the books poured out. Oddly enough, Balzac was always a bugbear of the critics, who compared him unfavourably with Eugène Sue and Paul de Kock, objecting that he painted a society that was dissipated and materialistic. They provided, however, no period with which this view could be strongly contrasted. André Maurois's own background is one Balzac would have loved to depict, with industry, peacetime successes and wartime vicissitudes.

Prometheus: The Life of Balzac,   1965
André Maurois,   *Daily Telegraph*
translated by Norman Denny,
Bodley Head.

DANTAN'S STATUETTE
CARICATURES

Caricature is not an art that can really ever be said to have flourished abundantly in this country. There have been brilliant by-products, but Max Beerbohm is the only great exponent of modern times who comes immediately to mind: and even Max Beerbohm is concerned chiefly with intellectual rather than physical comment. I distinguish, naturally, between caricatures and cartoons, the latter opening up a completely different field. The *Vanity Fair* series by 'Ape' and 'Spy', first-rate in their way, although drawn with great restraint, are excellent examples of the English approach to caricature, a genre further explored from time to time by the artists of *Punch*. The essence of caricature is, of course, to seize on physical peculiarities, and exaggerate them in such a way that a joke is made about an individual's body – not clothes, or political opinions, or even personality, but *body*: arms and legs and nose and head.

At this point of my exposé of the art of caricture one faction will immediately point out that the English are too kind, and have too much good taste, to make fun of people's physical defects; while another will insist that the English are too prudish and too lacking in that kind of graphic skill. There is perhaps something to be said for both views; but I suggest that the chief reason is that we are, in this country, in some way less aware of physical characteristics, in short, not at home with 'the body' like the Latins, or even the Central Europeans.

Anyway, caricature takes its name from Italy, where its popularity can be seen all the time, not only in drawings in newspapers or advertisements but plastically, from Pompeiian excavations to Capo di Monte china. It is with this plastic form of caricature that we are here concerned: caricature in its purest form, in which almost all the emphasis is upon the outstanding physical characteristics of the subject.

Jeanne-Pierre Dantan (1800–69), although now largely forgotten, was regarded in his day as one of the greatest exponents of this art who has ever lived. He came from a Protestant Norman family with a tradition of craftsmanship. Together with his caricature statuettes, which are as a rule about nine inches high, he also executed 'serious' sculpture of no great interest. The Musée Carnavalet in Paris possesses

386

the greatest collection of his comic works, of which his statuette of Paganini is perhaps the best known in this country. It may sometimes be seen in the window of music shops, almost frightening in its vitality and physiological detail.

For some reason musicians are particularly popular subjects for miniature sculpture, and to this day small busts of Beethoven and other famous composers are to be seen exposed for sale. It is therefore appropriate that Dantan should have executed figures of Berlioz, Rossini, Meyerbeer, Strauss and a host of lesser known musicians and singers. Balzac, Dumas *père* and Victor Hugo were also among his victims. He paid several visits to England and made statuettes of William IV, Wellington, Brougham, and a number of other noblemen and men about town. Cantankerous and eccentric himself, he would not necessarily caricature individals on request; for it soon became known that there was no better advertisement for any public figure than to be a model for Dantan.

Janet Seligman gives an excellent account of him, although, considering his contemporary fame and the obvious oddness of his own character, comparatively little is known about his personal life. He was, however, a great collector of *curiosa,* and some of his statuettes were made only for the eyes of friends. His style shows the influence of Daumier, though in no slavish fashion, the statuettes existing entirely in their own right. It is an excellent thing that this book should have been written about him. It includes photographs of twenty of his works. One cannot help wondering whether a market still exists for public figures caricatured in this manner. During the war there were statuettes of Winston Churchill to be seen. There is perhaps an opening for some enterprising comic artist to try his hand at such sculpture. They might be sold at places like airports as souvenirs for foreign visitors. After the lapse of nearly a century it is an opportunity for some artist to make a name in a new medium. As it happens I possess a group depicting Napoleon III and Lord Palmerston in caricature, certainly in Dantan's manner, but unrecorded here – perhaps by a pupil of Dantan.

Figures of Fun: The Caricature-   1957
Statuettes of Jean-Pierre Dantan,   *Punch*
Janet Seligman, Oxford University
Press.

VICTOR HUGO

Victor Hugo (1802–85) is one of the monsters of literature; and, speaking for myself, I have no desire ever to reopen *Les Misérables* or sit through another performance of *Ruy Blas*. Where poetry is concerned one must accept the judgment of the race to whom the poet belongs. French opinion overwhelmingly hails Hugo as a great – perhaps the greatest – French poet. It is said that without him poets like Baudelaire and Mallarmé would lack half the basis of their technique. That may be so. As a novelist he is stiff, humourless and improbable to a degree; as a playwright, as far away from Shakespeare as you can get.

There is, of course, nothing original in saying that Hugo was often a bore. Whatever we may feel about him in that respect is slight compared with the sufferings he inflicted on his gifted contemporaries. Stendhal, Flaubert, Baudelaire, Amiel, Huysmans, Anatole France, all had their moments of agony at the awful banality of his wooden psychology and self-important moralising. True, they had to acknowledge his gifts as well. To some people life presents itself as a web of infinite subtlety; to others a picture daubed in the crudest colours. A case can be made for either view, or indeed for a combination of both. Hugo belonged decidedly to the school of crude colour.

It has to be admitted that Hugo's own life was full of the most extraordinary incidents that might be held to excuse a taste for the melodramatic. His father was a Napoleonic general who came near turning himself, and his family, into Spanish nobles. If the Bonapartist regime had survived this might well have happened to the Hugos. The writer's parents were far from happy together. Victor's great gifts were apparent at an early age, and the brother nearest to him seemed almost equally talented. The two of them fell in love with the same girl. Victor married her; his brother went raving mad at the wedding and spent the rest of his life in an asylum.

By the time he was twenty-five Hugo was a famous figure in the French literary world. He had political ambitions and became a Peer of France under Louis-Philippe. From a Royalist beginning, he moved steadily towards the Left. At first he was a supporter of the Prince-President, but they soon quarrelled and, during the Second Empire, Hugo lived in exile in the Channel Islands, where his inability to comport himself in a manner appropriate to a refugee made him little liked in the neighbourhood.

By this time his stature in France was immense. His political capabilities strike one as inadequate to the point of being laughable; but he possessed physical courage and a strength of personality that carried him almost to the top. He remained, however, always the literary man. It is impossible to trace in him the smallest atom of statesmanship. His political ideals were the romantic political ideals of the literary man; his methods of attempting to achieve them, wholly literary in their conception. But as a literary man he had probably the greatest public – and, in a sense, political – success in history. It was rather as if Dickens, Tennyson, Hardy, Kipling and Galsworthy were all rolled into one at the period of their greatest public popularity and held the stage for sixty years.

With all this complicated material André Maurois deals with skill. Maurois is absolutely determined that as a writer Hugo must be presented in the highest class. In France it is no doubt true that the characters of Hugo's novels are household words; in this country, not so. For twenty people to whom Emma Bovary or Swann are living persons, scarcely one would be likely to say, by way of verbal illustration, that such-and-such a person was like a given character from *Les Misérables*. At times Maurois becomes almost irritable with Hugo for making sustained praise so difficult to a biographer, himself of such very different character and personality.

Many will find the greatest interest of the book in Hugo's personal life, which was also lived on a Gargantuan scale. Starting off with a primness that would have done credit to the most straitlaced of Victorian married men (he admonished his fiancée for showing too much ankle when walking over mud) he became in due course a figure from whom no member of the opposite sex was safe. The involutions of his more permanent emotional life would have sent any ordinary man off his head. It is necessary to be broadminded where figures of Hugo's vitality and egotism are concerned; even so it is impossible not to feel that a lot of his adventures were unnecessarily sordid.

Victor Hugo,   1956
André Maurois, Cape.   *Punch*

ALEXANDER DUMAS

It would be interesting to know how much Alexander Dumas *père* (1802–70) is read in this country today. Certainly *The Three Musketeers* and *The Count of Monte Cristo* have passed into the language as phrases; but how many people who speak of them have read no more than excerpts from the former, and have only a rough idea of the latter's story? How many truly regard them as their favourite books would be hard to guess. I suspect that the first class – those familiar with the names only – greatly predominates.

Dumas's Memoirs, written at immense length, have here been boiled down to manageable proportions. They are oddly enjoyable. One cannot believe all that he says, in the sense that no life is lived in the simple terms here presented. On the other hand, if Dumas's career is to be recounted in the terms of his own romances, the story rattles along and gives you a good idea of what life was like for a young man with literary ambitions in the Paris of the Restoration.

Dumas's grandfather, a member of the *noblesse,* had gone to San Domingo, where he had a son by a Negress. This son became a general in Bonaparte's army. For one reason and another – Dumas says the jealousy of Bonaparte himself – General Dumas died broken and poor. The General's widow, to whom her son was greatly devoted, kept a *tabac.* This volume describes how Dumas began his career as a dramatist. It ends when he was thirty, about to turn to the writing of novels.

The qualities that make *My Memoirs* attractive are their zest, their lack of pretentiousness, Dumas's determination to write with integrity within the aims he set himself. He did a great deal of collaborating. The friendships and quarrels which resulted from this inevitably tricky form of writing are of some interest.

Dumas was, of course, in the vanguard of the Romantic Movement. He had a passionate regard for Shakespeare, and, at a suitable distance behind Shakespeare, greatly admired Scott and Fenimore Cooper. One of his great contemporaries of whom he speaks without enthusiasm – and then almost apologising for his own opinion – was Balzac.

Like so many writers, he was unsatisfactory in his early jobs because he was only good at writing – this was true not only of writing books,

390

and plays, but also of his calligraphy; one of his early employments was that of copying clerk. He describes an office row when thus engaged. Its vividness is enjoyable.

The struggle began immediately I took up my new duties. They wanted to herd me together with five or six of my fellow-clerks in one large room, against which I revolted. Instead of this large office, thick with supernumeraries, clerks and assistants, I had my eye on a sort of recess separated by a simple partition from the office-boy's cubicle, and in which he kept the empty ink-bottles.

I asked if I might move there, but I might as well have asked for the Archbishopric of Cambrai, which was just vacant. A fearful clamour greeted my request, involving the office-boy as well as the head of the department. The head of the department thundered that it was not only contrary to administrative customs, but that my claim was most presumptuous!

I was trying to fit myself into the unlucky recess, which, for the moment, formed the sum of my ambition, when the head clerk walked haughtily from the office of the head of the department, bearing the command that the rebellious employee, who had dared to leave the ordinary rank, should at once return there.

There was joy throughout the department. A fellow-clerk was to be humiliated and, if he did not humbly accept his humiliation, he would be dismissed. The office-boy opened the door between his cubicle and mine, with all the empty bottles he had managed to muster together.

'But, Féresse,' I said, watching him uneasily, 'how do you think I can manage here with all those bottles, or rather how are all those bottles going to fit in with me – unless I live in one of them, in the manner of *le diable boiteux?*'

'That's just it!' sneered Féresse as he deposited fresh bottles by the old ones. 'M. le Directeur don't look on it like that. He wants me to keep this room for myself and doesn't expect a newcomer to lay down the law.'

I strode towards him, blood mantling my face. 'The newcomer, however insignificant is still your superior,' I said, 'so you should address him bareheaded. Take your cap off, you young cub!' At the same time I gave the lad a backhander that sent his hat flying against the wall, and left.

The scene is as exciting as some of d'Artagnan and modern conditions have made it scarcely less romantic.

In spite of the strong feeling that office-boys should know their place, Dumas took no active part in the Revolution of 1830. The indifference with which he speaks of shooting soldiers and policemen who had the misfortune to be on duty during those days is in contrast with the more humane account of the same subject given in Alfred de Vigny's *Servitude et Grandeur Militaires*. Vigny was a friend of Dumas, who was also on boisterous tems with Vigny's mistress, the charming actress, Marie Dorval.

It is indeed, extraordinary how many of Dumas's friends became famous. He leaves a description of a party he gave for several hundred people in four empty rooms on the landing where he lived. All his painter friends helped to decorate these, Delacroix himself executing a huge fresco of a battle-scene. One wonders what happened later to those rooms. Were they white-washed or covered with wall-paper?

Adventures with my Pets is the first translation since 1909 of Dumas's *Histoire de mes Bêtes*. In the English edition of fifty years ago, it was felt necessary to omit the chapter called 'Historical Researches into the Origins of the Peculiar Fashion of Greeting Among Dogs'. Recent judgments in the courts will no doubt ensure that the inclusion of this section in the present volume will risk no prosecution. The book consists of jottings by Dumas about himself, his animals, his hunting, his travels, his books, his servants and his political views. He had a dog called Pritchard. His cat, Mysouf, he describes as a 'hardened criminal and hypocrite'. Like the Memoirs, this book, which might easily have been intolerable from some pens, can be enjoyed for its unselfconscious high spirits.

My Memoirs, Alexander Dumas,   1961
translated by A. Craig Bell, Owen.   *Daily Telegraph*
Adventures with my Pets, Alexander
Dumas, translated by A. Craig
Bell, Grey Arrow.

PROSPER MÉRIMÉE

The fame of the opera may be chiefly due to Bizet. That does not prevent *Carmen* from being an extremely good story. In fact Prosper Mérimée (1803–70) provides a landmark in short-story writing. After him the art was never quite the same. *Tamango,* the African chief who led a mutiny on a slave-ship and ended up playing the cymbals for the British 75th Regiment (the Gordons) is another admirable story of its kind – though whether Highland regiments ever, in fact, recruited Negro musicians, I am not sure. In short, had Mérimée done nothing else, he would have a niche, and, in some respects the variety of his talents was a positive handicap to him as a writer. That might not have been so had his temperament been even a little different.

Mérimée was the only child of a reasonably successful, if not greatly talented, painter of classical subjects. His mother was also an artist of some ability. One of his great-grandmothers had written fairy stories, among them 'Beauty and the Beast'. There was the usual start in a lawyer's office, then his parents, with whom Mérimée was on good terms, saw that writing was their son's line, and did their best to be helpful. He made a success of things at a surprisingly early age.

A situation now arose perhaps more characteristic of French writers than those of this country, certainly one which the nineteenth century in France makes familiar. Mérimée wanted to make a career in government service, preferably diplomatic. This might be thought the crux of the matter. Mérimée desired worldly success, rather than the rewards, such as they are, brought by writing. Certainly that is one way of looking at his career, even allowing for the fact that some sort of employment other than writing may have been required for earning a living, anyway at the rate he liked to live. On the other hand, there is always the example of Stendhal – a close friend of Mérimée's and twenty years older, a considerable influence on him – who to the end of his days craved success in the civil service. Yet Stendhal certainly cannot be blamed for failing to deliver the goods so far as literature is concerned.

Nevertheless, reading about Mérimée, one does have the feeling that, with his talent, he fell between two stools. When he was about thirty, appointed Inspector-General of Public Monuments, he seems to have done the job very well. He had a lot of energy, and, although his cold, deliberately 'English' manner alienated people, he was good on committees. Something of an Anglomaniac, he was even more keen on Spain (he spoke both languages), a taste that led to an incident with extraordinary repercussions on his own life. Travelling in a Spanish stagecoach, he made friends with a gentleman of that country, out of favour because a liberal, not particularly well off because a younger son. This Spaniard asked Mérimée to visit him. He had two daughters. Mérimée took a fancy to the little girls, and tried to teach them French.

Mérimée continued to see and correspond with this Spanish family. The elder brother died, Mérimée's friend became Count de Montijo; subsequently the two daughters Duchess of Alba and the Empress Eugénie. Mérimée started with fairly revolutionary views, but he moved to the Right. He was never, in fact, what might be called a Bonapartist, in spite of friendship with Eugénie and close association with Napoleon III's court. All this, and a great deal more that is of interest, is described in A. W. Raitt's biography, which brings the many books about Mérimée up to date in a thoroughly readable and scholarly manner. It also deals with sides of Mérimée that may be less well known, like his learning Russian after he was fifty, thus becoming a key-figure in introducing Russian literature to France – and in consequence, Russian writers to this country, where they were first read in French.

Mérimée was a passionate rather than happy womaniser. He proposed marriage a few times in his youth, but never brought it off, devoting himself to serious, sentimental love affairs, stray mistresses and brothels. He also liked writing obscene letters and telling hair-raising stories.

A good deal of his personality remains mysterious, full of paradoxes, which Raitt is the first to admit. One suspects there was some rather disabling psychological trouble, though hard to guess what. The whole story is an interesting one, both of the man and the writer. Setting off as a follower of the Romantic School, Mérimée has their characteristic interest in violence, primitive passion, all that is exemplified in *Carmen*. At the same time, he found any sort of 'realistic' delving – in a sense the logical follow-up of an examination of violent or passionate feelings – altogether unsympathetic. This attitude caused him to be almost shocked by his friend Stendhal's *Le Rouge et le Noir*; to underrate Baudelaire (though objecting to his prosecution); disapprove of Gogol (though translating him); find Dostoevsky 'too much influenced by Hugo'. Such odd judgments partly explain why Mérimée himself was always a little self-conscious about writing fiction, and turned to history, because 'history was true, and novels are not true.' One sometimes wonders.

Prosper Mérimée,   1970
A. W. Raitt, Eyre & Spottiswoode.   *Daily Telegraph*

CHARLES SAINTE-BEUVE

Charles-Augustin Sainte-Beuve (1804–69), if not necessarily France's greatest critic, was certainly the most remarkable guide to French literature that ever lived. Recently, he has taken something of a beating, in general because he guessed wrong about a lot of his contemporaries, backing nonentities, missing Balzac, Stendhal, Flaubert, Baudelaire and Verlaine; in particular, because Proust vehemently disliked his methods and delivered a terrific and damaging attack on him in *Contre Sainte-Beuve*. A. G. Lehmann has written his book with these facts in mind. It is an immensely detailed and excellently expressed account of the first half of Sainte-Beuve's life. 'I have no wish to invent a new Sainte-Beuve – handsome, straightforward, fearless, saintly, heroic,' says Lehmann, going on to explain why, on the other hand, Sainte-Beuve is unusually open to caricature. This is sound. One can enjoy Proust's excoriation, and some of the disobliging stories about the great critic, while still bearing in mind that Sainte-Beuve's name has lived for a variety of good reasons.

Fatherless, impoverished, brought up by two doting women, drab, devout, immensely hard-working, apparently ugly (though the earlier portraits do not look too bad), Sainte-Beuve, when at the age of twenty-three he changed from medical student to literary journalist, did not appear to have the ball at his feet. There can be no doubt, however, that something exceptional about him impressed people. Victor Hugo, a year or two older, then bounding into fame, took him up as a close friend. A few years later, Stendhal's first act on being appointed French consul at Trieste (a post he, in fact, never filled) was to ask Sainte-Beuve to stay with him for 'six months or a year'. We must keenly regret that Sainte-Beuve found himself unable to accept this invitation. It could have been switched to Stendhal's subsequent consulate at Civitavecchia, and we might have had a description of each of them by the other.

One of Sainte-Beuve's most firmly held convictions was that, if criticism were to be treated – as he believed it could be treated – as a 'science', everything possible should be discovered about the author. He took precisely the contrary view to the theory that only the book matters. It is, therefore, just that Sainte-Beuve himself should be examined in this light; although the fact that he thought so, and to some extent prepared the way for future biographers, means that material known about him require careful examination.

The great emotional upheaval in Sainte-Beuve's on the whole uneventful life was his love affair with Victor Hugo's wife. This, even on the face of it, presents a situation of unusual interest. Hugo was everything a successful writer might wish to be: a poet immediately recognised as a man of genius; everywhere talked about; a political force; unusually good-looking; not merely a lady-killer, but a man with quite unusual aptitudes for that role. Sainte-Beuve, on the other hand, although he set up as a poet, soon found that such gifts as he possessed were chiefly of a critical order. In his younger days he was almost obsessed by his own unattractive appearance; he was desperately poor; he was not only gauche with the opposite sex, but possessed, so it appears, some physical disability that made normal relations difficult. Lehmann does not mention that last aspect of Sainte-Beuve's case and one feels that something should be said of it if only to deny, or modify, the story.

It is not absolutely certain that Sainte-Beuve's love for Adèle Hugo was consummated. On the whole one would suppose that at some stage that was so. There is, however, no doubt whatever that for a number of years they saw each other as often as possible – which was not very often – and probably exchanged about 600 letters. It was the great adventure of Sainte-Beuve's life. To what extent the situation would have existed without Hugo himself is hard to say; for triumphing over Hugo certainly played an undeniable part. In the end Adèle seems to have cooled and the whole affair flickered to a close.

Lehmann draws attention to Sainte-Beuve's many different sides:

Now a poet writing up his idol, now a religious polemicist, now a political commentator, portrait-writer, literary historian, reviewer of the week's best-seller, professor, gossip columnist. For any of these aspects of his writings there is a sizeable choice of aphorisms to choose from.

His likes and dislikes were equally complicated. Stendhal seems, in a sense, to have taken to him more than he to Stendhal – certainly more than Sainte-Beuve took to Stendhal's novels. His attacks on Balzac, at the level at which they are made, are certainly hard to refute. The point remains, however, that unspeakably vulgar as Balzac may have been, that was a small matter compared with his extraordinary energy and inventiveness as a novelist.

Sainte-Beuve seems to have moved with exceptional speed towards a middle-aged point of view. It was perhaps the result of his own upbringing: he had been treated as a grown-up when still a small child, always called 'Sainte-Beuve' by his mother. It would perhaps be true to say that he never had any youth. At thirty-five we find him complaining that there was no 'movement' among French writers, no 'moral preoccupation'. How up-to-date the complaint sounds. Let us hope that those now making it are not committing the same error as Sainte-Beuve and missing the contemporary winners.

Although the present book deals with Sainte-Beuve's earlier life, Lehmann looks ahead to some extent in his examination of *Port-Royal*, Sainte-Beuve's great reconstructive work on the famous Jansenist stronghold. This book took form in a series of lectures when Sainte-Beuve was for a year at Lausanne. It has many digressions, outlining the history of the monastery, its triumphs, its persecutions, giving individual studies of figures like Montaigne and Pascal. For those who enjoy literary coincidences, there is a good one in Sainte-Beuve's life. He was returning from Italy to Marseilles in 1838 after a holiday, and, as the journey was only two days, had economised by not taking a cabin. Trying to get some sleep on the deck, he made friends with a Russian, who spoke bad French, but was evidently a man of remarkable intelligence and distinction. It was Gogol. In such patterns is life arranged.

Sainte-Beuve: A Portrait of the   1962
Critic, 1804–1842, A. G. Lehmann,   *Daily Telegraph*
Clarendon Press: Oxford
University Press.

MICHAEL LERMONTOV

The importance to non-Russians of Michael Lermontov (1814–41), a considerable poet in Russian, lies in that he also wrote *A Hero of Our Time*. This is a novel which on first reading may seem a mere collection of short stories, linked by the character of the Byronic figure, Pechorin, but is, in fact, a work of great originality (from which Tolstoy learned a lot). It is a book which I can read again and again.

Ideally, readers of Laurence Kelly's biography should be familiar with *A Hero of Our Time*, but Lermontov's brief life was so extraordinary that he is well worth hearing about in any case. It is most surprising that Kelly's should be the first really full biographical study in English to be devoted to this remarkable figure.

The family of Lermontov (Learmonth) came originally from Scotland, no doubt as soldiers of fortune, and he himself had romantic feelings about this ancestry. The Lermontovs were not particularly well off, but his father, a dissipated character, had made a good marriage, which went wrong. As a result, Lermontov was brought up by a rich grandmother, ambitious for him. He was therefore put into one of the smartest regiments, the Life Guard Hussars, as not at all a rich young man.

Lermontov was incredibly talented. Kelly is admirable in supplying all sorts of details about him, which will be quite new even to many of those who already admire the writings. For example, this book is illustrated with many of Lermontov's own drawings and painting, which, if not in the top class, show that he could perfectly well have earned a living as a painter. At the university he had been a highly praised violinist. To these qualities he added extreme physical bravery in hand-to-hand fighting.

It is amazing to realise that Lermontov was only eight years older than Dostoevsky, so much does he seem to belong to an earlier period; he was a boy at the time of the Decembrists' revolutionary rising, crushed by the unpleasant Emperor Nicholas I. Again and again this Tsar's autocracy reminds one of Soviet circumstances: strict censorship; dissident political figures represented as being mad; forbidden literature secretly disseminated. Perhaps most interesting of all is the fact that some of the imperial censors ran considerable risks in showing sympathy for what was politically unacceptable.

Lermontov, from his earliest days, was a difficult customer. He seems to have had that propensity, trying to friends, of not knowing when a joke (especially a practical joke) had gone on long enough. In the end this was to prove a literally fatal failing. Pushkin, Russia's national poet, was killed in a duel in 1837 by the French adopted son of the Netherlands Minister to Russia. This was an affair involving the supposed adultery of Pushkin's wife. Kelly (though he does not elaborate) says there were also homosexual undercurrents in the circles involved. Lermontov did not know Pushkin personally but, greatly admiring him as a poet, wrote a searing lament for Pushkin's death, casting blame on the corrupt hangers-on of the imperial court. For this he was removed from his regiment and sent to some comparatively scallywag dragoons, serving in the Caucasus, where Russia was fighting an expansionist war.

Lermontov had been several times to the Caucasus as a boy, loved the country, and was in many ways in his element in a regiment made up of aristocratic officers who had blotted their copybooks, Poles suspected of separatist activities, straight adventurers. In addition the regiment was permanently on active service. His gallantry was such that he was gradually forgiven, in due course reinstated in the Life Guard Hussars.

Nicholas I, however, had taken a particular dislike to this gifted and prickly young man. He did not allow Lermontov to receive the decorations for gallantry for which he had been recommended. Not for the first time one is reminded that, in spite of Russia's great size, the number of people who actually operated things politically, socially, culturally, was very small. Thus a poetry-writing subaltern could be a real thorn in the side of the Tsar himself. When *A Hero of Our Time* appeared, as Kelly enjoyably points out, the Tsar 'reviewed' the book in a letter to his wife (a much livelier person than himself), and it is absolutely true that Nicholas's feelings about the book, the points he makes are precisely those of a thick-headed novel-reviewer.

Finally Lermontov got packed off to the Caucasus again, where – quite against orders – he went to the Caucasian spa at Pyatigorsk, on the grounds that he needed to recover his health, no doubt partly true. At Pyatigorsk, he said, one was 'enflamed by the ladies during the days, and the bed-bugs at night'. Unfortunately Lermontov's habit of not knowing the moment when making personal jokes becomes a bore overcame him. He teased an old schoolfriend about his taste for wearing Caucasian dress. Quite ludicrously, a duel was fought. Lermontov was killed. So, alas, he was never able to write the great work he planned, a kind of *War and Peace*. His poetry, like Pushkin's, does not really come over in English translation.

Lermontov: Tragedy in the   1977
Caucasus, Laurence Kelly,   *Daily Telegraph*
Constable.

FEODOR DOSTOEVSKY

I

Of all the great Russian writers, Feodor Dostoevsky (1821–81) is the one whose books most brilliantly portray the complexities of Russian character. They should be made compulsory reading for every member of the Foreign Service and all politicians who aspire to speak on Soviet policy. Dostoevsky's own experiences and ideas were no less typically Russian in character than the novels that mirrored them. Born in 1821, he was a decade younger than Dickens, whom he sometimes resembles.

How would Dickens have reacted, one wonders, to having his father murdered by his employees, being himself transported to hard labour in an Australian convict prison for four years for a mild political indiscretion, followed by two years as a private soldier on the Indian North-West Frontier, and by two more in the same place as a second-lieutenant? That would have made the blacking factory seem rather a minor affair.

David Magarshack, who has revolutionised the reading of Dostoevsky's novels in English by his translations that have appeared during the last few years, now gives us a biography, clear, readable, throwing new light on its subject.

There are two sides to Dostoevsky as a novelist: the first, his capacity for illustrating in his characters the contradictions and perversities of human nature; the second, his wish to propagate certain specific theories of his own. Magarshack is particularly good at sorting out and explaining these often complicated ideas, which became at times hopelessly entangled with Dostoevsky's personal life, producing the wildest contradictions of behaviour.

Although Dostoevsky's father, an army doctor, possessed about 1,300 acres and 100 serfs, he was a relatively poor man, and Dostoevsky himself was always essentially one of the 'have-nots' with a grudge against society. After a bad start at the Army College of Engineering, he managed to become an engineer officer, but retired almost immediately with the rank of lieutenant to earn his living by writing. At this period he was, in principle, on the side of revolution, with a leaning towards socialism and atheism, although his opinions were obscure and tentative. They certainly took no very active form. However he was arrested and sent to Siberia. The story of how Dostoevsky and his companions were lined up to be shot, pardoned only at the last moment (all a piece of ghastly Russian play-acting) is well known. After four years of frightful conditions as a convict he did another four as a soldier in a garrison town on the borders of China.

The interesting thing about this treatment of Dostoevsky by the authorities is that it did, so to speak, do the trick from the authorities' point of view. If he went to Siberia more or less a socialist, more or less an atheist, he came back a convinced Greek Orthodox Christian, a passionate believer in the authority of the Tsar, and ultimately a Pan-Slav who advocated Russian Imperial expansion at all points and over all Slav communities.

It is not always easy to see how Dostoevsky's political system would have worked in practice had he ever had the opportunity to experiment with it. It might be described as the Ill-Fare State. He refused to accept 'as the epitome of all desires a big house with model flats for the poor on a lease of 999 years' even if free treatment by 'the dental surgeon Wagenheim' was thrown in. At the same time he insisted on absolute government. Dostoevsky believed that misery and suffering were a necessary part of the human lot; that to remove them was only to produce an existence of boredom and horror that would lead men to suicide. 'Happiness does not lie in happiness but in its attainment' was his view. He detested the Roman Catholic Church, and he drew a sharp distinction even between the Greek Orthodox Faith and the Greek Orthodox Church.

There certainly seems to be some psychological justification for the view that too much 'welfare' and 'civics' lead to a need for violence as an antidote to boredom, but it is hard to see how an autocracy of Dostoevsky's sort could be maintained. Would it have been at all different from what existed already? He would perhaps have answered that he considered the status quo as satisfactory as could reasonably be expected. Dostoevsky has naturally proved a most unassimilable dish for the Soviet regime to digest. He is at once so near, and yet so far.

Magarshack has much to say that is of interest about Dostoevsky's personal life, his two marriages, his love affairs, his horrible stepson, Pasha, his literary rows, his passion for gambling, his epileptic fits. His second wife, Anna Snitkin, was a twenty-year-old stenographer who came to work for him. The marriage was a success, though not without its trying moments. One of these was when Anna (as described in the chapter of her Memoirs called 'My Joke') sent him an anonymous letter copied from a serial she had been reading, telling her husband that his wife had been unfaithful to him. The joke fell extremely flat.

Dostoevsky, David Magarshack,   1962
Secker & Warburg.   *Daily Telegraph*

II

Although Dostoevsky achieved success as a writer relatively early in life, his books did not at first reveal his startling genius. He was forty-four when *Crime and Punishment* appeared, putting him at once into the highest class of novelist by its force and originality. The notebooks he filled before writing *Crime and Punishment* were examined by the Soviet authorities in 1921, with other papers bequeathed by Dostoevsky's widow, whom they had allowed to die in misery two or three years before. The *Notebooks for Crime and Punishment* were in due course published in Russia in 1931. This volume is a translation of them, intermixed with explanatory passages by Edward Wasiolek, Professor of Russian at Chicago University. Dostoevsky's biographers have, of course, already made use of the Notebooks, but this is the first opportunity for those who do not read Russian to have access to them.

The story of *Crime and Punishment*, it will be remembered, was one of notable simplicity for Dostoevsky, who as a rule went in for complicated narratives. A student called Raskolnikov murders an evil old pawnbroker and her sister; after eventually confessing to the crime, he is sent to Siberia. The complexity of the book lies not in what happens factually, but in the analysis of the murderer's mind, his motives and final reasons for giving himself up to the police. The interest of the Notebooks lies – for those who like probing into literary method – in seeing Dostoevsky's various experiments in discovering the best way of expressing what he wanted to say. For those who enjoy that sort of thing, much that is revealed here is absorbing – for example, the fact that at one moment *Crime and Punishment* was going to be written in the first person. Dostoevsky finally decided that the autobiographical form was unsuitable – would not carry conviction – for much of the material that had to be analysed.

It has been suggested in the past, partly because of the remarks and behaviour of Dostoevsky himself, that his approach to writing was rather slapdash. The Notebooks show that, on the contrary, scenes and characters were worked out in the smallest detail. One marvels at the vitality which he brings to these notes. So far from being a happy-go-lucky writer, he was a very great craftsman.

Crime and Punishment is perhaps the first of Dostoevsky's novels clearly to reveal their two-sidedness, one aspect exploring human psychology – in which he was, of course, a pioneer of 'modern' writing – and the other expressing certain pet theories of his own. These theories can be briefly summarised in 'If there is no God you can do what you like,' and a detestation of Socialism in any of its manifestations. Naturally Dostoevsky is a great embarrassment to the Soviet authorities. Although his books voice opinions and illustrate ideas that stimulate (from their point of view) immeasurably more dangerous criticisms of the USSR than any of the unfortunate Sinayevsky and Daniel, sent to hard labour, they are impossible to suppress.

Raskolnikov owes something to Stendhal's Julien Sorel and Dostoevsky adds to the psychological portrait of his murderer by stating specifically in the Notebooks: 'His mother's caresses are a burden,' and 'Even thoughts of his mother are painful.' This, naturally, provides a step for the psychiatrically minded to see the woman murdered as a mother-figure. Without going all the way in this kind of criticism, the Notebooks do show Dostoevsky's extraordinary instinct for ideas later to be associated with Freud. Dostoevsky himself said that his approach was no more than a 'higher realism', which, rendered as 'Surrealism', makes him a scarcely less remarkable innovator.

Crime and Punishment offers Dostoevsky's first 'saint', Sonya Marmeladov, a prostitute, and Svidrigaylov, a satanic figure, to find ultimate expression in Stavrogin of *The Devils (The Possessed)*. The Notebook contains various preparatory sketches for this couple:

> Sonia, always meek, always without humour, always serious and quiet; then suddenly she would burst out laughing terribly at trifles and this affected the young man as gracious.
>
> Svidrigaylov's conversation about the 16-year-old; how she deceived him and said she would be a good wife. N.B. 'What does happiness consist of?' asked Sonia. 'Happiness is Power,' he said.

We see in the Notebooks how Sonia and Svidrigaylov are gradually knocked into shape as characters, together with the comic figure, Lebezyatnikov, a nihilist, who was going to insist on his wife being unfaithful, if he ever married, and considered cleaning out cesspits 'more noble' than the activities of 'Raphael and Pushkin'.

Notebooks for Crime and Punishment,   1967
Fyodor Dostoevsky, edited and   *Daily Telegraph*
translated by Edward Wasiolek,
Chicago University Press.

III

The Marxists had begun to attack Dostoevsky as a writer while he was still alive. The interesting (anonymous) introduction to Leonid Grossman's *Dostoevsky: A Biography* outlines the various changes in Soviet official attitude, after the Revolution, to the man Lenin (in 1913) had called 'the archobnoxious Dostoevsky'. At first Dostoevsky's works, though never actually banned, were published very selectively – only *Poor Folk, The Insulted and Injured, Crime and Punishment*. All were equipped with extensive commentaries, emphasising their portrayal of the oppressed masses in a capitalist society. Dostoevsky's name was rarely mentioned in textbooks.

By the mid-1920s this attitude had somewhat relaxed, and, perhaps because Dostoevsky's reputation was ever increasing abroad, a Soviet edition of his complete works, in thirteen volumes, was produced between 1926–30. By 1935, a Communist Party journalist with an eye on what was coming, wrote in *Pravda*, 'The novel *The Devils* is the filthiest libel against the Revolution,' and added that one should not 'open wide the gates of literary sewage . . . confidence in our young people does not under any circumstances release us from vigilance in that question.'

During the Stalin period even *The Insulted and Injured* was deemed a betrayal, because of its praise of meekness, and war was openly declared against Dostoevsky's 'canonization by the arms-bearers of foreign reaction'. Grossman, who had always been a Dostoevsky student, had to lay off. After the brief thaw of 1956, Dostoevsky was allowed back again, his status in Russia increasing sufficiently to allow celebration in 1971 of the 150th anniversary of his birth.

Leonid Grossman (1888–1965) was a professional literary critic who had made some name before the Revolution. His biography is therefore of interest in showing what could be said by 1962. A revised edition of the book appeared in Russia in the year of the biographer's death. Grossman had talks with Dostoevsky's second wife but nothing striking emerges from these. His biography is long, solid, fair, interpolated with no more than a reasonable number of pious references to the horrors of capitalism and free enterprise; emphasis on Tsarist repression obviously being double-edged, perhaps deliberately so.

Grossman's biography is not nearly so good a book as David Magarshack's *Dostoevsky* which, as it happened, appeared in this country in the same year, 1962, though no doubt Grossman had graver problems to contend with, as to what he might say. Two small variations between these books are that Grossman accepts the Dostoevskys' legend that their family was of noble and ancient origin. Magarshack from the evidence regards this as in the highest degree improbable.

Another small disparity is that, when Dostoevsky was arrested in 1849 for conspiracy (woken from sleep by the police), Grossman says: 'A major of the gendarmerie uttered these words in tones of great solemnity, and then, changing to an ordinary tone of voice.' But, in his own account, Dostoevsky himself (quoted by Magarshack) twice emphasises the extreme gentleness and sympathy of the (lieutenant-colonel) police officer's 'tone of voice'.

One of Grossman's oddest suggestions is that Stavrogin, in *The*

Devils, is to some extent modelled on the Russian revolutionary, Bakunin. Admittedly Bakunin was a remarkable man, but surely this is rather like saying that Steerforth (to whom Stavrogin may well owe something, Dostoevsky being a great Dickens enthusiast) is modelled on Robert Owen, the philanthropic socialist cotton-spinner.

Dostoevsky thought that the sentimental half-baked 'progressive' inevitably fathered the child of destruction and violence. He illustrated this theory literally, in *The Devils* by his picture of Mr Verkhovensky – one of the great comic figures of European literature –whose son, Peter Verkhovensky, while accepted by local society and more or less having an affair with the provincial governor's wife, is organising a Nihilist cell, and arranging a political murder.

In Ronald Hingley's brilliant study *The Undiscovered Dostoevsky*, he refers to Virginia Woolf's astonishing judgment that Dostoevsky had 'little sense of humour'. It would be scarcely wider of the mark to suggest that Dickens suffered from that, but true that some relaxation from total seriousness is occasionally required, too, from those who write about Dostoevsky. In this respect Magarshack and Hingley are to be seen at an advantage over Grossman's unrelieved seriousness, at the same time it must be recognised that Grossman was handling dynamite, and, in the light of that, has done an honourable and thorough job.

Dostoevsky: A Biography, Leonid   1974
Grossman, translated by Mary   *Daily Telegraph*
Mackler, Allen Lane.

IV

Joseph Frank is justifiably determined to avoid sensationalism in what is at times an undoubtedly sensational life story, and he plays down Dostoevskian family relationships almost to the extent of suggesting happy home circumstances. Certainly they all wrote each other high-flown letters though one suspects that too much weight should not be allowed to these. In this family field Frank does, however, introduce (in a postscript note) a recently investigated matter that is of great interest. Although a relatively poor man when it came to ready money Army-Doctor Dostoevsky had managed to make himself a landowner, and, owing to his disagreeable behaviour towards his serfs, some of them are supposed to have murdered him in an even more disagreeable manner. Certainly Dostoevsky himself seems to have believed that. There now appears reason to think that Dr Dostoevsky died of apoplexy, and that a neighbour, anxious to acquire the property at a cheap rate, put it about that a horde of serfs had murdered his fellow-landowner. If that had been proved, most of the estate serfs would have been deported to Siberia, and the land would have gone for a song. Such an invention is almost more Dostoevskian in conception that an actual murder.

Much against their will Dr Dostoevsky sent two of his sons as cadets to the military Academy of Engineers. Frank pointed out that the education there was good, much wider than might be expected. Dostoevsky, at the age of sixteen or seventeen, was by now pondering the deeper problems of human existence, and already wrote with extraordinary facility. He soon got out of the army, and, although he had a hard time of it, managed to establish himself as a writer. When only twenty-four he made a hit with his first novel *Poor Folk* not a great work, but showing traces of what was to come. Inordinately vain, Dostoevsky's success went to his head, and he became most unpopular with other Russian writers, on the whole a backbiting crowd. In any case, Frank makes two points about this period: that it is sometimes forgotten how capable a journalist Dostoevsky was; and, however regrettable as a matter of artistry was Dostoevsky's caricature of Turgenev in *The Devils*, Turgenev had, in fact, lampooned Dostoevsky in print first.

Frank gives the clearest account I have yet read of Dostoevsky's political situation as a young man, and the circumstances that led up to his arrest and exile to Siberia; the arrest being the final incident of this first volume. The generally accepted Dostoevsky myth – propagated to some extent by himself – is that the influential critic Belinsky (who certainly gave him a lot of help as a young writer) had turned him from a devout Christian to a Socialist and atheist. His experiences in Siberia brought him back to Christianity, and an extreme nationalism which included the creed that Russia should dominate all the Slav countries and ultimately the whole world.

This story has been accepted by Christians as turning Dostoevsky's own life into a kind of parable; by Soviet criticism, as linking him with what Frank calls 'that Golden Legend of Russian history', a unified revolutionary tradition (even though Dostoevsky subsequently betrayed it), and incidentally support for limitless Russian predatory expansion.

The author indicates that Dostoevsky's beliefs at this period were far less clear-cut: a semi-religious utopian socialism (however disapproved of by Belinsky) never quite uprooted – certain forms of Slavophilism always lurking in the background. Nevertheless, Dostoevsky's mind was not made up between such mutually exclusive beliefs. In a sense this all came to a head in the 'Petrashevsky Conspiracy', of which Frank gives an absorbing account.

Dostoevsky is sometimes represented as having been arrested for frequenting what was little more than a mild discussion group, mainly interested in socialist theory. To some extent that was true, but within the group, existed secret elements that believed in terrorist action, the aim in fact to establish a Communist dictatorship. Indeed, it would be true to say that few if any of the members believed in 'democracy' as understood in the West. How deeply Dostoevsky was committed to violent action is not wholly clear from the evidence, but one might suppose considerably. The leader of the Terrorist faction (Petrashevsky was only the group's host) was a striking figure named Speshnev, aristocratic, rich, womanising, dominating, who unquestionably contributed a great deal in *The Devils* to the character of Stavrogin. One is greatly struck in Frank's book by how much of the Petrashevsky situation Dostoevsky used in that novel twenty years later.

Dostoevsky: The Seeds of Revolt,   1977
1821–1849, Joseph Frank, Robson.   *Daily Telegraph*

V

This second part of Joseph Frank's projected five-volume study of Dostoevsky begins just after the writer's arrest when he was twenty-eight years old. The Secret Police had clamped down on those involved in the Petrashevsky affair. It takes him through four years' incarceration as a convict in Siberia; then a further four years in the army; closing with Dostoevsky's first marriage and return to Petersburg. Frank's detailed and scholarly handling imparts an element of newness, even positive excitement as to what is going to happen.

One of the points made in the first volume was that at least some of those who met at Petrashevsky's excellent dinners were not members of a harmless discussion-group with mildly socialist leanings but ruthless conspirators bent on replacing Tsarist rule with something perhaps not so very different from the Soviet regime. To what extent Dostoevsky was associated with the violent element is hard to estimate; much of the fascination of Frank's work is in the close examination of what Dostoevsky thought then. How much of that was changed by Siberian exile?

Dostoevsky had eight months of imprisonment in the Peter and Paul fortress before being subjected to the fearful mock execution and packed off in shackles to serve his four-year sentence. During the interrogations he behaved – unlike some of his fellows – with considerable firmness, confusing his judges by oblique answers. Having already served briefly as officer of Engineers he was the first of those blindfolded, tied to the stakes to grasp that he was not going to be shot when he heard the drums beat Retreat; a characteristically dramatic touch.

Dostoevsky set off for Siberia in surprisingly good spirits in spite of the hardships of the journey. He is on record as imagining that he would meet more 'worth-while' people among the convicts than he had been in the habit of associating with. That was the consequence of swallowing whole the romantic utopian socialism of novelists like Victor Hugo and George Sand. Perhaps not surprisingly this turned out to be far from the case. The convicts at Omsk were perfectly detestable. They also did everything they could to make life additionally uncomfortable for any prisoners of a higher class.

Frank analyses the complicated question of the changes that actually took place in Dostoevsky's point of view after emerging from captivity, changes which he himself so strongly emphasised. These were, roughly speaking, renewed faith in Christianity, reverence for the Tsar, devotion to the convicts in spite of their behaviour, belief in the Messianic mission of Russia. It is never easy at any given stage of his life to define precisely what Dostoevsky thought, not least because one of his great contributions as a novelist was to illustrate the contradictions of the human personality of which he himself provided a good working example. In relation to these changes Frank comments that Dostoevsky seems never altogether to have abandoned the Christian faith; that he had no theoretical objection whatever to autocracy (what he hated was serfdom); that anyway towards the end a few individual convicts (one of whom Dostoevsky taught to read) were relatively amenable (though they did not stop stealing from him nor from each other); and he always seems to have been in favour of Russia increasing her frontiers at the expense of border countries like Poland.

Dostoevsky's novels display such a peculiar hatred of Poles that it might be wondered whether the Polish political exiles imprisoned with him (with several of whom he was on friendly terms) had in some manner caused him to feel inferior (possibly by doing him a kindness). Prison had demonstrated to Dostoevsky that the convicts were at their best at private work to earn a few kopecks which as Frank says, 'guaranteed the individual a sense of self-possession and moral autonomy'. Such employment acted as a means of instinctive self-preservation against the destructive forces of prison life.

This made Dostoevsky a passionate antagonist of socialism, although the then popular theories of Fourier shared to some extent Dostoevsky's own taste for absolute government. Like the rich Russian socialist expatriate Herzen, Dostoevsky believed it an advantage to Russia that contracts and codified laws had never been properly understood there; an attitude which also made him intensely antagonistic to the Church of Rome.

On being released Dostoevsky had tried to be sent on active service in the Caucasus, which might have proved a step towards pardon, but he was ordered to serve as a private for an indeterminate period in a Siberian regiment of the line stationed at Semipalatinsk, a town of great dreariness in Central Asia. Semipalatinsk undoubtedly contributed a great deal to 'our town' as portrayed, at perhaps a slightly superior level, in the great novels.

House of the Dead, Dostoevsky's comparatively neglected account of convict life, has been thoroughly examined with excellent effect by Frank. But in Semipalatinsk, we begin to feel ourselves at home with the familiar Dostoevsky, at first as an infantry private becoming a social asset at local parties, and eventually being promoted ensign. He falls madly in love with his first wife, whose first husband was still alive. She was born Maria Dimitrieva Constant, not a Russian surname. (Could she have been a remote relation of Benjamin Constant whose Swiss family included many soldiers of fortune?) At last they get to Petersburg, but already there are signs of marital trouble.

Dostoevsky: The Years of Ordeal,
1850–1859, Joseph Frank, Robson.

1984
Daily Telegraph

VI

In 1859 Dostoevsky's ten years in Siberia ended, he returned to Petersburg passionately anxious to get to work again, plunge into journalism which he loved, write the novels germinating in his mind. The comparatively short period under examination here covers the time before he began to produce the works for which he is most famous, but when events of decisive importance in his future career took place.

Dostoevsky was a man of inextinguishable energy. That is the essential thing to understand about him. To have undergone what he had in prison, suffer from epileptic fits, find his marriage in an increasingly rocky condition, have to make an entirely new start in his profession, might have daunted some people; not Dostoevsky. He started a magazine, most of which he tended to write himself, also became secretary of what would in this country have been the Royal Literary Fund. To raise funds for this cause he took part (as did Turgenev) in an amateur performance of Gogol's *The Inspector-General*, where Dostoevsky played the corrupt Postmaster in a manner universally acclaimed.

The House of the Dead now came out, first in magazine parts. Naturally it had to pass the censor. It is of interest that the second instalment was at first held up because the authorities thought it gave too attractive a picture of prison life in Russia. The book would threaten a positive incitement to crime. It would be difficult to find a better example of bureaucratic literary criticism.

Frank steers the reader through the appalling jungle of Russian politics of the 1860s in the most skilful manner, relating the personalities and parties concerned to Dostoevsky's own position – not at all an easy task, as Dostoevsky himself was always changing, at least adjusting his views: except that he took a stand on supporting the Russian Orthodox Church and was always violently anti-Roman Catholic. It might be thought, not altogether unreasonably, that these squabbles between Westerners, Pan-Slavs, Radicals, Nihilists, Feminists, and so on, taking place more than a century ago, have lost their immediate impact. Nothing could be further from the truth. They are all the problems that beset the Soviet Union – and everyone else who deals with the USSR – now, if in different forms. To attempt to understand Russians there is no better guide than much that is to be found here.

As well as *The House of the Dead* and torrents of journalism, Dostoevsky produced *The Insulted and Injured* and that curious work *Notes from the Underground*. The former, a try-out for more impressive novels to come, was full of melodrama and crime, material for a newspaper serial, blended with what were to develop into all the typical Dostoevskian characters and situations.

Notes from the Underground has been compared with Diderot's *Neveu de Rameau* (which Dostoevsky may well have read), an anti-hero depicted who was meant to outrage in the manner of Defoe's *The Shortest Way with Dissenters*, or Swift's *A Modest Proposal*. As usual, irony was not understood, and Frank emphasises this has been the fate of *Notes from the Underground*, which was intended by the author as a parody.

To turn to Dostoevsky's private life, he and his first wife were attached to each other, but not getting on well at this time. Her health was bad (she was tubercular) and finally she died during the years Frank's book covers. Dostoevsky's devoted brother Mikhail also died, a disastrous loss. He left a pile of debts incurred when he had been trying to run the magazine in Dostoevsky's absence.

Meanwhile Dostoevsky himself was going through some bad experiences with Apollinaria (Polina) Suslova, prototype of several frightful girls who were to figure in the later novels. Suslova, an emancipated young woman of the epoch, had a story (no better, no worse, than the average, says Frank) accepted by Dostoevsky for the magazine and, although he was considerably older than she, it was not long before they were having an affair. Dostoevsky in any case wanted a trip abroad (although intensely xenophobic and convinced that Russia was superior to any other country) both for rest, and to avoid creditors. He arranged to meet Suslova in Paris.

Hardly had Suslova arrived there before she met, and immediately fell for, a good-looking young Spaniard called Salvador. Dostoevsky was greeted at his hotel with a letter saying all was over. Suslova then heard Salvador was ill with typhus; she must not come to see him as that would cause scandal. Walking in the street a day or two later, she ran into Salvador, who, of course, was not suffering from typhus at all. Accordingly, Suslova went to Italy with Dostoevsky, who was still mad about her, but only as his 'sister'. It was all exactly like one of his novels.

Dostoevsky: The Stir of Liberation, 1860–1865, Joseph Frank, Robson.

1987
Daily Telegraph

GUSTAVE FLAUBERT

I

'What a man Balzac would have been if only he'd known how to write!'
said Flaubert in a letter to his mistress, Louise Colet. This is perhaps
the briefest, clearest way of expressing Flaubert's own literary point of
view. Enid Starkie takes her fences at a gallop, producing a well-
arranged, readable, individual account of Flaubert's career up to the
publication of *Madame Bovary*. This makes a good division, because
Flaubert's life altered considerably after that event. The reader is
accordingly not bothered with a lot of material of rather a different sort
from the earlier years.

A striking thing about Gustave Flaubert (1821–80) was his extraordinary maturity as a child, contrasted with the comparatively slow
start he made as a writer – slow enough for an ambitious friend like
Maxime Du Camp to accuse him, one of the most industrious of men, of
sloth. Flaubert seems to have decided to be a writer at the age of about
five, actually getting down to it at ten, and by eleven or twelve already
talking of disillusionment and suicide. This did not prevent him from
being a ringleader in various school rebellions, incidents that remind
one that the insurgent students of today have not entirely invented
rebellion as a line. Enid Starkie's book emphasises the consequences of
Flaubert's seizure, apparently of an epileptic kind, when he was
twenty-two. Although he was on good terms with his father, it was this
attack that resigned his parents to allowing him to give up the Law and
settle down to a career as an author.

Much is known about Flaubert; much, too, remains mysterious. As a
young man he was not only unusually intelligent, but also tall,
handsome, attractive. When, at the age of eighteen, he was sent on a
holiday to Marseilles he was at once seduced by a woman of thirty-five.
The incident was followed up on the woman's part by passionate
love-letters, and all his life Flaubert himself regarded it as something
significant in forming his character. It set the pattern of the 'older
woman'. One might expect that some sort of ease in dealing with the
opposite sex would follow, but this seems not to have been the case.
How much was the nervous disorder to blame? How much was that
disorder the consequence of venereal disease, admittedly contracted in
Paris?

It has been suggested – one would say without very good reason, taking the overall picture – that Flaubert lived a drab life. However, allowing for the moment that he did, one cannot fail to be struck by the extraordinary intensity he brought to whatever he did, drab or not. This intensity comes out in his human relationships, in spite of his almost pathological horror of finding himself too deeply involved with a woman. The idea of marriage, still more of children, was abhorrent to him, though one agrees with Enid Starkie that he would have made a kind father.

Enid Starkie sees an element of homosexuality in Flaubert's deep friendships with men. Certainly he wrote letters to men that are sentimental, almost passionate. All the same, I find it hard to agree in any but the most 'subconscious' sense. There never seems to have been the slightest suspicion of a homosexual relationship of a merely sexual kind. His close attachments to other men were always to those with whom he shared red-hot intellectual interests. As he felt strongly about intellectual matters, he felt these relationships strongly. That would be my own reading of the case, though Enid Starkie may know more than she puts on paper.

Flaubert's *Intimate Notebook* to which he commits his eighteen-year-old thoughts, has been mislaid by his heirs, but a typewritten copy was made of its contents in the 1930s. This is now published. Francis Steegmuller points out that the themes which preoccupied Flaubert at this age were those that pursued him all his life. There is a youthful try-out for the blood-soaked pages of *Salammbô* here and Sade already appears in his role of philosopher and psychologist, which one is apt to think of as a 'modern' discovery.

Flaubert: The Making of the Master,   1967
Enid Starkie, Weidenfeld &   *Daily Telegraph*
Nicolson.
Gustave Flaubert: Intimate
Notebook, 1840–41, translated by
Francis Steegmuller, W. H. Allen.

I I

One is apt to think of Flaubert as working away at Croisset, bored to death with the neighbours, making an occasional trip to Paris to see literary friends or visit a brothel, in general, wholly given over to writing his books. That was not so. In the latter half of the novelist's life, after the publication of *Salammbô*, he was greatly taken up with social life, which he much enjoyed, getting on surprisingly well with Napoleon III, and becoming a close friend of Princess Mathilde. This Bonaparte princess (who figures in Proust) seems to have been a rather tiresome woman without intelligence or taste, but she was kind to

Flaubert. In the same mistaken way, one also thinks of Second Empire
and Third Republic Paris as a city crowded with writers and literary
life; but, on the verge of the Franco-Prussian war, when he was
approaching fifty, Flaubert complains that he does not know one single
soul among his friends with whom he could spend an afternoon
discussing poetry.

By an odd chance, when *Flaubert the Master* turned up for review, I
was halfway through a reread of *L'Education Sentimentale*. Flaubert
looked upon *L'Education Sentimentale* as his most successful work, though
there was a good deal of critical grumbling about it at the time. I am
interested that Enid Starkie regards Flaubert's opinion as that now
generally held.

That *L'Education Sentimentale* is Flaubert's best book, I heartily agree,
but I should have thought that many critics nowadays would adopt the
slightly doubtful approach of Enid Starkie herself, who complains that
the hero – or anti-hero – Frédéric, is 'ineffectual', the other characters
in the novel 'unpleasant'. This seems so typical of a lot of academic
literary criticism that one wonders whether it does not derive from what
is basically a dislike for reading novels at all – at least a kind of yearning
for novel writing with the moral viewpoint of, say, Walter Scott. A
moment's thought never seems to be spared for what the author is
trying to do, still less a ray of humour, in which Flaubert himself was by
no means deficient.

One of Flaubert's exploratory accomplishments is that he grasped
that 'ineffective' people, in terms of art, are just as interesting as
'effective' ones, while Frédéric's romantic passion, Mme Arnoux – who
surely 'lives' in the novel as a person – would have required no
comment, if she had been not only good-looking, but witty, sexy,
energetic, good at devising places for assignation, at methods of keeping
her husband quiet and preventing him from going bankrupt. Is it not
precisely because she can claim none of these things that Frédéric's
lifelong romantic passion (and final disillusion) is worth investigating?

Flaubert looked on his own contemporaries, those who were young in
the 1840s, as a 'Lost Generation'. He deliberately allows the novel to be
dated with local allusions, yet certainly many sequences of it might well
have been placed in London of the 1920s – the fancy-dress party, for
example – and I have little doubt that much remains equally true
today. The political talk is astonishingly up to date. Henry James oddly
thought *L'Education Sentimentale* was 'dead', a fate that far more often
threatens his own novels. One is surprised that James does not level a
more damaging technical criticism – unexpected in connection with
Flaubert – that there is a certain arbitrariness in the manner in which
the narrative is from time to time told from a point of view other than
Frédéric's.

Enid Starkie won't hear a word against Flaubert as a man, and there can be no doubt that he had many qualities of niceness and kindness, not always characteristic of his profession. He literally ruined himself financially by the good nature he showed towards his odious niece and her shady husband.

The objection to this devoted approach to Flaubert is that the reader has constantly to remind himself that he is hearing about a great novelist, with all the complicated inner workings of a man of strong imagination, not a jolly old buffer, who for some reason gets caught up from time to time with a lot of strange people, some of them with unpleasant habits. As it were to offset this view of her subject – of which the author herself seems a little aware – she emphasises Flaubert's taste for pornography, and refers, in so many words, to his homosexuality. When I read her earlier volume, *Flaubert: the Making of the Master,* I thought the imputation of homosexuality thin, unless she knew more than appeared in her book. Here there is mention of letters to a friend beginning 'vieux péderaste', with fantasies about the subject, but the joking tone suggests to me far more a preoccupation with what Flaubert regarded as comically exotic behaviour, rather than personal practice. After all, *Salammbô* is undeniably sadistic, but there is no evidence that Flaubert went further than writing, so far as sadism is concerned.

Flaubert the Master: A   1971
Critical and Biographical Study, 1856–   *Daily Telegraph*
1880, Enid Starkie, Weidenfeld &
Nicolson.

III

When Gustave Flaubert was twenty he made a tour of the Near East with his friend Maxime Du Camp. He kept a diary. Later, when he came to write his Carthaginian novel *Salammbô* and the revised version of *The Temptation of Saint Anthony* he drew on these notes for local colour. Francis Steegmuller has abstracted the portion of the diary which deals with Egypt, included certain extracts from Du Camp's travel books, written on the same subject years later, and added short informative passages to reinforce the narrative. The result of all this is an enjoyable work, produced in a handy form, which might be taken by any tourist to Egypt with advantage today; Flaubert went to most of the places normally still visited. It was all a little different in 1849–50, but not all that different. Abu Simbel, now moved to the top of the hill, was only just appearing above the sand. The temple of Isis at Philae did not yet emerge from a sheet of water. Arab slave-dealers floated down the Nile with their cargoes of Negro slaves.

Some of this material has, of course, already appeared, but a certain amount remained unpublished until quite recently, even in France. For example, Flaubert's experiences with the noted courtesan, Kuchuk Hanem ('Pretty Little Princess', or possibly just 'Dancing Woman') at Esna are well known to Flaubert fans. Here we are given a blow-by-blow account of the night they spent together – and more casual encounters – with quite a few other items in the way of fresh trimmings to the sex life of the great novelist. It was not surprising he returned home with health permanently impaired. This side of Flaubert is not to be disregarded. He was oddly geared. Even by French standards, the passionate letters he wrote to his mother stand out. When he found no letter from her on arrival at Aswan, he wrote: 'Perhaps no one thinks of me any more . . . I am too angry to collect my thoughts.' The fuss made by both his mother and himself when he left on this oriental journey would have been excessive had Flaubert been straight on his way to execution. The other side of these maternal sentimentalities was addiction to prostitutes, bawdy jokes and fresh experiences of any sort, preferably macabre.

Du Camp was a good foil to Flaubert. Somewhat richer, in one sense more sophisticated, intelligent, a competent stylist, he was without anything approaching Flaubert's writer's grasp of a situation; nor, it might be added, Flaubert's humour. Du Camp thought Flaubert was bored much of the trip. Flaubert certainly does at times complain. That did not mean he was not piling up stuff for subsequent use. Du Camp was in any case writing much later, and there is reason to suppose he is not always reliable in detail. It should be borne in mind that travelling in Egypt at this period was tough and dangerous. Du Camp was an early photographer. His pictures, some of which are reproduced here, are excellent, including one of Flaubert (who would hardly ever allow himself to be photographed) at long range, wearing Nubian costume, in the garden of their Cairo hotel. One of the proprietors of that hotel was called Bouvaret, the sound of the name later to be immortalised in *Madame Bovary*.

Steegmuller includes among the illustrations a reproduction of Delacroix's picture 'Women of Algiers' (1834) in the Louvre. He points out the extraordinary similarity of Delacroix's scene to that described by Flaubert, when he and Du Camp visited a prostitute called La Triestina in Cairo.

Little street behind the Hôtel d'Orient. We are taken upstairs into a large room. The divan projects out over the street; on both sides of the divan, small windows giving on the street, which cannot be shut. Opposite the divan, a large window without frame or glass; through it we see a palm-tree. On a large divan to the left, two women sitting cross-legged; on a kind of mantelpiece, a night-light and a bottle of raki.

La Triestina comes down, a small woman, blonde, red-faced. The first of the two women – thick-lipped, snub-nosed, gay, brutal, '*Un poco matta, Signor*', said La Triestina; the second, large black eyes, straight nose, tired plaintive air, probably the mistress of some European in Cairo. She understands two or three words of French and knows what the Legion of Honour is. La Triestina was violently afraid of the police, begged us to make no noise. Abbas Pasha, who is fond only of men, makes things difficult for women; in this brothel it is forbidden to dance or play music.

The woman who led them to Kuchuk Hanem

was thin, with a narrow forehead, her eyes painted with antimony, a veil passed over her head and held by her elbows. She was followed by a pet sheep, whose wool was painted in spots with yellow henna. Around its nose was a black velvet muzzle. It was very woolly, its feet like those of a toy sheep, and it never left its mistress.

Such descriptions put over vividly what they saw. There is a strong tradition of French interest in the Near East, added to Flaubert's powerful romanticism for all that was savage or exotic – a romanticism which, as a writer, he was so severely to discipline. Even so, one is at times impressed at the way in which violence, eroticism, disease, squalor, never seem to pall when in oriental shape. To say that is not to doubt for a second the genuineness, both of fact and sensibility, of what Flaubert records. He conveys none of the feeling (at times found in contemporary writers) that some hair-raising incident has been put in purely for effect.

Flaubert in Egypt, translated   1972
and edited by Francis Steegmuller,   *Daily Telegraph*
Bodley Head.

THE BROTHERS GONCOURT

I

Edmond de Goncourt (1822–96) and Jules de Goncourt (1830–70) are a strange phenomenon in the French literary world of the nineteenth century. They have been written about extensively. André Billy's biography may be called definitive; Robert Baldick supplies an excellent summary of their lives and works. The two Goncourts wrote as one. Their historical research, their novels, their Journal, their art collection, each was conducted in unison. They lived together, at times shared the same mistress, smiled or frowned at the same moment, in general, presented a completely united front to the world, brought to an end only by the younger brother's death.

Their stock-in-trade was various and original: French social history of the eighteenth and early nineteenth centuries: novels experimenting with the new element of 'realism': the re-establishment of painters like Watteau, Fragonard, and Boucher, who had fallen out of fashion: the introduction to the West of the art of Japan: and, above all, the Journal, which provides an account of the life lived by the two brothers, and an unrivalled picture of French literary society of the time. All this is described well, if at times a trifle diffusely, by Billy. We are given an excellent picture of the Goncourts' world, their work, their relaxations, their foibles. At the same time, we feel that too little attempt is made to give an adequate answer to the question: why were they like that?

Perhaps that question is impossible to answer. Contemporary biography has certainly had its fill of psychological explanations. Even so, some effort seems required to interpret the behaviour of such an unusual pair of brothers. To begin with, the Goncourts were greatly preoccupied by their 'aristocratic' birth. This, in itself, seems odd in the circumstances. The Huot family, to which they belonged, had taken the suffix 'de Goncourt' in 1786, when a great-grandfather bought the seigneurie of a small village in the Meuse valley. Their father had had a distinguished career as an officer in the Napoleonic army. Another relation was French Minister to the Vatican. It was all perfectly respectable and above-board; only not very exciting. The family, it is true, was not at all well off, which no doubt increased an emphasis on its own good standing.

The approach of the two brothers to the opposite sex is also

418

unexpected. In one sense they seem to have been almost an old-maidish couple, dominated by a vigorous servant who looked after them, cooking their meals, tucking them up in bed at night, dealing with their correspondence when they were away from home. They were both attracted and repelled by women. Attraction took the form of visits to brothels, and affairs of a decidedly squalid kind; their hate was brought to boiling point when they found, on the death of the servant who had been a kind of Nanny to them, that she had been robbing them right and left, and living a life even more dissipated than their own.

They were kept going, not by any external affections, or even much worldly success, so much as by their feelings for each other, and their deep devotion to art. As Jules de Goncourt wrote, when he was eighteen or nineteen:

I have made a very firm resolution and nothing will make me change it, neither sermons, nor good advice, even from yourself whose friendship I have fully experienced. *I shall do nothing* to employ an expression which is incorrect but in general use.

If producing some forty books can be so termed, they both stuck to this resolution. When Edmond de Goncourt was living on an income of 1,200 fr. (even in the 1840s, not a fortune, say £60) he was buying water-colours by Boucher and drawings by Watteau. For a rare edition of *Télémaque* he paid 400 fr. – a third of his income.

Self-satisfied and pernickety, the brothers were also in their way great. Their memorial is the Journal. In this diary they do not attempt to hide their own failings. They may be unfair to others, but they have a left a superb tapestry of their age. The influence of the Goncourts is to be found in all directions. Zola – whom they detested – learned a great deal from them. Their interest in sex and nervous diseases heralds much that was to follow in our own day in the field of psychological research. Proust was devoted to their pages and amusingly parodied their style. André Billy points out that one of their flaws as novelists – perhaps one should say as a novelist – is to place too much reliance on the documentary side of what they observed. They became slaves to actual incidents they had seen, or words literally spoken; both of which, in a novel, must be adapted to the imaginative rhythm of the narrative.

The Goncourt Brothers,
André Billy, translated by
Margaret Shaw, Deutsch.
The Goncourts, Robert Baldick,
Bowes.

1960
Daily Telegraph

II

The complete version of the Goncourt Journal, which must now run to about twenty volumes, appeared in France only three years ago. Here we have the whole work boiled down to 400 pages by Robert Baldick. He has done a brilliant job of selection. General ideas, personal preoccupations, encounters with famous people, visits to brothels, are balanced in such a way that one closes the book feeling as if a panorama of nineteenth-century Paris had been displayed in a film of startling originality. The diarists have in a high degree that peculiar power of making you see what they describe.

Although so quintessentially French, the Goncourts, one feels, might also have existed in an English incarnation. These two old-maidish brothers, devoted to each other, immensely conscious of being 'gentlemen', dedicated to the arts, at odds with the rest of the world, sensual yet chilly in their sexual tastes, could have found some parallel on our own side of the Channel.

Edmond de Goncourt was the stolider, more serious. Jules, lively and frivolous. All the same they were so much in tune stylistically that it is impossible to say which contrived what passages.

The Goncourt Journal cannot be accepted as speaking the absolute truth about every subject mentioned. The entries should be thought of as the most amusing sort of dinner-table conversation – alas, all too rarely encountered – in which the speaker is highly intelligent, passionately interested in life and literature, not at all discreet, able to express himself briefly and well. It is not the evidence of a witness speaking on oath. For example, Balzac is described as having a mistress of seventy, a former lady-in-waiting to Marie-Antoinette. Baldick points out in a note that the lady in question was the daughter of one of that Queen's ladies-in-waiting, that she was forty-five when Balzac, aged twenty-three, had his affair with her, and she died at fifty-nine. In the same way, we are told in 1865 that the Duc de Morny, Napoleon III's illegitimate half-brother, possessed a cabinet of photographs of his unclothed mistresses; but in 1886 attention is drawn to Morny's particular prejudice against a state of nature.

However, these are small matters beside the overwhelming impression that we are hearing in general what actually happened, even if the story is repeated in the personal idiosyncratic manner of the narrator. After all, that is true of all good stories. The scraps of reported dialogue the Goncourts give from time to time are especially convincing.

It would be possible to embroider endlessly on the various aspects of the Goncourt Journal. One thing that strikes the reader is that these years, the second half of the nineteenth century, were the period when Frenchmen acquired the stamp by which they are thought of in other countries today. It was the Second Empire which offered – to use a favourite contemporary catch-word – this image, a caricature which needs constant modification. The diary helps to show how the caricature came into being; also where it should be scaled down.

An an example of Edmond de Goncourt's shrewdness, he noted in 1895, the year before he died, when boys climbed trees to shout abuse at Dreyfus during his public military degradation:

> This provided me with the opportunity to say, with regard to that poor wretch, that I was not convinced of his guilt, that the judgments of journalists were the judgments of little boys up in the trees.

This was the view of a man by no means a professional humanitarian, or even at all times a confirmed anti-anti-Semite.

Some of the Journal was published in Edmond de Goncourt's lifetime. Not surprisingly, these extracts gave a lot of offence. No doubt there was an element of Goncourt getting his own back for the fearful slatings his novels and plays often received at the hands of the critics. At the same time, it is hard to dismiss Goncourt's contention that, although he might draw attention to the wants of others, he made no effort to hide his own failings. The picture he gives of himself may not at times be specially attractive; at the same time he does not indulge in orgies of self-examination and confession which are so often merely a form of self-adulation.

One notices a certain change of tone during the last twenty years of his life. Earlier on, the brothers were at pains to insist that, much as they needed women, neither of them had ever been in love for more than a day or two – a state they shared with Flaubert and Zola. In the later pages, Edmond unbends a little. At times he is almost sentimental when he thinks of the past.

There are innumerable splendid stories. Flaubert quotes one of the reviews of *Madame Bovary* in which the critic ended with the words: 'How can anyone allow himself to write in such an ignoble style when the throne is occupied by the greatest master of the French language, the Emperor.'

Or this:

> Brown, the painter of horses, told me this story about Pointel, the very Christian editor of an illustrated paper . . . Pointel sent for Brown to do some woodcuts for his paper, and asked him what he painted.
>
> 'Why, horses,' said Brown.
>
> 'Horses!' Pointel strode feverishly twice round his office and came back to Brown.

'Horses!' he repeated. 'Horses lead to whores. Whores lead to the death of the family. There will be no horses in my paper.'

Alphonse Daudet's wit is constantly recorded. Daudet said that 'Renan's brain was like a deconsecrated cathedral, full of piles of wood, bales of straw, and heaps of assorted lumber but retaining its religious architecture.' Mme Daudet commented that Mme Zola looked 'like an old doll in the window of a bankrupt toy shop'. Both ladies had rather a rough time with their respective husbands.

Pages from the Goncourt Journal, edited and translated by Robert Baldick, Oxford University Press.

1962
Daily Telegraph

LEO TOLSTOY

I

About halfway through *Tolstoy and the Novel*, I began to wonder whether we have a better literary critic than John Bayley. To write in a stimulating manner about Tolstoy at this stage is not an easy thing to achieve. Bayley brings this off with such good effect that by the end of the book one is pondering about his own critical method almost as much as about Tolstoy's characteristics as a great novelist – anyway at first sight – is his 'ordinariness', which is somehow magnified to a colossal scale. On closer examination, it is true, this appearance can be shown to be a kind of illusion that results from his particular approach. Even so, objections as to mannerisms that can be put forward about Proust, Dickens, Flaubert, Dostoevsky, Joyce, Conrad, almost anyone else you like to name, cannot be levelled against Tolstoy.

If one picked up a book by any of the above novelists, for example, and opened a page at random, it would be unlikely that one would not immediately be struck by individualities of style. Tolstoy in a small dose, on the other hand, can convey positive banality – an impression, of course, dispelled when the deeper draught is swallowed. Tolstoy's really appalling vitality and virtuosity included producing two of the world's greatest novels in opposing genres – that is to say the vast panorama of *War and Peace* and the close examination of domestic life (and adultery) of *Anna Karenina*.

I have hitherto always felt the latter more interesting, but I suspect Bayley of preferring the former. He writes so compulsively on the subject that I was conscious of a distinct rearrangement of my own opinions. Bayley shows that the absence of *tone* in the telling of *War and Peace* – which might be expected to be a handicap to the narrative – in fact binds it together taking for granted the fact that 'all his characters see reality as it really is.'

'Reality' in this case is, of course, Tolstoy's own view, which he imposes on the reader by sheer brute force. Bayley, unlike so many critics, has an excellent grasp of the effect – and if necessary, the limitations – of certain techniques. It is common enough to read reviews in which the reviewer complains of some failing or omission in a given novel, but very rare for the same reviewer to relate this to what is probably an unavoidable requirement of that novel's technique.

War and Peace enjoys certain enormous advantages where 'telling a story' is concerned. The scene is set in the past, when what has happened is historically settled. The individual behaviour of the characters, especially the older ones, has taken on the quality of myth. The horrible people are, accordingly, less horrible, and violence less violent. In addition, there is the stylised social pattern of the Russian scene. Even so, Bayley points out that there are certain moments when Tolstoy becomes 'novelettish': certain moments, too, when we do not believe what he says. Bayley emphasises the novel's 'Voltairean, Mozartian, side; the fact that male sexuality is kept in the background – we are unconvinced by the 'debauchery' of Pierre and others – in a book that is in many ways a study of women and life seen from a woman's point of view. It was one of Tolstoy's favourite themes that there was a parallel between male sexual activity and the aggressions of war – of any violent action. *War and Peace* was to have ended with the Decembrists – the 'Officers' Plot' that was to have replaced Tsarist autocracy with a constitution. Finally Tolstoy decided against this material.

Many similar alterations in early drafts are referred to here, some of them of the greatest interest. For example, Anna Karenina, in an earlier abandoned version, was to have been a *jolie laide* 'far too plump – a little more and she would have seemed monstrous'. Shades of Garbo. It comes as almost a shock to be reminded that Tolstoy himself thought 'Russians did not know how to write novels,' and hardly put forward *War and Peace* as a novel. Henry James could not wholeheartedly approve, while others, like Percy Lubbock, were highly critical, as Bayley says, reminding 'us of eighteenth-century objections to Shakespeare's violations of dramatic rules'.

In the end Tolstoy himself rounded on his own novels, classing them in general as valueless. He was also a passionate antagonist of Shakespeare, whose works he held to have survived only through a series of extraordinary mischances. In short, these theories about art are a side of Tolstoy that admirers have to accept with regret. Since Russia, in her history as a country, has not produced a single painter of even the second rank, it is perhaps not surprising that Tolstoy admired pictures in the manner of 'The Letter From the Front'. This taste was based on his theory that all art should be organic: for instance, you should not go to Italy to see the galleries there, but (one imagines), it was all right – anyway at the time – for the Dutch School to paint evocative peasant interiors.

Tolstoy was no fool, so that his attack on art for art's sake at the same time lands some heavy fire on minor writers of his own period. All the same, it was a point of view that could only lead in the last resort, by its romantic, sentimental basis, to incongruous, even inane, judgments. These unhappy ventures into the critical field were all part of Tolstoy's effort to probe into 'what life was about'. The extraordinary thing is, one feels, that a man of his particular temperament should have become a novelist at all, much less one of the greatest. It is only necessary to consider the temperament of almost any other novelist.

John Bayley shows a mastery of his subject, indeed, a remarkable familiarity with Russian literature in general. Above all, one feels that he enjoys the books, does not, in the manner of some contemporary critics, treat Tolstoy as if he were a criminal for having written them at all. There are interesting side issues – the influence of *The Cossacks* on Hemingway, who himself refers to this book in *The Green Hills of Africa*, though it is hard to believe that he then read it for the first time.

One of the less fortunate legacies of Tolstoy to the Russian novel was a vast and casily adaptable *War and Peace* framework, which the less talented could use with comparative effect, but without any of Tolstoy's brilliant feeling for life. Bayley quotes an example of this parodied Tolstoyan manner from one of the works by the Nobel Prize winner, the Soviet novelist, Michael Sholokhov: 'Their comrades took their rifles and cartridges: dead men have no need of weapons.'

Tolstoy and the Novel,   1966
John Bayley, Chatto.   *Daily Telegraph*

II

After rereading *War and Peace* (or *Anna Karenina*, I cannot remember which, it is immaterial), a friend once remarked to me: 'Wonderful – but what a relief to get back to a Western mind like Balzac's.' Edward Crankshaw's book – concerned with Tolstoy as a novelist rather than sage – brought this comment back more than once.

Tolstoy was perhaps the most dominating personality of modern times. His status as a personality was, so to speak, quite separate from his literary gifts. From earlier boyhood he was determined to seek perfection, an ambition that made him totally self-engrossed. He was not interested in other people. Yet here there were two paradoxes: first, that he invented hundreds of believable characters; second, that he regarded himself as unremittingly serving his fellow men.

Tolstoy must always be seen in his own very special circumstances. He was an aristocrat. He was one of the foundations of the classical Russian novel – an aspect almost impossible to exaggerate in his country's development. He lived in the age of Russian expansionism, himself fighting in the Crimean War, which, as Crankshaw points out, checked Russia in her attempt to force a way to the Mediterranean. This war experience had a deep effect on Tolstoy who never ceased to regard Russians as a chosen race.

Crankshaw takes the bull – in this case Tolstoy – firmly by the horns, not attempting to deny his subject's gifts, also not concealing his many unpleasantnesses as a man – his self-righteousness, passion for power, lack of honesty with himself and others, craving for notoriety. There is a school of thought that regards any drawing attention to Tolstoy's failings as mean-minded and petty. If Tolstoy were merely a novelist that might be at least arguable. Again Balzac makes a good contrast. Not all Balzac's financial dealings were admirable, but they had nothing to do with his writing; nor was he always telling other people how they ought to behave. Telling other people how they ought to behave was Tolstoy's foremost activity. Accordingly, it must be important to know how Tolstoy behaved himself.

As a writer Tolstoy's abilities were immediately recognised. This did not prevent him from showing an uncontrollable envy for other writers, which rose to a peak of odiousness in dealing with Turgenev who was about ten years older than himself. The two novelists had an obsessive interest in each other. A row between them about Turgenev's plans for educating his illegitimate daughter caused Tolstoy to issue a challenge to a duel. He behaved thoroughly badly and Turgenev could hardly have behaved better. At that very moment Tolstoy was taking no steps whatever to educate his own illegitimate son, who subsequently became a coachman at Yasnaya Polyana, the Tolstoy country house.

Crankshaw remarks that Tolstoy judged himself by his aspirations, all other people by their deeds. In such considerations, sex played a spectacular part, Tolstoy being exceedingly highly sexed. The peasant girls and prostitutes who were normally his source of satisfaction always brought a subsequent sense of disgust. Tolstoy's reaction to this was that women were sinful to tempt him; finally, that all sex was wrong. When, at the age of thirty-three, his daughter wanted to marry an eminently respectable widower, Tolstoy wrote: 'I can understand that a depraved man may find satisfaction in marriage. But why a pure girl should want to get mixed up in such a business is beyond me.'

At the same time, Tolstoy believed that self-satisfaction was synonymous with happiness, and he loathed any suggestion of mystery in his life. This extreme literalness, allied to his own gigantic powers, was by no means a handicap as a writer. His ability to describe selected small incidents with a kind of inspired ordinariness builds up to the marvels of the long novels. Crankshaw, who does not involve himself in a lot of literary criticism, picks out the scene where Vronsky inspects his racehorse in *Anna Karenina* and, in *War and Peace*, the morning mists before the battle of Borodino – both descriptive masterpieces of Tolstoy's art. He also draws attention to the colossal powers of organisation shown in putting together the material for these novels.

Edward Crankshaw, who notes the essential propagandist side of

War and Peace as a limitation, makes an interesting comment on the paradox of Tolstoy disregarding all other individuals, yet inventing them in fiction with such skill. He suggests, convincingly, that Tolstoy is often dealing with projections of himself, in which his enormous self-interest provided him with almost infinite variety. Alternatively, Tolstoy produces greatly talented, yet in the last resort stylised, versions of what people are like. His characters (unlike those of, say, Dostoevsky) always remain consistent to their author's label.

One of the ironies of Tolstoy's insistence on the unbelievability of the plot of *King Lear* was, as has been pointed out (notably in an essay by George Orwell), that his own end at the Astapovo railway station waiting-room could scarcely have resembled more that of a modern Lear.

Tolstoy: The Making of a Novelist,   1974
Edward Crankshaw, Weidenfeld &   *Daily Telegraph*
Nicolson.

III

Dozens of books have been written about Tolstoy, but it is no bad thing that his story should from time to time be retold in contemporary terms. A. N. Wilson does this well. He has that touch of quirkiness particularly acceptable in dealing with Tolstoy, whose biography does not respond to over smooth treatment. Clearly, Tolstoy is to be considered in the top class among novelists. Having granted that, one may have reservations about his books. Wilson remarks that Tolstoy 'in his greatest fictitious creations seems second only to Shakespeare'. I would not agree. There is none of Shakespeare's subtlety – nor, to mention only two other writers, Proust's or Dostoevsky's. Tolstoy's stories unfold more like movies of genius, into which they have been very successfully fashioned, his characters always to be easily understood in popular terms.

Tolstoy as a politico-philosopher is a far more complex matter. After he wrote *Anna Karenina* (1876), Tolstoy had a kind of breakdown. This was perhaps not surprising after so great a release of energy, but his view that a novel should reflect the ups and downs of life, its pleasures and pains, altered to the conviction that everything he wrote should teach mankind how to live. This, as we know, led to extraordinary developments in both Tolstoy's public and private life. In the end, the Russian Government showed itself incapable of dealing with this unassimilable individual; his hitherto happy marriage became the prototype of unsatisfactory unions.

There is so much material in Tolstoy's life that, inevitably, different biographers emphasise different aspects. Wilson brings up various points sometimes forgotten. For instance, although Tolstoy belonged to a grand family, particularly on his mother's side (the Volkonskys), his branch was not particularly well off, such money as he had rapidly disappearing because of his own extremely rackety habits in respect of gambling and whoring. His books, selling well as they did, filled a financial need, which latterly he was always threatening to throw away.

Tolstoy went to Kazan University (also Lenin's Alma Mater), an academic backwater, where none of the undergraduates exchanged revolutionary ideas as they would have done in Moscow or St Petersburg. As a young man he read Sterne's *A Sentimental Journey* in French, being so bowled over by it that he determined to learn English. No doubt Tolstoy eventually spoke English well, but it should be mentioned that his first biographer (one hopes mistakenly) says that Tolstoy reported attending a lecture by Dickens on economics, when in fact Dickens was giving one of his famous readings, impersonations of Marley's Ghost, or the spirit of Christmas Past.

Tolstoy was for several years an officer in the Artillery, including service in the Crimean War. From time to time his goings-on resulted in contracting venereal disease, as most of his sexual encounters were with prostitutes. To this period of his life belongs the entry in his diary: 'I have never been in love with women . . . I have very often been in love with men.' His first act on getting married was to give his young wife the diaries to read, which was to cause a good deal of trouble later. Countess Tolstoy believed her husband had affairs with his innumerable disciples, some of them decidedly shady. In fact, nothing seems less likely, but the possibility added to the troubles of Tolstoy married life.

In reading about Tolstoy, one must constantly remind oneself that often he is simply being Russian. This certainly should be borne in mind regarding the behaviour of the characters in his novels, even if the recommendations may seem obvious. One of the most interesting speculations is that Soviet Russians – the national behaviour apt to remain much the same in changed circumstances – are no doubt behaving in just the same sort of way.

Tolstoy must have been one of the most egocentric men who has ever lived: witness his passion for drawing attention to himself (particularly shown in his behaviour on the train, just before his death, when he was supposedly escaping in secret from his wife). But he was oppressed from time to time by the feeling that he was not being egocentric enough.

His horror [writes Wilson] shortly after getting married, had been that marriage was the enemy of egoism. 'Where has my self gone?' he asked. 'The self I once loved and knew.' He was still writing in the same vein at the age of eighty.

Wilson says well that Tolstoy's 'moral aspirations – as they occur in his fiction, and in his life – are moving, while his moral presumption is so repulsive.'

After the abortive revolution of 1905 there was an aftermath of civil disturbance throughout Russia. Marauding peasants cut down 129 oak trees on the Yasnaya Polyana estate, taking away the timber. Then a night watchman was murdered. The property had by then been made over by Tolstoy to his wife, who called in the police. The Governor came to see what he could do to help. It was rather embarrassing because Tolstoy's son was having an affair with the Governor's wife. All most unTolstoyan.

Tolstoy, A. N. Wilson,   1988
Hamish Hamilton.   *Daily Telegraph*

PAUL VERLAINE

There seems no particular reason why Paul Verlaine (1844–96) should have been thrown up by his background. His father was a good-natured army officer; his mother, doting certainly, but apparently in no way unusual. The family was ultimately of Walloon origin. There were some disreputable relations, but no more than in most families. His parents began by being quite well off, but were bad at investments. Verlaine himself showed signs of brilliance at an early age; a tendency to alcoholism not much later. He was the sort of alcoholic who became dangerous when drunk – threatening his mother with a sword or dagger, and really meaning business.

A graph of Verlaine's sex life would mark remarkable readings. In a general way, from quite early on, he showed signs of being homosexual. But he fell deeply in love with a girl of sixteen when he was twenty-five; marrying her; producing a son; and feeling deeply about her – hate and love – for the rest of his life. Verlaine's marriage was broken up by Arthur Rimbaud, then not quite seventeen. Rimbaud wrote to Verlaine; came to see him; decamped with him. Rimbaud was also an army officer's son, his father unusually intelligent, his mother immensely dominating, rather than doting. Rimbaud, apart from his genius as a poet, was a kind of apotheosis of the hippy; disagreeable, sadistic, filthy, criminal. As is well known, Verlaine did two years' imprisonment in Belgium for wounding Rimbaud, and it is surprising that neither managed to kill the other in the course of their violent relationship.

Verlaine and Rimbaud eloped to London, where Verlaine gave English lessons as a consequence of advertising. Later Verlaine returned to England, and taught at boys' schools in Lincolnshire, Bournemouth and Lymington. Verlaine always loved England. He liked the food:

Next appeared the roast beef. Not one of those crimson lumps that are set before us in our best restaurants, but a well cut joint, daintly streaked with fat and lean, emitting rich and appetising odour, full of promise of nourishment. No sauce, no gravy! The vegetables were

430

potatoes boiled in their jackets, and bursting through their skins. They were served on a plate to the left, and were the substitute for bread . . . It is true that the latter article of food, which here is only eaten when cut in slices with butter or jam, appeared in a pudding with lemon peel (lemon pudding), a delicious sweet.

He adored the London fogs, English beer and the hymns in church. In fact, he made a translation of Bishop Ken's 'Awake my soul, and with the sun', and English hymns left an appreciable mark on his poetry. Even when he returned to England in 1893, towards the end of his life, when things in Paris were on the whole just about as bad as they could be, the visit was an enormous success.

As Joanna Richardson points out, Verlaine's was an intensely divided nature. There was always a side of him that yearned for bourgeois life (for example, election to the Academy), but his bohemian side was no joke. It entailed real depths of squalor and horror, in which he maintained a kind of court of admirers in the cafés, but was never far off starvation and murder. It is, indeed, extraordinary that he managed to survive as long as he did. In 1889, when he went into hospital – he spent a great deal of his life in hospitals, where it was smart for ladies of fashion and literary men to visit him – he was suffering from syphilis, gonorrhoea, rheumatism, diabetes, cirrhosis of the liver, bronchitis, and water on the knee. Money was a permanent problem. This was not so much because no one was prepared to give financial aid, but from difficulty of doling that out in a manner that prevented it being immediately appropriated by one or other of the poet's obnoxious hangers-on.

There are many good accounts quoted here, of persons who visited Verlaine. He was apt to be lying in bed with all his clothes on, dirty boots appearing where the bedclothes ended. George Moore paid one of these calls. Almost all emphasis is laid on the sinister look in the poet's eyes.

Verlaine, a convert to religion during his period in prison, is fond of excoriating himself in his poems for the sins of the flesh – in his case not to be underestimated – but his least attractive side is a kind of cunning, a slyness in dealings, not uncommon in persons of his temperament. 'To him,' said Jean Lemaître, 'men are not individuals with whom he has relations of duty and of interest, but forms which move and pass.' Nevertheless, quite apart from the greatness of his poetry, there must have been tremendous charm and laughter, if he were in good form. When he arrived in Ghent to give a lecture, Maeterlinck, who had gone to meet him, saw a third-class train window open with a great clatter, framing the 'faun-like' face of the poet, then in his fiftieth year. 'I take sugar with it!' Verlaine shouted.

This meant that (in the old-fashioned manner) he drank his absinthe by dripping water over a lump of sugar poised above the glass.

Verlaine, Joanna Richardson,   1971
Weidenfeld & Nicolson.   *Daily Telegraph*

ARTHUR RIMBAUD

The more you pile up material about a person like Arthur Rimbaud (1854–91), the more, in some ways, you get away from the point. One is absorbed by every item that is brought to light (washing-bills would be an inappropriate metaphor in Rimbaud's case), but at the same time it is the general picture rather than the detail that must always be kept in mind.

One of the interesting discoveries of Enid Starkie's latest investigation is that Rimbaud seems to have inherited his rackety side from his mother's, rather than his father's, family. Mme Rimbaud, bigoted, avaricious, dominating, puritanical, was – in spite of Enid Starkie's occasional pleas in her favour – one of the most odious of women. She came of yeoman farming stock. Her husband, a man of considerable intelligence, had risen from the ranks to be a captain in the army. He had held important administrative posts in Algeria and published translations from the Arabic. His marriage was a consolidation in the social scale, but both his wife's brothers went to the bad. They were alcoholic and dishonest. When they came to their sister for help, she would make them show their identity papers like tramps. Captain Rimbaud wisely abandoned his wife at an early stage.

Rimbaud's gifts as a boy of about fifteen were of such a fantastic order that it is hard to imagine anything suppressing them. Indeed, circumstances could scarcely have been more discouraging than those he found round him at home. Did the almost wholly adverse pressure to which he was subjected bring out what was most remarkable in Rimbaud, or was it – anyway in the long run – a handicap to him as an artist and a man?

On the one hand we have Rimbaud the poet, an entity that can be grasped in itself; on the other, Rimbaud the adventurer – a conception in some ways more complex – who abandoned poetry, and hoped to make a fortune on the Somali coast. Where these sides meet in Rimbaud is as an exponent of the will. The will was surely what preoccupied Rimbaud most; more than his poetry; more than his efforts to make money. All his life he was interested in magic, the Kabala, the Illuminists. Starkie is at great pains to trace and explain these magical references in the poems, but she never states in so many words that 'magic', as expounded by, say, Éliphas Lévi (one of Rimbaud's preceptors in the art) is no more than the development of the will by the use of certain traditional disciplines. At least, without setting up as a thaumaturge, that appears to me to be the crux of the matter.

It is this obsession with the will that offers some explanation of Rimbaud's otherwise inexplicable sex life. That Verlaine, a weak man, with an earlier homosexual background, should have fallen under the influence of this extraordinary young poet is believable; but that Rimbaud, apparently not at all homosexual in later life, should have returned this passion is odd. In fact, it seems capable of explanation only by Rimbaud's determination to dominate Verlaine – finally resulting in the shooting scene and Verlaine's imprisonment at Brussels. In the same way, exercise of the will, as such, seems to be the only clue to Rimbaud's five years' wanderings (at one moment he was a private in the Dutch army in Indonesia) and his life as a trader in Abyssinia.

It is extraordinary that the astonishing dangers and privations he endured should have brought him no more than about £600 – and that only by stinting and starving himself almost to death. Rimbaud had a genius for picking up languages. This was the period of history, of all others, when it might be thought a man of his courage and attainments – and, it might be added, lack of scruple – could have piled up a fortune by prospecting for large business concerns.

The fact was that the will came in again. Rimbaud would not endure the smallest discipline imposed by others, although capable of accepting the most terrible disciplinary burdens imposed by himself. Enid Starkie speaks of his kind, even saintly, behaviour to the Africans. But Rimbaud's sympathies with African tradition actually led him to toy with the slave trade, at that time much inconvenienced by British efforts at suppression.

Rimbaud died at Marseilles in 1891, his leg amputated, but still hoping to return to the area of the Red Sea.

Arthur Rimbaud,   1962
Enid Starkie, Faber.   *Daily Telegraph*

LUDWIG II OF BAVARIA

Ludwig II of Bavaria (1845–1886) is an arresting figure for three reasons: his relationship with Wagner; his building of beautiful palaces; the manner in which he throws light on the behaviour of a certain type of neurotic – for it is convincingly argued by Wilfrid Blunt, in his no-nonsense, sympathetic biography, that, unmanageable as the King may often have been, he was not mad.

The Wittlesbachs had ruled Bavaria for some 700 years, not without their ups and downs. Ludwig's grandfather, for example, had been forced to abdicate on account of Lola Montez. His father, on the other hand, was a dullish man, who said that he would have liked to be a university professor had he not been a king; his Prussian mother was an anti-intellectual who never opened a book and expressed surprise at people who did so.

Ludwig, talented, handsome, physically strong, was rather strictly brought up, without any understanding. He came to the throne when he was nineteen. There was insanity in the family, and in due course his younger brother quite simply went mad. However, there is madness in many families which also produce their sane members, and it is clear that what Ludwig mainly suffered from was arrested development. In many respects he remained a child. When it came to discussing foreign affairs, or Papal Infallibility (a doctrine to which he took exception), he was formidable in argument and remarkably well informed. At the same time he found all official dealings excruciatingly boring, and was only happy living a life of fantasy in which the Arts played a considerable, though almost wholly undisciplined, part.

Ludwig's first act on succeeding (although he was only superficially 'musical') was to get in touch with Wagner to make arrangements for his operas to be produced on a colossal scale in Munich. The Wagner-Ludwig story is of great interest, with important practical results to music. It needed all the composer's gifts, energy and lack of scruple to cope with the King. Much of their association is, so to speak, Wagner's own story.

The question of Ludwig's homosexuality arises in his relationship with Wagner, and one would wholly agree with Blunt that the extraordinary letters exchanged between them must be seen in the

435

context of the period, German sentimentality, the fifty-one-year-old Wagner's astonished delight at Ludwig turning up as a patron just at a moment when disaster threatened, and Ludwig's own taste for violently emotional friendships. Homosexuality in this case has no part. At the same time there seems no doubt that Ludwig was homosexual, but that, deeply religious, he went through agonies of guilt on this account, and did his utmost to control himself physically.

When, for a variety of reasons, Wagner passed out of Ludwig's life, the King began to develop his passion for building, producing the extraordinary array of palaces for which he is now primarily remembered. As he grew older his ministers found him increasingly difficult to deal with. Finally, there was a *coup d'état*, and Ludwig's body, with that of the doctor who certified his madness, was found floating in the lake of the castle.

One of the most remarkable examples of Ludwig's childishness was his habit of circling round and round the riding school, after he had laid down that he was on a journey to some particular place, for example, 'Munich to Innsbruck'. This might start at 8 p.m. and go on until 3 a.m., with an interval for a picnic supper.

It is tempting to think that his mother's failure to supply some sort of imaginative nourishment to a highly strung child was partly responsible for this longing for a dream world. Ludwig never got on with her. At the time of the Franco-Prussian war he once refused to see her on the grounds that he was 'in no mood to receive a Prussian princess', and used normally to refer to her as 'the widow of my predecessor' or 'the Colonel of the 3rd Artillery Regiment'. If any assertion of Bismarck's striking abilities were required, the fact that he persuaded Ludwig to write the formal request (desired by the Iron Chancellor, but not at all by Ludwig) that the King of Prussia should become Emperor of Germany, would come high as an example of man – or rather king – management. (When there was later a question of his visiting Paris, the French press remarked that there was no objection because Ludwig had only accompanied his troops on the piano.)

One of those enjoyable paradoxes produced by history is that the reason the Bavarian ministers finally decided that Ludwig must go was not on account of his eccentricities, nor even his growing unwillingness to take part in government, but because of the appalling debt he was piling up by his frenetic building. Half a million people now come to Bavaria every year, pouring money into the country, chiefly to see Ludwig's palaces.

The flaw in Ludwig's character which cannot be excused was his taste for being a king – which was enormous – without accepting a monarch's responsibilities. He had undoubtedly paranoiac tendencies. Wilfrid Blunt mentions, but does not develop, one point. Ludwig was a great taker of chloral. Was not that, or some similar drug or concatenation of drugs responsible in Waugh's *Ordeal of Gilbert Pinfold* for the hallucinations?

The Dream King: Ludwig II
of Bavaria, Wilfrid Blunt, with a
chapter on Ludwig and the Arts by
Dr Michael Petzet, Hamish Hamilton.

1970
Daily Telegraph

AUGUST STRINDBERG

August Strindberg (1849–1912) is a major dramatist who, for better or worse, was one of the pioneers of the modern world, particularly the modern theatre. He is Sweden's greatest figure since, say, Charles XII. He seems to have looked rather like Frans Hals's portrait 'The Laughing Cavalier' who, as is often pointed out, is neither laughing nor a cavalier. Strindberg presents similar contradictions.

Michael Meyer's biography is long, full and exceedingly well done. He picks his way through enormous complications of work, bohemian life, and three disastrous marriages, in a manner that is never dull. I think perhaps Meyer slightly underrates what roughly comes under the heading of Strindberg's novels. They are sometimes tedious, but contain remarkable things. It is a long time since I read any of them, but the sinister coincidences from which the author suffered in real life are often striking.

Meyer rightly begins with the incredible provincialism of Sweden in the mid-nineteenth century. Stockholm, with a population of about 90,000, had no water system, one bath-house, and the main sewers (disagreeable when they unfroze after winter) often running down the middle of the street. Everyone knew everyone else and, when Strindberg had some slight success with a play in his early twenties, the King wanted to meet him.

Almost all those who knew Strindberg personally were insistent that he was not insane. He was, however, to say the least, badly balanced, and clearly possessed odd gifts of an hypnotic and clairvoyant kind. The amount of absinthe (in those days the real stuff) he drank at certain stages of his life did not improve a persecution mania (apparently to some extent hereditary). Although he could be generous, he had the hysteric's disagreeable habit of suddenly turning against a friend without the least reason.

Strindberg was the son of a shipping agent who had married his housekeeper from a lower social stratum. One is astonished at what an early age he began to write plays of some sort and managed to scratch a living, though he was hard up to the end of his days, if latterly not seriously. He began much on the Left (in spite of fairly virulent anti-Semitism), notwithstanding being thought of as the great anti-feminist, to which the plays best known in this country – *Creditors, Miss Julie, The Father* – bear witness. In fact, some of his views (separate beds, equal

438

education, filling of any post, etc.) were comparatively feminist for the period. All the same, Strindberg regarded Woman as The Enemy, and particularly disliked what he considered the 'Feminism' of Ibsen, of whom he was chronically jealous. He complained that what was objected to in his own writings was merely treating women on the terms that would have been regarded as perfectly permissible to treat men.

Like those hypochondriacs who really have something seriously at fault with their health, Strindberg always managed to associate himself with women who, with the best will in the world, would have taken a lot of coping with, especially his three wives, the first of whom was a Swedish-Finn, the second an Austrian, the third a Norwegian. Strindberg began his married life by running away with the wife of an officer in the Swedish Life Guards, met through the latter's interest in starting private theatricals within his regiment. This in itself illustrates Stockholm's small interconnected social world. Captain Baron Wrangel took this pretty well. He was having an affair himself, and, in spite of Strindberg's frenzied suspicion of all his wives, Siri (née von Essen) Wrangel does seem to have had lesbian tendencies. She had an extremely tough time after parting from Strindberg, and I should like to know rather more definitely what Michael Meyer himself thought about her.

Frida Uhl, a journalist, was daughter of comparatively rich parents. She and Strindberg honeymooned in London. There was a scene outside a pub on Hampstead Heath when the landlord asked where they had slept the night before. It was a Sunday, and the landlord had to comply with some absurd law about only serving travellers. Strindberg had to be prevented from striking him with his walking stick. That the second Mrs Strindberg was formidable is proved by the fact that many years later she returned to London, slept with Augustus John, who was then reduced to an attempt to leave the country to avoid her persecutions, at which she turned up at Charing Cross and insisted on accompanying that seasoned philanderer to Paris, 'her only luggage a revolver'. She started a night-club called The Cave of the Golden Calf, decorated by Wyndham Lewis and Jacob Epstein. It was just before my time, but I have known many who frequented it.

Strindberg's third wife, Harriet Bosse, was just twenty-two and beginning a career on the stage, where she was ultimately extremely successful. She was playing Puck in *A Midsummer Night's Dream*, when Strindberg, then fifty-one, met her. He had been induced to see the performance. In some ways this was the most disastrous of all the three marriages, and, with its heavy weather, perhaps the most Scandinavian.

Strindberg: A Biography,   1985
Michael Meyer, Secker &   *Daily Telegraph*
Warburg.

LOU SALOMÉ

Just as the Modern Movement in the arts had progressed, radically speaking, as far as it could well go before the outbreak of war in 1914, the Modern Woman had also appeared and run her course to the fullest extent by the same date. Lou Salomé has some claims to be considered as perfect a specimen of that latter phenomenon as the nineteenth century could produce. Her biography is of the greatest interest and sets all kind of persons who were connected with her in a new and interesting light.

She died in 1937 at the age of seventy-six. The Nazis inveighed against her as a 'Finnish Jewess' – incidentally, a very rare thing to be – but, although she is sometimes described as Jewish in serious literary works, she had in fact no Jewish blood. Her father was a Russian general of French Huguenot descent, her mother, North German and Danish. To attempt to summarise her life would be to risk spoiling the good story the book has to tell, but, briefly, Nietzsche, then thirty-seven, fell madly in love with Lou Salomé when she was twenty-one; Rilke, reversing the age ratio, had an affair with her that lasted for some years when he was twenty-two and she thirty-eight. In her fifties she became a close friend – one imagines no more – of Freud, although she was still for years intimately associated with other men.

Her husband, Friedrich Carl Andreas, a scholar, partly German, partly Malayan, partly of royal Persian stock, although a man of strong passions, never contrived to persuade his wife to sleep with him. For most of their lives they did not live under the same roof, though they remained married. H. F. Peters writes without vestige of humour and, it has to be admitted, ample use of cliché. At the same time, in fairness to him (he always takes Lou's side), her life is so full of extraordinary situations that a good rough-and-ready sentimental approach is in many ways the best method of dealing with a narrative so packed with solid, complicated material.

Tastes differ, but the photograph of Lou Salomé at the age of twenty-one certainly presents a young lady about whom it seems not unreasonable to lose one's head. Added to her outward appearance, she was immensely intelligent, serious – even if her novels sound unalluring – and a woman of quite unusual vitality. However, the aspect of her that is perhaps most striking is the manner in which she used sexual relations as a weapon, apparently remaining a virgin well into her thirties. This would be understandable enough if she had been a woman who disliked physical relations with men but, in due course, this was seen to be far from the case.

There can be no doubt that her father loomed large in the formation of her character and also her extraordinary early amorous interlude with Gillot, a Dutch clergyman in Russia, who proposed to her, although he already had a wife and two children. Lou, aged seventeen, used to sit on his knee in his study while he explained doctrinal points.

Nietzsche, in the end, said that Lou was a thoroughly evil woman. Others who became involved with her agreed. All the same, there can be little doubt that her men, so far as one can see, without exception wished to remain with her, while she after a time preferred to move on to other lovers. After they had been discarded, Lou's lovers' behaviour differed. One unfortunate reject appears to have castrated himself before committing suicide. George Ledebour, the writer and politician, sent back unopened a letter she wrote him twenty-five years after their break. Rilke, on the other hand, a person of quite remarkable emotional toughness, retrieved sufficient from the association to remain on good terms with Lou all his life. He wrote her some of his best letters. At the time when they were still lovers, they went to Russia *en famille*, and there is a splendid account there of a super-embarrassing visit to Tolstoy.

Lou Salomé's later life was devoted to psychoanalysis, to which she appears to have made a useful contribution. Her own experience well equipped her to show no surprise at the experiences of others.

It is a remarkable thing, as I. F. Peters points out, that when she was still under thirty in 1890, before psychoanalysis was known, she could write in an article about artists and neurotics:

> Those types of people with psychologically undigested remnants of life who can find relief only if fortunate circumstances or a successful hypnosis make them give vent to the cause of their disease, of which they are not consciously aware until it has, as it were, been thrust out of their souls.

My Sister, My Spouse is, apart from its picture of Lou Salomé herself, a valuable study of what might be called the Central European side of intellectual life untouched by any of the characteristics in that field that France or this country has to offer.

My Sister, My Spouse: 1963
A Biography of Lou Andreas-Salomé,   *Daily Telegraph*
H. F. Peters, Gollancz.

AXEL MUNTHE

The Story of San Michele was first published in this country in 1929. By now (1953) it has sold nearly a million copies and is said to be still selling. Its readers at the present day are mostly quiescent, but when the book first appeared they were vociferous enough in its praises. Their extraordinary range in those days could not fail to strike any one interested in human behaviour. Elderly maiden ladies in cathedral closes; hard-drinking American heiresses married to dissolute French noblemen; Kipling; Paul Bourget; Mussolini. All these found it enchanting. But the highbrows would have none of it; and indeed, in literary circles, *The Story of San Michele* became a byword for cheap and pretentious writing.

What sort of a man was its author, Axel Munthe (1857–1949), who produced this best-seller in his seventies? The present biography does not get us much further. His cousin, Dr Gustav Munthe, contributes an adequate account of the family, and says something of Munthe's early days and subsequent career. The remaining two-thirds of the book, by Baroness Uexküll, consists of rather random memories of its subject. Baroness Uexküll already finds it necessary almost to apologise for Munthe's extremely pro-British and anti-German attitude in two wars; though naturally in this country we feel his approach more sympathetic than that of some of his countrymen, who fell over backwards in efforts to assure both the Kaiser and Hitler of their neutrality.

Munthe came of an ancient and decidedly eminent family, having its origin in Flanders, though Scandinavian since the end of the sixteenth century. His grandfather was a distinguished cavalry officer with a large family, among whom Munthe's father, the youngest son, went through life with a background of bad health, puritanism, and lack of money, alleviated by interest in chemistry and music. Munthe himself started his career as a sick man. It was due to a visit to the Riviera to overcome a weakness in his chest that he decided to study medicine in France.

It appears that he was marked down at an early age for a brilliant medical career; but as soon as his grown-up life begins the reader enters a realm of fantasy, created by *San Michele*, which Munthe's present biographers fail to illuminate at all clearly. He seems to have possessed hypnotic gifts which were used with great effect both directly and indirectly. When the cholera epidemic struck Naples in 1884 he made his way to Italy from Lapland, where he was spending a holiday, and worked with the medical relief services there with the greatest courage.

Gradually his fame grew as a doctor and an eccentric. He moved in the highest circles, and it was his boast that there was not a royal palace in Europe in which he had not spent a night. But like other men of giant egotism, the ordinary rewards of material success were not enough for him. They must be emphasised by a kind of outward denial. Decorations were showered on him; he lost them or gave them away. With a post at court, he made difficulties about wearing official uniform. When he accompanied a royal train he would not wait for the royal party to alight, but would immediately jump to the platform and stride off with his two dogs. He declared that he liked the company only of the poor and lowly, and no doubt on Capri he spent some of his time with the peasants, as he had done while working in the Paris hospitals. But, all the same, it was with the great that his life was finally associated, ending as a guest in the King of Sweden's palace.

Loving the sun, yet almost blind; highly courageous, yet always in deadly fear of death; hating ceremonial, yet a voluntary courtier; is it to be wondered that he complained of unhappiness? Did his own protests against convention become almost a form of obsequiousness? After all, everyone knows the success that a professional 'rough diamond' or 'plain speaker' can achieve in far less exalted circles. If Munthe had really wanted a quiet life (even at an agreeable high social level) he could perfectly well have enjoyed one without so much exhibitionism. Yet there can be no doubt that he was a remarkable man, and, whatever its failings (and the third-rateness of much of its tone as pseudo-philosophy can scarcely be exaggerated) that *The Story of San Michele* is, in its way, a remarkable book. For example, the anecdote of the hunch-backed *Leichenbegleiter* and the two coffins that became confused is admirably told by any standard.

Curzio Malaparte (author of *The Technique of the Coup d'Etat*), another Capri resident, (also a student of life not suffering from too much diffidence), supplies an interesting vignette in *Kaputt*.

When Axel Munthe is in a good mood, he amuses himself with improvising mischievous jokes at the expense of his friends. And that was perhaps his first good day after some months of raging loneliness. He had gone through a dismal autumn, a prey to his black whims, his irritable melancholy, shut up day after day in his tower, stripped bare and like an old bone gnawed by the sharp teeth of the southwest wind that blows from Ischia, and by the north wind that carries the acrid smell of the Vesuvian sulphur as far as Capri . . .

stiff, lean, wooden, like an old tree trunk, worn and withered by the sun, by the frost and the storms, and with a happy smile hidden amid the hair of his small beard like that of an aged faun.

The Story of Axel Munthe,
Gustav Munthe and Gudrun
Uexküll, John Murray.

1953
Punch

MARIE BASHKIRTSEFF

Do people know about Marie Bashkirtseff (1860–84) nowadays? Not many, so it seems. Yet she was a familiar name even twenty-five years ago, and Stephen Leacock wrote a characteristic parody of diaries written in her manner. ('Yesterday, he touched me . . . today, he touched me again – and touched father, too, for five roubles.') She set a fashion for intense, introspective, intellectual, entirely humourless young ladies, a few of whom no doubt persist in some circles until this very moment. The present little volume is perhaps the best way of dealing with Bashkirtseff (perhaps more correctly Bashkirstseva). In small doses her traits show to the best advantage. In bulk her really appalling self-love makes the diary almost unreadable, as we plough through page after page of how beautiful she finds herself. Indeed, her conceit emphasises the strain of real stupidity that ran parallel with her undoubted, and extraordinarily precocious, talents. 'My body like that of an antique goddess, my Spanish-looking hips, my small and perfectly-shaped bosom, my feet, my hands, and my childlike head – of what use is it all, since nobody loves me?' (9 May 1884.)

It was really not surprising that men were a bit alarmed, although a certain number of them made declarations. As a matter of fact Mlle Bashkirtseff does not seem to have been greatly interested in the opposite sex, in spite of having fallen hopelessly in love with a Scotch duke at the age of thirteen. What she liked was success and notoriety: and a good deal of money.

These letters, charmingly decorated by Danuta Laskowska, certainly make Bashkirtseff look attractive in the pictures. Contemporary photographs are less convincing. Ann Hill, in her introduction, is inclined to accept the diarist entirely at her own estimation, beautiful, well born, wealthy, moving in the highest society, conversant with English, Italian, German, Greek, Latin, drawing and music; and it must be admitted that there is some truth in all this. All the same, each item has to be considered on its own merits, and perhaps it was not quite as glamorous as it appears on paper. One of the most striking features of the journal is her almost insane jealousy of her Swiss fellow girl-student, Breslau.

Bashkirtseff was of Russian landed stock (an old Tartar family on her mother's side), and although she sometimes visited her own country her Russian was imperfect. She spent most of her time in Paris, Nice, or Naples. No doubt she possessed an overpowering nervous energy. She never shows much grasp of any but the most superficial view of the arts she talks of so endlessly; though her picture, 'Le Meeting', made a hit in the Salon. Even so far as her own self-examination is concerned, she can write down her overflowing emotions and ambitions, but can never go far in analysing them.

When she began her correspondence with Maupassant it was the year of her death. He was thirty-three, at that time producing *Bel-Ami*, *La Parure* and *Yvette*. She signed the letter 'Miss Hastings', asking to become the author's confidante, adding 'But I warn you that I am charming; this sweet thought will encourage you to reply to me.' Maupassant was not so easily caught as all that, but undoubtedly intrigued – what author would not be? He replied in terms to suggest that he was too world-weary to be overexcited by such a letter. He asked what was the point of corresponding if they were never to meet, and explained to her that he received many fan letters of her kind.

Bashkirtseff's tone is deliberately provocative. On the whole she may be said to get the best of it, though tormenting a busy writer, and remaining hidden behind anonymity, has about it something of a bull-fighter who leaps behind the barricade to safety when the bull charges. It seems that she herself really lost interest at last, attracted by other literary prey. Besides, her own end was near.

With all her faults – although, personally, she must often have been an excruciating bore at dinner parties – Bashkirtseff is not without interest as a type. She exemplifies the temperament which is not so much concerned with doing a thing – in her case singing, painting, writing, flirting – as in seeing themselves do it. For example, she is all the time watching herself provoking Maupassant. If she had gone farther, perhaps had a real love affair with him, it might have done her a great deal of good. Unfortunately her interests were too concentrated on herself for anything of that sort to happen.

I Kiss Your Hand,   1955
The Letters of Guy de Maupassant and   *Punch*
Marie Bashkirtseff, introduced
by Ann Hill, Rodale Press.

MAURICE MAETERLINCK

Maurice Maeterlinck (1862–1949) occupies a peculiar position in modern literature. Enormously successful in his day, even then there was about him always something a trifle suspect. This was not merely because in some circles his work was received with the wildest enthusiasm, in others, with the greatest ridicule. That is true of many distinguished figures in the world of art. There is a kind of professional (rather than personal) 'bogusness' about Maeterlinck; and yet at the same time he is a remarkable figure, in his own way full of interest. In this brief, unpretentious study, W. D. Halls packs a great deal of useful information. It is one of the few books one wishes to have been longer. Maeterlinck requries to be set against the changing intellectual tides of his long life. He himself altered his line superficially from time to time, but in essentials very little.

He was born of a family of *haute bourgeoisie* in Ghent. In the face of considerable conventionality and stuffiness on the part of his relations, he managed as a young man to get to Paris, where he met, rather surprisingly, the symbolist poets Villiers de l'Isle Adam and Mallarmé. This was the lasting influence of his life. The whole atmosphere of his upbringing and background of Belgian society were inimical to writing, but Maeterlinck made a name for himself at a surprisingly early age. Physically he was a big man who, even by Flemish standards, was a hearty eater. He joined the Ghent Civic Guard because he liked handling firearms, and when he was fifty took boxing lessons from the great Georges Carpentier, giving for charity an exhibition bout with that famous pugilist, whose fight with the British boxer, Gunboat Smith, I remember the papers being full of just before the First World War. Maeterlinck combined a good deal of aggressiveness in personal dealings with great diffidence in making public appearances. For example, he challenged Debussy to a duel when the musician was collaborating with him in the production of the opera *Pelléas and Mélisande*, but made some excuse about going to Sweden to receive the Nobel Prize.

Halls hints that Maeterlinck was addicted to adventures with women, but he is discreet on this point. It certainly appears that Maeterlinck did not feel at all deeply in such relationships (although he would like to have done so) until he encountered Georgette Leblanc, in his early thirties. She was an actress, sister of the author of the Arsène Lupin detective novels. Maeterlinck lived for many years with Mlle Leblanc, a dynamic character who contributed a certain amount to his own flow of ideas. Finally they drifted apart. In his late fifties he married Renée Dahon, also an actress, much younger than himself, who survives him. The marriage was a successful one.

One might perhaps think of him as a kind of Flemish J. M. Barrie, although sufficient has been said above about Maeterlinck's characteristics to indicate that there was little or no personal resemblance. There was between them, however, a sympathetic literary feeling, and Maeterlinck himself admitted that *Peter Pan* and *The Little White Bird* gave him impetus for his own *L'Oiseau Bleu*. Barrie had been born a couple of years earlier, and had a somewhat similar early success in making fantasy his line. Maeterlinck's great preoccupations were Death and Destiny. Barrie, of course, approaches his subjects in a deliberately lighter vein, but he, too, is capable of bringing into *Peter Pan* a line like 'To die will be an awfully big adventure.' Both writers hit off just what a certain public required at the moment.

Maeterlinck was immensely productive. He wrote about thirty plays, several volumes of verse, and innumerable essays. His ideas were limited, and he did not mind borrowing, on the whole acknowledging, his sources. He does not appear to have been at all interested in individuals – he detested Proust's novels – only in the general idea of Man and his unhappy destiny. He reached his peak before he was fifty, never achieving after that age much that was new in his writing. One of the things that makes Maeterlinck interesting is that he seems, relatively speaking, not to have courted his huge success. Naturally, like all writers, he wanted to be appreciated, but his career is in many ways one not at all designed by himself for the kind of popularity he received. In Great Britain and America he was particularly adulated. Even the French, who might be expected to find some of Maeterlinck's work too whimsical for their love of *logique*, tried to find special ways of making him a member of the Academy, without his having to relinquish his Belgian nationality.

In reading about Maeterlinck, one feels that he was a writer in whom something went badly amiss. There was a moment when, so to speak, he took the wrong turning. Perhaps this was due to his faithfulness to symbolism – a creed played out by the time Maeterlinck reached maturity, or at least was to find an entirely different form from that in which he had first known it. He never showed any awareness of the great changes in the arts that were developing at the turn of the century. Indeed, his name conjures up an approach to art that was to receive a series of shattering blows from the painters and writers born about twenty years later than himself. There is something Edwardian about him, rather than Victorian; decadent in the sense that he was handling material which – although in a sense original – was also outworn.

When he was rich and famous he acquired the vast abbey of St Wandrille in Normandy, destroyed during the fourteenth century, and rebuilt during the seventeenth century. Here he used to spend all his summers before the First World War. Georgette Leblanc would dress as an abbess; Maeterlinck, for exercise, would roller-skate – a wonderful period touch – through the interminable cloisters. So extensive were the abbey's apartments that the two of them devised special cries of distress when they were lost in its labyrinth. This picture of Maeterlinck roller-skating through Gothic ruins seems a kind of allegory of his own literary life. All the same, it must be admitted that, even today, to invoke his name at once suggests a particular kind of fantasy; and to leave a stamp of this sort is not wholly to be disregarded.

Maurice Maeterlinck: 1961
A Study of his Life and Thought,   *Daily Telegraph*
W. D. Halls, Clarendon Press:
Oxford University Press.

GABRIELE D'ANNUNZIO

Even in his palmiest days d'Annunzio was never really a success in this country. That was not altogether just, because, although the elaborately rhetorical and melodramatic side of his art was a sort on the whole unsympathetic to English taste, the *Decadence* had a good run for its money in England. It is an extraordinary story, which Philippe Jullian has told to perfection. Gabriele d'Annunzio (1863–1938) is an interesting example of the men and movements stemming from the late-nineteenth century, *not* leading to the Modern Movement, which, long out of fashion, have become relatively disregarded. His standing as a writer is not easy to assess, but, even in translation, enough is quoted here to show him far from the mere *pasticheur* he was sometimes labelled. Jullian compares d'Annunzio with Gustave Moreau (in whose studio Matisse worked), painter of exotic classical subjects. This is perhaps a good rough-and-ready parallel to bear in mind while d'Annunzio is considered in what was after all his main role, man of action.

Everything that happened in d'Annunzio's life was d'Annunzian, including the fact of finding himself with his immensely appropriate name. He had been born Rapagnetta (undistinguished sounding in Italian), but his father, a provincial mayor and insatiable womaniser, had changed the surname. From earliest childhood, in the Abruzzi, d'Annunzio seems to have been something of a prodigy. His father, who does not otherwise sound a very attractive figure, grasped this, giving his son a good education and – astonishing in view of the family's financial position – when he produced some poems at the age of sixteen, had them privately printed; good will which d'Annunzio repaid by recording with savagery his father's many physical defects.

From the moment these poems were printed, d'Annunzio never looked back. All his life he was involved in extravagance that made money a problem, but even in his early days, when he was a gossip-writer, he was steadily building up to fame. Jullian draws attention to how much d'Annunzio owed, as a writer, to the particular position of late-nineteenth-century Italy, a new national state that needed a 'great' literary figure, and how profoundly suited d'Annunzio was to fill the bill. Side by side with his literary output was d'Annunzio's inordinate ability to dominate women.

450

The liaison with the actress Duse is probably the best known of d'Annunzio's love affairs, but there were myriads of them, often with ladies themselves of considerable interest for one reason or another; even without the relatively famous ones, like Ida Rubenstein, Isadora Duncan (a push-over), Romaine Brooks and Luisa Casati. His powers of fascination (apart from by no means setting his face entirely against homosexuality) were scarcely less in evidence with men. So intelligent and cool a customer as Valéry, although he laughed about their interview, admitted to have felt d'Annunzio's power, while Robert de Montesquiou (at once an easier and more difficult subject, for whom d'Annunzio wrote a preface) remarked that he said 'such beautiful things that one would have thought he was speaking of himself'.

Living in Paris in 1914, d'Annunzio (just then for the first time become a victim of syphilis) had entered his fifties. His literary career had been dazzling, and (knocking spots off the Theatre of Cruelty) covered much of the ground considered up-to-date at the moment. He now turned to bringing Italy in with the Allies. During the Italian campaign he had a morale-boosting appointment, which took him all over the place in the front line. Though this had (like all his activities) a certain farcical side, it was certainly physically dangerous. One is glad to learn that a general told d'Annunzio that he too was a poet, and insisted on reading aloud two madrigals; just punishment for a man with whom humour was not a strong point. D'Annunzio was in a sea plane crash that temporarily blinded him, permanently destroying one eye. This did not prevent him from staging his *putsch* which captured Fiume. At that moment he might have been Dictator.

His connections with Fascism have done his reputation much harm, but, although he seems never to have assisted persecuted writers, he condemned the murder of Matteotti, and always loathed Hitler. He quickly retired from the Fascist world to live his last years in a dream-palace like Ludwig II of Bavaria. Jullian's enormously readable narrative of this entralling monster throughout a longish book never lets up for a moment. It is written with the ease that is the consequence only of hard work and, like a Victorian novel, tells the reader at the end of the story what ultimately happened to the subordinate characters, that is d'Annunzio's mistresses.

D'Annunzio, Philippe   1973
Jullian, Pall Mall.   *Daily Telegraph*

RAINER MARIA RILKE

Like all very inward-looking writers (Joyce, D. H. Lawrence, etc.), Rilke is apt to receive treatment from biographers and commentators which, by its desperate and humourless seriousness, distorts the picture of the man himself. Eudo C.Mason is a great relief in this respect. He writes with wit and understanding, not only giving a lively picture of the poet approached from a new angle, also examining many incidental matters of interest to those not specially concerned with Rilke and his poetry.

Born of a German family living in what is now Czechoslovakia, Rilke disliked the idea of a Prussia-dominated Germany, deploring Austria (especially the Empire's 'Merry Widow' side) almost equally; and, without possessing any known Czech blood, had been brought up to depise the Czechs. Mason shrewdly points out that the ultra-individualistic attitude adopted towards his own country by Rilke – characteristic of the period – would have been intelligible to Rousseau, even to Milton. It would have been incomprehensible to Homer, Virgil, Dante, Shakespeare and Racine.

Having sloughed off his Teutonic skin, Rilke had to find some garment to replace it. The covering created by him was woven chiefly of Latin material, with elaborate Russian and Scandinavian (especially Danish) trimmings. He had, however, a great distaste for the English-speaking world, in which he lumped together Great Britain and the United States of America almost as one. This is the side of the poet which Mason examines here, sometimes with entertaining results. In the first place, Rilke is found to be in the paradoxical position of translating Mrs Browning's *Sonnets from the Portuguese* into German at a comparatively early age; then gradually knowing – or pretending to know – less English, the older he grew. He had, in fact, an extraordinary facility for learning languages.

Mason, whose admiration does not at all blind him to the occasional absurdities of Rilke, becomes at times understandably cross with this view of a foggy puritanical island, devoid of intellectual or aesthetic life. All the same, there were moments when he had to fall back on English words and phrases. One of the few English-speaking writers Rilke came across was Bernard Shaw, when Shaw was sitting for Rodin, to whom

Rilke was then secretary. (He was also, apparently general factotum, expected to shunt about the studio vast pieces of sculpture.) The meeting with Shaw – Narcissus sighting Narcissus – was, at the time, a great success on both sides. Later Shaw was, for some reason, reticent about it.

Rilke also saw something of Gwen John, that talented painter, sister of Augustus John, mistress of Rodin. Little or nothing is known of their friendship, but there seems to have been warm sympathy between them. On the whole, however, Rilke, expecting to be bored by the English, was not disappointed. Perhaps the curious naïveté Rilke so often showed made him accept an unfriendly and stylised view of the Anglo-American world.

This naïveté is well illustrated by the fact that he was capable of writing of the Sonnets of Louise Labé (which he had himself translated): 'It is extraordinary for poems published in 1555 to interest and move us so much at the present time.' This view (he was himself then forty-two) shows an amazing narrowness of vision for a man who was, supposedly, the prophet of instinct and inner feeling. The fact was that, Rilke, as Mason points out, was by no means without what might be called his Hollywood side – liking the obvious and sometimes missing the subtle.

Rilke, although he enjoyed attending church services, was vigorously anti-Christian. *The Book of Hours*, translated by A. L. Peck, the one volume of his early poems which he excepted from his condemnation of the others, is, therefore, something of an oddity. Peck's translation aims at giving a version to convey something of the poetic quality of the original for those who do not know German. My impression is that he has been successful. *The Book of Hours* shows a side of Rilke less emphasised than that most in evidence in Eudo Mason's book. It is therefore helpful to read it immediately afterwards. It adds to the picture of this striking figure, who has been compared with W. B. Yeats (ten years older), but remains an essentially different kind of man and poet.

Rilke, Europe and the   1961
English-speaking World, Eudo   *Daily Telegraph*
C. Mason, Cambridge University
Press.
The Book of Hours, Rainer Maria
Rilke, Hogarth Press.

II

René Karl Wilhelm Johann Josef Maria Rilke (1875–1926), usually abbreviated to Rainer Maria Rilke, is commonly billed as the foremost

German-speaking poet of the twentieth century. Certainly literary figures, even when their careers extend before and after the period – d'Annunzio and Gorky, for instance – seem to belong essentially to that most interesting interlude between the death of Queen Victoria and the outbreak of war in 1914. Rilke is one of them. He has that crankiness, self-conscious professional exhibitionism, of an artist or poet in a bad Edwardian play or novel. It is no surprise to learn that he went through a stage of bare feet and Russian shirts buttoned up to the neck.

Rilke was born in Prague, then part of the Austro-Hungarian Empire, son of a railway official who had done well in the army though failed to gain a commission. Rilke's claims to distant aristocratic origins seems to have been quite imaginary, but he always groused a lot about bourgeois life and certainly might be said to have himself achieved the *beau monde* quite early on.

At the age of eleven Rilke went to the military school at St Pölten, of which Robert Musil has left a fairly hair-raising account in his novel *Young Törless*, one of the few school novels written from the point of view of the bullies rather than bullied. Rilke afterwards used to speak with great horror of his schooldays, but in fact received first-rate reports (reproduced here) except for gymnastics and fencing. So far from being disapproved of for being a poet, he was apparently sometimes summoned to read one of his poems to the class who listened with awe. It is certainly true that Rilke was upset when he had to leave the school on account of health, because he had wanted to enter the army. He proceeded to a business college where he also had excellent reports, passing out second of fifty-three. The fact was that – perhaps like most poets – he was in certain aspects extremely competent at keeping an eye on his own mundane interests.

Rilke's life, in the manner of those who have powers impossible to convey on paper, then started explosively. He had a little money from his family, and was working away at plays and poems, so that he just managed to keep going. At the age of twenty he began an affair with the redoubtable Lou Salomé, then thirty-six. From that moment Rilke never really looked back.

Wolfgang Leppmann takes his readers well and clearly through all that follows, not always easy to chronicle, as Rilke was constantly moving about and experiencing different forms of social life, which have to be recorded side by side with tracing the developments in his poetry. Wolfgang Leppmann resists the temptation to tell a richly comic story. Rilke's remarkable talents, ability to fascinate people, instinct for knowing all those who were up and coming in the world of art and letters, did not include the smallest grain of humour (which Austrian birth, a remote Jewish ancestress, a passion for things

Russian, might any of them have given him), and in consequence there are moments in his life of the purest farce.

Women seem to have found Rilke irresistible. He could never stay in an hotel without a new lady taking charge of him, something that always led to trouble. There is no doubt that a Proustian knowledge of the Central European social world of the period would greatly add to appreciation of Rilke's progress in it. Incidentally, Leppmann is surely wrong, I think, to call it a gaffe when Rilke closes a letter '*Chère comtesse*', with a request to give his regards to 'Monsieur de Gallarati-Scotti'. A friend would not refer to her husband as *Comte* de Gallarati-Scotti. It wasn't because Rilke didn't know he was a Count.

Wolfgang Leppmann describes well the usual Rilke situation by saying 'Whether his momentary need was for money or a dozen handkerchiefs (of course with embroidered monogram), a bit of practical advice or merely human solace', there was always a woman to give it; and as often as not a Princess.

Rilke life and writings are not easy to discuss in a few words. This biography gives a good no-nonsense account of both, including copious quotations, sometimes in both languages. It is to be recommended for reading about a poet who is perhaps still not sufficiently known in this country. One more thought occurs to me. Rilke had a friend called Edgar Jaffé who was briefly Minister of Finance in the still-born Bavarian Soviet Republic of 1919, with members of which Rilke had tenuous connections. But this was D. H. Lawrence's brother-in-law, the estranged husband of Frieda's sister Else. In his Letters, Lawrence shows signs of being rather proud of the appointment. How enjoyable if Rilke and Lawrence had met through that.

Rilke: A Life, Wolfgang
Leppmann, translated with the
author by Russell M. Stockman,
verse translations by Richard
Exner, Lutterworth Press.

1985
Daily Telegraph

FRANZ KAFKA

I

It was reasonable to set out on the 550 pages of these letters from Kafka to Felice Bauer (the woman to whom he was twice engaged without marrying) thinking they were likely to be heavy going. I knew they had been compared unfavourably with *Letters to Milena* (the married woman with whom Kafka had an affair some years later) which I had enjoyed when they appeared here in 1953. These apprehensions were altogether unfounded. *Letters to Felice*, written without the faintest idea that they would ever be published, read like a well-constructed novel – a somewhat harrowing one.

Franz Kafka (1883–1924) is chiefly known for such works as *The Castle* and *The Trial,* which describe in fantastic terms such situations as the arrest of the hero, for some unknown misdemeanour, which he himself feels he has committed. They are, at one level, the image of a man's inner psychological troubles; at another, their scenes were to take dreadful shape some years later, in the Communist countries' political trials. Kafka himself was inclined to prefer other writers' autobiographical material to their novels. Personally, I feel this preference in his own case. The fascination of the present volume, the action of which takes place between 1912 and 1917, is that not only do we see Kafka in love, but the whole setting is revealed: the home of his Jewish family, in middle-class Prague, in the period when the typewriter and the telephone were just coming into general use. Kafka used quite often to type his love letters.

He worked in an insurance office. I knew this, and had always imagined that his job there was an extremely modest one. On the contrary, this writer whose name has become (rather unjustly) a byword for intellectual obscurity, was at the age of twenty-nine in charge of a department of seventy persons. He would arrive at the office at 8 a.m.; leave about two o'clock or 2.30; eat; sleep; then work until two or three in the morning at his writing. He was the eldest of six children. I had also imagined that his father bullied him. Again things were quite to the contrary. Kafka's agonies appear to have stemmed from living with one of those large genial Jewish families.

Felice Bauer, four years younger than Kafka, was a sensible, energetic, intelligent young woman, more orthodox in her Jewishness

456

than he. At the time she was working in Berlin; first as a shorthand typist in a gramophone-record firm, then in a better position, with a manufacturer of dictating machines. Kafka had a curious dream (he often relates his dreams) that seems to have foretold the teleprinter and wrote a longish letter to Felice suggesting in practical terms that an invention of this sort should be put in hand.

He might be said to have fallen in love with Felice at their first meeting. She did not have at all an easy time in their relationship, and the reader often wonders how she stood it so long. She lived in Berlin, Kafka in Prague. He would write to her most days, sometimes twice a day, and there was trouble if she did not reply by return. However difficult he might be, Kafka had great humour and charm. He gives an extremely funny account of the helpless laughter to which he was reduced when there was a ceremony to celebrate the promotion of two members of the Workers' Accident Insurance Institute (the large firm where he worked) and its President made gestures like the Emperor.

Kafka suffered from bad health (he was a vegetarian, which irritated his father, a butcher's son) and he himself said that not only did TB physically undermine him, but it was his moral weapon too. This awareness of his own psychology, at a period when such traits were not, as now, universally discussed, indicates one of his remarkable characteristics. He also speaks of the power-element in reading aloud, saying he used to enjoy dreaming about reading aloud 'the whole of *Education Sentimentale*' at one sitting to a crowded hall.

In spite of Kafka's lack of physical robustness (he always feared sexual impotence), he wrote, when the war came:

Why don't you realise that it would be my good fortune . . . to become a soldier, provided of course my health would stand up to it, which I hope it will. I shall be called up at the end of next month, or the beginning of the next. You ought to hope that I shall be accepted, as is my wish.

Soon after writing this letter, Kafka reports that Robert Musil (Austrian author of *The Man Without Qualities*), then a lieutenant of infantry, called on him. Kafka's political standpoint was that of a patriotic, if neurotic, subject of the Empire.

An extraodinary sub-plot in *Letters to Felice* exists in those written to Greta Bloch, Felice's friend. In 1935, Greta Bloch made known these letters, together with the information that, in about 1914 or 1915, she had had an illegitimate child, who died at the age of seven in Munich. Her implication was that this child was Kafka's. Such facts as are known are clearly set down here, and it would be true to say that the evidence is strongly against Greta Bloch having had an illegitimate child at all. And yet there are certain odd phrases. One feels that the editors have been clear and sensible about the whole story in all but dismissing it. And yet . . . Felice herself does appear to have briefly become Kafka's mistress at Marienbad (where he stayed at the Hotel Schloss Balmoral and Osborne).

Letters to Felice,   1974
Franz Kafka, edited by Erich Heller   *Daily Telegraph*
and Jürgen Born, translated by
James Stern and Elizabeth Duckworth,
Secker & Warburg.

II

An enormous amount of interesting material is to be found in these Letters, not only about Kafka himself, but regarding the vigorous intellectual developments taking place in Central Europe during the years leading up to the First World War. They show the young Kafka entering his Prague insurance firm almost with enthusiasm, apart from the time business took from his own writing hours. At first he thought he would be sent to Trieste, and one toys with the possibility, had that been so, of a falling in with Joyce and Svevo in that city. Unexpected sides emerge, like Kafka being keen on racing and himself learning to ride. We get the picture of an attractive humorous figure though always suffering appalling nervous tensions, any form of noise being a torture, such as a workman whistling while mending a pipe in the next room. Then Kafka was struck down with tuberculosis, and life gradually ebbed away.

Although not at all unwilling – indeed rather keen – to serve in the Austro-Hungarian forces during the war, Kafka's health was much too bad to allow him to do so; but in the manner of army bureaucracy, he was kept on the end of a string. In November 1917, he writes from his sanatorium: 'An interesting item for the military programme of the Central Powers for 1918: The expiration of my exemption has been set for January 1, 1918. For once Hindenburg has come a bit too late.'

A great many of the letters are to Kafka's lifelong friend, Max Brod, now remembered chiefly for his association with Kafka, but at the time a much more successful writer. Of his meeting with Felice, the girl to whom he was twice engaged, Kafka (July, 1916) wrote to Brod:

When she came towards me in the big room to receive the engagement kiss, a shudder ran through me. The engagement trip with my parents was sheer agony every step of the way. I have never feared anything so much as being alone with F. before the wedding. Now all that is changed and is good. Our agreement is in brief: to get

Franz Kafka   459
married soon after the end of the war; rent an apartment of two or
three rooms in some Berlin suburb; each to assume economic
responsibility for himself. F. will go on working as she has done all
along while I – well, for myself I cannot say.

Should one try to visualise the situation, there is the picture of two
rooms somewhere in Karlshorst [5 miles south-east of Berlin], say, in
one of which F. wakes up early, trots off, and falls exhausted into bed
at night, while in the other room there is a sofa on which I lie and feed
on milk and honey. So there the husband lolls about, the wretched
and immoral lout (as the cliché has it). Nevertheless in this there is
calm, certainty, and therefore the possibility of living.

This idyll never came about though Kafka did live in Berlin for a
time in 1923, when he was very ill. Through the background of the
Letters move the emotional problems of Kafka's friends, especially
Brod, who was having trouble with wife and mistress. As so often one
wonders to what extent truth and irony are mixed when (January 1918)
Kafka writes to Brod: 'You are right in knowing that the deeper realm
of real sexual life is closed to me; I too think so.' Above all Kafka always
returns, though in a totally objective manner, to his own fear of death.

There are enjoyable glimpses of the literary life of the time and place,
Kafka requests (September 1917) a book on sexual psychology by Dr
Wilhelm Stekel ('You must know this Viennese who reduces Freud to
small change') on account of its mention of *The Metamorphosis*, Kafka's
story of a man who is transformed into a bedbug. Kafka gives a shrewd
and characteristic estimate of the philosopher and wit, Karl Kraus. He
has what appears to be a tiff with Robert Musil about a contribution to
a magazine Musil was editing. The picture is all immensely alive.

Franz Kafka: Letters to   1978
Friends, Family, and Editors,   *Daily Telegraph*
translated by Richard and Clara
Winston, Calder.

GIUSEPPE DI LAMPEDUSA

On the whole aristocrats do not become novelists. I use the word 'aristocrats' here purely as a convenient term to describe persons who are the actual holders of comparatively ancient titles together with landed possessions of considerable extent, and an ancestry connecting them closely with other families of the same sort. Poets, yes; but, offhand, Tolstoy is the only novelist of that kind I can name. The case of Lampedusa, author of *The Leopard*, has therefore this oddity in addition to what is already an odd story.

Don Giuseppe Fabrizio Tomasi, last Prince of Lampedusa (1896–1957) undeniably falls within the definition, coming from a world very different from, say Conrad's, although Conrad, often described as an 'aristocrat', was of an ancient Polish family and, in one sense, shaped in an 'aristocratic' tradition. The point is a psychological rather than social one, the implication being that persons brought up, and living later in that particular way, although they may have remarkable literary gifts, do not as a rule express them in the form of a novel. This fact, if it can be established, seems a matter of some literary interest.

Lampedusa was of the Tomasini family, one of great antiquity in Italy, the founder of the sept having married, it is claimed, the daughter of a sixth-century Byzantine emperor. Tomasini are found all over Italy – the great poet, Leopardi, belonged to them – and a branch settled in Sicily before the turn of the sixteenth century. Lampedusa's more immediate lineage is just what might be expected: soldiers, saints, eccentrics. The family owned several huge estates and town houses in Sicily.

Lampedusa himself became a regular officer of Artillery – again like Tolstoy, as it happens – fighting in the Balkans during the First World War, being captured, escaping. He remained in the army until 1925, although he seems to have suffered from some sort of a post-war nervous crisis. He was always anti-fascist and would not hold any public office under Mussolini, retiring to his estates and reading much, although not writing himself. He was particularly devoted to Shakespeare and Stendhal.

Lampedusa did not marry until he was thirty-four. His wife, of Baltic origin, was stepdaughter of the Italian Ambassador in London, also a Tomasi, and it was in London that he met her. She was to become a distinguished psychiatrist, and it appears that at her instigation her husband took to writing, primarily as a means of counteracting the melancholia from which he suffered. This was a state to which he was no doubt always to some extent subject, and it was exacerbated by the destruction of his home and most cherished possessions by an Allied bomb in the Second World War. These biographical details, with others, are to be found in the present volume together with some of his own memoirs of childhood, a short story and the opening of a novel. All these are well worth reading in themselves.

They are important because they show that *The Leopard* was not one of these games of nature by which a non-professional writer can produce one book of a certain force, but is never able to write again. Lampedusa had all the marks of a professional writer.

The childhood memoirs, suggesting familiarity with Proust, have at the same time a completely individual atmosphere. The short story about the siren, 'old-fashioned' perhaps in conception, is written with complete assurance. The beginning of the novel *The Blind Kittens* might have grown into a work of considerable power. *The Leopard* itself, not intended for publication, had to be arranged posthumously from bits of manuscript found in different places. It is interesting to learn, for example, that the sequence about the priest, which never seemed to me properly to 'belong', was really written as a separate story.

Where *The Leopard* will settle in the literary field cannot, of course, be said at this stage. It certainly looks as if Lampedusa contributed a minor classic to Italian writing. What is no less interesting is that *The Leopard* has had large sales, not only throughout Europe, but in Italy itself, a country where novelists, even internationally well-known Italian ones, have a modest circulation. This has not caused universal satisfaction. In Italy, as elsewhere, the literary Establishment, the fashionable taste of the critic-mandarins, is Leftish. It is bad enough that a rich prince, even if now deceased, should have written a good book; adding insult to injury that the public should clamour to buy such decadent stuff.

Two Stories and a Memoir,   1962
Giuseppe di Lampedusa, translated by   *Daily Telegraph*
Archibald Colquhoun, with an introduction
by E. M. Forster, Collins and Harvill.

INDEX